FREEDOM SHIP

Also by Marcus Rediker

FREEDOM SHIP

❈

The Uncharted History
of Escaping Slavery by Sea

❈

Marcus Rediker

Viking

VIKING
An imprint of Penguin Random House LLC
1745 Broadway, New York, NY 10019
penguinrandomhouse.com

Image credits may be found on pages 333–35.

Designed by Amanda Dewey

Map illustrations by Daniel Lagin

LIBRARY OF CONGRESS CATALOGING-IN-PUBLICATION DATA
Names: Rediker, Marcus, author.
Title: Freedom ship : the uncharted history of escaping
slavery by sea / Marcus Rediker.
Description: New York : Viking, 2025. |
Includes bibliographical references and index.
Identifiers: LCCN 2024035833 (print) | LCCN 2024035834 (ebook) |
ISBN 9780525558347 (hardcover) | ISBN 9780525558354 (ebook)
Subjects: LCSH: Underground Railroad—Atlantic Coast (U.S.)—
History. | Stowaways—Atlantic Coast (U.S.)—History. |
Fugitive slaves—United States—History—19th century. |
Antislavery movements—United States—History—19th century. |
Classification: LCC E450 .R29 2025 (print) | LCC E450 (ebook) |
DDC 973.7/115—dc23/eng/20250203
LC record available at https://lccn.loc.gov/2024035833
LC ebook record available at https://lccn.loc.gov/2024035834

Printed in the United States of America
1st Printing

The authorized representative in the EU for product safety
and compliance is Penguin Random House Ireland, Morrison
Chambers, 32 Nassau Street, Dublin D02 YH68,
Ireland. https://eu-contact.penguin.ie.

For my brothers,
Shayne Rediker and Peter Linebaugh

CONTENTS

�varsquare

FREEDOM SHIP

Introduction

A Wave of Resistance

The storm-winds wildly blowing,
The bursting billows mock,
As with their foam-crests glowing,
They dash the sea-girt rock;
Amid the wild commotion,
The revel of the sea,
A voice is on the ocean,
Be free, O man, be free.

—*The Anti-Slavery Harp: A Collection of Songs*
for Anti-Slavery Meetings (1848)

Thomas H. Jones was born in 1806 on a plantation owned by the cruel John Hawes in coastal New Hanover County, North Carolina. Hawes sold him at age nine to another enslaver in Wilmington, the state's leading port. In an account of his life first published in 1854 Jones recalled, "Mother wept bitterly, and in the midst of her loud sobbings, cried out in broken words, 'I can't save you, Tommy; master has sold you, you must go.'" His new enslaver lashed him repeatedly with a cowhide strap for various "offenses," including his determined efforts to learn to read and to find true religion. As a young man Jones married a woman named Lucilla and had "three dear little babes," Annie, Lizzie, and Charlie, but his wife and children were all sold to the labor-hungry cotton planters of Alabama. He would never see them again. Jones described his early life as one of "poverty, suffering and shame," of "dark fears and darker realities."[1]

Little did Jones know at the time that his life would take a turn toward freedom in 1841 when an enslaver named Owen Holmes purchased him and allowed him to hire out his labor on the Wilmington waterfront. Jones would pay Holmes $150 per year and keep whatever he earned above that amount. Jones explained, "I worked, loading and unloading vessels that came into Wilmington," laboring on the docks and in the dark holds of vessels, stowing cotton, lumber, shingles, tar, and turpentine. Dock work was grueling and hazardous, but it "afforded many advantages." The result was, "I was able to lay by quite a sum of money." Living and working among the dozens of ships and hundreds of sailors who entered and departed the port each year, Jones met a cosmopolitan crowd and learned how Atlantic shipping worked.[2]

Jones toiled long hours and saved his money, storing it in a box he buried in the floor of his cabin to hide it from the slave patrols. He met and married a woman named Mary, formed a new family, and used his savings to buy the freedom of Mary and their three young children, whom he placed aboard a packet ship for New York City in July 1849. He planned to join them three weeks later. Around this time his enslaver fell sick and was no longer able to supervise his labor on the docks. Out of money and desperate to join his family in New York, Jones decided that this was his opportunity: he would seek his freedom, not by self-purchase but by making a deal with a fellow worker on the waterfront. If his design failed, he would likely be sold off to the cotton South like his first family.

During the late summer of 1849 the brig *Bell* sailed into Wilmington harbor from New York. Jones went aboard and quietly sought out the steward of the vessel, who was likely African American and someone already known to him, to make a bargain. They spoke in hushed, urgent tones: Jones would pay $8 ($329 in 2024) if the steward would "stow me away in the hold of the ship, and take me on to New York." Jones had offered the steward all the money he had, so he was relieved when he accepted the offer. Jones got himself "an allowance of biscuit and water" and hid out in the hold amid tightly stowed forty-gallon barrels of turpentine.

The freedom voyage was not as easy, nor as exhilarating, as Jones had hoped. Once the ship got out to sea, Jones fell violently seasick and decided on the second day at sea that "I could not live out the passage" in the hold. In a condition of "great weakness," he appealed to the steward, who snuck him into a passenger cabin, where he would be more comfortable. This was a dangerous move, but Jones apparently felt he had no choice. The brig's captain soon discovered him and recognized immediately that he was a fugitive. He vowed, Jones solemnly explained, to "send me back by the first opportunity that offered."

The drama of the discovery was soon eclipsed by a bigger drama engulfing the entire ship—"a severe storm." For several days, wrote Jones, "we were driven by the gale." The runaway went to work, cooking for the crew. After the storm subsided, the ship lay becalmed for several days. When the voyage resumed, the captain put Jones under guard and gave orders to sail straight to New York. It was clear to Jones that as soon as they came to anchor, the captain would "send me back."

His dream of a free life with his family ebbing away, Jones made "a last effort to get on shore" once the *Bell* anchored in New York. When the captain left the ship to tend to business and "the mate was busy in the cabin mending his clothes," Jones escaped surveillance, went below deck, and lashed together some loose wooden staves to create a makeshift raft. He grabbed a paddle, put his trust in God, and "launched forth upon the waves." He was about a mile from shore, but the tide was in his favor. After he had paddled about a quarter of a mile, the mate discovered the escape, lowered a boat, and took off with three sailors rowing hard in pursuit of him.

Thomas H. Jones escaped in a self-made raft, waving his hat at two sailors in a nearby boat to rescue him from those trying to return him to slavery.

Jones saw that the mate was gaining on him; he would not make it to shore. He took his "old hat" off his head and waved it frantically for help. He spied a small boat "coming round" not far away. The boat's two sailors came to his rescue and took him on board. They understood what was happening and asked Jones straightaway if he was a slave, adding that he should not "fear to tell the truth, for I was with friends, and they would protect me." Jones explained "my circumstances just as they were." When the mate pulled up alongside and demanded the return of Jones, the sailors proved "as good as their word." They ordered the mate "to keep off" and vowed to "prosecute him if he touched me." Slavery had been abolished in New York in 1827 and the sailors knew it. The mate retreated in defeat. The sailors then gave Jones "a little money and some clothes in addition to all their other kindness." They took him to his friend, African Methodist Episcopal church minister Robert H. Cousins, who lived on John Street in lower Manhattan, where his family was staying. Jones wrote, "The meeting with my wife and children . . . was a moment of joy too deep and holy for any attempt to paint it . . . my dear wife lay sobbing in her joy in my arms, and my three dear little babes were clinging to my knees, crying 'Pa has come; Pa has come.'" Jones then made his way to Boston, Canada, and Great Britain, where he became an important preacher and lecturer in the circuit of transatlantic abolitionism. His story of escape by sea was of "thrilling interest" to all who heard him.

SEEING THE UNSEEN

The story of Thomas H. Jones is common in the long annals of slave resistance across the Americas. Thousands of people escaped slavery by sea, leaving behind voluminous documentation. Yet the history books have had little to say about them. Why have these dramatic tales of dockside conspiracies, below-deck hideaways, billowing sails, and ultimately liberation been so rarely told? The importance of the question is compounded by the extraordinary quality and depth of scholarship on the "Underground Railroad," a hallmark of research among historians for more than a century.[3]

Part of the answer is that the metaphor "underground railroad" has, from the late 1830s onward, pointed us in the wrong direction, limiting most historical investigations to the landed routes by which people traveled northward to freedom. Indeed, those escapes almost never took place underground and rarely on railroads. The phrase thus occludes from our historical vision as much as it illuminates. Scholars and the general public have explored endless secret passageways to freedom on land without considering the ones that led to the hold of a ship.[4]

Deepening our ignorance is a largely uninspected bias in modern thought I have called *terracentrism*—the unconscious tendency to think that history occurs only on land and, relatedly, that the oceans and seas of the world are somehow temporal voids, places where history does not happen. We therefore exaggerate, in retrospect, the importance of the railroad, the dominant symbol of American industrialization, which in the antebellum era was much less significant to commerce and economic growth than was maritime transport.[5]

A third limitation flows from the previous two: historians often neglect maritime sources even though large-scale historical processes such as the formation of class, race, and culture have happened on the decks of deep-sea sailing vessels. We have been ignorant not only of the mass of maritime escapes but of their rate of success, which was likely much higher than those attempted by land. Maritime escapes appear in many traditional histories of the Underground Railroad, but never do historians inspect the system that lay behind them. We learn of the "runaway army" but not the "runaway navy," the landscape of flight but not its seascape.[6]

Another reason for our oversight lay in the images of American popular culture. The dominant image of the runaway from the nineteenth century to the present is a woodcut that appeared in many newspaper advertisements: a man, simply dressed and usually barefoot, walking on land, carrying a bindle or a sack over his shoulder. This representation implies that escaping was a landed and individual act. Historians have deepened the power of the image by treating running away as an individualistic response to enslavement, in contrast to the much less common resistance of insurrection. Not only was running away commonly undertaken as a collective act, as the following pages will show, it was fundamentally social, requiring collaboration and alliance even for someone like Thomas H. Jones who tried to go it alone. Jones needed social connections and cooperation to make his successful passage. A focus on the heroic individual has limited our vision of how escape worked.[7]

This book is about Thomas H. Jones and the thousands of other enslaved people who escaped slavery by sea during the three decades

This image accompanied thousands of runaway advertisements, falsely implying that people escaped individually by land, disguising the social and maritime dimensions of self-emancipation.

before the American Civil War. They escaped from dozens of places, but principally from Savannah, Charleston, Wilmington (North Carolina), Norfolk, and Baltimore. They arrived throughout the Northern states that had abolished slavery, but mainly to Philadelphia, New York, New Bedford, and Boston. A significant proportion moved on to Canada, especially after Congress passed the Fugitive Slave Act of September 1850. Some even sailed southward to the Caribbean, while others crossed the Atlantic to Great Britain. Examining docks and ships as places of work, cooperation, discipline, policing, and subversion—in short, as zones of struggle and infrastructures of escape—this labor history reconstructs the lost social world of Thomas H. Jones, the steward who stowed him away, and the sailors who rescued him and gave him money and clothing, all willing and essential hands in the struggle against slavery. The emphasis of this book is how the maritime system of escape worked, from beginning to end.[8]

What would Jones and the thousands of others like him have known about the role of ships in the lives of their ancestors? Many of them would have heard the stories of an older generation, perhaps members of their own families, about the extreme violence and terror of the dreaded Middle Passage in the Atlantic slave trade. To the victims of that awful commerce, the oceangoing tall ship was a place

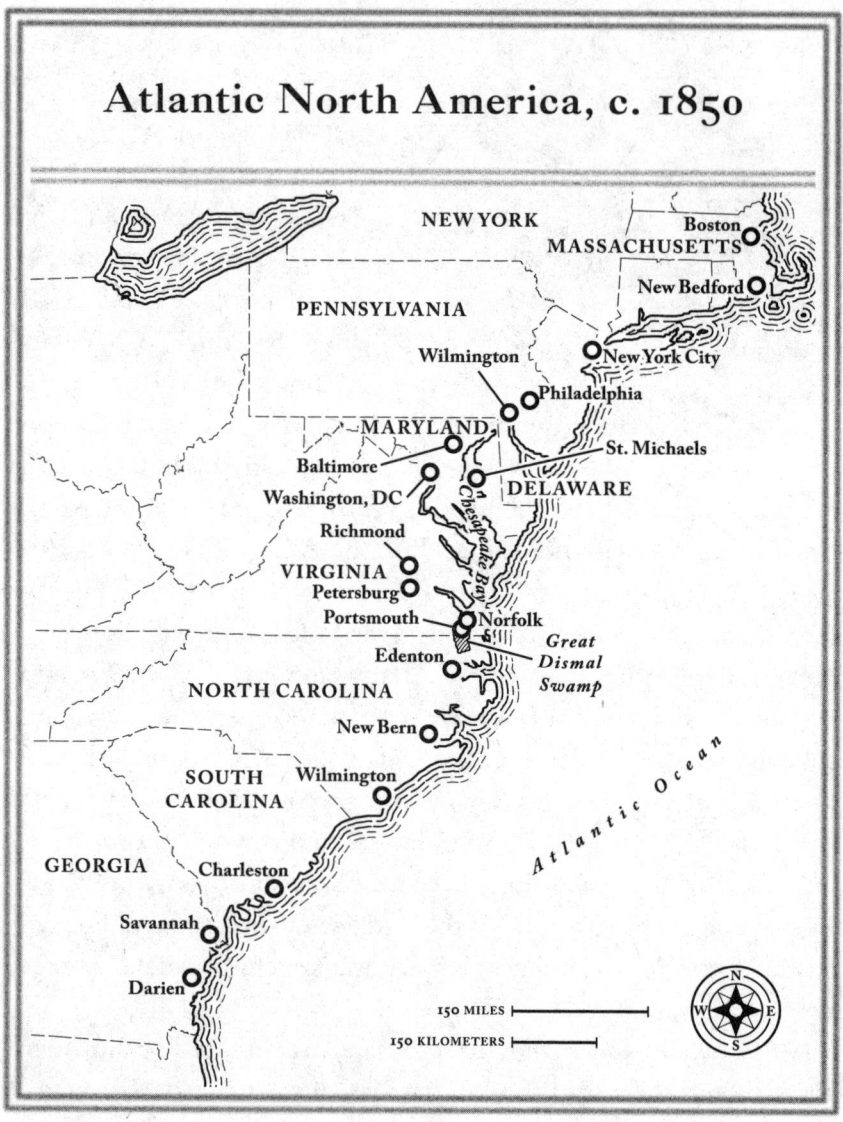

Atlantic North America, c. 1850

of brutal enslavement, unimaginable horror, and premature death. To Jones and his generation, the same vessel offered freedom. They seized it, turning the docks, the ship, and the ocean into sites of struggle and self-emancipation.[9]

HISTORYMAKERS AT SEA

The drama of escaping slavery by sea in antebellum America featured a variety of historical actors: first and foremost, the enslaved men and women who occupied the front line of the battle. As insurrectionists, maroons, and runaways, they challenged the slave system, deeply and continuously. When they slipped away aboard North-bound vessels, they robbed their enslavers of labor and capital and struck a blow against the institution of slavery. Whether these men, women, and children came from plantations, farms, urban workshops, or the docks, they were the ones who took the initiative, planned the escapes, and bore the primary risks. Their irrepressible radical attacks drove the system of maritime escape set forth in the pages of this book.

Alongside them in the struggle were free Black citizens, most of whom had themselves escaped slavery by one means or another. In the Southern ports, free people of color hid runaways in their own communities and, through dockside labor connections, helped many to board ships. In the Northern ports, the free Black communities took the recently arrived escapees into their homes, fed them, clothed them, and helped them to get jobs. Black churches and civic organizations provided material aid. The Reverend Leonard Grimes and the Twelfth Baptist Church in Boston, better known as the Fugitive Slave Church, welcomed hundreds of the self-emancipated, as did the various Black abolitionist organizations such as the Massachusetts General Colored Association and the New England Freedom Association. An anchor of fugitive assistance in the free Black community was the Colored Sailors Home in New York, where the proprietor, Black sailor-abolitionist William P. Powell, defended the rights of Black seamen as he took in maritime runaways seeking aid.[10]

Free Black sailors played a central role in the maritime system of escape. They signed on to Northern vessels, sailed to Southern ports, and went ashore as subversive symbols of freedom. In October 1850, shortly after the passage of the Fugitive Slave Act, the editor of the *Wilmington Aurora* complained about "a crew of free negro sailors, seven or eight in number," who had arrived in North Carolina on a vessel from Philadelphia. In a majority African American port town, "it may safely be assumed that they are dangerous visitors." The danger posed was both ideological and practical. Black seamen were, according to the editor, "all of them, from the very nature of their position, abolitionists, and have the best opportunity to inculcate the slaves with their notions." Common work on the docks and ships permitted the circulation of radical ideas that could result in direct action: "More—they enjoy, as sailors, facilities of aiding their escape to the North or other free soil."[11]

These free Black sailors were part of a waterfront motley crew, made up of mariners, dockworkers, porters, carters, and draymen, Black and white, who assisted runaways on both ends of escape and during the sea voyage in between. They got the fugitive secretly aboard the vessel and into a secure hiding place. They also joined protests against slavery; as a writer for the Washington, DC, newspaper the *Daily Union* noted after the passage of the Fugitive Slave Act in 1850, the people in the streets were "the most motley gangs, of all colors, castes, and characters, that ever assembled in the face of the world." These multiethnic workers occupied a strategic position in the waterfront division of labor, standing at the gateways of departure and arrival.[12]

Abolitionist Thomas Wentworth Higginson revealed another important, although usually invisible, actor in the social world of maritime escape. In 1886 he looked back on his work in the Boston

Vigilance Committee, which "owned a boat, in which men used to go down in the harbor to meet Southern vessels." Their common practice was "to take along a colored woman with fresh fruit, pies &c." A woman vendor was common on the waterfront, so "she easily got on board & when there, usually found out if there was any fugitive on board" by talking to the members of the crew. A group of sailor-abolitionists would return to the vessel later that night to liberate the captive.[13]

Vigilance Committees were especially important organizations for fugitive aid. Formed by Black and white abolitionists in New York in 1835, then in Philadelphia in 1837 and Boston in 1841, the primary purposes of the groups were to assist fugitives who arrived in their cities and to prevent the kidnapping of urban free people of color, who were routinely "blackbirded": thrown aboard a ship, sailed to the South, and sold into slavery. Independent of William Lloyd Garrison's pacifist American Anti-Slavery Society, members of the Vigilance Committees often embraced the principle of armed self-defense and frequently took direct action against slavery.[14]

The maritime chain of labor and solidarity stretched from people emancipating themselves from Southern bondage to free Black communities South and North, to free workers on the Atlantic waterfront and on ships, to abolitionists in port cities. Thousands of people freed themselves though this variable, flexible, secretive, and therefore hidden network. Nineteenth-century Southern elites understood this system much better than have modern historians.[15]

ATLANTIC MARITIME RADICALISM

Escaping slavery by sea was part of a long tradition of Atlantic maritime radicalism. As capitalism expanded around the globe beginning in the late sixteenth century, multiracial sailors and other maritime workers provided the labor that linked the continents. They also pioneered new forms of anticapitalist resistance, forming democratic and egalitarian pirate communities, taking to the streets in rowdy protest in almost all early modern port city riots, inventing the strike in 1768, and exploding into mutiny on an Atlantic-wide scale in the 1790s. Enslaved peopled deepened the radicalism by shedding their chains and rising up aboard slave ships, and by escaping the plantation system to build autonomous maroon communities. The maritime radical tradition depended on mobility, as, for example, when sailors and other waterfront workers spread the word of the Haitian Revolution around the Atlantic. William P. Powell held close to his heart an image of Crispus Attucks, the half-Black, half–Indigenous Natick sailor who led a revolutionary crowd into protest in 1770 and through the Boston Massacre became the first martyr of the looming American Revolution.[16]

This story of maritime maroons begins in 1829, when African American dockside abolitionist David Walker published *Walker's Appeal, in Four Articles; Together with a Preamble, to the Coloured Citizens of the World, but in Particular, and Very Expressly, to Those of the United States of America*. Walker called on enslaved people throughout the Americas to follow the example of the Haitian Revolution and cast off their fetters. Walker used seamen Black and white to carry his pamphlet into the slave states, where enslavers responded with panic— and repressive legislation. After Walker's opening shot, a series of profound events made the next dozen years a formative period in the struggle against slavery: Nat Turner's rebellion and the founding of *The Liberator* in 1831; major slave revolts in Jamaica and Brazil in 1831–32 and 1835; the British abolition of colonial slavery in stages, between 1834 and 1838; the *Amistad* rebellion in 1839; and the *Creole* slave ship revolt in 1841. Against this fiery backdrop the American abolitionist movement advanced dramatically. Self-emancipation acquired a new political valence at the very moment when ever-larger numbers of Northern-based merchant vessels, powered by sail and steam, entered Southern ports to trade. Fugitives and their comrades contributed to the rising radicalism of the 1830s by helping to generate the new Vigilance Committees. What we have come to know as the Underground Railroad had its origins on the waterfront.[17]

AN OVERVIEW OF FLIGHT BY SEA

Escaping slavery by sea is an old practice, coterminous with the establishment of slavery in North America. Political elites of colonial Virginia and South Carolina legislated against it in some of their earliest laws on the institution of slavery, in 1705 and 1710, respectively. Escaping slavery was also prohibited by federal law, beginning with the writing of the United States Constitution in 1787. Anyone "held to Service or Labour"—a euphemism for an enslaved person—who escaped would by law be delivered back to his or her enslaver. Congress strengthened the law in 1793, empowering magistrates and federal officials in all states to arrest and return fugitives to their so-called owners. The new law also criminalized the solidarity of anyone who helped fugitives, promising a fine of $500 ($15,000 in 2024). The Fugitive Slave Act of 1850, which reflected rising national tensions over slavery, went even further, requiring all US citizens to assist in the return of fugitives and establishing commissioners (not juries) to quicken the removal of fugitives back to the South. The law also increased the penalties for those who assisted runaways. None of these laws succeeded, as hundreds, sometimes thousands, absconded to freedom year after year. The Fugitive Slave Law had no deterrent effect; indeed, it created fierce resistance in the North and by 1851 had pushed public opinion to support fugitives and other abolitionists.[18]

Many fugitives escaped by land and by sea, but precise numbers remain unknown—and largely unknowable. The Library of Congress has estimated that enslavers placed roughly two hundred thousand advertisements for runaways in newspapers between 1730 and

1865, but this number vastly underestimates the actual number of runaways. Tens of thousands ran away from slavery year after year. Most escapees planned to be away for a short period and to return to the plantation, farm, or workshop. They ran to protest some aspect of their enslavement: to escape physical punishment, to see a loved one, or to avoid being sold or transferred to another place. Enslavers did not advertise in newspapers for the great majority of these escapees. Some they hunted down; others they knew would eventually return on their own. Shackles, stocks, and whips awaited them. This kind of temporary escape was called *petit marronage*.[19]

A minority, but still a huge number, of fugitives practiced *gran marronage*, trying to escape slavery once and for all, never to return. They faced bigger challenges by usually needing to travel much farther to escape. Historians have suggested that over the full history of slavery in North America, as few as 50,000 and as many as 100,000 successfully escaped, roughly one-quarter to one-half of the advertised total. The great majority of these escaped after 1830, a large proportion of them by sea.[20]

Our uncertainty about the numbers arises from the very nature of the activity, which was illegal and therefore clandestine. The perfect escape left no documentation. Many who escaped by sea did not divulge the secrets of how they did it, especially if they ran away before slavery was abolished and therefore might, by telling their tale, endanger both fugitives and their helpers. Frederick Douglass, America's most famous maritime runaway, criticized those who tipped off enslavers. The dilemma of disclosing the subversive knowledge of escape was best summed up by a man who had been a maroon in the Great Dismal Swamp of Virginia/North Carolina before escaping to the North, most likely through Norfolk: he said to a Boston abolitionist, "'I expect I better not tell the way I came: for there's lots more boys coming the same way I did." Women and children came by sea too.[21]

Those who published their accounts of escape after the Civil War, in the 1870s and 1880s, felt freer to discuss their experiences in detail. Douglass revealed specifics about his escape in his autobiography of 1881 that he had withheld in the first two versions, published in 1845 and 1855. George Latimer, a celebrated sailaway who arrived with his wife Rebecca in Boston in 1842, waited more than half a century to tell the story of his escape. William Still, whose *The Underground Railroad* was published in 1872, narrated the histories of more than nine hundred people who had passed through the office of the Philadelphia Vigilance Committee during the 1850s, offering abounding details of escape.[22]

Estimating the number of fugitives who escaped by sea poses additional challenges because many enslavers who thought their human property had sailed away did not bother to advertise locally. They were, after all, long gone, beyond the reach of local newspapers, so why waste money? Enslavers would occasionally place ads in the newspapers of the port to which they thought the escapee had sailed, but more often they would simply employ slave catchers to go in search of them. Timothy D. Walker has noted that of the "103 extant pre-Emancipation slave narratives, more than 70 percent recount the use of oceangoing vessels as a means of fleeing slavery." His figure is supported by another statistical measure: more than half of those who arrived in New York and more than two-thirds of the fugitives who arrived in Philadelphia during the 1850s came by sea. The percentages would have been even higher in New Bedford and Boston. Thomas Wentworth Higginson, who was deeply involved with escapees in Boston, noted that "fugitive slaves commonly came by water, as stowaways in vessels."[23]

Maritime fugitives, and the motley crew behind them, exercised growing national influence from the 1830s to the outbreak of Civil War in 1861. From 1837 to 1843, several escapes by sea triggered prolonged, heated conflict between Northern and Southern states, resulting in interstate Southern cooperation and solidarity, fierce legal battles about Northern-owned vessels operating in Southern ports, sectional strife, and the passage of "personal liberty laws" on behalf of fugitives in New York and Massachusetts. These conflicts, initiated and exacerbated by continued escapes by sea, helped to create a national crisis that led to the passage of the Fugitive Slave Law of 1850, after which those who fled slavery by sea continued to inflame national debate. Three of the highest-profile cases prosecuted under the Fugitive Slave Law involved Shadrach Minkins (1850), Thomas Sims (1851), and Anthony Burns (1854), who had sailed to Boston from Norfolk, Savannah, and Richmond, respectively. Even though Sims and Burns were both returned to bondage, the mobilization, publicity, and expense around their return effectively nullified the Fugitive Slave Act in Massachusetts, as both Northerners and Southerners agreed. A final wave of escapes by sea crested in 1861, as the turmoil of the Civil War created new maritime opportunities for freedom seekers.

HISTORY FROM BELOW

The maritime system of escape, from beginning to end, was organized by people who are largely unknown to us—poor people with calloused hands, often nameless in the historical record and therefore unremembered, the wretched of the earth. They are the heart and soul of this book, which chronicles their actions, ideas, stories, and improbable victories over the powerful and highborn. Theirs is a history from below: the pages that follow resurrect and narrate their experiences and consciousness, recover their voices, and illuminate their collective power. They acted out courageous, death-defying stories. They escaped slavery in ingenious ways. Their labor on the docks and ships, within the dynamic political economy of port cities, drove the freedom story. These workers used the material structures of capitalism, in particular its ships and trading patterns between North and South, to free themselves and alter the trajectory of history. A few escapees, like Frederick Douglass and Harriet Jacobs, both once en-

slaved, became famous, but most others, like sailor-abolitionists Jonathan Walker and William P. Powell, are little known. Most of the
names found in these pages will be completely new to readers. These
men and women cast a fresh light on the history of resistance to slavery, on abolitionism, and on the coming of the Civil War, all of which
look different when seen from below.

This narrative draws on a wide array of sources to reconstruct the
stirring stories of maritime maroons—their motivations, methods,
and impact. The most important evidence comes from newspaper advertisements and accounts, first-person narratives of the enslaved
themselves, and the records of abolitionist groups who assisted runaways. Maritime fugitives generated massive documentation, which
makes it possible to reconstruct their history from below.

The doleful cry of the enslavers went up again and again, in every
newspaper published in or near an early-nineteenth-century port city:
after describing someone who had absconded, their advertisements
frequently warned, "All masters of vessels are cautioned against harboring or concealing him, or in any way aiding him in his escape, as
the law will be strictly enforced." Sailors, stewards, and cooks, most
of them Black, smuggled freedom seekers aboard, but enslavers expected shipmasters to police their own vessels, which many were
more than happy to do, not least because their future ability to trans-
act business in a Southern port was at stake. Despite the best efforts
of constables, guards, and captains to police the docks, maritime
workers and fugitives found their way aboard ship after ship.[24]

The same advertisements that warned masters of ships not to take
runaways on board often told revealing personal stories in miniature
about those who took flight, detailing their looks, demeanor, and social networks. In June 1833 an enslaved young man named Edward—
dark-skinned, round-shouldered, middle-sized, and downcast in the
eyes in conversation—escaped from Richmond. His enslaver, Lewis
A. Collier, traced his flight to the connections of Edward's father,
Solomon, a drayman of many years who got to know "the crews of

vessels sailing to this port." "From that acquaintance," wrote Collier, "I have no doubt he will endeavor to get him off to the North on some vessel." Collier knew enough to pin suspicion on two schooners that left Richmond the day Edward went missing: the *Effort* and the *George Wheaton*, both bound for New York. Collier also noted that the captains of those vessels may or may not have known that Edward was stowed away on board. Edward might have boarded the vessel secretly, with the assistance of dockers or sailors, men his father would have known and trusted. The likes of Edward, Solomon, and the sailors were the reason why the officials of Richmond formed the Society for the Prevention of the Absconding and Abduction of Slaves in 1833, targeting both runaways and those who assisted them.[25]

Many who crossed the sea for freedom wrote their own stories of escape after they reached a Northern city, sometimes with the assistance of abolitionists. William Grimes, who escaped Savannah by sea in 1815, self-published the first narrative of escape in 1825. The book, he proudly announced, was "written by himself." Abolitionists published escape narratives with increasing frequency in the 1830s and 1840s, as flight and other kinds of resistance increased. Frederick Douglass, a man of the waterfront, penned the most famous narrative in 1845 as a contribution to the abolitionist movement and no doubt encouraged many others to do the same. These sources must be used with care, not least because white, middle-class abolitionist editors sometimes interpolated their own individualist values and ideas into the narratives. But there can be no doubt that the voices of the fugitives themselves, like that of Thomas H. Jones, usually shine through. Narratives of escape became a weapon in the struggle against slavery, creating sympathy for fugitives among the Northern public.[26]

Just as important in recovering the stories of maritime escapees are records kept by two abolitionists: Sydney Howard Gay in New York and William Still in Philadelphia, both of whom helped hundreds of escaped people, recording their personal stories and assisting them with money, food, clothing, shelter, and transport to destinations beyond the reach of their enslavers. Gay, editor of the *National Anti-Slavery Standard*, published by the Garrisonian American Anti-Slavery Society, kept a "Record of Fugitives" in which he noted names and various kinds of information about the two hundred men, women, and children he assisted from January 31, 1855, to December 30, 1856. Gay created the rare document in the perilous time of the Fugitive Slave Act. Had federal officials discovered it, they would have fined Gay $1,000 ($36,000 in 2024) and sentenced him to six months in prison. Everything he was doing was criminal according to the controversial federal statute.[27]

African American abolitionist William Still did even more. Beginning in December 1852 Still assiduously recorded information about fugitives who passed through his office. He wrote down the names of the self-emancipated and for many of them noted details such as age, physical appearance, where their escape began, why they decided to run, and how they made their getaway, by land or by sea. Still listened sympathetically as the veterans of bondage told chilling tales of murder, flogging, rape, and other cruelties that staggered the imagination. His "Journal C," as he called it, is filled with practical testimony from the enslaved themselves about the very nature of American slavery and how to resist it. Still understood the historic nature of what he was witnessing and its importance for posterity. He kept the journal for more than four years, penning its final entry in February 1857.[28]

Still folded his journal into a larger book, *The Underground Railroad: A Record of Facts, Authentic Narratives, Letters, &c., Narrating the Hardships, Hair-Breadth Escapes and Death Struggles of the Slaves in Their Efforts for Freedom*, originally published in Philadelphia in 1872. In this stunning eight-hundred-page compendium, Still fleshed out the accounts of some of the individual runaways beyond what he had recorded in the often spare, telegraphic notes of Journal C, adding details stored in his own memory as well as those he gathered from other abolitionists. Still also included in the book dozens of letters written to him by runaways he had assisted as they enjoyed freedom in the Northern states or in Canada. He took pleasure in tracking down and publishing the runaway advertisements and the rewards offered for some of the people who had sat across from him in the Vigilance Committee office. He sometimes played the role of amanuensis, committing to paper the specific words fugitives spoke to him. He added hundreds of new names and miniature biographies, mostly from the period after Journal C left off, from March 1857 through December 1860. Still produced some of the richest surviving evidence about the workings of the Underground Railroad, which included many harrowing accounts of people who escaped bondage by sea. The notes of his interviews are a gift for the ages.[29]

Every escape subverted the social order of slavery. Thomas H. Jones, along with every man, woman, and child who boarded a freedom ship, struck a blow against bondage and at the same time helped to advance the abolitionist movement and bring on the Civil War. The power of such escape lay not in this or that event, no matter how ingenious and heroic, but rather in the constant collective force of resistance. For the fugitives, sailing away from slavery was an assertion of agency and a repeated act of political will. For Northern abolitionists, it was an inspiration, a source of education, and a means to expand the movement. For Southern rulers and their cherished "peculiar institution" of slavery, it was an agonizing death by a thousand cuts. A voice called from the ocean and thousands answered. Maritime escape was a long, slow-moving, and unstoppable oceanic wave of resistance, bigger and more powerful than we have ever known.

Chapter 1

The Art of Escape

E scaping slavery by sea was an art. It required thought, planning, and several kinds of knowledge, which is to say, getting away successfully and permanently was as much an intellectual challenge as a physical one. Edward Hicks, a serial fugitive from Lunenburg County, Virginia, highlighted the importance of what he called "head-work" in the process of escape. In his early adventures, he admitted, he was "running about in the bush without much object." But soon he began to study the process of running away. "I lay down studying," he recalled after escaping to Canada, "and got up studying, how to get out of the condition I was placed in." He "studied" his way to freedom, as did many others.[1]

What did would-be fugitives need to know to escape? They had to be able to read people and situations deftly and quickly, to figure out who could assist the flight and who would try to foil it. Successful desertion required no small amount of acting, often involving pretending to be something you were not. In the run-up to departure, one had to disguise all intentions in interactions with enslavers and with other enslaved people too, sometimes one's own family members. Some fugitives disguised their bodies, literally adopting entirely new, deliberately misleading, public personae. Some escapees passed for white; some dressed as gentlemen; some female runaways disguised themselves as male sailors to get aboard a ship. The hope of escape demanded extreme patience. Plans to abscond might lie hidden in the mind of the fugitive for years awaiting the right circumstances for action.[2]

A would-be runner needed to know about climate, ecology, and geography on the route of escape. Which season was best? What kind of weather would one face? Where to find food and water? How to survive in the wild? Escape by sea also depended on understanding rivers, estuaries, and oceanic currents. What was the ever-shifting political geography of freedom? Where could it be found and how would one traverse the earth's surface to get there? The means of escape required technological knowledge: What kind of vessel would carry one to freedom? The smallest canoe, raft, or skiff? The more sophisticated sloop or schooner? Or the technological wonders of their age, the largest oceangoing ship or steamer? Answers to these questions could mean the difference between life and death.

Above all, the escapee needed social skills, especially the ability to establish relationships of trust. This could not be a solitary venture. Friendships with sailors, dockworkers, market women, and other waterfront workers would be critical to successful escape, as would the solidarity of free people of color who had been through similar ordeals. No small number of successful escapes depended on the kindness of strangers both North and South, some of whom were abolitionists, some of whom were not; a few were enslavers. A variety of brilliant strategies and tactics were required to overcome the formidable obstacles of police, bounty hunters, and federal marshals. The art of escape among maritime fugitives demanded thought, planning, knowledge, and in some cases downright genius.[3]

THE PROGENITOR, 1815

William Grimes was the first person to write and publish a personal narrative about escaping Southern slavery, and he absconded by sea.

His autobiography, *Life of William Grimes, the Runaway Slave*, appeared in 1825. It was "Written by Himself," without the assistance of Northern abolitionists, who were few at the time and little engaged with fugitive aid. The first half of the book is an unflinching exposé of the extreme violence and cruelty of slavery—and Grimes had the scars on his back to illustrate them. His book cataloged floggings by enslavers after every failed escape attempt.[4]

Grimes worked on the waterfront of Savannah, where in 1815 his enslaver, Francis Harvey Welman, allowed him to hire out his own time. He would find his own work, pay Welman the bulk of his wages, and keep the rest for himself. He found work on a large, handsome new brig, a two-masted vessel named the *Casket*, captained by Samuel Doak. Grimes joined the crew to load large bales of prime upland cotton into the hold of the vessel. Talking as he worked, Grimes said he "got acquainted with some of these Yankee sailors, and they appeared to be quite pleased with me." Conversation soon took a serious turn, in muted tones beyond the ears of Captain Doak and the mate: "The sailors growing more and more attached to me, they proposed to me to leave in the centre of the cotton bales on deck, a hole or place sufficiently large for me to stow away in, with my necessary provisions." Their action was what American dockworkers would later call a "Baltimore front"—a deliberate arrangement of cargo designed to hide subversive designs from the bosses. The small, dark, open space among the stacked and lashed bales of cotton, created by sailors on the main deck of the vessel, would be Grimes's first free abode. How he felt about pinning his hopes on a vessel named the *Casket* as he occupied a dark space not much bigger than a coffin, he did not say.[5]

From his hiding place Grimes heard the first sounds of freedom as the mate barked orders to raise the anchor and set sail. The vessel's timbers creaked and groaned as the wind filled the sails. When the *Casket* sailed past Tybee Island lighthouse and crossed the south end sandbar out into the Atlantic, the "sailors gave three hearty cheers, and gave me to understand that I was clear." Yet Grimes remained hidden because the ship's officers did not know about his presence. He sometimes crawled out of his hot, airless compartment at night to "lie down with the sailors on deck," to breathe the fresh salt air and stretch his limbs. In the dark "the captain could not distinguish me from the hands, having a number on board of different complexions." Disguised among the motley crew, his short voyage proved happily uneventful.

When the *Casket* arrived at the quarantine ground on the northeastern shore of Staten Island, New York, Grimes left his hiding place for the ship's forecastle, the sailors' living area, to change clothes. The mate came down unexpectedly and found Grimes putting on a clean shirt. Grimes stood there, frozen, with his shirt half on. The mate, who had supervised his labor loading the cargo in port, recognized him instantly and asked, "Why, Grimes, how came you here?" Grimes was too terrified to answer. The mate then summoned the crew and put the same question to them. Fearing trouble for their own role in the escape, they answered with evasive sympathy: the "poor fellow, he stole aboard." The mate returned his gaze to Grimes and asked if the steward or the captain knew he was aboard. Grimes recovered his power of speech: they did not. The mate told Grimes to "let no one know anything about it" and added with a sigh, "I wish that I myself knew nothing of it." By Georgia law all ship officers were subject to prosecution, fine, and imprisonment for being party to an escape. But that did not mean that the mate would turn Grimes over to the New York port authorities to be returned to bondage in Savannah. Using his natural habit of command, the mate said, "Here, boys, put him over the bows, and set him ashore on Staten Island." It was a brave call and not an uncommon one.

Going ashore increased the danger of discovery because slavery was still legal in New York, a place of slave catchers, blackbirding—in which slave catchers and outright kidnappers targeted free people of color—and an illegal slave trade. Anyone assisting a fugitive could expect rigorous prosecution and jail time too. A sailor of the *Casket* took Grimes aboard a small boat to connect him to a wider circuit of solidarity. After landing on Staten Island, Grimes wrote, his guide "found another sailor with whom he was acquainted, and told him my circumstances, requesting him to assist me in getting to New York." The new sailor had never met Grimes but was sympathetic and promised to help. A few hours later the sailor took Grimes to a packet boat, near which a doctor was inspecting newly arrived sailors and passengers for signs of illness. As his companion distracted the doctor on one side, Grimes slipped by on the other. He was so wracked with fear, he later wrote, "I almost fainted." Grimes "rejoiced heartily" after the packet pushed off.

When they landed in Manhattan, the sailor took Grimes to the home of yet another sailor, passing along the instructions to help the young runaway, which the man did, expanding the network of mutual aid. Grimes spent the night with the third sailor and concluded that it was too dangerous to stay in New York. In the morning, he bought "a loaf of bread and a small piece of meat" and started on foot for New Haven, a place he had heard about from a visitor to Savannah.

Looking back over his motivations for escape, Grimes concluded that he had too much "sense and feeling" and too little fear to be enslaved. At an early age he had grown ungovernable in spirit—and realized that it would not be long until he would have "resisted with my life." Thanks to the kindness of a dozen maritime strangers, he would spend the next fifty years of his life as a free man, although a poor one, in New England.

"I SHOULD BE FREE," DATE UNKNOWN

When William Still, a key player in the fugitive solidarity movement in Philadelphia, invited Lewis Tappan, a leading abolitionist for more than thirty years, to contribute "a few reminiscences" to his forthcoming book, *The Underground Railroad*, Tappan, although eighty-three years old and in poor health, shared four memories for posterity. One concerned a fifteen-year-old girl who had escaped bondage, arrived in New York, and now took part in a Sunday school class, where Tappan met her. When he asked her about "the mode of her escape," she answered,

> I was walking near the water . . . when a white sailor spoke to me, and after a few questions, offered to hide me on board his vessel and conduct me safely to New York, if I would come to him in the evening. I did so, and was hid and fed by him, and on landing at New York, he conducted me to Mrs. Smith's house, where I am now staying.

Tappan was shocked by her answer. He asked if she had parents and a family. She replied that she was an only child, that both of her parents were living, adding, "I love them very much." Still perplexed, Tappan probed, "How were you treated by your master and mistress?" The young woman answered, "They treated me very well." "How then," asked Tappan, "could you put yourself in the care of that sailor, who was a stranger to you, and leave your parents?" The young woman's answer burned itself into his memory: "I shall never forget her heart-felt reply," he wrote to Still: *"He told me I should be free!"*[6]

MESSENGERS, 1829

David Walker—tall, slender, athletic, and dark-skinned—was a man of the waterfront. He grew up as a free person of color in the port town of Wilmington, North Carolina, and lived for several years in Charleston, South Carolina, during the slave conspiracy of 1822, after which Denmark Vesey, a former sailor who had visited revolutionary Haiti, ended up in the gallows with thirty-four others. Appalled by what "his people" had suffered, Walker decided, "I cannot remain where I must hear their chains continually." He traveled northward by sea and by 1826 had become a slopseller to sailors on the Boston waterfront. Sailors, laborers, and self-emancipated former slaves gathered at his shop, originally located on Dock Square, to share news and stories. He took sailaways into his home. His generosity to the poor and oppressed meant, according to Black abolitionist Henry Highland Garnet, that he "was a poor man—he lived poor, and died poor."[7]

Walker's Appeal . . . to the Coloured Citizens of the World (1829) scorched the hands of anyone who picked it up. Walker denounced the horrors of slavery, prophesied the end of the evil institution, and exhorted the "Coloured Citizens of the World" to follow the example of the Haitian Revolution, assuring them all the while that a just God was on their side. Walker refuted the racist ideas that suffused Thomas Jefferson's *Notes on the State of Virginia* (1785) and appropriated the Declaration of Independence for the Black freedom struggle. He rejected the version of Christianity that offered a gospel of "blood and whips."[8]

Walker devised innovative ways to disseminate his ideas by sea. He sewed copies of the pamphlet into the clothing he sold to sailors, concealing the contraband they would carry ashore. He shipped a box full of pamphlets to a specific person in a Southern port who would then distribute them. He dispatched an agent to travel with copies to make sure they got ashore and to the right people. Walker sought to get the pamphlets into the hands of boatmen, craftspeople, and market women, who would fan out into the hinterland and spread the word of revolution by water and by land. He also hoped that literate people would read the work aloud to those who could not read, as sailors routinely did both ashore and at sea.

Walker knew that African American maritime workers were already under serious suspicion in Southern ports. Several of them had participated in Charleston's conspiracy of 1822, which resulted in the

WALKER'S

APPEAL,

IN FOUR ARTICLES;

TOGETHER WITH

A PREAMBLE,

TO THE

COLOURED CITIZENS OF THE WORLD,

BUT IN PARTICULAR, AND VERY EXPRESSLY, TO THOSE OF

THE UNITED STATES OF AMERICA,

WRITTEN IN BOSTON, STATE OF MASSACHUSETTS,
SEPTEMBER 28, 1829.

THIRD AND LAST EDITION,
WITH ADDITIONAL NOTES, CORRECTIONS, &c.

Boston:
REVISED AND PUBLISHED BY DAVID WALKER.

1830.

David Walker, a Black Boston abolitionist, wrote a revolutionary pamphlet that sailors Black and white smuggled into Southern ports and circulated among the enslaved.

passage of South Carolina's Negro Seamen Act, decreeing that all Black sailors were to be "quarantined" when they arrived on merchant ships for fear of subversion. One of Walker's own (white) sailors noticed the removal of a Black cook from a nearby vessel when he arrived in Charleston in 1830. An African American man onshore said to him, "there goes another one," to which the white sailor replied, "it was a great Shame as it turned Every thing into confusion on board the vessel." The Black man replied "that was not half" of the problems such arrests caused.[9]

Walker's Appeal first reached Savannah, Georgia, on December 11, 1829, by the hands of a white sailor. The following month a Black sailor brought copies to Richmond, Virginia. In March 1830 a courier got the pamphlet to four Black men in New Orleans, two free, two enslaved, who were promptly arrested for possessing it. In August 1830 another anonymous maritime worker brought two hundred copies of the *Appeal* to enslaved worker Jacob Cowan in Wilmington. Using a group of maritime "runners" or "messengers," Cowan circulated the pamphlet far and wide, connecting to "sixty armed slaves" who would rise in insurrection in New Bern four months later. Captured and sold to the Deep South, where "he would be deprived of the opportunity of a Sea port town to receive and distribute such books," Cowan became a vector of rebellion himself, "exciting" and "encouraging" a slave conspiracy near Mobile. Other maritime workers connected Walker's ideas to arsonists and conspirators in Georgia and to slave rebels near New Orleans.[10]

The inner workings of David Walker's communication network were revealed when the captain of the guard of Charleston, South Carolina, arrested white sailor Edward Smith in March 1830. Smith had smuggled six copies of the *Appeal*, which the authorities considered "a very seditious, inflammatory" pamphlet, into the port city and distributed them to Black dockworkers and sailors who came aboard his vessel, the *Columbo* out of Boston, to discharge cargo. Smith recounted a conversation with a "Black sailor, who asked for a copy only to be told that all copies had already been claimed." Smith, who worked a on packet ship that sailed regularly between Boston and Charleston, added that he could get more copies when he returned to his home port. The captain of the guard overheard the conversation and arrested Smith immediately. Under interrogation, Smith used the only excuses available to him—that he did not know David Walker (he thought he was perhaps a minister), nor did he know the content of the pamphlets. Yet he agreed to take the publication even though Walker warned him that "he must do it privately and not let any white person know any thing about it." Smith added that he had not been paid to deliver the pamphlets and that he did so, even after reading a few pages and learning what the pamphlet was about, because he had "pledged his word" to Walker that he would do so. Smith was sentenced to a year in jail and fined $1,000 ($33,000 in 2024), more than a year's pay for a working sailor.[11]

The spread of Walker's revolutionary ideas incurred the wrath of Southern enslavers, who put a price on his head. They passed additional Negro Seamen Acts to limit the movement of Black sailors, but his ideas continued to circulate, inspiring resistance among the enslaved. Walker understood that taunting Southern tyrants might result in his own imprisonment or death. "Somebody must die in this cause," he said, and die he did, at age thirty-three, on August 6, 1830. Many around him suspected that he had been poisoned.[12]

Maritime subversion, like ships and sailors, ran in two directions. Seamen arrived in Southern ports, passed out their abolitionist literature, then weighed anchor and set sail back to the ports where their voyages had begun, sometimes with maritime fugitives in tow. The networks mobilized by David Walker to disseminate his pamphlet were the mirror image of the constellations of people who would, in reverse, carry runaways to Philadelphia, New York, and Boston in a maritime circuit of liberation.

"THOU SHALT NOT OPPRESS HIM," 1834

On one of his many efforts to escape slavery across the southeastern United States, from Florida to North Carolina, a tall, athletic, "keen-eyed" young man named Moses Roper experienced an epiphany. He had already crossed several rivers as he fled toward freedom. He waded and swam the smaller ones and paddled small canoes or rode ferries across the larger ones. On this escape, as he made his way toward Savannah, he "found the advantage of being six feet two inches high" as he tiptoed in the water along the riverbed. He knew that alligators inhabited the river, but they did not deter him. He also knew that his enslaver, the brutal cotton planter John Gooch, was leading a small mob of slave catchers after him, as other enslavers had all too successfully done many times in the past. The scars on his back reminded him of the price of recapture. Roper suddenly realized that "if my master was in pursuit of me, my safest place from him was in the water, if I could keep my head above the surface." The land was controlled by Gooch and his fellow enslavers, but the water, he imagined, was a place of freedom, though a dangerous one. Praying that he might "be kept from a watery grave," Roper moved slowly and deliberately toward a better life.[13]

Roper was one of the most determined runaways in American history. He made his first escape attempt at the age of thirteen and ran away at least a dozen more times over the next six years. As a teenager he battled seventeen different enslavers in a never-ending cycle of flight, recapture, grisly punishment, and resale. The slave-owning terrorists "ploughed" his back with hundreds, perhaps thousands, of lashes; crushed his fingernails in a vise; smashed his toenails on an anvil with a hammer; and poured tar on his head and set it on fire. They forced him to carry burdensome log chains, wear iron collars, and walk around with heavy bars on his feet. Roper fought a life-and-death struggle against John Gooch, who tried for three years to break

him but failed. At a certain point, Roper recalled with a sense of triumph, "the whole stock of his cruelties seemed to be exhausted." But
Roper was not yet free.

On his final escape Roper traveled 350 miles alone, by land and
river, through slave country, from Apalachicola, Florida, east-northeast
to Savannah, Georgia. He sustained himself on the long journey by
scavenging for fruit in the forest. He also begged meals here and there
and persuaded a sympathetic white person to write a pass for him.
(The light-skinned Roper was able to "pass" for white.) When Roper
finally arrived in Savannah—"a place where they are always looking
out for run-away slaves"—he went straight to the docks "and inquired
for a berth as a steward to a vessel to New York." He knew the job, as
he had done it aboard a steamer on the Apalachicola River in Florida.
In five minutes, he got a position aboard an old, rotten, leaky schooner, the *Fox*, under the authority of a Captain Deckay, "a very kind
man." When the vessel finally put to sea in August 1834, Roper was
"unable to express the joy [he] now felt." The moment of seaborne
emancipation was at hand.[14]

His joy was short-lived. Roper had never sailed the high seas and
discovered that the rolling motion of the ship wracked his gut and
made him terribly seasick. His fellow sailors—most of whom, he was at
pains to point out, were white Southerners—took umbrage and "asked
me why I shipped, as I was not used to the sea?" Roper remained ill almost the entire passage, five of the six days the *Fox* spent at sea, requiring
others to do his work. When the vessel arrived at Staten Island, several
of the sailors roughed him up before leaving the vessel.

Roper finally made it safely ashore in New York, where he immediately learned that the waterfront was crawling with slave catchers. Freedom kept edging away from him. He kept moving, working his way by
ship up the Hudson River to Albany. He then traveled overland to Vermont, New Hampshire, and finally Boston. He settled into the port for
a few weeks, working in a shop on the waterfront, but soon two "coloured men," probably sailor-abolitionists, searched him out to deliver

bad news: a bounty hunter had come to Boston looking for him. Roper took off for New York and boarded a ship named the *Napoleon* for Liverpool, where he arrived in late November 1835.

Roper published an account of his life and maritime flight, *Narrative of My Escape from Slavery*, in 1837. The book went through more than ten editions in Great Britain (three in Welsh), the United States, and Canada, selling thirty-eight thousand copies, and bringing him considerable fame as an abolitionist. He toured England, Wales, Scotland, and Ireland, giving what he figured was "upwards of 2,000" lectures, displaying "instruments of torture" and making slavery real to British audiences. He not only published one of the earliest accounts of escape by sea but added to the liberation theology of running away, finding righteous sanction in the King James version of the Bible for those who assisted their fugitive fellow creatures: "Thou shalt not deliver unto his master the servant which is escaped from his master unto thee, he shall dwell with thee, even among you, in that place which he shall choose, in one of thy gates, where it liketh him best; thou shalt not oppress him" (Deuteronomy 23:15–16). Roper traveled 4,400 miles over sixteen months, making his passage to freedom one of the longest and most grueling on record.[15]

WAR ON THE DOCKS, 1835-1836

Acting on tips from dockworkers and sailors, David Ruggles hopped from ship to anchored ship in the port of New York looking for enslaved people to emancipate and stowaways he might carry toward freedom. He had what in his day was called "mad courage"; he was always ready to fight on behalf of freedom, no matter how strong and ruthless the adversary. Born in the free Black community of the port city Norwich, Connecticut, Ruggles had gone to sea at an early age, plying the northeastern coast of the United States on one vessel after another. According to his biographer Graham Hodges, "Seafaring exposed Ruggles to militant black abolitionism." He learned "the mechanics, dangers, and successes of ocean-borne fugitives" from sailors. He left the sea after a few years but maintained his connections to waterfront workers. When he committed himself fully to the abolitionist cause in 1834, Ruggles approached the waterfront as a strategic site of struggle—a place where merchants and workers, profits and freedom met, crashed, and mixed. It was a front line in the battle against bondage.[16]

Beginning in early 1835 Ruggles fought blackbirders in New York. Some of these body snatchers were ship captains who sought to sneak men, women, and children aboard their vessels and sail away as quickly as possible out of New York, where slavery had been abolished in 1827, to anywhere it was still legal. Ruggles began to patrol the waterfront, which literally became something of a war zone. Ruggles had eyes and ears all over the docks through which he monitored the coming and going of ships. He warned the Black community by bravely publishing the names of blackbirders as well as local "traitors" who snitched to them. Rallying abolitionists and community members alike against what the Bible denounced as "man-stealing," Ruggles helped to form a new kind of abolitionist organization called the Committee of Vigilance in November 1835: its founding purposes were to defend those being kidnapped and to protect any fugitive who arrived in New York seeking freedom. The methods of resistance were confrontation and direct action, the most radical tactics of the abolitionist movement at the time. Ruggles insisted on the right of self-defense and, against the wishes of his pacifist Garrisonian abolitionist colleagues, always reserved the option to use violence if necessary. New York would not be the slaveholder's hunting ground if David Ruggles could help it.[17]

In late 1836 waterfront workers alerted Ruggles to the presence in New York Harbor of an illegal slave trade operation. The Portuguese brig *Brilhante*, captained by I. C. A. de Silva, had lately come from Gambia with several enslaved people on board. Ruggles leapt into action, publishing accounts of the slaver in the *New York Evening Post* and the *New York Sun*. He then boarded the vessel himself to verify with his own eyes that people were being held in bondage illegally. Five enslaved people were taken off the ship and placed in jail. He had de Silva arrested. Abolitionist attorney William Jay prosecuted de Silva, but a judge released him and sent the enslaved people back to their ship.[18]

If the law would not uphold the hard-won right to freedom, other means would be necessary. On Christmas Day 1836, before the *Brilhante* could exit the harbor, "a gang of negroes, some of whom were armed," went aboard the slaver, attacked the crew, and liberated two of the five being held in bondage. The crew of the *Brilhante* did not resist, but when a mate came on the main deck to try to stop the rescue, a member of the gang "cocked a pistol at him, and threatened to blow his brains out." The gang returned to the ship two hours later to try to remove the remaining three people, but this time the shipmaster and mate fought them off. Ruggles denied that he was part of the gang, but there can be no doubt that he helped to organize the raid.[19]

Two days later the notorious slave catcher Daniel D. Nash, Joseph Michaels (the mate of the *Brilhante*), and several other ruffians showed up in the middle of the night, armed with pistols, dirks, clubs, handcuffs, and a gag, at Ruggles's home on Lispenard Street. They planned to blackbird him: they were armed with a writ declaring him to be a slave whom they were now entitled to take aboard the *Brilhante* and ship southward for sale. Ruggles fought them off long enough for the city watch to arrive and arrest Nash and Michaels. When Ruggles went to city hall the next morning to press the case, he was himself arrested by another slave catcher, Tobias Boudinot, and locked up in Bellevue Penitentiary. Ruggles gained his release and continued to agitate about the case, while de Silva sailed away with the three remaining captives. Publicity surrounding the militant liberation of the two captives likely spurred other abolitionists to found new Vigilance Committees in Philadelphia (1837) and Boston

(1841). What would soon be known as the Underground Railroad had its origins on the waterfront.[20]

NOT MUCH OF A SAILOR, 1837–38

Jim Matthews prowled the waterfront of Charleston, South Carolina, in December 1837, looking for a ship. His first two efforts to escape slavery had resulted in recapture and vicious floggings that left thick scars on his back, so he fully realized the risk he was taking. He now stood at the stevedore's stand on the dock, hoping for work. Having grown up in Four Holes, a swampy region thirty miles inland, he knew little about life on the waterfront. A dock boss came along and asked Matthews if he wanted work, and he said yes. Off he went in a gang of workers to stow bales of cotton aboard a vessel in port. At midday the stevedores retired to a local cookhouse for a meal. Matthews followed the group but he had no money, so he slipped away and returned to the ship, where he met the steward on deck. The white man proved friendly and gave him something to eat.[21]

Later in the week Matthews returned to the vessel to work and "saw something shining on the ground" amid the dockside bales of cotton. He did not know what it was, but he nonetheless stooped down, picked it up, looked it over, and put it in his pocket. That night a waterfront guard boarded the vessel and yelled to the boss, "Holloo, have you got any run-away n——s here?" The head stevedore protected both himself and his fellow worker: "no,—no runaways in this lot." The guard then asked to see everyone's badges, a license the city required of every stevedore to prevent exactly what Matthews was doing: working his way aboard a ship for the purpose of escape. Matthews watched nervously as one dockworker after another displayed his badge to the guard. When the officer came to him, Matthews reached into his pocket with a trembling hand and pulled out the shiny object he had found on the dock. The guard looked at it, nodded, and moved on. Had Matthews not found that lost badge, he would have been taken directly to the "Sugar House," a dungeon-like workhouse for runaways where he had already spent three months of literal torture. Fugitives needed luck.

Charleston authorities required enslaved workers to be licensed to labor on tall ships. Jim Matthews luckily found a badge on the docks and used it to escape slavery in 1837.

Matthews kept meeting with the steward who one day "asked me what I would give him to carry me to the free country," meaning Boston, where the vessel was bound. Matthews had no money, but he eagerly promised two months of future wages. Labor would buy his freedom. The steward answered that he could help him but would not take any money for it. He told Matthews to come back late that same night. When Matthews returned, the steward led him down into the hold of the vessel and told him to crawl into a narrow space between bales of cotton and stay there. The next morning the ship set sail for Boston. The steward brought Matthews food and drink every night and after a long voyage welcomed him to the "free country." Waiting until the entire crew had disembarked, he took Matthews ashore and pointed him toward the "colored sailor's boarding house," a safe haven.

On his way Matthews met a Black man—probably a sailor—who asked, Matthews recalled, "if I was a sailor." Matthews was tired, weak, and unsteady on his feet, but he still had a sense of humor: "I told him not much of one, but that I had just come from a ship." The man looked him over closely and saw that his ragged clothes were covered by pills and wisps of cotton. He realized that he was a fugitive and said, "I understand it all." The man took Matthews to the boardinghouse and the next day escorted him to a local abolitionist, "who gave me some warm clothes." Matthews eventually moved farther north, working as a laborer in Hallowell, Maine, where another abolitionist took down his story of escape and published it the following year.

FROM MARITIME ESCAPE TO PERSONAL LIBERTY LAWS, 1839

The men talked as they worked aboard a schooner called the *Robert Center*, anchored in Norfolk in 1839. Three Black sailors, Isaac Gansey, Peter Johnson, and Edward Smith, all based in New York, conversed with a local enslaved man, also named Isaac, who had come aboard as a ship carpenter to make repairs on the vessel. Impressed by Isaac's skill, one of the sailors remarked that he would be "foolish to remain in Virginia as he could get good wages in the north." No fool, Isaac hid among a cargo of oak timber and sailed to New York with his three new friends. Meanwhile, Isaac's enslaver, John G. Colley, figured out how he had escaped and dispatched to New York two slave catchers, who promptly captured Isaac and dragged him back to Virginia. Colley then insisted that Gansey, Johnson, and Smith be arrested and returned to Virginia to be tried for the felony of "slave stealing." Virginia lieutenant governor Henry L. Hopkins supported Colley and wrote to New York governor William H. Seward, insisting that he send the sailors back for trial.[22]

Served with a requisition demanding the return of the three sailors, Seward read it and concluded that "the case was novel, the papers curt, the proofs defective, and the aspect of it repugnant." Slavery had been abolished in New York in 1827, and according to state law the men had done nothing wrong; they had neither legal nor moral guilt. Seward refused to comply with the request. The sailors had already been locked up, but soon a local abolitionist submitted a writ of habeas corpus on their behalf to a jail official, who promptly freed them. The sailors disappeared, but the dispute did not.[23]

Virginia's enslavers were furious—about Seward's decision and about the growing numbers of bondmen and bondwomen who had in recent years escaped north by sea. They were eager to make examples of Gansey, Johnson, and Smith. Virginia governor Thomas W. Gilmer entered the fray, announcing to the members of the state's senate and house that these sailors "strike boldly at the foundation of the social relations of the states, if they do not disturb the very elements of society itself, in all the slave-holding states." Virginia's rulers were ready to fight to protect the vital interests of the South.[24]

Seward coolly replied that New York's laws "did not admit the possibility that one man could be stolen from another." Gilmer replied that "property rights in man" were protected by the US Constitution, while Seward made the case for the primacy, in this instance, of states' rights. Seward then escalated the battle by passing legislation to guarantee fugitives legal representation and jury trials in New York. He led the repeal of the existing law that allowed Southerners to bring the people they enslaved to New York for nine months, thereby establishing a "free soil"—or more accurately in this case, a "free harbor" doctrine. He also reserved to himself the right to appoint agents who would negotiate on behalf of free people of color who had been kidnapped and sold into slavery in the South. These personal liberty laws would become foundations of the struggle against slavery in the Northern states.[25]

Virginia's indignant elites responded by passing "an act to prevent citizens of New York from carrying slaves out of the Commonwealth," a vessel-inspection act meant to tax and punish shipowners and captains from New York. They then upped the ante by threatening secession from the Union and appealing to other Southern states for support. The ruling classes of South Carolina and Georgia, who had their own problems with sailors and fugitives, complied with similar legislation against New York shipping. The controversy would smolder for seven years.[26]

Seward, who personally disliked slavery, was by no means an abolitionist when the three Black sailors and the fugitive forced his hand and educated him on the issue of bondage. Between 1839 and 1843, he nonetheless put the power of the state of New York behind abolitionist sailors and fugitives. Southerners heard in his actions "the maniac yell of fanaticism" and the threat of "universal emancipation." What began as a conversation about labor on the deck of a schooner became an interstate battle over political power and constitutional rights. Maritime runaways had become a national controversy, covered by newspapers from Massachusetts to Louisiana.[27]

SONG AND DANCE, 1830s

Much of the secretive culture of maritime escape has been lost, but seaborne resistance sometimes erupted into visibility in surprising ways. The practice of escaping in the holds of North-bound vessels was so frequent in the 1830s that an account of the life of the fictional Jim Crow, the folk trickster, stage sensation, and Blackface minstrel who emerged from African American dance competitions on the docks of New York included these lines:

> I jump aboard the boat, ah, early in the mornin'
> And I leave [New] Orleans, just as the day was dawnin',
> I hide under the wood where the n——s had tossed 'em.

Jim Crow was said to have hidden in the hold of a timber ship and made his way to New York. Thousands of others found refuge among barrels of rice, hogsheads of tobacco, and bales of cotton.[28]

Another subversive musical performance was recorded in New Orleans, where enslaved maritime workers taunted their bosses with a song about escaping slavery by sea. Sailors frequently made up such spontaneous and oppositional ditties as they worked. The refrain of the "Runaway's Song of Defiance" was:

> It's true they cannot catch me
> There is a schooner on the sea
> It's true they cannot catch me

The dockers and sailors sang the threat, in English and in French, as they worked and as they celebrated the famous one-armed runaway and bandit known as Bras-Coupé.[29]

"THAT BROTHER'S PRAYER," 1840

The deepening racism of the early nineteenth century transformed maritime labor, dividing workers ashore, on the docks, and at sea, where growing numbers of skilled African American mariners found themselves confined to the lower-paying positions of cook and steward aboard ships. In 1837 these Black "Sons of Neptune" turned the racialization of the division of labor into a source of strength, organizing in New York a new mutual aid organization called the Stewards' and Cooks' Marine Benevolent Society.[30]

Much of what is known about the society appeared in a single article published in the *Colored American* newspaper on May 2, 1840, recounting the group's annual dinner celebration held at the Phoenix Saloon, 60 Lispenard Street, less than a block from the home of David Ruggles, a center of activism of the recently formed New York Committee of Vigilance. According to President John Mitchell, the society proudly boasted eighty-nine members and cash on hand of $548.42 (more than $17,100 in 2024), although he also noted the death of five members over the past year and another who was ill.

The society had its own constitution, rules, and seal and sought rec-
ognition by the New York state legislature.[31]

The mood of the meeting, according to a reporter for the *Colored
American*, was one of "general hilarity," within which the sailors exchanged "the best and noblest sentiments" among themselves and
with the "landlubbers" and "teetotalers" present among them. On this
festive occasion, the supporters of temperance winked at the use of
alcohol among those who suffered long, dangerous voyages across the
vast Atlantic, missing the comforts of home. The tone of the meeting
turned serious when it came time for toasts—to William Lloyd Garrison and the American Anti-Slavery Society, and to equal rights for
"colored people" as "enjoyed by other men." The politics of the society
were explicitly abolitionist, based on the Biblical injunction "do unto
others as you would be done by."

The fundamental purpose and guiding principle of the society was
solidarity, which its members extended to fellow sailors and to their
wives and children, many of whom lived in poverty. The goal of the
group was "to participate in another's woes, to sympathize with distress, and feel a glow of satisfaction at the happiness of others." The
society also vowed "to administer comfort and cheer the hearts of the
widow and orphan," the collateral victims of a deadly occupation.
President Mitchell summarized the ethos of the society in verse:

> 'Tis not to pause, when at our door
> A shivering brother stands,
> To ask the cause that made him poor,
> Or why he help demands.
> 'Tis not to spurn that brother's prayer,
> For faults he once had known—
> 'Tis not to leave him in despair,
> And say that we have none.

Every sentiment expressed in these lines toward a poor, shivering, de-
spairing brother seaman applied equally well to a would-be fugitive

slave, who might be taken aboard by a member of the society with no questions asked. This kind of solidarity is precisely why Black stewards and cooks were routinely snatched from their ships and jailed for the duration of the vessel's turnaround time in Southern ports. The men of the Stewards' and Cooks' Maritime Benevolent Society embodied the nightmare of the Southern port city ruling class: they were the very people who might distribute abolitionist literature and assist their brothers and sisters who sought to make their way to freedom by sea.[32]

TOOLS, CORDAGE, SAILS, 1843

Sarah Moore escaped bondage in New Bern, North Carolina, in 1843, concealed by a ship's steward in an "unoccupied state-room forward of ye cabin," a place used for the ship's stores such as tools, oakum, tar, cordage, canvas sails, and "other articles of daily necessity." The steward helped Moore to cover herself with these items and lie still to avoid being found out by the ship's mate, who routinely visited the room, lantern in hand, to pick up this or that. Moore explained to abolitionist Sydney Howard Gay that the mate "never discovered her, so well was she concealed in a place only partially lighted, + so quiet did she keep herself." Moore never left the cabin and spent the entire seven-day voyage disguised by the materials of maritime labor. She arrived safely in New York.[33]

THE GHOST, 1847

Eager to escape slavery and willing to die in the effort, John Andrew Jackson spoke urgently with the Black cook of a ship anchored in the harbor of Charleston, South Carolina, on the day after Christmas 1846. Jackson asked if the vessel was bound for Boston. The cook replied that it was. "Can't you stow me away?" Jackson asked. The cook was sympathetic but nervous: "Yes," said he, "but don't you betray me! Did not some white man send you here to ask me this?" Jackson swore that he had come on his own initiative.[34]

The cook told Jackson that he and several other Black sailors had just been released from jail after their captain posted bond. Jackson, who had grown up in Sumter, South Carolina, about one hundred miles inland from Charleston, was surprised: "What did they put you in jail for?" The cook then explained the Negro Seamen Act: "They put every free negro in jail that comes here [by sea], to keep them from going among the slaves," and let them out only twenty-four hours before the ship went back to sea. The cook then reiterated his willingness to help—if "you are sure no white man has sent you here." Merchants and enslavers sometimes sent people aboard vessels to test the willingness of captain and crew to break the law by offering to carry someone to a free state. The stakes were high for the cook, who could end up back in jail or even sold into bondage. He told John to return the next morning.

The next day Jackson found the cook lighting a fire in his galley and asked him "to redeem his promise" and "stow me away," only to discover that the cook had lost his nerve. Having thought the matter over, the cook ordered Jackson off the ship: "Walk ashore," he said, "I will have nothing to do with you; I am sure some white person sent you here." The would-be fugitive protested, "No, no one knows it but me and you." The cook countered, "I don't believe it . . . so you walk ashore." Jackson turned toward the gangway, but he would not be easily discouraged.

As Jackson looked back, he saw the cook reenter the galley and close the door. He then "crept stealthily on tiptoe to the hatch," the large, covered opening to the ship's hold. He stood there "fearing and hoping"—afraid that the cook might come out of the galley at any moment and at the same wishing that the captain or mate might emerge from the cabin and open the hatchway for him. Luckily, the mate stepped out, Jackson presented himself as a stevedore, and he was let into the hold. His bluff had worked.

The hold soon began to fill up with real stevedores, all Black, ready to load the vessel's cargo of cotton bales. A member of the work gang asked Jackson, "Are you going to work here this morning?" The would-be stowaway replied no. The man was puzzled; "Arn't you a stevedore?" Jackson again said no. With growing suspicion the man then asked, "Who do you belong to?" The quick-witted John answered, "I belong to South Carolina." He thought to himself, "It was none of their business whom I belonged to; I was trying to belong to myself."

Jackson then found a hiding place: "I slipped myself between two bales of cotton, with the deck above me, in a space not large enough for a bale of cotton to go." By this time the workers had begun to lower the bulky bales of cotton down into the hold. They placed a bale "at the mouth of my crevice," hiding him from the ship's captain and crew. Jackson was now enclosed in a musty-smelling space "about 4-ft. by 3-ft., or thereabouts," "left in total darkness," and "stifled for want of air." He had luck on his side: the wooden bulkhead at his back, on the other side of which was the steerage, where the sailors slept, had a broken board that allowed air to come through. He had also taken a useful precaution: he brought with him a gimlet, a hand tool for drilling holes in wood, just in case. He also had two knives, some hardtack biscuit, and a bottle of water.

Jackson awakened the next morning to the sailors singing their farewells as they weighed anchor. The vessel began to rock from side to side, thrilling Jackson that his "journey from slavery to freedom" had begun. His heart filled with joy at the prospect that "I soon should be able to call myself FREE." Yet the feeling was not to last, as seasickness and soon the "horrors of thirst" made him wish for even "the filthiest water in my native swamp" near the plantation on which he had grown up. Jackson pulled out his gimlet and bored two holes into the ship's deck above his head. He saw the sailors walking about the deck above him, but since no one had authorized his boarding, he was afraid to reveal his presence by asking for water. He sat silent and thirsty in the dark for the remainder of the day.

The next morning Jackson saw a sailor standing right above him "with his arms folded, apparently in deep thought." Desperate, he called out, "Pour me some water down, I am [al]most dead for water." The seafarer, disoriented by the sound, did not look down but rather looked up at the ship's rigging, "apparently thinking the voice came from there." Jackson then cut off a long splinter of wood with his knife and pushed it up through the hole to attract the man's attention. The sailor saw it and ran immediately to the captain, crying, "There is a ghost aboard!"

The captain arrived, got down on his hands and knees, peered through the holes, and saw Jackson in the hold. He demanded to know how he got there. Jackson replied with careful ambiguity: "I got stowed away." The same fear that had gripped the cook two days earlier now possessed the captain, who asked "if some white man did not stow him away to get him in trouble?" Jackson assured him that this was all his own doing. Soon the cook arrived and verified the story; the man "wanted me to stow him away at Charleston, but I would not." The captain called to the sailors, "Boys, get the chisel and cut him out." Once on deck John grabbed from the cook a half-gallon bucket of water and "drained it to the last drop."

The captain swore to "put me into the first vessel he met, and send me back" to Charleston, but luck was with the fugitive. They met no vessel and soon they approached Boston. The captain's view of Jackson softened when the pilot came aboard to guide the ship to the wharf. Rather than turn him in, he sent Jackson into the forecastle, where he would not be seen. Later that evening, February 10, 1847, Jackson arrived in Boston, in the free state of Massachusetts. He thanked God that he "had escaped from hell to heaven." Now he "felt as I had never felt before—that is, master of myself." In his joy he felt like "a bouncing sparrow."

The solidarity of the sailors now took over. Three tars, Jim, Frank, and Dennis, took the runaway to the sailor's boardinghouse on Richmond Street near Rowe's Wharf. They got him both a room and a job with Henry Foreman, the proprietor of the boardinghouse, where John worked for his lodging and meals until he left Boston for Salem. Not long afterward a slave catcher named Neddy Anderson showed up at the boardinghouse and demanded to see Jackson. Foreman protected him, claiming not to know where he was. Several sailors, incensed that a "slave-hunter" had entered their establishment, drove Anderson out. Foreman wrote to Jackson that "they were hunting for me there" and that he should stay away from Boston. Jackson traveled on to Canada and finally to England and Scotland, where he lectured in the abolitionist circuit of churches and meetings from Edinburgh and Glasgow to London.[35]

CONFIDENCE MAN, 1848

Thomas Chambers, as he called himself, or "Morris," as his enslaver J. W. Ellis called him, mastered the details of social life in the South to escape bondage by sea. Ellis, who lived in Salisbury, North Carolina, hired Thomas out to F. A. Hoke, proprietor of the American Hotel in Charleston, South Carolina, where Chambers had the opportunity to meet and interact with scores of mobile people. He made the most of it. On July 13, 1848, he got aboard the *Columbus*, bound for Philadelphia. When the steamship arrived at the dock, Chambers disembarked onto the free soil of Pennsylvania and would be lost to his enslaver ever after. His victory of head-work, or intelligence, over brute force was based on a clever, elaborate ruse.[36]

Chambers pretended to be free—and in the most convincing ways. A couple of days before the *Columbus* was to depart Charleston, he went boldly to the man in charge of the steamer, Captain S. M. Welsh, about coming aboard as a passenger. He showed the captain his "free papers." Welsh referred Thomas to H. F. Baker, the business agent of the *Columbus*, whose job it was, among other things, to inspect the documents of the many free Black passengers who wished to travel to Philadelphia. Welsh and Baker knew that enslaved people routinely tried to board their ship. Indeed, Chambers was not the only person seeking a passage to freedom on the next voyage of the *Columbus*. Welsh later observed that three other enslaved people had also tried to escape by sea. All three were "thwarted."

Chambers met with Baker in his office, brandishing his papers, which had a seal and a signature from a magistrate in North Carolina. To Baker's experienced eye, which had pored over "many free papers," those carried by Chambers "appeared to be genuine," suggesting that he had either purloined papers belonging to someone else or engaged in high-level forgery. But Baker was not yet convinced. He sent Chambers away, saying that "he would not be taken as a passenger, unless he produced a white man to certify that the papers were genuine."

The next day Chambers returned to Baker's office in the company of a white gentleman, "genteelly dressed," named Hackey, who explained that "he had known [Chambers] from his early youth, and knew him to be free; and that they were both from the same place" in North Carolina. Convinced by the class of the man's clothing and demeanor, Baker "saw nothing to excite suspicion" and approved Chambers's bid for a ticket. Chambers paid the fee and prepared to depart, but Hackey's part in the drama was not yet over. To make Chambers even more believable as a passenger, Hackey then went to Captain Welsh to explain that he was booking "a passage for his servant." To both Baker and Welsh, everything seemed to be in order.[37]

Chambers went aboard the ship "without concealment," nattily dressed and acting the part of a well-to-do free person of color. He moved freely around the main deck, conversing over several days with other passengers, including William Kelly, who noted that among the fifty to sixty on board, there were "four or five other colored persons," all of whom were "said to be free." Kelly spoke with Chambers every day. The other Black passengers, who were common on the packet ship's regular voyages, were part of his cover.

Kelly noted that when the vessel pulled up to the dock in the City of Brotherly Love, Chambers was the first person to go ashore, although he attached no particular significance to the fact at the time. Soon a courier from the telegraph office rushed to the *Columbus* to report that a fugitive named Morris had been aboard. Kelly jumped into action but quickly discovered that not everyone shared his enthusiasm for recapturing Chambers. Even Captain Welsh, after learning of the escape, did not, according to Kelly, "make any exertion for the capture" of the escaped bondman. When one of the owners of the *Columbus* offered a police officer a reward to capture and return him, "he declined the undertaking." Chambers had disappeared, and no one was in pursuit.

When Ellis subsequently sued Welsh for the value of his lost property—the "intelligent" man said to be worth $1,000—the attorney defending Welsh blamed the enslaver for what had happened. First, he claimed, "he should have kept [Chambers] at home." Hiring him out so far away in Charleston had dramatically reduced control over the bondman's movements. Even more important, the attorney claimed, Ellis had "educated [Chambers] in port and manners, as to give him the arts of deception, and the semblance of a freeman." The attorney was certainly right about the arts of deception, but he was wrong to give the credit to Ellis. From acquiring the "free papers," to enlisting a white ally, to acting out a drama as a free person aboard the *Columbus*, Chambers had pulled off one of the most audacious escapes in the long annals of seeking freedom by sea. His confidence was duly rewarded.[38]

"I COULD ACT," 1848

Daniel Drayton, a white captain who grew up on the New Jersey shore and lived most of his working life in Philadelphia, attempted the largest mass escape from slavery during the antebellum era. On April 15, 1848, he took seventy-seven men, women, and children aboard the *Pearl*, docked at the remote Seventh Street Wharf in Washington, DC, bound for freedom in Philadelphia. Owing to poor weather and bad luck, the escape failed. Drayton, his two crewmates, and the freedom seekers were captured and returned to the nation's capital, where police held at bay an angry mob eager to lynch Drayton. Convicted in a high-profile show trial and sentenced to twenty years in prison, Drayton served four years and four months before abolitionist senator Charles Sumner from Massachusetts petitioned President Millard Fillmore to pardon him in the summer of 1852. Drayton's trial provoked a heated debate in the House of Representatives, broadcasting maritime escape to a national audience.[39]

The enslaved people of Chesapeake Bay had recruited Drayton to the abolitionist cause. Every time he docked his trading vessel, they clambered aboard to handle cargo—and they had an agenda. They told Drayton about their harsh treatment, how their children were sold away to the Deep South. Drayton learned "by intercourse with the negroes, that they had the same desires, wishes and hopes, as myself." He explained that "there is not a waterman who ever sailed in Chesapeake Bay who will not tell you that, so far from the slaves needing any prompting to run away, the difficulty is, when they ask you to assist them, to make them take no for an answer." Drayton, having "read in the Bible that God had made of one flesh all the nations of the earth," was moved by these conversations. He began to say yes.

On the Potomac River docks in 1847, a free Black man named Paul Jennings, formerly enslaved by President James Madison, approached Drayton to take an enslaved woman, her five children, and a niece to her free husband in Frenchtown, Maryland. The woman had already paid for her freedom, but her enslaver had refused to honor the deal. Drayton agreed take them and successfully completed the voyage. Word of the deed circulated through the free Black and enslaved communities of Washington and northern Virginia, which led to his venture on the *Pearl* and subsequent arrest a few months later.

By the time Drayton got out of jail in 1852, his health and his spirit had been broken. With the assistance of a friend, he wrote a memoir. He gave lectures on the abolitionist circuit. But he and his family remained destitute. He even proposed another large-scale rescue in Norfolk, a foolhardy action he was not physically capable of carrying out. In 1857 he went to New Bedford and checked into the Mansion House Hotel. He was found dead the next day of a laudanum overdose. He had no baggage and only $12 on his person. Drayton had already written his own epitaph in his memoir: he admired those who protested slavery using "burning words and eloquent speeches," in books and sermons. But he, as a humble seaman, "could not do that." Yet he found his own way: "I could not talk, I could not write; but I could act."[40]

DEFYING DEATH, 1848

William Curtis worked on a big plantation in Darien, Georgia, sailing up and down the Altamaha River as a boatman. His enslaver, Jacob Famous, had so many bondspeople, he did not know their names. The overseers who ran his plantation treated the enslaved "very roughly." Curtis recalled the fate of a fourteen-year-old girl who "positively refused to have intercourse with her master, said she would sooner die." Her defiance earned her a hundred lashes with a cat-o'-nine-tails. She fainted after the first fifty. The whipper waited until she came to, then flogged her fifty more times. She passed out again, never regained consciousness, and soon "was buried like a dog," Curtis bitterly remembered.[41]

"Taking out" for freedom had been on Curtis's mind for a while, as he watched the ships come and go in Darien. He paid special attention to "colored sailors" as a possible lifeline to freedom. He noted the effect of the Negro Seamen Act: "Those who come in American vessels are always taken out as soon as they arrive and are imprisoned until the vessel sails," but those who came on British ships from Liverpool or Halifax, Canada, were not jailed. When he learned that Famous planned to sell some of his workers, Curtis planned with Samuel Glenn to take immediate action: they would try "to escape to the north which they thought was a free country." On the evening of October 30, 1848, they boarded "a small boat of about 14 feet keel" and set the vessel's two sails to glide down the Altamaha River, into the Atlantic.[42]

Curtis and Glenn reached the Atlantic near the mouth of the Savannah River two days later and now had to get past the guard boat that "lays there to search vessels . . . and prevent the escape of Fugitive Slaves." Fortunately for the fugitives, rain was pouring, and all the patrol vessel's hands were below deck. The men slipped by safely. Because their vessel was small, they planned to sail northward within sight of land, but a "stiff North East Storm" forced them to make a fateful choice: either go ashore or sail farther out to sea. It is not clear how much they knew about the danger they would face in a small open boat sailing in stormy Atlantic waters, but they courageously chose to head out to sea "in hopes of falling in with a vessel that would take them north."

The fugitives battled a "heavy sea" for six days, then catastrophe struck. A wave smashed the small boat, throwing Glenn, who was "a very expert swimmer," overboard. He swam from "the top of the waves" to "the trough of the sea" as Curtis tried to pull him back into the boat. He failed and Glenn perished. Now all alone in a desperate situation, Curtis held out amid the storm for another five days, the last four without provisions or water, which had been washed overboard. On the twelfth day out, someone aboard a ship sailing from the Windward Islands to Boston spotted him and picked him up. The storm had carried him hundreds of miles. Curtis later noted that "the captain took him on board and treated him well," even though he must have known that the man he rescued was a fugitive. Curtis arrived at Boston on November 22. A member of the Massachusetts Historical Society wrote down his death-defying freedom tale for posterity.

"STICK TO IT," 1852

Born free in Poughkeepsie, New York, Nate Lobam went to sea at age thirteen and spent the next thirty years traveling around the world on steamers and sailing vessels. According to the journalist who interviewed him about his eventful life in 1874, "He has traveled from Maine to Mexico, from New York around the Horn to San Francisco, and even to Hong Kong, China." He was a crew member aboard the steamship *Henry Clay* in 1852, when its boiler burst and the entire ship went up in flames on the Hudson River, killing eighty. He was also aboard the steamer *Golden Age* when it was wrecked near Coiba Island on the Pacific coast of Central America in 1855. He once ventured into a gambling den in Panama to rescue a drunken shipmate, fought off several men who attacked him with machetes, and killed four of them as he escaped. He was sent to prison with a date to be executed before Captain Thatcher of the US sloop of war *Decatur* somehow rescued him and brought him home. After Lobam retired from the sea he became a well-known figure on the streets of New York, selling bananas and telling his vivid life stories at the corner of First Street and the Bowery on the Lower East Side.[43]

Lobam had played a critical role in the liberation of eight enslaved people aboard the steamship *City of Richmond* in September 1852. Jonathan Lemmon of Bath County, Virginia, came aboard and asked Lobam for the captain, saying that "he wanted to carry some 'n——' north, then reship them to Texas," where he planned to settle. He also had to get tickets for himself, his wife, and their seven children. Lobam summoned the captain, with whom Lemmon made a deal to keep the enslaved "closely confined" aboard the *City of Richmond* until they boarded a steamship to New Orleans and Galveston. Lobam knew that the practice was common but illegal: "When [the enslaved] arrived in a free state, they were free," according to New York's personal liberty laws.[44]

Once the *City of Richmond* had gotten out to sea, Lobam crept into the steerage to meet with the eight enslaved people, two women and six children: Emeline, age twenty-three, with her younger brothers Lewis (sixteen) and Edward (thirteen) and her two-year-old daughter Amanda; and Nancy (twenty), along with her twin sons Lewis and Edward (seven) and her daughter Ann (five). They were all kin. Lobam asked the women a simple question, "whether they would like their freedom." They responded enthusiastically that they did. Lobam told them that he had a plan and all they needed to do was "keep quiet" and "stick to it" once they docked in New York.

When the vessel arrived in port, Lobam sent shipmates with messages to three abolitionists: Black porter Louis Napoleon, prominent free Black businessman David Curry, and white attorney Erastus Culver. Napoleon secured a habeas writ, which freed the enslaved people of their shipboard incarceration and soon, after they spent a brief stint in the town jail, brought them before Judge Elijah Paine, who liberated them again. After two more arrests, several vigilant protests in the streets and courtrooms by the Black community of New York, and two more rulings in their favor, the eight moved on, with the assistance of Napoleon and other abolitionists, to freedom in Ontario, Canada. Meanwhile, the rich merchants of New York feared that the successful emancipation from below would damage their business dealings with Southerners and raised $5,240 ($207,000 in 2024) to reimburse Lemmon for his loss.[45]

Lobam's whispered question in the bowels of the steamship in 1852 moved in a direct, unbroken line to the crisis of the Union and the coming of the Civil War a decade later. Even though the eight freed people were safely ensconced in Canada and beyond the reach of the American legal system, Jonathan Lemmon continued to pursue his property rights in court, which prompted a protracted battle between the legislatures and legal systems of New York and his native Virginia. The Lobam-Napoleon connection detonated a fierce national struggle. The appeal process, which was fundamentally about people "in transitu," kept the issue of the mobile maritime struggle against slavery before an increasingly inflamed public. The Lemmon case made its way slowly through the New York court system, and many believed it would reach the Supreme Court, where it had the potential to nationalize slavery by overturning all state laws against it and reestablishing the full property rights of enslavers in all Northern states. Debate over the Lemmon case raged in the press. The authors of South Carolina's "Declaration of the Immediate Causes which Induce and Justify the Secession of South Carolina from the Federal Union" (December 1860) invoked the case, as did the Confederate constitution. Nate Lobam and others who worked on the Atlantic system of escape hastened the coming of Civil War.[46]

A SAILOR'S SEA CHEST, 1857

James Noble of Baltimore had a pretty good idea about what had happened, even though he had been powerless to stop it. He claimed a young woman named Lear Green as his property. She was "about 18 years of age, black complexion, round featured, good looking and ordinary size." She was likely a "fancy girl"—someone forced into prostitution and repeated rape. The clue lay in her stylish silken clothes—bonnet, dress, and cape. This was not how most enslaved people dressed. Noble also knew that Green's boyfriend, the quick-spoken, scar-faced William Adams, and his mother, both free people of color, were likely involved in the escape. Adams "had been heard to say he was going to marry" Green and take her to New York by ship.[47]

Baltimore was known for a rigorous train and ship inspection system designed to prevent escape from bondage, so it took special headwork and planning to beat it. Green, Adams, and his mother designed a plan, the centerpiece of which was a seaman's chest, the rough wooden box in which mariners carried everything they needed for a long sea voyage. Inside the chest, the plotters placed a quilt, a pillow, a few articles of clothing, "a small quantity of food and a bottle of water," and finally Green herself. The sea chest would be her vessel within the vessel. Adams and his mother then fastened strong ropes around the box and placed it as freight aboard one of the overnight steamships of the Ericsson Line, which ran regularly from Baltimore to Philadelphia (not in this case to New York, as Noble thought). Adams's mother would accompany the chest on the voyage, knowing that the racist policy of the shipping company required all people of color to remain on deck, which was exactly where she wanted to be, near the chest that carried Green. Even so, she fretted terribly and wanted to open the wooden box to provide fresh air, and even "to see if the poor child still lived."[48]

Eighteen hours later, the steamer arrived at the wharf in Philadelphia, where all freight was unloaded, including the box with the stowaway hidden inside. Green and Adams had arranged to have the chest delivered to friends of his mother on Barley Street, where her relieved and joyful liberation took place. Acting on behalf of the Philadelphia Vigilance Committee, William Still took the young woman into his own home for several days, to protect her and to help her recover her health. Green explained to her benefactor that through it all "she had no fear."

Still, who had assisted many hundreds of runaways, was impressed

Lear Green escaped bondage in Baltimore in 1857 by hiding in a sailor's sea chest. Her means of escape was one of the most ingenious methods ever devised.

by the spirit, courage, and audacity of the plan: "Such hungering and thirsting for liberty, as was evinced by Lear Green, made the efforts of the most ardent friends, who were in the habit of aiding fugitives, seem feeble in the extreme." Of all of those who successfully escaped to the northern United States or to Canada and "purchased their liberty by downright bravery, through perils the most hazardous," not one of them, Still insisted, "deserve more praise than Lear Green." Still had her photographed while sitting inside the sea chest and kept the improvised vehicle to freedom "as a rare trophy." He concluded that the impression made by the two women involved in the escape upon the abolitionist movement "can never be effaced."[49]

"THEY NEVER MOVED," 1850s

The solidarity of sailors could take various forms, even on the same freedom voyage, as an unnamed escapee explained to Quaker abolitionist Elizabeth Buffum Chace of Valley Falls, Rhode Island. A Black steward had led two fugitives aboard his vessel in Portsmouth, Virginia, hiding one in the hold and the other in his own cabin, feeding them at night during the voyage. When the vessel arrived in Wareham, Massachusetts, the captain discovered one of the men, vowed to ship him back to slavery, and locked him in the cabin. The man broke through the locked door and jumped onto the wharf. "The Captain," he recalled, "called to the men to seize me, but they never moved, and I ran up the street as fast as I could." He escaped. One member of the crew had hidden and fed the men, while the other sailors, who may not have known that the fugitives were on board, disobeyed an order at a crucial moment and thereby facilitated the escape.[50]

SENATOR MASON'S FUGITIVE, 1858

William Carpenter probably appreciated the irony more than anyone. He escaped his enslaver, James Murray Mason, who was the grandson of Founding Father George Mason, the descendant of a long line of Virginia enslavers, a member of the United States Senate, and, most important of all, the primary author of the Fugitive Slave Act of 1850. Carl Schurz, a freedom fighter in the European revolutions of 1848–49 who had emigrated to the United States, described Mason as "a thick-set, heavily built man with a decided expression of dullness in his face. What he had to say appeared to me to come from a sluggish intellect spurred into activity by an overweening self-conceit." The fierce Southern chauvinist was animated by "the surly pretension of a naturally stupid person to be something better than other people, and the insistence that they must bow to his assumed aristocracy and all its claims." Carpenter refused to bow and took to his feet.[51]

When Carpenter arrived at the office of William Still in 1858, his presence caused a stir. Still observed, "It was highly pleasing to have a visit from a 'chattel' belonging to the leading advocate of the infamous Fugitive Slave Bill. He was hurriedly interviewed for the sake of reliable information." Carpenter carried within him intelligence from the front line of the struggle, locally in Frederick County, Virginia, and nationally in Washington, DC.[52]

Carpenter began by acknowledging that "incidents of extreme cruelty might not have been so common on Mason's place as on some others" in Virginia, but he did not share the senator's view of the superiority of the Southern way of life. He summed up his experience:

> I belonged to Senator Mason. The Senator was down on colored people. He owned about eighty head—was very rich and a big man, rich enough to lose all of them. He kept terrible overseers; they would beat you with a stick the same as a dog. The overseers were poor white trash; he would give them about sixty dollars a year.

Still quietly noted Carpenter's victory over "the Father of the Fugitive Slave Law—Senator Mason" and announced with joy that the "Year of Jubilee has come."

TWO BONNETS AND A PARASOL, 1859

An enslaved person known as "Irvin" boarded the steamship *Wilson Small* "in full female apparel" in June 1859, carrying in one hand a box with two bonnets and in the other a parasol. They "had stuffed [their] bosom with old rags for a delicate purpose." Hailing from Snow Hill on the Atlantic coast of Maryland's Eastern Shore, "Irvin" sailed to Baltimore as a first passage toward freedom. The fugitive's height, "six feet tall," and "giant like proportions . . . excited suspicions to [their] sex" during the voyage. Once the ship docked, the first mate of the steamer turned "Irvin" over to a constable, who took the fugitive to jail "in the unbecoming apparel [they] had assumed" to await "the requisition of his master." Cross-dressing was another weapon in the freedom struggle.[53]

HEAD-WORK

These escapes by sea originated in ports in Georgia (Savannah and Darien), South Carolina (Charleston), North Carolina (New Bern, Wilmington), Virginia (Richmond, Norfolk), and Maryland (Baltimore), and ended farther up the Atlantic in Philadelphia, New York, Providence, and Boston. Because of the heavy traffic of cotton ships from Boston and New York to Liverpool, several of the fugitives sailed on to Great Britain, where slavery had been abolished on August 1, 1834. Others went on, by land and by sea, to Canada. The geography of escape by sea changed with the passage of James Murray Mason's Fugitive Slave Act by the US Congress in 1850, which rendered precarious the lives of many who had escaped to Northern ports. Yet, for the entire antebellum era, the maritime system of escape was Atlantic in scope. The broader the fugitive's geographic knowledge, the greater the likelihood of successful escape.

Various motivations drove these fugitives to the docks and ships of the Atlantic. As our examples earlier reveal, fugitives fleeing the South sought to escape violence, receive pay for their labor, marry, or connect to family; all sought freedom in one form or another. Those who met them on the docks or ships were motivated occasionally by money, but more often by solidarity, the desire to abolish slavery, or even the hope to foment revolution. Practical and political elements were interwoven in the maritime circuit of escape.

The overwhelming majority of the fugitives began their escape on the docks or on a vessel of some kind, usually within a relationship that grew out of work, either forced, chosen, or sometimes a combination of the two. The enslaved Thomas H. Jones, for example, hired out his labor as a dockworker and put himself into a position to escape. Others, like Sarah Moore and John Andrew Jackson, gravitated to the docks as part of their plan to abscond. Over the course of their journeys, escapees had to navigate away from, or around, enslavers, slave hunters, constables and watchmen, hostile ship captains, and whippers who would lash them if caught. They needed knowledge to outwit and evade a complex system of policing.[54]

A staggering array of people helped the fugitives make their escapes. The most common figures were sailors, Black and white, at sea and ashore. Black sea cooks and stewards also played special roles, as did, less often, captains and mates. Dockworkers occupied a strategic position in the network of maritime maroons, as did free Blacks who assisted on either end of the escape. Others who pitched in were an occasional sympathetic white person (one, surprisingly, dressed as a gentleman), a minister, and a boardinghouse keeper. A motley crew of sailors invited dockworker William Grimes to sail away with them to New York. Once there, his ship's first mate helped him at a crucial moment. Three sailors, two of them total strangers, then guided him through the final stage of his escape.

The tactics of escape offer a typology of how fugitives got aboard various vessels and into the free waters of Northern states. The examples reveal six means of escape, all requiring head-work. These plans of escape will recur throughout this book: working one's way to freedom; using disguise and deception; hiding aboard a ship, usually with the assistance of a crew member but sometimes without; shipping oneself as cargo aboard a vessel; purchasing passage from a sailor or captain; or commanding and sailing your own small vessel away from slave society. Sometimes these creative forms of fugitive agency were deployed sequentially within the same escape.

Enslaved people planned and carried out their own escapes and therefore bore all the risks of discovery, arrest, and punishment. They did their own head-work. William Still of Philadelphia spoke of the arrangements for escape made by fugitives and maritime workers: "In this matter the Committee did not feel disposed to interfere directly in any way, further than to suggest that whatever understanding was agreed upon by the parties themselves should be faithfully adhered to." Dedicated Northern abolitionists like Still rarely got involved in escapes until the fugitive arrived in Philadelphia, New York, or Boston. In many cases they did not get involved at all, as sailaways moved through other, autonomous networks organized by the overlapping communities of maritime workers and free people of color. "Self-emancipation," wrote runaway Henry Bibb in 1854, was "the order of the day."[55]

Chapter 2

The Structure of Escape: Port Cities, Trade, and Capitalism

North American port cities grew up at different times, for different reasons, and with different origins and geographies. They nonetheless shared common characteristics based on their relationship to the rapidly expanding system of global capitalism, which moved money and goods around the world, largely by sea. All ports connected their hinterlands to the growing world market; all were essential to the production and worldwide circulation of commodities. Port cities connected direct producers inland (slaves, farmers, artisans) to laborers in the port (dockers and porters), who were, in turn, connected to workers aboard ships and, after the voyage, to other port-city workers and finally to consumers in the metropoles and broader markets. Ports were always Janus-faced—inward-looking toward productive hinterlands and outward-looking toward the world market. Port-city workers forged global commodity chains and a vast, highly profitable system of production and exchange.[1]

Port cities have been crucibles of class formation and dynamic sites for the development of capitalism since the sixteenth century. The two went hand in bloody hand as the rulers of Europe and the Americas organized and disciplined workers to produce and transport commodities for the world market. Although the types and combination of waterfront workers varied over space and time, all ports had an occupational structure in which half or more of the population worked in trade or in support of it, in shipbuilding and repair or in the building of infrastructure, like the docks and roads that made commerce possible. All ports featured a motley proletariat, a mix of multiethnic, usually international men, women, and children, skilled and unskilled, waged and unwaged. African American workers enslaved and free were central to all American ports in the antebellum era. Port workers did not always produce commodities, but they did produce value by moving commodities through space and time. They occupied a strategic position in the accumulation of capital on a global scale.[2]

Escaping slavery by sea in nineteenth-century America took place within what has been described as the golden age of American maritime trade, when "canal fever" expanded inland waterway commerce and coastal and oceanic shipping grew in new and dynamic ways. Slavery boomed and expanded across the American South, manufacturing prospered in the North, and the United States acquired vast new territories to become a continental empire. This was the era of the "Second Slavery," a distinctive regime in which commodity production by enslaved workers intertwined with industrialization to drive global capitalist development. The expansion of commodity production for domestic and international markets by both free and unfree labor in this era in turn generated a transportation revolution. Technological innovation fueled the expansion of shipping as steamboats multiplied on oceans, rivers, and canals, and trains crisscrossed the country. The completion of the Erie Canal in 1825 made New York the country's biggest maritime port.[3]

Since every commodity chain was necessarily a chain of human labor, every trade route was a potential route for a runaway, which is to say, hinterlands for commodities were identical to the hinterlands for those escaping slavery by sea. The regional trade that flowed into Norfolk made that port a magnet for fugitives who escaped from southern Virginia and northern North Carolina. The same was true for Savannah, to which the famous memoirist Charles Ball traveled eighty miles over land in 1830 to escape by sea, and for Charleston, as John Andrew Jackson showed when he traveled one hundred miles in 1846 from Sumter County, South Carolina. Port cities were transit points for people escaping slavery over hundreds of square miles inland. Cooperative labor had both sanctioned and subversive dimensions.[4]

Port cities grew at a dazzling pace as workers constructed maritime infrastructure alongside one body of water after another. Port authorities mobilized these motley crews to expand docks, improve harbors, and build warehouses. Merchants and captains hired thousands of dockers and sailors, Black and white, to move the commodities being traded and shipped. The waterfront division of labor grew more complex. Shipyards in Norfolk, Philadelphia, New York, and Boston boomed, constructing more and ever-larger vessels. In 1820 American shipbuilders turned out 557 vessels with a carrying capacity of 51,394 tons. In 1855 the number of vessels produced had increased almost fourfold (to 2,027) and the amount of tonnage by a factor of eleven (583,450). The average size of a vessel produced in American shipyards grew from 93 tons in 1820 to 288 tons in 1850. The bulk vessels and those who sailed them were employed in the coastal trade, the volume of which during the 1850s exceeded the total of transport on canals and railroads combined. The maritime sector played a leading role in this dynamic phase of American economic development.

Central to maritime expansion was a particular kind of shipping—the packet ships, sailors, and routes that linked Southern and Northern ports on regular schedules from the 1810s through the Civil War. Prior to the ascent of the packet trade, maritime trade was episodic and often unpredictable. New York merchants led the way in organizing a new, more reliable commerce, building a fleet of vessels along the East River that would sail in two directions: southward to the cotton ports of the United States and eastward across the Atlantic to Liverpool and the textile factories of Lancashire. A small army of clerks and agents, soon denounced in the South as "Yankee merchants," fanned out from New York to Atlantic ports everywhere, especially Charleston, Savannah, Mobile, New Orleans, and Havana. More than a hundred vessels arrived in the cotton ports every year, on a quick and predictable schedule. A vessel could deliver cotton—and a fugitive—to New York from Charleston or Savannah in about a week, or from Mobile or New Orleans in about two and a half weeks.[5]

Southerners did not fully understand how thoroughly New Yorkers had come to dominate their trade until the 1830s. They complained that for every dollar earned on cotton, forty cents went to Northern shippers. As *DeBow's Review* lamented in 1837, "The South thus stands in the attitude of feeding from her own bosom a vast population of merchants, ship-owners, capitalists, and others, who without the claims of her progeny, drink up the life blood of her trade." By 1850, half of the tonnage of the American merchant fleet came into or out of New York. New Yorkers would use their packet ships, and later their steamers, to keep the South in "economic bondage" until the Civil War.[6]

In the early nineteenth century the industrialization of seafaring and sea travel strengthened the commercial connections between Northern and Southern ports. Steamship operators in New York and Philadelphia established regular service to New Orleans, Mobile, Savannah, Charleston, Norfolk, Petersburg, and Richmond in the 1850s. By 1853 seventeen vessels with a combined carrying capacity of 22,000 tons (one ton equaled forty square feet of carrying capacity) were routinely steaming into Southern ports. This small fleet of vessels had the same carrying capacity of more than a hundred 200-ton schooners, which also made their way to Southern ports.[7]

The huge size of the steamers meant more places for fugitives to hide—in the engine room, in the steerage, sometimes even in an empty first-class cabin. The free people of color who traveled as passengers on any given steamship voyage provided cover. The *Augusta* and the *Keystone State* brought fugitives from Savannah, while the *Jamestown*, the *Pennsylvania*, the *Roanoke*, the *Stag*, and the *Virginia* transported freedom seekers from Richmond, Petersburg, Portsmouth, and Norfolk. Of special importance was a vessel called the *City of Richmond*, which, thanks to an active "pilot" named John Minkins, delivered more than a dozen escapees to the Philadelphia office of William Still between 1853 and 1854. That number was of course only a fraction of those who had hidden away aboard the steamers.[8]

By 1850 almost 200,000 seamen sailed annually into and out of the major Atlantic ports of the United States on more than 18,000 American- and foreign-owned ships. The greatest number by far, 38,000, sailed the ships entering and exiting New York City. Another 20,000 manned the vessels of Boston. Around 5,000 worked the ships bound for Charleston, Baltimore, and Philadelphia. Even the smaller ports—Savannah, Wilmington, Norfolk, and New Bedford—saw a thousand or two sailors disembark their vessels over the course of a year. Nationwide, as many as 20,000 of these sailors were free or enslaved men of color. The sheer number of ships and sailors suggest the potential magnitude of maritime escape.[9]

Resistance to slavery, and the agency of those who escaped by sea, was thus closely linked to the structure and technology of trade. Every profit-seeking ship that departed a Southern port for a Northern one, carrying cotton or other commodities into the world market, represented a potential line of escape. Yet getting aboard a ship was never easy, and fugitives sometimes waited months before finding a "safe ship" on which to stow away. The key to successful escape would be lateral connections within the port city proletariat, the relationships between the runaway and workers on the docks and ships.

LIFE AND WORK ON THE WATERFRONT

Early nineteenth-century port cities were bustling, noisy, rowdy, often violent places—not for the faint of heart. The several blocks closest to the water hummed with activity as sailors brought ships to anchor and then labored with dockers, porters, carters, and draymen to unload and transport their valuable cargo. Maritime craftsmen swarmed around the ships, repairing and preparing vessels for the next passage. Saws buzzed, mallets cracked, wooden cartwheels creaked and groaned. Shipwrights barked orders to their journeymen, apprentices, and laborers about the sawing, hauling, and hammering of planks. Market women roared their wares, selling food to sailors who arrived in port half-starved but flush with wages, which they carried into the taverns and grogshops. Black dockworkers sang slowly to each other, to control the pace of work as they loaded and stowed bales of cotton:

> Lift him up and carry him along
> fire, maringo, fire away,
> Put him down where he belong
> fire, maringo, fire away,
> Ease him down and let him lay,
> fire, maringo, fire away,
> Screw him in and there he'll stay.
> fire, maringo, fire away,
> Stow him in his hole below,
> fire, maringo, fire away,
> Say he must and then he'll go.
> fire, maringo, fire away.

The work was hard, physical, and dangerous. In a time when most ports had limited technology (tackle, hoists, and derricks), raw human strength was essential to moving commodities, whether massive timber or 450-pound bales of cotton. Hernias and back injuries were common among wharf hands, as was maiming or death by body-crushing heavy cargo. Patrick Snead, who escaped to Canada, had worked on the docks of Savannah: "I had to work hard, lifting heavy bales of goods. This lifting caused me to wear a truss some time before I left."[10]

Cities had a special allure for runaways, who craved anonymity and the safety that came from it. Enslaved people who "stole themselves" by running away committed a serious crime against property and could expect bloody punishment if captured. They therefore sought to melt into the urban crowd, to become invisible to authorities of all kinds. Sparsely populated rural areas and small towns always bred suspicion about strangers, and all white people were encouraged by financial reward to report, arrest, and return suspected runaways. The waterfront, by contrast, was the most multiethnic place in the world in the nineteenth century, full of locally unknown people who drifted in and out of town with the tides. The very word "port" derives from the Latin *portus*, which means both harbor and haven, a place of relative freedom in contrast to the slavery of the ancient countryside. Cities by the sea have been "places of comers and goers, dodgers and drifters, grafters and grifters and anyone who prefers the cool welcoming fugitive night." Runaways disappeared into densely populated Black urban communities, where they might avoid detection and receive vital assistance.[11]

Escapees also needed money: a second major attraction of the port city was the availability of work on the waterfront. Any runaway with skill in carpentry, cooperage, metalwork, or seafaring found work easily. Even more important to most runaways was the availability of unskilled laboring jobs. Finding work on the waterfront was a big step toward successful escape, as anyone could see simply by surveying the forest of ship masts near the docks. Dockside labor "was an ideal halfway house on a runaway's road to freedom."[12]

Prospects for escape might be found anywhere people worked

together, on ship or shore. The various labor processes of the waterfront, whether building ships or moving cargo, required the cooperation of many hands, free and enslaved. Fugitives met those who could help them on the docks and aboard the ship, in places beyond the prying eyes and straining ears of municipal authorities. Black workers in Charleston, for example, had considerable autonomy on the job, as white stevedores complained in 1859: forty to sixty enslaved dockworkers might occupy the same large ship as it was being loaded or unloaded, often "without any White Person among them."[13]

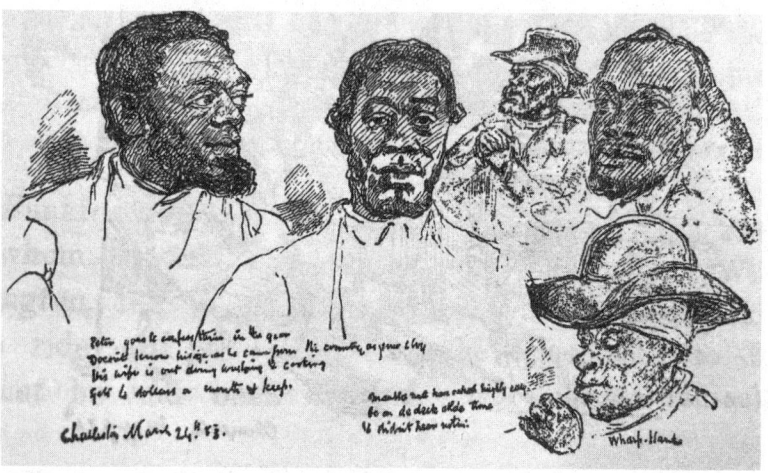

British artist Eyre Crowe visited the Charleston waterfront in 1853 and drew portraits of dockworkers, often key players in the maritime system of escape.

Sailors and would-be fugitives hatched many an escape plan in port city grogshops and "low tippling houses," some of them Black-owned. These establishments offered drinking, gambling, dancing, and singing to waterfront workers and often served as bases for sex workers. They were also depots in the second economy, where appropriated goods were bought and sold. A Charleston newspaper denounced the "filthy little groggeries, where the most debased and abject of our black and white population assemble to drink and gamble" and to engage in "obscene language and drunken orgies." On ships and docks and in cellar speakeasies, subversive news and information circulated among mobile maritime workers. Fugitives and their allies planned escapes amid the loud, rowdy merriment of multiracial taverns.[14]

A small vessel could also offer sanctuary—traditional watercraft such as lighters, flatboats, ferries, skiffs, periaugers, punts, rafts, galleys, pilot boats, cutters, or sloops, with their crews of mostly African American seafarers who often labored under little white supervision. Vessels in service to port-city commerce ranged from the smallest canoe to the largest steamship, any of which could carry men, women, and children northward to freedom. Frederick Douglass called the vessels of the maritime circuit "freedom's swift-winged angels."[15]

Free Black communities in all ports were crucial to designs of escape, at the points of both origin and arrival. Free people of color in all ports defended themselves against slave catchers, kidnappers, and white mobs as they inspired, attracted, and protected fugitives. Their local organizations of self-defense—what maritime runaway Harriet Jacobs called "impromptu vigilance committees"—would be building blocks for larger Vigilance Committees beginning in 1835. Many of these urban maroons lived near the waterfront and worked in maritime industries. Their labor and its setting put them in a strategic position to find and help those seeking to escape by sea.[16]

No small number of these free people of color living in seaports had been maritime maroons themselves. When Harriet Jacobs arrived in Philadelphia and New York from the small port of Edenton, North Carolina, she found in each place a community of people she knew from her hometown, most of them likely having escaped by the same route she had. On the docks of New York, Frederick Bailey (soon to be Douglass) ran into a Maryland sailor he knew as "Allender's Jake," a recent runaway who had taken the new name William Dixon. In New Bedford several hundred of the town's one thousand free Blacks were fugitives, most of whom had arrived by sea.[17]

THE SOUTH'S DILEMMA

Maritime escape presented serious challenges to Southern elites for several related reasons. They shipped a large portion of their exports on Northern-owned vessels, especially those based in New York, as we have seen. In 1850, 78.6 percent of all American shipping tonnage was registered in Northern ports, and more than 60 percent of that figure in New York. Every Northern vessel arriving in a Southern port brought within it a different labor system, based on wage labor, and a different kind of authority in the person of the captain, who presided over an autonomous space largely beyond local control. To make matters worse, from the Southern elite point of view, the main deck of the Northern ship was a place where labor was mobilized and business was transacted: enslaved people routinely boarded the vessel to work, loading or unloading cargo, while various traders, legal and illegal, came aboard to buy and sell. Worst of all, each Northern vessel potentially carried within it abolitionist principles, the likelihood increasing with each Black sailor on board. In this complex social and economic situation, Southern legislatures sought to regulate maritime work, mobility, contact, and communication, and to criminalize solidarity between enslaved people and anyone else working on a ship. Southern rulers created a large body of maritime law to prevent escape by sea.[18]

Behind the actions of Southern legislators lay a difficult calculation: they had to weigh the potential loss of slave property by escape against the expense of enforcing their laws, both within the calculus of profits to be made by Northern-based trade. Virginia and North Carolina lacked dominant ports and therefore depended on a more decentralized, geographically dispersed system of commerce, which made such laws expensive and hard to enforce. The normal functioning of the Southern economy in production and trade created ties of cooperation between Northern and Southern shipboard workers who produced wealth but at the same time could easily be turned to subversive purposes. How to police the cooperative work on the decks and in the holds of ships that went on almost every day of the year?

Preventing escape by sea required that the Southern ruling class control a large and diverse array of maritime workers, beginning with the captain of the Northern vessel. He was made legally responsible for policing his own ship and ensuring that no would-be fugitives came aboard. A Virginia law of 1856 stated that if a "slave is found on board after leaving port, or in the night time," the captain "shall be presumed to have knowingly received him [or her]." At certain moments of high tension between North and South, ship captains would also have to provide bonds, or securities, to be held and used by state officials to pay for any enslaved person who should escape on that captain's vessel. Any captain proven to have "carried off" a fugitive in Virginia might be imprisoned for up to ten years and barred from future trade in the Southern state.[19]

The second person to be controlled was the sailor, especially the Black sailor, who was the object of special legislative repression. The infamous Negro Seamen Acts, passed by every Southern state between 1822 and 1848, specified that Black seamen were to be "quarantined," or locked up, as soon as they arrived in port until a few hours before their ship was to depart. South Carolina led the way with such legislation in the aftermath of the conspiracy of 1822. In 1829, after the publication of David Walker's *Appeal*, the state of Georgia made it a crime for any Black seaman to "communicate with any free negro or person of color," promising death to any sailor who incited insurrection. The legislators of South Carolina decreed in 1835 that any captain who did not place his Black seamen in jail would have his ship hauled out "one hundred yards distance from the shore and remain until said vessel shall proceed to sea." Other controls required a "certificate" of freedom for any Black sailor boarding or exiting the vessel. A few jurisdictions required that the names of free Black sailors be entered into a registry to track their movements.[20]

Legislators sought to punish sailors or anyone else who enticed, advised, assisted, or harbored a runaway. The prohibition of false passes, money, clothing, and provisions reveals the kinds of assistance commonly provided to escapees. "Slave stealing," as Southerners preferred to call escape by sea, was punishable by death in Virginia as early as 1732, but in the nineteenth century several states reduced the sentence to a prison term ranging between two and ten years. North Carolina's huge losses to maritime marronage led to a reinstatement of the death penalty in 1855. In that same year, a Black seaman from New York, Alfred Woodly, was convicted of hiding away a fugitive named Anthony and sentenced to death. In 1860 a Charleston judge sentenced a young white mariner named Francis Michel to death for assisting a young enslaved person aboard a freedom ship.[21]

The third and most important group to be controlled were the enslaved people who boarded the vessels. Most state legislatures insisted that any enslaved person who went aboard a ship needed to have a pass from his or her enslaver. This applied to both maritime workers and to the enslaved market women who boarded ships to sell their cakes, vegetables, and other foods to hungry sailors. Legislators also tried to limit the amount of time enslaved people spent aboard the ship. The governments of Maryland and Washington, DC, for example, specified that the enslaved board ships for no more than an hour at a time, laws that would be routinely disregarded in the loading and unloading of vessels. Other states forbade the enslaved to board ships at night or on Sundays. Yet others, knowing that captains "coasted" to trade with one place after another, tried to limit how far enslaved workers could sail away from their home port. Maryland stipulated ten miles, while Virginia placed the limit at the county line.[22]

Fugitives who were caught faced violent punishments imposed by enslaver or state authorities. Severe whippings were the most common punishment for failed escapes, although various other torture methods, such as branding or bearing chains and logs, were also employed to deter the runaway and terrify like-minded others. Another frequent outcome was for the runaway to be jailed and sold to a slave trader who would carry the offender to the Deep South, a place from which escape would prove more difficult.

Legislators also targeted a fourth group of maritime workers—enslaved and free Black laborers on the rivercraft who brought commodities, sometimes their own produce, into the port cities. They too were required to have passes. Virginia decreed in 1836 that every head man of a vessel must keep a list of all workers; anyone found on the boat and not on the list would be presumed a fugitive. Shipmasters in North Carolina could be fined, and their vessels impounded, if they sent their boatmen to work without passes. The workers who brought with them "corn, cotton, peas," and other items they had produced on their own, to peddle to the ship's crew, also attracted legislative attention. Maryland legislators made the specific link between "clandestine trade" and the intention to abscond: traders who boarded the ships negotiated over the price of food and perhaps the terms to get someone, perhaps themselves, aboard the outbound vessel as a stowaway.[23]

The commonplace specter of all-Black crews independently sailing, poling, and rowing vessels up and down the rivers that fed the port cities created special worries for Southern rulers. Their legislatures therefore passed laws regulating the use of small craft of all kinds, clearly acknowledging their role as vehicles to freedom. Virginia and Maryland trusted white solidarity enough to create laws requiring that the crew of every river vessel include at least "one white man," eighteen years of age or older. Similar regulations applied to ferrymen, bridge keepers, and pilots, many of whom were African American and many of whom presided over a means of escape. Permitting an enslaved person to cross a river without a pass would merit two to five years in prison. Pilots, who routinely boarded Northern ships and guided them into or out of port, would be fined for assisting a captain who had evaded inspection. They would also be rewarded should they find an escapee aboard a vessel they were guiding out toward the Atlantic.[24]

Southern regulators did not stop with waterfront workers. They also tried to make Northern capitalists and their merchant shipping companies responsible for those who sailed away aboard their vessels, even though the businessmen were far away and had little idea what happened on the ships they owned. A South Carolina law of 1841 singled out "several lines of packets now trading . . . regularly between Charleston and New York" to be closely watched. Maryland, Virginia, and North Carolina all tried to hold steamship companies liable for escapees who got aboard their vessels. But these merchants and companies were too important to the Southern economy to be pressured about runaways, even though they would want to return them to the South to maintain business comity in any case. There is no evidence that Southerners ever went after a Northern businessman to pay for a sailaway; captains and sailors, yes, but not the big bosses.[25]

When tensions between Southern and Northern states over maritime escapes escalated, in a prolonged dispute between 1839 and 1846, with Virginia, South Carolina, and Georgia on one side, against New York and Maine on the other, Southern authorities created a new system to control arriving vessels and seafarers: a small army of officials to inspect every departing vessel owned in New York. Virginia mandated that their inspectors be placed "at or near the mouths of rivers of the Commonwealth that empty into the Atlantic Ocean." Several Southern states also required New York–based captains to post a bond or security on first docking, often as much as $1,000 ($35,000 in 2024), against which deductions would be made if any local enslaved person disappeared when the ship left port. Southern lawmakers also mobilized dockside spies and informers, offering $500 to anyone with information about an escape plot. By 1846 Virginians had come face-to-face with economic reality and repealed these draconian measures. Maritime marronage continued, and after a surge in the early 1850s, Virginia legislators created another expensive inspection system in 1856. That reform would also fail, as we shall see in chapter 8.[26]

SAVANNAH

Thomas Sims walked up and down the Savannah docks in February 1851, stopping alongside a two-hundred-ton brig, the *M. and J. C. Gilmore*, to talk with crew members about getting work on board. The smallish, thin twenty-three-year-old man had been trained as a mason, but now he wanted to be a cook—and to work his way to Boston, where the vessel would soon be bound. Perhaps he had heard the story of a local enslaved man named Henry who had "passed himself off as a French cook" and gained passage on a ship to Boston not many months before. Told that the vessel did not need a cook, Sims left but returned the night before the brig sailed, sneaking below deck and hiding in the hold among the bales of upland cotton. If any sailor encouraged or helped him in his illegal boarding, he kept the secret. He later announced that "no one but God and himself knew when he went aboard the vessel."[27]

Sims sought his freedom in a dynamic port city, fifteen thousand strong, that lay along the Savannah River, eighteen miles from the Atlantic. From hundreds of miles upcountry, flatboat and raft workers steered cotton, lumber, and rice downriver from the hinterland to the port, where dockers and sailors loaded the commodities into warehouses and an array of oceangoing vessels. According to a survey of 1850, twenty-seven steamers, seventeen packet ships, and another sixty vessels of all kinds, from skiffs and schooners to brigs, barques, and ships, anchored in the harbor, taking on cargo. The soundscape of the docks included the roar of cotton presses, the rasping noises of sawmills, and the hissing, clanging sounds of cars from the nearby Central Railroad of Georgia. Poor Black and white women loudly hawked their goods on the docks, selling fish, cakes, eggs, fruits, and vegetables to sailors and any other hungry workers they encountered, while Black washerwomen thumped wet laundry with their "battlin' sticks." The ships, the people, and the noisy chaos made Savannah a magnet for runaways from both Georgia and South Carolina.[28]

The city itself lay above the river, atop a forty-foot bluff at the edge of Bay Street. Sims would have known the geography of the port city's sites of pain, suffering, and struggle: a new jail had been built in 1846 at Hall and Whittaker Streets, where runaways, vagrants, prostitutes, and sailors all mixed together, and where every morning "dreadful groans and shrieks" reverberated out of the iron-grated windows as the town whipper performed his grisly chores. Not far away were the slave pens at Habersham and Bryan Streets, where slave auctions took place opposite the city market. Sims would have seen sick and broken-down seamen begging around the city, even after a Marine Hospital had opened—for white sailors only—in 1819. Ministers and members of the port's Female Seamen's Friend Society looked after the sick and the destitute, while "landsharks," "crimps" (labor agents), and boardinghouse keepers chomped at the able-bodied sailors who had just been paid off by their captain.[29]

Savannah experienced a different sort of problem with sailors in 1826, when, on two occasions, in July and again in November, "colored seamen of the most depraved and dangerous character" encouraged flight among the local enslaved population. Savannah authorities considered their efforts to assist runaways to be "kidnapping." The city council asked the Georgia legislature to pass a law confining these men to their ships because "their influence . . . upon our slaves is . . . great in the depraving of their morals, inducing them to desertion and possibly, occasionally, inciting them to insurrectionary attempts." The local struggle reactivated in 1829 when (white) sailors smuggled David Walker's *Appeal* into Savannah, prompting the Georgia legislature to pass a Negro Seamen Act, requiring that Black sailors be "quarantined" when they arrived in port.[30]

Runaways like Sims tended to congregate in one of two places as they sought out a vessel for escape. Those coming from the countryside gathered in transient camps outside the city, raiding local plantations at night for food and venturing into Savannah to make the kind of connection Sims sought. Inside the city they gravitated to an area called Yamacraw in Oglethorpe Ward, located on swampy ground between the river to the north and the railyards to the south. Oglethorpe was the city's largest ward, home to a thousand enslaved people (most of whom hired out their labor), three hundred free Blacks, and another thousand poor whites, many of them recent immigrants from Ireland. As many as eight families crowded into small wooden tenements, which were described as "dingy, dirty, squalid, cheerless." Dogs, cows, goats, and pigs wandered around the urban commons.[31]

Yamacraw was a traditional sailortown replete with saloons, grogshops, tippling houses, cheap boardinghouses, gambling houses (cards, dice, dominoes, billiards), dancing cellars, and nine brothels, all of which were illegal. "Disorderly" grogshops served as markets where "tiefed" goods were bought and sold. Workers routinely helped themselves to a handful of cotton from transient bales, repacked it into new round bales, and sold it in the second economy. Enslaved African Americans and poor whites united in literal conspiracy against the city's white elite.[32]

In November 1846, a few years before Sims sought a ship, a group of enslavers had made clear the connections between the second economy and resistance from below. Lamenting the decline of the plantation owner's paternal authority as an effective form of class discipline and the emergence of a new relationship in which enslavers and the enslaved saw each other as "natural enemies," they formed the Savannah River Anti-Slave Traffick Association, taking aim at the fraternization of poor Black and white workers in unregulated dramshops, where plantation property—cattle, hogs, poultry, tools, produce stored in barns, and even "standing crops"—was traded for liquor and other favors. The enslaved believed that "they have the right to steal the fruits of their own labor," that is, to take back what had originally been stolen from them. "Nightly expeditions" to the dramshops were followed by "days of languor," which undermined plantation labor productivity. The members of the new organization saw the drinking establishments as schools of resistance: poor whites who engaged in the illicit trade were an active arm of the abolitionist movement, moving the enslaved toward "insurrection, burning, and murder," and ultimately the "violent dissolution of our domestic institutions," most terrifyingly slavery itself. A special part of the nightmare was the involvement of "desperate gangs of runaways" in the network.[33]

In the aftermath of Sims's successful escape and several others, the dock police expanded, but problems remained: the eighty to one hundred waterfront watchmen who worked long hours at low pay to stop the appropriation of goods and the escape of people often slept on the job, a habit that soon energized more far-reaching reforms. In 1854 naval officer and slave trader Joseph Bryan reformed the night watch, established a regular uniformed police force, erected gas streetlights, and dispatched spies to brothels, grogshops, and sailor boarding-houses. The struggle nonetheless continued: the *Savannah News* announced in 1855 that the river piracy conducted by the motley crew was "almost an established right."[34]

Thomas Sims himself would go on to become one of the best known—and most controversial—maritime runaways of his day after he and his fellow abolitionists in his new home, Boston, fell afoul of the infamous Fugitive Slave Law of 1850. Sims emerged from the "sailors, slaves, and rowdies of all grades and colors" who peopled the Savannah waterfront to become a major player in the debate about slavery in the 1850s. His dockside act of resistance would echo from Savannah to Boston and beyond.[35]

CHARLESTON

Charlotte escaped her enslaver, the jeweler and silversmith John Stiles Bird of Charleston, on December 21, 1831, no doubt taking advantage of the relaxed discipline of the holiday season. Three days later, on Christmas Eve, Bird published a runaway advertisement in *Charleston Mercury*: she "is about 5 feet, 3 inches high, and about 18 years of age." He added two other distinguishing characteristics: she had lost her upper front teeth and "she holds her head down when spoken to," both perhaps signs of trauma. Bird offered a reward and requested that she be delivered to the "Master" of the Charleston Work House (the "Sugar House"), whose staff awaited her with various instruments of torture. Bird thought she had help getting away. He offered a larger reward for evidence leading to the conviction of any person "white or black" who harbored her. He gave one more clue about how she intended to get away: "All Masters of Vessels are cautioned against carrying the said Wench out of the State, as the law will be rigidly put in force against all such offenders."[36]

Charlotte sought escape from an unusual Atlantic port city, where a majority of residents were Black and almost half of them enslaved. Located at the confluence of the Ashley, Cooper, and Wando Rivers, Charleston had 43,000 residents in 1850: 20,000 whites, 19,500 slaves, and 3,500 free people of color. The extreme inequality of the city was embodied in the huge number of enslaved people and in the 155 white men who owned half of the city's wealth. Together they made Charleston the hub of a regional economy: six major railroads, built in the 1820s, brought cotton, flour, grain, naval stores, livestock, and people to the city. Workers carted the commodities to the docks along East Bay Street on the Cooper River, where "vessels from all parts of the world" anchored.[37]

Even though Charleston was in relative economic and demographic decline compared to the more dynamic Lower South cotton region in the antebellum era, it remained an important port. More than 1,700 vessels sailed into its harbor in 1842 alone, many of them part of the regular packet service to and from New York established in 1822. Charleston merchants sent 60 percent of their exports and received 80 percent of their imports through Northern ports. During the 1850s New York, Boston, and Philadelphia had a combined 1.5 million tons of shipping, while Charleston shipowners claimed only 33,000 tons. Most of the vessels that arrived in Charleston were

The Port City of Charleston, South Carolina, c. 1850

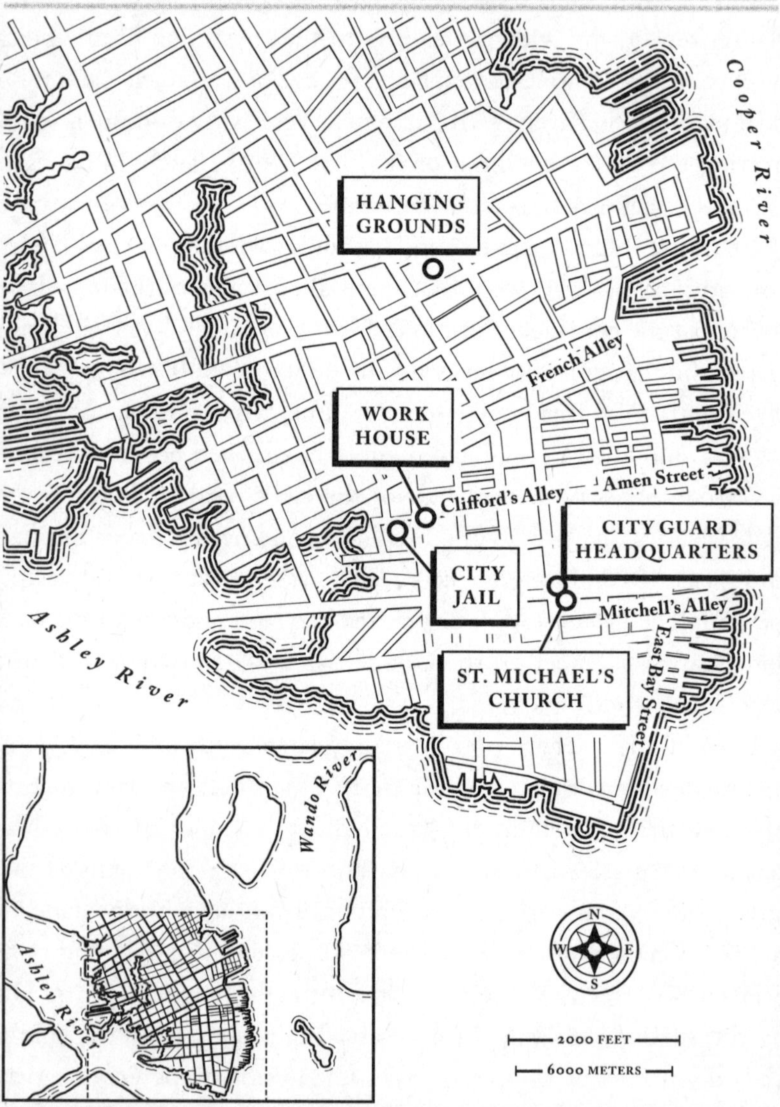

Cooper River

HANGING GROUNDS

French Alley

WORK HOUSE

Clifford's Alley — Amen Street

CITY GUARD HEADQUARTERS

CITY JAIL

Mitchell's Alley

ST. MICHAEL'S CHURCH

East Bay Street

Ashley River

Wando River

Ashley River

N
W E
S

2000 FEET

6000 METERS

Northern- or foreign-owned. Hundreds of departing vessels presented Charlotte with an opportunity for escape.[38]

Unless she had family connections, Charlotte probably did not receive assistance from members of Charleston's free Black community. The largely mulatto elite, almost all of them children of white enslavers and enslaved women, was highly skilled and strongly inclined to identify with white culture. Four out of five (82 percent) held skilled or semiskilled jobs, and no small number (131) owned slaves of their own. Relatively few worked on the waterfront. The top ten occupations for free Blacks featured only one with a maritime orientation: the coopers who built the casks and hogsheads used to ship rice, turpentine, and other commodities. As the Civil War approached, most of Charleston's free people of color declared their loyalty to South Carolina and defended the Confederacy.[39]

Charlotte's escape likely depended instead on the hundreds of enslaved people who worked on the waterfront—dockworkers and sailors on locally owned coastal vessels and steamers. A few worked as riggers and sailmakers. They tended to live in the crowded alleyways near the wharves, particularly Clifford's Alley, which ran from King Street between Queen and Clifford, and French Alley between Magazine and Anson Streets, where sex workers plied their trade. On Amen Street, a block from the docks, sat Cornell June's sailors' boardinghouse, a brothel "of the very lowest and degraded character." Many propertied citizens no doubt cheered when it burned down in 1835.[40]

Workers Black and white met in waterfront grogshops to drink, dance, and play "rattle and snap," a dice game played with beans. In these free spaces the motley crew interacted with what an observer described as "an equality of sociability." Every night at nine the revelers heard drums beating from the headquarters of the City Guard and bells ringing from St. Michael's Church, tolling curfew for all enslaved people. Anyone who remained out risked being locked up and flogged by the guards at the city jail, known for its "morbid stench," or the dreaded "Sugar House," the very place John Stiles Bird wanted slave catchers to send Charlotte.[41]

Another notorious place of cooperation was Mitchell's Alley, which ran from East Bay Street to Bedon's Alley, two blocks from the wharves. Eight feet wide at one end and only five feet wide at the other, it was too narrow for carts or carriages and too dark for genteel pedestrians. It was, rather, a nighttime meeting place for "negroes and disorderly white persons," who planned "the escape of negroes who have been detected in Stealing from the wharves," dockworkers who had appropriated "loose cotton" or coal on the waterfront. Planters outside Charleston worried about sending their bondsmen anywhere near the "free blacks and low and worthless white people" in port, from whom they would get "ideas of insubordination and of emancipation."[42]

By the time Charlotte ran away, "ideas of insubordination and of emancipation" had long been percolating in Charleston. Indeed, the city government's strategy for dealing with maritime escapees was shaped by the uproar associated with Denmark Vesey in 1822. Following that occasion, authorities arrested 131 suspects, discharged thirty-eight after questioning, tried and acquitted twenty-seven, banished thirty-one, and hanged thirty-five just north of Boundary Street. Big changes followed. Charleston's municipal government reorganized its City Guard, strengthening its headquarters at Broad and Meeting Streets. Slaveholders organized the private South Carolina Association, which would assist local authorities in policing the enslaved. The South Carolina legislature passed laws in 1822 and 1823 making it possible to reenslave free Blacks who returned to Charleston, invoking the infamous Negro Seamen Acts.[43]

By the late 1850s Charleston authorities had grown so frustrated with Northern seamen, they decided to reproduce their own maritime labor. Merchants and governmental officials put up $8,000 (almost $300,000 in 2024) to establish the Charleston Marine School aboard a two-hundred-ton brig, the *Lodebar*, which they purchased in 1859. They recruited students from the urban poor—"boys who had theretofore been wandering about the streets of Charleston," from fifteen to eighteen years old. The leadership of the school required the boys to sign an indenture and to learn how to run a ship under rigorous work/time discipline. The impulse to build the new organization came from long observation of Northern sailors in Charleston: the founders of the new school noted that the seamen "certainly can not be deemed friendly to an institution with which [the state's] welfare is closely identified." The replacement of Northern seamen with homegrown mariners would protect "our peculiar Institutions . . . from their evil communication with our negroes." Over the previous three decades those communications had resulted in hundreds of escapes by sea.[44]

Charleston authorities grew so weary of subversive Northern sailors they decided in 1859 to gather poor white teenagers from the streets and train them to sail ships.

After the repression of the conspiracy of 1822, the enslaved of Charleston switched their primary form of resistance from insurrection to arson—fires were a chronic plague in antebellum Charleston—and to running away. It is impossible to know the full frequency of escape, but it is instructive that city authorities apprehended 115 runaways between 1838 and 1839, many of them no doubt trying to board a ship. One of them may have been a skilled carpenter named Carolina who had packed his "broad cloth suit" to escape with "the Yankey Capt[ain] of a fishing smack" in 1839.[45]

Charleston was America's most heavily policed city in the antebellum era. The police force doubled in size from the 1830s to the 1850s as maintenance costs increased fivefold, reaching $100,000 a year ($3.8 million in 2024). By 1850 the city boasted a police force of 250, many of them Irish, working at low wages, earning a mere sixty cents for a long night's work patrolling the waterfront. Reorganized by Mayor William Porcher Miles after 1855, and now including twenty-five officers on horseback, the force came to be known as "Paddy Miles' Bull Dogs." A special detachment called the Charleston Neck Rangers was created to deal with that lawless zone, while the South Carolina Association added private and frankly political muscle to policing, especially along the docks. Authorities staged floggings and executions as public acts of terror.[46]

On a visit to Charleston in 1853, Frederick Law Olmsted witnessed the drumming, the cannons, the guard house, and the "numerous armed-police . . . under military discipline" and thought that the city must be "in a state of siege or revolution." Four years later William Kingsford saw "a strong [police] force constantly in readiness to act" as patrols combed the city "at all hours." He asked a companion why this was so and was told that such "surveillance was necessary because of Charleston's position as a seaport, which resulted in 'a great many desperate men' congregating there." Kingsford added, "it struck me that the principal cause of anxiety might be, after all, the slave population," who were, if anything, more desperate and eager than anyone to cooperate with the seaport workers. The intersection of slavery and commerce, and the ever-present prospect of escape by sea, animated the heavy-handed policing of the city.[47]

WILMINGTON, NORTH CAROLINA

Amid the Civil War, a blockade-runner based in Wilmington headed out to sea with a cargo of cotton. As he and his shipmates steamed twenty-five miles down the Cape Fear River to the Atlantic, port authorities boarded to look for fugitives: the vessel would be "searched and smoked." An hour into an intensive fumigation, "an unfortunate wretch—crushed almost to death by the closeness of his hiding-place, poked with a long stick till his ribs must have been like touchwood, and smoked the color of a backwoods Indian—was dragged by the heels into the daylight, ignominiously put into irons and hurled into the guard-boat." He had been trying to make his way to the "Yankee fleet" offshore. Wilmington's Commissioners of Navigation and Commerce wielded an unusual weapon in their effort to prevent escape by sea.[48]

The unnamed man was one of hundreds who, over many decades, had tried their luck on an outward-bound vessel from the shores of North Carolina. The practice stretched back to the colonial era, but it took on a new urgency in 1784, when the state legislature passed laws aimed specifically at maritime runaways and their comrades, enacting a law that would be renewed and kept in force until slavery came to an end—with limited effect. As early as 1809 Wilmington was known as "an asylum for runaways." North Carolina elites passed another law in 1841 to keep enslaved people off steamboats "without written permission of their owners." In a state defined by the vast Albemarle-Pamlico estuarine system, more than a dozen rivers, and more than three hundred miles of Atlantic coastline, none of the laws seemed to work.[49]

"A Citizen" who sought to protect the property of enslavers wrote to the *Wilmington Journal* in October 1849, explaining that escape by sea had become "almost an everyday occurrence." The badges port authorities required of dockworkers were not enough. He identified the port's Black dockworkers as the problem and offered a "plain and palpable" solution. The authorities of the port must "change the character of Stevedores": "We must have *white* men in the place of *negroes* engaged in that business" to have the vessels properly stowed and inspected. Only a racial recomposition of the waterfront workforce would break the cooperation that got fugitives aboard outward-bound vessels.[50]

Infuriated by endless clever and successful escapes, the commissioners struck back in May 1850, although not in the way "A Citizen" had recommended. Replacing Black dockers would have been too expensive, so instead they issued a decree requiring that searches aboard departing vessels include a new practice: the harbor master would fumigate all departing vessels "in search of runaway slaves." Surviving documents show that between 1858 and 1861, fumigators boarded 1,968 vessels at Smithville, located at the southwestern corner of the Cape Fear River, and Federal Way, situated on the eastern edge of the river. The pungent smell of sulfur hung heavy over the docks as fumigators dipped strips of old sail canvas into melted brimstone and burned them inside a barrel in the hold. They repeated the process on one vessel after another, on average forty-eight a month, most of them schooners and brigs, along with a few barques and a handful of steamships. A ship captain named Martin tried to escape the procedure but was chased down by the captain of a pilot boat, captured, and fined by William Love, the Commissioner of Navigation and Pilotage for Cape Fear River. Port authorities forced illicit passengers from their hiding places coughing, choking, and gasping for air, then returned them to their enslavers to face punishment. An inventive new form of policing used chemical means to break the circuit of escape.[51]

Wilmington authorities thus drew upon and extended a metaphor that had circulated around the Atlantic since the time of the Haitian Revolution: resistance was a disease, and it required a similar treatment. The decree of 1850 made the point directly, explaining that a law had long been in place for incoming vessels with "sickness on board." It would now be applied to outgoing vessels to protect against the "sickness" of running away from bondage, a practice that Southern physician Samuel Cartwright would describe as a mental illness, "drapetomania," a year later.

Located on the Cape Fear River, which cut through a large hinterland, Wilmington had a population of 7,264 in 1850, more than half of it (3,683) African American. Only 9 percent (652) of the population were free people of color, which meant that a great majority of those who worked on the docks were enslaved. They loaded onto mostly Northern ships commodities from the hinterland's extractive forest industries: naval stores and wood products (timber, lumber, shingles, staves), crude and distilled turpentine, rosin, tar, and pitch. Swamps and bogs made overland transport difficult and expensive, so most exports were floated and poled downriver on rafts and flats by Black river workers. These autonomous and mobile human gangplanks, who connected local and Atlantic maritime cultures, were essential to the economy and always a danger to its labor system.[52]

Black maritime workers who arrived in North Carolina from afar posed an additional challenge to local authorities. A writer for the *Peoples' Press and Wilmington Advertiser* was convinced that Northern sailors were abolitionists as early as 1835, before the founding of the Vigilance Committees in New York, Philadelphia, and Boston: "Our insulted commonwealth can find no salve in the presumption that those who are guilty [of helping the enslaved escape bondage by sea] are misled by unprincipled fanatics—that Garrison & Tappan, and other diabolical intriguers have perverted the understandings and excited a false sympathy in the breasts of those who come among us for commercial purposes." That subversive sympathy might arrive in

Wilmington at any time. In 1852 Black seaman Samuel Dowler offered a local dockworker a sail to freedom, saying that this "was the way he escaped from South Carolina some years ago."[53]

Calculated terror through extralegal policing was another tool to prevent escape by sea. In 1850 port authorities arrested and jailed a Black sailor recently arrived from Philadelphia who had used "impertinent, if not seditious language" upon questioning. The patrol employed a local enslaved man to give the sailor two public floggings; "witnesses assert that it was never done better." The editor of the *Wilmington Aurora* announced with satisfaction, "This may be Judge Lynch's Law, but we think it a very good one."[54]

Two enslaved men, Abraham Galloway and Richard Eden, decided to test their lungs, wits, and will against Wilmington's fumigation policy as they sought out a sympathetic mariner in 1857. They found an experienced captain who was willing to stow them away amid a cargo of tar, rosin, and spirits of turpentine. The men had already secretly fashioned their own tools of escape: two large "silk oil cloth shrouds," which they would slip over their heads and draw tight at the waist. They also carried with them wet towels to hold to their nostrils. They sneaked aboard the ship, "determined to struggle against death for liberty," and they got lucky. They escaped the fumigation process: "the law was not carried into effect in this instance." It was not easy for three fumigators to search the hundreds of vessels clearing the port each year.[55]

Abraham Galloway (pictured) and Richard Eden fashioned oilcloths with drawstrings at the waist to outwit the fumigators and escape slavery in Wilmington, North Carolina, in 1859.

Yet Galloway and Eden were not out of danger, for they soon encountered a new and potentially more lethal problem: trapped below deck, their prolonged exposure to turpentine during the voyage caused a serious suffusion of blood through the skin, weakening both men. When they arrived in Philadelphia, William Still and his colleagues on the Vigilance Committee gave them medical assistance and asked for a favor in return. They requested that Galloway and Eden give them one of their silk shrouds, which they wanted to keep as a souvenir of the struggle against slavery. The fugitives were happy to comply with the request, after which Still summoned "an artist to take the photograph of one of them; which keepsakes have been valued very highly." Their act of resistance, concluded Still, was "inventive genius." It was one of many victories of intelligence and will over brute force.[56]

NORFOLK

Daniel Carr lived in the Norfolk-Portsmouth area before being sold south to North Carolina. He attempted to escape his new enslaver, who recaptured, stripped, and flogged him mercilessly. As William Still acidly noted as Daniel sat before him a free man in Philadelphia in November 1855, "This did not cure him." He ran away again, into the Great Dismal Swamp, where for three months he was "surrounded with snakes, wild cats, Bears, Coons &c." He survived using the skills and knowledge of commoning, hunting and gathering his subsistence. He made his way through the swamp and traveled the last few miles in the open to Portsmouth to visit his wife Hannah and their three children, Sam, Dan, and "baby." While he was there, he told Still, he had a moment of "unspeakable joy": he met "the noble Captain F., whose big heart was delighted to give him a passage North." Captain James Fountain's schooner would be his freedom ship. Carr sailed out of Norfolk among "the twenty-one" who made the largest successful mass escape in the history of the Atlantic circuit of self-emancipation.[57]

Carr's experience was common in the 1850s, as freedom seekers escaped by the Chesapeake Bay's rivers, ports, and almost twelve thousand miles of coastline. Between 1,000 and 1,500 ships sailed into the Hampton Roads region yearly, many of them docking at Norfolk, which boasted the deepest harbor on North America's Atlantic coast, permitting easy access to Northern vessels that docked close to landed urban neighborhoods. William Still in Philadelphia and fellow abolitionist Sydney Howard Gay in New York received and assisted more than three hundred fugitives fleeing Virginia between 1852 and 1861, almost two-thirds of whom had traveled northward by sea. This was of course only a small fraction of those who got away.[58]

The vast majority of the runaways from Norfolk and Portsmouth for whom Still and Gay did not record a means of escape had almost certainly arrived by water too, for the topography of these cities made it difficult to escape by any means *except* by sea. Norfolk is surrounded on three sides by water. Unless a runaway wanted to travel south and circle west toward Richmond before heading north by land, they would have to sail northwest across Hampton Roads toward Yorktown or northeast toward the tip of the Delmarva Peninsula before setting off by foot on paths vastly more perilous than any route a ship might take.

A port of roughly fifteen thousand people by 1850, Norfolk was the beating heart of a region that pumped an endless stream of runaways into Chesapeake Bay and the Atlantic Ocean. It was an epicenter of freedom seeking. Daniel Carr's experience shows that the zone of escape surrounding Norfolk included Portsmouth, just across the Elizabeth River, as well as the Virginia–North Carolina hinterlands. Norfolk and Portsmouth offered everything a runaway might want: established free Black communities; the anonymity of urban life;

work to be found along the waterfront; and, perhaps most crucially of all, dozens of Northern ships lying at anchor and taking aboard cargo. Nearby swamps offered a protective interior that discouraged slave catchers and allowed runaways to hide out as they awaited a ship.

Norfolk's waterfront workers were a key to its subversive history. Both free Blacks and enslaved people worked as dockers, sailors, porters, and ship carpenters; some labored in the US Navy shipbuilding yard and aboard naval vessels. Others toiled out of the same port as fishermen, oystermen, and ferrymen. Women hucksters sold their wares along the waterfront. Free Blacks provided "a haven for runaways." Just beyond the city limit, away from the waterfront watchmen, stood a "disorderly house of ill fame resorted to by idle and dissolute persons both white men and negroes for the purpose of gambling and drinking." White and Black seafaring workers met, drank, and exchanged stolen property in "a negro dancing house."[59]

Perhaps the greatest reason why runaways flocked to Norfolk was the self-organization of the free Black and enslaved communities, which was superior to that of any other Southern port. The emancipated people who arrived in Philadelphia and New York repeatedly and gratefully bore witness to a strong, secret network of movement and communication, many of them indicating that they had been in hiding for months before a sympathetic sailor offered passage to the North. Daniel Carr was one of the lucky ones, waiting only three months; Susan Brooks waited four; Robert McCoy five. Harrison Bell and her daughter Harriet Ann went undercover for "several months." Anthony Blow hid out for an astonishing ten months. A communal effort of heroic proportions was required to feed, maintain, and hide people for such extraordinary lengths of time. The ability to care for runaways for a longer time also contributed directly to the success of their escape: the longer someone was able to hide out, the less likely their enslavers were to be looking for them, making it easier to get aboard a ship.[60]

In most Southern ports the social organization that made escape possible was relatively simple and usually temporary, based on family, friends, and fellow workers—small, fluid networks that formed and dissolved quickly to avoid discovery. But in Norfolk the Black community built more durable organizations to handle the logistics of escape. One runaway described a secret "soc[iet]y," which in the middle of the nineteenth century meant an organized group with common goals and regular means of operation. The "society" may have referred to the United Order of the Tents, an all-women group that operated before the Civil War, then declared its official existence in 1867 as the first Black women's benefit society in the United States. Its earlier fugitive operation helps to explain how and why runaways were able to survive for months before finding a "safe ship."[61]

Hiding places in Norfolk were many and various, necessarily changing over time to allay suspicion. Some people hid out in free-Black city neighborhoods, for example between Water Street near the docks north to Queen Street or in Cow Bay amid its "labyrinth of alley-ways." Others moved out of town, to less densely populated places, where they were sheltered and fed, in specially constructed rooms or basements belonging to trustworthy supporters. Some hid in small dark spaces beneath floorboards. Many moved from place to place to keep the slaveholders and constables guessing.[62]

Some, like Daniel Carr, went all the way to the Great Dismal Swamp, originally a massive two-thousand-square-mile ecosystem of marshlands. The swamp was slowly whittled down by developers beginning in the 1820s but remained attractive to runaways through the Civil War. Known for its green moss and muddy landscape, its amber-colored water, and its stands of pine, Atlantic white cedar, maple, black gum, and cypress trees, its elevated hummocks supported a population of bears, bobcats, and snakes as well as massive swarms of mosquitoes and yellow flies. Poet Henry Wadsworth Longfellow imagined a runaway in this unusual ecology in 1842:

Where will-o'-the-wisps and glow-worms shine,
        In bulrush and in brake;
Where waving mosses shroud the pine,
And the cedar grows, and the poisonous vine
        Is spotted like the snake;

Frederick Douglass acknowledged the swamp as an important zone of struggle in 1848 in an article he published in the *North Star* entitled "Slaves in the Dismal Swamp."[63]

Difficulty of access made the swamp a liberated zone to runaways and squatters from the seventeenth century onward, as a rich body of historical scholarship has made clear. Fugitives ran to the swamps to protest a beating or to gain leverage in negotiation with an enslaver. The move permitted a brief stint of freedom known as *petit marronage*, after which one might return to family and work. In a few cases those who escaped created permanent bases from which to wage war and pillage against nearby plantations. Taking up residence in the swamp was often the first phase in a longer process of sailing away to freedom.[64]

Living in the swamp required skill, knowledge, and courage. Moses Grandy, a seafaring man who knew the swamp intimately and used it to work his way to freedom, learned the skills of commoning early in his life: "I remember well my mother often hid us all in the woods, to prevent master selling us. When we wanted water, she sought for it in any hole or puddle formed by falling trees or otherwise: it was often full of tadpoles and insects: she strained it and gave it round to each of us in the hollow of her hand. For food, she gathered berries in the woods, got potatoes, raw corn, &c." Folk knowledge of where to find and how to prepare food was a key to surviving in the swamp and continuing the journey toward freedom.[65]

Another part of Norfolk's superior organization was a reliable and effective group of pilots who connected runaways to specific ships. One of the best known was an enslaved dockworker named Henry

Lewey, whose movement name was "Bluebeard." William Still spoke of Lewey as "one of the most dexterous managers in the Underground Rail Road agency in Norfolk." He assisted numerous people onto ships, until finally arousing the suspicion of the authorities, who jailed him but could not find evidence to convict. He returned to action, helping his twenty-eight-year-old wife, Rebecca, who was described as "healthy, stout & genteel," to get aboard Captain Fountain's schooner in July 1856. Lewey also worked with steward John Minkins to make the steamer *City of Richmond* a freedom ship. Lewey himself ended up escaping by sea, alongside the soon-to-be-famous runaway Shadrach Minkins; he reunited with Rebecca in Canada. Pilot Eliza Baines worked at Crawford House, which "catered to those in the maritime industry"—a perfect place to pick up intelligence about activity on the docks. Less is known about pilots such as Sam Nixon, William Bagnall, and a man called "Ham and Eggs," all of whom opened ship hatchways for fugitives voyaging to Wilmington, Philadelphia, and New York. A young woman named Annetta M. Lane, a founding member of the United Order of the Tents, gave her "prized coral necklace" to a ship captain to take a penniless family aboard his ship, saying, "Take this and let them go free."[66]

BALTIMORE

William Jones took a creative although dangerous path to freedom in April 1859. Worried that his enslaver, Robert H. Carr, planned to sell him just like all the other items he sold in his Baltimore grocery, Jones conspired with a friend, a pilot in a maritime network, about how to get to Philadelphia. He decided that he would confine himself in a box, add straw, and ship himself as freight aboard a steamship of the Ericsson Line. He may have heard of Lear Green's successful escape two years earlier. During the voyage Jones almost fainted and at one point thought he would die. He had an urge to cry out in fear but managed to suppress the impulse. Soon a cold chill came over him, almost freezing "the very blood in his veins" and causing "intense agony." He eventually fell asleep, survived the seventeen-hour voyage, and arrived in Philadelphia on a Sunday morning. Another friend engaged a carriage and met the vessel at the wharf with the bill of lading, only to discover that the box was too large. The driver refused to carry it. The friend spent a frantic hour and a half looking for a furniture car and finally secured one. While the friend and the driver were loading the box, Jones "gave a sudden cough"—had the driver heard it? He had not. He dutifully delivered the box to its given address without a clue as to its contents. William Still observed the scene at the end of the journey: "The box is opened, the straw removed, and the poor fellow is loosed; and his rejoicing, I will venture to say, as a mortal never did rejoice, who had not been in similar peril." Jones's friend and the welcoming members of the Philadelphia Vigilance Committee joined in the jubilation, which lasted several hours. It was time, wrote Jones's anonymous abolitionist friend, to "sing hally luja." A "mighty host" had passed over the waters.[67]

Many fugitives made a first passage to Baltimore, one of the most dynamic port cities in the young United States. In the late 1830s Baltimore had a growing population of 75,000, which included 13,000 free Blacks and roughly 4,500 enslaved people. By 1860 the total population of the city had almost tripled to 212,000, making it the third-largest urban area in the country. In the 1830s European immigration to Baltimore surged, bringing German and especially Irish workers to the city and its docks. The free Black community had grown to more than 25,000, while the number of the enslaved had shrunk to 2,200. The Baltimore and Ohio Railroad, completed in 1827, expanded the port's hinterland and made it the leading export center for commodities produced in western Maryland, southern Pennsylvania, and beyond. A long transition in the region from tobacco farming to less labor-intensive wheat production began in the late eighteenth century, slowly diminishing the demand for slave labor and increasing the manumissions that swelled Baltimore's free Black population. Maryland planters with surplus labor also hired out many bond workers to the port, often directly to merchants and master artisans who organized maritime industry. Fugitives recognized that the port city offered opportunities for escape that were inconceivable in the plantation society they had left behind.[68]

A key location for Baltimore's port-city proletariat was Fell's Point, the dockside community where vessels of all kinds—ships, brigs, schooners, and sloops, along with smaller craft such as fishing and oyster boats—anchored in the deep water of the Patapsco River near the local shipyards, docks, warehouses, taverns, inns, coffeehouses, and grogshops. Animated by English, German, Scots-Irish, Irish, Acadian, Haitian, and African American workers, Fell's Point hosted all kinds of maritime industry. Artisans and apprentices made sails, rope, blocks, tackle, and pumps. Carpenters, caulkers, and riggers worked on the vessels that almost always needed repair before the next voyage. Stevedores Black and white loaded and unloaded hundreds of ships, carrying cargo to and from the spacious warehouses. Porters, draymen, and carters transported commodities around town. Thousands of multiethnic sailors came and went with the Atlantic tides. Most workers lived near their dockside workplaces, in a warren of alleyways—Happy Alley, Argyle Alley, Strawberry Alley, Petticoat Alley, and Apple Alley. Fell's Point was a magnet for fugitives who flocked to the neighborhood in the hundreds, finding work on the waterfront as they awaited their opportunity to get aboard an outward-bound vessel.[69]

The large free Black community of Baltimore was dominated by people who had gained their freedom in one of three ways: by an enslaver's manumission; by self-purchase, usually after acquiring money through hiring themselves out; or by escape. More than half of Baltimore's free Black men worked on the waterfront, most of them as laborers, with smaller numbers of sailors, carpenters, caulkers, draymen, and porters. Most of the women were domestics, seamstresses, cooks, hucksters, and washerwomen, a line of work common among sailors' wives. The community had a rich civic life, celebrating Haitian Independence Day (January 1) and, after 1834, British Emancipation Day (August 1). Black neighborhoods in Fell's Point and Old Towne also organized local Vigilance Committees to patrol the streets and prevent kidnappings by blackbirders. Several members of the Black community were active in the early 1830s in the annual National Convention of Free People of Color, one goal of which was to encourage freedpeople "to participate in the anti-slavery movement by shielding escaped slaves and organizing for more overt political actions."[70]

The first half of the nineteenth century was a time of vigorous self-organization in the free Black community—the establishment of new church congregations and benefit societies. Churches on Sharp Street featured "shoutings, singing, clapping of hands, and stamping with the feet"—in short, what Baltimore authorities denounced as a dangerous "degree of fanaticism" and "religious enthusiasm." According to a survey taken April 1838, the free Black community had formed thirty beneficial associations, many of them explicitly for waterfront workers such as "mechanics" (artisans), porters, and caulkers, as well as for barbers, coachmen, brickmakers, and a great many others.[71]

The importance of Maryland's waterways and Baltimore's free Black community intersected in the life and activism of Harriet Tubman, the state's other legendary fugitive, along with Frederick Douglass. Tubman was a fearless, inspirational leader in ferrying people to freedom. She relied on landed routes in her mass escapes, but since she operated in Maryland she inevitably used the state's spidery set of waterways that opened to the Chesapeake Bay. She had a base in Baltimore in the persons of her brothers-in-law, free Black dockworker Tom Tubman and free Black sailor Evans Tubman, both of whom were known to assist fugitives in Fell's Point. As Harriet told historian Wilbur H. Siebert in an interview in 1897, "she would take a boat with her travelers" from Baltimore "and get off at some convenient landing in Delaware," usually en route to Philadelphia or New

York. She arranged a maritime escape for her niece Kessiah and her two children, working with Kessiah's sailor husband John Bowley. For the Tubman family as for so many others, steamships and "other vessels were the vehicles of deliverance for maritime journeys to freedom."[72]

PHILADELPHIA

Robert Purvis, the son of a white English businessman and an enslaved Black woman he described as a "Moor" from Morocco, led the campaign to assist fugitives in and around Philadelphia for almost a quarter century, from the time he helped found the American Anti-Slavery Society in 1833, then the Vigilant Committee in 1837, through the outbreak of the Civil War. He led multiple antislavery organizations and hid runaways in his own home at the corner of Ninth and Lombard Streets, in a secret basement room accessible only through a trapdoor. When Purvis passed away in 1898, his obituary in the *New York Times* deemed him the "President of the 'Underground Railroad.'"[73]

Looking back on his long involvement in the struggle, Purvis noted that he and his comrade abolitionists in Philadelphia had helped around "one person per day," which would, over his long career, have meant almost nine thousand escapees. He provided a key insight into how the system worked, recognizing the "most efficient helpers, or agents we had" over that long span of struggle: two market women who worked on the docks of Baltimore, one of whom "was white, the other 'colored.'" Purvis did not say how many runaways these women assisted, nor how long they were active. But they did stand out in his memory as exceptional, ranking alongside the Quaker Thomas Garrett of Wilmington, Delaware, who toward the end of life recalled that he had helped 2,700 fugitives, most of whom went on to Purvis and William Still in Philadelphia. These waterfront workers were two among the thousands of unnamed, unknown heroes of the struggle against slavery.

Purvis also explained how the market women worked. He noted that "by some means"—he knew not how—"they obtained a number of genuine certificates of freedom," most likely seamen's protection certificates, such as the one Frederick Douglass used on his escape to freedom in 1838, or some other kind of legal document, perhaps manumission papers, indicating that formerly enslaved persons had achieved free legal status. The women gave these documents to would-be runaways and funneled them toward Philadelphia. These "freedom papers" were so authentic, rare, and valuable, Purvis and other abolitionists in the City of Brotherly Love took care to collect and return them to the two market women so that they could be "used again by other fugitives." The success of these "passports," as Purvis called them, depended on a prevalent form of racism. Local officials in Baltimore, whether at the railroad station, the docks, or any other site of departure and surveillance, Purvis recalled, embraced "the generally received opinion, that 'all negroes look alike.'" They did not scrutinize the documents, allowing fugitive after fugitive to escape.[74]

Philadelphia was a leading port in antebellum America, but for many years it was by no means clear that the city would become a trading center, much less a key destination for escapees by sea. Located more than a hundred miles from the Atlantic by boat with a narrow hinterland and an unsheltered harbor, Philadelphia grew up along the Delaware River, which was inclined to freeze in winter. The route of the largest river from the interior of Pennsylvania, the Susquehanna, made it easier to ship cargo to Baltimore. Philadelphia's hinterland lacked export commodities until settlers felled the trees of the primeval forest, exported timber, and planted wheat. Anthracite coal shipments first arrived in the city in 1806 and slowly expanded as Irish navvies dug miles of canals during the 1820s and 1830s. By the 1840s more than 3,000 ships exported 350,000 tons of coal. Manufacturing, which included a dynamic shipbuilding sector, took off, and the city rapidly became a major seaport and industrial center.[75]

Some maritime escapees were drawn to Philadelphia because of its history and politics. With a population of eighty thousand in 1830 and half a million by 1860, the vibrant city boasted North America's longest history of abolitionism. Quakers established the world's first antislavery organization in 1775, the Society for the Relief of Free Negroes Unlawfully Held in Bondage, and abolished slavery in their own ranks in 1776. They then helped to pass the Gradual Abolition Act of 1780, the first major antislavery legislation in the western hemisphere. The organization they founded in 1775 evolved over the next fifteen years into the Pennsylvania Abolition Society.[76]

Quaker abolitionist Isaac Hopper helped to make Philadelphia a popular destination for those seeking freedom in a Northern port. Drawn into fugitive assistance in his youth by an encounter with an escaped slave-sailor named Joe from Bermuda, Hopper worked with Black stevedores and took fugitives into his home at Dock and Walnut Streets, a block from the waterfront. He helped to make Philadelphia a relatively safe place for fugitives, as an exasperated enslaver confessed to him: "There is no use in trying to capture a runaway slave in Philadelphia . . . the devil himself could not catch them when they once get here." Hopper sharply replied, "He would have less difficulty in catching the masters; being so much more familiar with them." Hopper's first biographer, fellow abolitionist Lydia Maria Child, estimated that over fifty years of activism in Philadelphia and New York, the obstreperous, frequently disowned Quaker helped roughly a thousand people, many of whom had arrived by sea, to make their way to freedom. Hopper organized the first "revolutionary cell" of a long-term movement.[77]

Partly because of Quaker practices of manumission and protection, Philadelphia attracted a large and robust free Black community. During the 1790s free people of color began to build enduring community institutions such as the African Episcopal Church of St. Thomas, founded by Absalom Jones in 1792, and the Mother Bethel African Methodist Episcopal Church, established by Richard Allen in 1794. A stalwart who stood alongside Purvis in the free Black community was his father-in-law James Forten, sailor, privateersman, American revolutionary war prisoner, and prosperous sailmaker, a man of the waterfront in every sense. Forten helped to establish the American Anti-Slavery Society in Philadelphia in December 1833 and became both a vice president of William Lloyd Garrison's new organization and an early important funder of *The Liberator*. The movement against bondage in Philadelphia made its way against fierce opposition, which included violent antiabolitionist, anti-Black riots in 1834, 1835, and 1842. In 1838 white rioters burned down the newly built abolitionist Pennsylvania Hall and state legislators stripped Black Pennsylvanians of the vote.[78]

An overview of Philadelphia's free Black population in 1849 demonstrates the centrality of maritime labor among male workers. Skilled "mechanics," who made up less than 10 percent of the total, included sailmakers as well as carpenters, blacksmiths, and sawyers who would have worked in shipbuilding or vessel repair. Roughly the same number worked as "seafaring men," manning the busy port's ships. The largest category of all, almost half of all male workers, were "laborers," which included waterfront porters, carters, and draymen as well as stevedores and, most significantly, unskilled day laborers.[79]

The founding of the Philadelphia Vigilant Committee in 1837 took inspiration from the dockside work of David Ruggles and the free Black community of New York two years earlier. With Black leadership, a majority of free Black members, a penchant for militant self-defense, and a strong connection to the waterfront, the committee sought to protect free Black men, women, and children from kidnapping and to assist fugitives who had escaped Southern slavery, most of whom were arriving by sea. They hid fugitives in their own free Black community, as they did with Harriet Jacobs when she arrived by sea from Edenton, North Carolina, in 1842. She stayed with the family of Jeremiah Durham, a carter on the docks and the minister of the Bethel African Methodist Church. She was assisted in her journey to New York by Lymas Johnson, a Vigilant Committee member and an African American porter who hauled shipping cargo around the waterfront and beyond.[80]

How many maritime maroons Johnson and his comrades helped in their early years is impossible to reconstruct because Robert Purvis burned the records when the Fugitive Slave Law was passed in 1850, fearing that if found, they would endanger both fugitives and their helpers. What few records do survive suggest that between 1839 and 1844 the committee helped no fewer than 352 freedom seekers, most of them from the maritime states of Virginia and Maryland. Some fugitives went back to sea after a sojourn in Philadelphia, continuing their voyages to New York, Trinidad, and Liverpool.

NEW YORK

Seventeen men and one woman docked their whaleboat at Whitehall Slip in lower Manhattan, not far from the battery. They carried the news and hope of rebellion within them. In July 1832, only a few months after Nat Turner's uprising broke out in Southampton County, Virginia, less than a hundred miles from their own homes in Northampton County, they had shoved off from Hungars Creek on the Delmarva Peninsula. Perhaps inspired by the uprising or by oystermen on Northern vessels who preached "universal emancipation" in Virginia waters, the eighteen freedom seekers brought the front line of the struggle against slavery with them to New York. No one knew it at the time, but their collective action would trigger a new phase in the history of New York: proslavery authorities in Virginia and New York would unleash a wave of violent repression against runaways and free people of color, many of whom would be kidnapped, thrown aboard ships, sailed South, and sold into slavery. The free Black and abolitionist communities would fight back, pioneering new tactics and a new kind of organization in the struggle against slavery.[81]

Outraged by the escape, the governor of Virginia dispatched an official state agent, William S. Floyd, to find and return the fugitives. Floyd rushed to New York, where he hired a spy and two armed police officers to prowl around Black neighborhoods. He found and arrested one of the freedom seekers right away, but when he discovered a second, late at night, a mob formed to protect the man. Floyd and the police drew their pistols, backed off the crowd, and successfully made the arrest. When forced to hold a hearing about the fugitive, under proslavery judge Richard Riker, Floyd noted that "not less than five hundred negroes appeared." When Floyd exited the courtroom after the hearing, the crowd surged forward to attack him. He and his private police drew their pistols again, and meantime Riker had summoned the city guard, who arrived and arrested "forty one or two of the most daring negroes," who were all sent to the "Bridewell." By the time Floyd departed the city with five captives in tow, he was "mad with the whole north." When he returned to Virginia, he resigned his position. The "dangers & difficulties" in New York had been too much. Floyd learned the hard way in 1832 that the free Black community of New York was already mobilized and militant on behalf of fugitives who had arrived in the city.[82]

The fugitives may have heard from sailors or oystermen that New York had completed the abolition of slavery in 1827, making the city a magnet for freedom seekers. The nation's leading port city boasted the largest fleet of merchant ships and the greatest maritime commerce of any port city, which gave freedom seekers in Southern ports many opportunities to steal aboard a ship and sail to New York. Yet upon arrival, fugitives faced extreme danger from slave hunters, as those from Northampton experienced firsthand. New York's ruling class had the North's strongest economic connections to Southern slavery, based on the transshipment of cotton, almost 80 percent of which passed through New York. J. D. B. DeBow, publisher of the South's leading economic journal, noted that New York was "almost as dependent on Southern slavery as Charleston itself." Black abolitionist Charles B. Ray agreed: New York was "perfectly pro-slavery." New York's political economy created a dangerous environment for fugitives.[83]

The fugitives from Northampton had escaped to a rapidly growing metropolis of almost two hundred thousand people, which included a robust free Black community of roughly fourteen thousand, many of them fugitives who lived around Canal Street in lower Manhattan and worked in maritime industries along the Hudson and East Rivers. Above the docks on both rivers stretched a dense forest of ship masts. The Eldridge Street jail, opened in 1836, followed by the Tombs in 1838, housed many maritime fugitives as the free Black/abolitionist community pursued legal and extralegal means of liberation. All the while these laborers moved the commodities of the world, from inland produce brought to port on the Erie Canal to the endless bales of cotton transshipped to New York from Southern ports.[84]

The arrival of the fugitives from Northampton County helped to create what Black abolitionist David Ruggles, and later historian Jonathan Daniel Wells, called the New York Kidnapping Club, a network of political authorities, police, judges, lawyers, and slave hunters who would terrorize the Black community for the next decade. Encouraged by businessmen and officials who were eager to cooperate with enslavers, the kidnapping club prowled the waterfront, searching for fugitives and capturing many free people of color who worked as sailors and dockworkers. Two of the main body snatchers of the decade, Tobias Boudinot and Daniel D. Nash, were both on the city payroll. In response to the arrival of the fugitives from Virginia, New York governor William Marcy awarded Boudinot a "blanket slave-

The Port City of New York, c. 1850

Hudson River

East River

| | 6000 FEET | |
| | 8000 METERS | |

N · E · S · W

A Whitehall Slip

B Colored Sailors Home, 61 Cherry Street

C Roosevelt Street docks

D Corlears Hook

E Eldridge Street jail

F City Hall Park

G Mother AME Zion Church, 158 Church Street

H Sydney Howard Gay's office, 138 Nassau Street

I New York Vigilance Committee office, 61 John Street

J David Ruggles Residence, 36 Lispenard Street

hunting writ," which the latter used so frequently he had to have it recopied on "sturdy parchment." Slave catchers recaptured fourteen of the Northampton fugitives and returned them to bondage. Only four gained their freedom.[85]

Against the repeated outrages of the New York Kidnapping Club, the free Black community of the city, in alliance with a small group of white abolitionists, formed the Vigilance Committee in 1835. The Black working class played a leading role in forming the group, not least because its members were the most vulnerable to blackbirding, the forcible reenslavement of free people, especially those who worked on the waterfront. The proletarian nature of the organization was revealed in its fundraising plans: a committee of a hundred people, mostly women, would be formed and each person would recruit ten other people to contribute one penny each. Women organizers would go on to form the Colored Women's Vigilance Committee a few years later.[86]

The annual reports of the Vigilance Committee issued in 1837, 1838, and 1842 make it clear that the waterfront was the primary zone of struggle and organization. The committee's three main concerns all came from the docks: finding and liberating enslaved people like Abraham Goslee on board ships that sailed into New York harbor; defending people like Hester Jane Carr, who was kidnapped on the waterfront, thrown into a ship, and sailed southward for sale; and fighting for the freedom of Black sailors like Anthony Freeman, who was illegally sold into slavery in 1836. David Ruggles complained bitterly about "the unhuman practices of captains of vessels, shipping masters, and seamen's landlords upon seamen in the city and port of New York." During the 1830s New York became a war zone, as those for and against slavery fought it out on the streets and docks until the outbreak of the Civil War.[87]

When the former sailor Ruggles "proclaimed Jubilee to the captive," he backed up the Biblical phrase with action. During its first year of operation the New York Vigilance Committee assisted 335 runaways, twenty-four a month, almost one a day. From the moment of its founding in 1835 to 1844, the committee assisted more than 1,800 fugitives, a majority of whom arrived by sea. The committee created "public odium" against slave catchers and slowly moved public opinion to their advantage, neutralizing some of the sentiment that had led to a massive weeklong antiabolitionist riot in July 1834. Abolitionists remained few and were despised by many, but their actions were enough to sway the New York political class to action.[88]

If this predatory phase of New York's history was initiated by the arrival of eighteen fugitives from Virginia in the late summer of 1832, it ended with another maritime event in the same state a few years later. In January 1839 an enslaved man named Isaac was helped aboard a New York vessel called the *Robert Center* by three Black sailors. As we saw in the previous chapter, Isaac was recaptured, but the governor and legislature of Virginia demanded that New York return the three sailors to stand trial for "slave stealing." New York governor William H. Seward refused—and retaliated by passing New York's personal liberty laws (1839–43) to defend fugitives. The New York Kidnapping Club slowly died off in the early 1840s.[89]

NEW BEDFORD

By 1858, when abolitionist Daniel Ricketson published *The History of New Bedford*, the port had a long tradition of assisting runaways: "in the early part of the present century there was hardly a house in the place which had not given shelter and succor to a fugitive slave." Ricketson exaggerated but he expressed an important truth: New Bedford had embraced and protected runaways for decades. Black and white churches rang their bells as warnings whenever slave hunters arrived in town. Ricketson recalled that the Fugitive Slave Act of 1850 had been received in New Bedford with such "universal contempt" that "the rendition of a fugitive from our city could not be effected." He concluded, with confidence and pride, "We trust that the attempt will never be made."[90]

A gritty seaport world famous for its whaling fleet, antebellum New Bedford was called the "Fugitive's Gibraltar": a crossroads for maritime escapees and a place of great strategic importance in the larger struggle against slavery. Smaller than the other Northern receiving ports with sixteen thousand residents in 1850, New Bedford boasted the North's largest free Black community by proportion— roughly 10 percent of the total population. Runaways found cover in the endless ebb and flow of sailors into and out of New Bedford; three thousand mariners would pass through in any given year.[91]

Because of the global reach of its whalers—and captains' constant need to recruit sailors due to desertion and death—New Bedford might have had the most diverse working class to be found anywhere in the world. The city's whalers routinely brought home Kanaka sailors from the Pacific, especially the Sandwich Islands (now Hawai'i), a major center for provisioning crews and repairing vessels. These sailors were joined, on ship and ashore, by Cape Verdeans, Azoreans, Chileans, and Native Americans from the Pacific Northwest, all workers from whaling ports of call. Self-emancipated Black workers easily slipped into the mix.

Two fundamental facts shaped attitudes in New Bedford toward maritime escapees. First, the social composition of the local elite: New Bedford had long been a Quaker town, in which many merchants, manufacturers, and middle-class professionals opposed slavery. They were sympathetic to fugitives and willing to offer them jobs and other kinds of assistance, even if they were not willing to treat them as equals. Relatedly, New Bedford's maritime economy, based primarily on whaling, was fundamentally different from that of Philadelphia, New York, and Boston. New Bedford merchants depended less on Southern markets, which made slavery easier to oppose for economic reasons. Herman Melville, who sailed out of New Bedford in 1841, observed that the patrician houses and gracious gardens of

New Bedford "came from the Atlantic, Pacific, and Indian oceans. One and all, they were harpooned and dragged up hither from the bottom of the sea."[92]

Second, and even more important, the unusually large and well-organized free Black community of New Bedford welcomed and assisted fugitives. The port's population of people of color increased from fewer than four hundred in the late 1820s to more than fifteen hundred in 1860. Many hundreds of them—a Quaker estimated seven hundred in 1850—had escaped Southern slavery, most of them by sea. The community preserved its maritime connection. In 1838 more than half of New Bedford's Black workers toiled on ships, many on whalers, while many more worked as common laborers and a few as skilled craftsmen on the waterfront. Black waterfront workers were the beating heart of the port's African American community.[93]

The free Black population lived throughout the city, with concentrations along the waterfront, especially the two boardinghouses for Black seamen, one of them operated in the 1830s by sailor-abolitionist William P. Powell. In the eighteenth century many Black New Bedforders lived in a community called New Guinea, which was destroyed by the British during the American revolutionary war. In the early nineteenth century, the toughest parts of town were mixed-race communities known as Hard Dig, a place of frequent riots where, according to a contemporary, the constable "seldom entered," and what would come to be called Dog Corner, which swarmed with proletarian revelers as soon as "the fiddle strikes up." A municipal survey reported in 1852 that New Bedford had seventy-eight liquor shops and fifty-six whorehouses, almost all of them located in working-class neighborhoods, many near the docks.[94]

A defining feature of New Bedford's free Black community was its extraordinary degree of self-organization. During the antebellum era, African Americans established five all-Black churches and eight abolitionist organizations, including David Walker's Massachusetts General Colored Association, and several militia groups such as the New

Bedford Attucks Frontiers, all well armed for self-defense. Black churches and abolitionist organizations were the institutional foundations for material aid to fugitives. The founders of the African Christian Church declared, "We hear the rattling of the chains and the cries of the wounded of this injured people. Slavery is a curse on the land. Who can wash away the stain! When will it be annihilated!"[95]

A fugitive arriving by sea could count on solidarity from the free Black/abolitionist community, while a slave catcher could expect militant hostility. The "tall and dignified" Nathan Johnson explained to a fugitive in 1838 that "no slaveholder could take a slave from New Bedford; that there were men there who would lay down their lives, before such an outrage could be perpetrated. The colored people themselves were of the best metal and would fight for liberty to the death." This he knew by experience. A local Black man and a fugitive had clashed, the former threatening to inform the latter's enslaver where he was. Someone called a meeting, announcing "Business of importance!" that required immediate community attention. The "would-be Judas" was given a special invitation and attended without knowing the purpose of the gathering. When the large meeting was gaveled to order, a church elder was appointed to preside. He "deliberately surveyed his audience, and then said, in a tone of solemn resolution, 'Well, friends, we have got him here, and I would now recommend that you young men should just take him outside the door and kill him.'" Several young men "bolted" toward the enemy of freedom, only to be intercepted by those "more timid than themselves." The betrayer escaped and never showed his face in New Bedford ever after. All threats to fugitives suddenly ceased.[96]

Maritime maroon John S. Jacobs of Edenton, North Carolina, had three main objectives when he arrived in New Bedford in May 1839: First, he wanted to educate himself, "to raise myself above the level of the beast, where slavery had left me, and fit myself for the society of man." Second, he wanted to make money to help his sister Harriet escape the lecherous clutches of enslaver Dr. James Norcom back home. Third, he wanted to stay out of the way of slave catchers for his own sake. After connecting with the free Black community in New Bedford, he resolved to work during the day and go to school at night. Finding that his long hours of labor caused him to miss his classes, he decided to take his books aboard a whaler, the *Frances Henrietta*, for a three-and-a-half-year voyage. He returned to New Bedford with a ship full of 3,100 barrels of whale oil and soon had several hundred dollars in his pockets. To his joy, he learned upon his return that Harriet had already escaped and come to town looking for him. New Bedford offered Jacobs community, education, work, and freedom.[97]

Fugitive John Thompson, an escapee from Maryland, also found New Bedford attractive. He had tried to sign onto a merchant ship in New York, but because of his inexperience, "I could get no berth on shipboard, as they only wanted to employ able seamen, so I was advised to go to New Bedford, where green hands were more wanted." In hopes of signing onto a whaling vessel as a cook or steward, he pretended to know the job. Once at sea, it became clear that Thompson was "wholly ignorant of a steward's duties," which did not make his shipmates happy. He confessed to the captain that he was a fugitive, trying to support his family in Philadelphia, and that he needed to take a long whaling voyage to dodge the slave hunters. A New York captain might have returned him to bondage, but the New Bedford man was touched by the story. Rather than flog him, he taught the "raw hand" how to cook and became, as Thompson recalled, "as kind as a father to me."[98]

The combination of a militant, well-organized free Black community; a maritime economy that offered work; and an established, largely Quaker abolitionist movement made New Bedford a city of refuge for maritime maroons. After the passage of the Fugitive Slave Law in 1850, prominent merchant Charles W. Morgan predicted that if enslavers came to New Bedford in search of fugitives, "bloodshed will ensue" because the free Black community "are a powerful body and determined to be free or die." Other free people recognized this

truth: as hundreds of fugitives embarked from other cities for Canada, New Bedford's free Black population expanded by 50 percent,
primarily because people who felt unsafe in New York migrated to the
city. The port that Southern enslavers denounced as "that den of
thieves and fugitive protectors" was, according to seaborne escapee
George Teamoh, "our magnet of attraction." New Bedford's people
embraced freedom "as a principle and nailed it to the mast-head of
their little bark [barque, a sailing vessel]." Those "loyal people,"
Teamoh continued, "had no argument for slavery but that of instant
death to the institution." As far as we know, no one who escaped to
New Bedford, by land or sea, was ever returned to bondage.[99]

BOSTON

On August 18, 1851, sailor-abolitionist Austin Bearse penned a letter
to fellow activist Samuel May Jr., general agent of the Massachusetts
Anti-Slavery Society in Boston. Bearse needed information from
May about a maritime fugitive, to whom he referred obliquely as "the
Soul." He then couched his inquiry in the Biblical parable of Jonah
and the whale, saying that he and two other abolitionists had

> *come to the conclusion that you was a getting down by the*
> *cold streemes of Babolon [Babylon] and by in quiring for a*
> *steeme Boat to go on the cape I thought you wanted to run*
> *away as Jonah did. Now if it should so happen that you*
> *should get over Bord and a whale should Swaller you and*
> *should spew you out on Cape Cod their is one thing that will*
> *not come to pass and thatt is the goard [gourd] will never*
> *grow up over your head on sandy Cape Cod.*

Bearse promised to send May a list of steamboats and their schedules. Babylon, a place of historic slavery, symbolized the South; Jonah

and the whale referred to Bearse's vessel, the *Moby Dick*, named for Herman Melville's not-yet-famous novel; Cape Cod was the transit point for the fugitive between that vessel and a steamboat, probably bound for Canada; the gourd plant was important to both Jonah (it shielded his head) and to the men and women who were enslaved and thirsty. Bearse concluded the letter by writing, "you will think that I have wrote a mess of nonsense, especially in theis times that tries men soules." The "nonsense" was a secret code used by abolitionists in the dangerous time of the Fugitive Slave Law. Bearse affirmed the revolutionary mission of abolitionism by alluding to Thomas Paine's famous words about the darkest moments of the American Revolution.[100]

As a member of the Boston Vigilance Committee, sailor-abolitionist Austin Bearse operated a small vessel to assist escapees who had arrived from Southern ports.

As a center of national and international communication, transportation, and production, Boston occupied a position of strategic economic importance that would amplify the actions of the city's abolitionist movement, which by the 1830s had become the strongest in the nation. Bearse's Boston was a primary shipping center for New England's booming industrial revolution. Capitalists imported millions of bulging bales of cotton, which required a huge fleet of merchant ships and a massive body of merchant seamen and dockers to transport the commodity from Southern plantations to New England factories or on to Liverpool. The

Boston waterfront was a key to a larger regime of labor and capital accumulation as well as to a series of spectacular maritime escapes that would inflame the national debate on slavery.

The free African American community of Boston was a critical component of the city's maritime complex. A significant number of Black Bostonians had been born into slavery in the South and had escaped, probably a large majority of them following the trade routes northward along the Atlantic seaboard to New England. Maritime fugitive Louisa P. Jones illustrated this point: after dressing as a man and sailing from Norfolk to Philadelphia and on to Boston in 1858, she wrote: "I have met with so menny of my acquaintance hear, that I all most immagion my self to bee in the old country." Male fugitives who arrived in Boston often found themselves frozen out of the trades by practices of racial exclusion; they huddled close to the less-regulated waterfront, where many men found work as dockers, dray-men, and porters. Three out of four performed semiskilled or unskilled labor. "Sailor" and "laborer" were the two most common occupations for Black male workers in the censuses of 1850 and 1860. The free Black community of Boston dwelled primarily in two neighborhoods, Beacon Hill and the North End, near the docks.[101]

Many of Boston's Black leaders cultivated ties with Black sailors and "men of the Wharf." The boldest African American leader in Boston, Lewis Hayden, a former runaway from Kentucky who sheltered fugitives in his own home and threatened to blow the place up if police tried to enter, led sailors and laborers into the streets on several occasions. Jehiel C. Beman ministered to seamen and dockers in the African Methodist Episcopal (AME) church near the North End docks. Samuel Snowden, pastor at the AME congregation on Beacon Hill and friend of waterfront militant David Walker, fought for the rights of Black seamen who were frequently jailed or "quarantined" in Southern ports. The Reverend Leonard Grimes also cooperated with waterfront workers in his antislavery activism, usually independently of majority-white abolitionist organizations. Moreover, Black sailors and dockers were themselves leaders, especially in moments of direct action.[102]

By the 1850s Boston's North End had two boardinghouses for "colored seamen"—and frequently for fugitives just off the ship. In 1838 a sailor helped a weakened and disoriented Jim Matthews, who had just arrived from Charleston, South Carolina, to one of the boardinghouses, where he stayed for a time before moving on to a life of freedom in Hallowell, Maine. Eight years later three sailors escorted another Charleston escapee, John Andrew Jackson, to the boardinghouse on Richmond Street near Rowe's Wharf, introduced him to Henry Foreman, sailor-turned-proprietor, and helped him to get both a room and a job. Boardinghouse residents helped to plan and carry out confrontational political actions and took part "in several fugitive slave rescues."[103]

In Boston as in New York, boardinghouses were swirling centers of knowledge and experience, where international seafarers came together for shelter, sustenance, and solidarity. Accommodating between twenty and thirty sailors each, the boardinghouses combined the functions of hotel, social club, and mutual aid society. Sailors visited local taverns and bars, drinking New York gin and feasting on raw clams. They got together to play cards and music or to visit the Belle Union Dance Hall. They met with "nightwalking" sex workers who were the bane of white middle-class moral reformers. When seaman John Tidde found himself locked away in a New Orleans jail in 1834, bereft of his freedom papers and facing sale into slavery, he smuggled out a letter appealing to his boardinghouse comrades and proprietor Arthur Jones for help. They interceded with Massachusetts authorities and secured Tidde's release.[104]

Boston's Black maritime workers joined Austin Bearse and three other members of the Vigilance Committee for a dramatic rescue in July 1853. As Bearse wrote in his memoir, "Some colored men on Long Wharf got the story somehow" of a fugitive, Sandy Swan, held captive on the brig *Florence* out of Wilmington, North Carolina, captained by

Amos Hopkins. Bearse and the motley crew boarded his thirty-six-foot vessel, the *Moby Dick*, and rowed out to the *Florence*, which was anchored off Fort Independence. Bearse rounded up alongside the *Florence* and went aboard with several of the men. Captain Hopkins had gone ashore, so Bearse went to the mate, second in command, and demanded that he hand over the captive. The mate replied that he was chained and incarcerated below deck. Bearse answered, roughly, "I want him, d——— quickly" and made a quick move to go below. The mate then asked to see "papers," to which Bearse responded, "I had all the papers I wanted," as he hurried down below and found that Swan had already escaped from his irons. The now-liberated prisoner joined the other men as they jumped into the *Moby Dick*. As they rowed toward Dorchester Bay, Swan changed from his ragged clothes into fisherman's attire so he would blend in with the other workers in case another vessel should stop and search them. Swan told Bearse that he saw his freedom by sea rescue coming: "God told him in the night that somebody would set him free in the morning."[105]

Chapter 3

Frederick Douglass's
Maritime Dream

Frederick Bailey—soon to be Frederick Douglass, the nineteenth century's greatest abolitionist—grew up in bondage on
a riverine system that emptied into Maryland's Chesapeake
Bay. As a child he moved to the bustling port city of Baltimore and
worked for years in Fell's Point on the north shore of the harbor near
the Patapsco River. He labored among a motley crew in the shipyards
and became a skilled caulker, wielding mallets, chisels, hooks, scrap-
ers, oakum, and hemp to seal the seams between the timbers in a
vessel's hull to make it tight and seaworthy.

The cosmopolitan Atlantic maritime milieu of Baltimore not only
enabled Douglass to escape bondage but also shaped his understanding
of the very nature of freedom. Because Douglass played such influential roles as a writer, public speaker, and publisher in the antislavery
movement, he must be considered America's most important runaway. The sea shaped his storied life in profound ways.[1]

Douglass left a rich record of his thoughts and actions about freedom and the sea. He wrote three different autobiographies at various
points in his life: he published *Narrative of the Life of Frederick Douglass, an American Slave* in 1845, seven years after his escape; *My Bondage*

and My Freedom in 1855, after he had achieved considerable fame as an abolitionist; and a final account, *Life and Times of Frederick Douglass*, in 1881, by which time he was a revered national symbol. These deep, insightful, rhetorically brilliant sources illuminate the role of the waterfront in the genesis of antislavery radicalism.[2]

Douglass was not, however, immediately forthcoming about his own escape; indeed, he criticized those who revealed details about how they had absconded from slavery. He wrote of Henry "Box" Brown, who escaped by shipping himself inside a crate to freedom in Philadelphia: had not "Brown and his friends attracted slaveholding attention to the manner of his escape, we might have had a thousand Box Browns per annum." Douglass therefore consciously decided "not to state all the facts" about his escape in his first two autobiographies. He did not want to implicate the comrades who had assisted him in a practice that remained a major crime against property. Nor did he want to provide useful information to slaveholders, who could then close "a door whereby some dear brother bondman might escape his galling chains." Such hesitations and omissions limit our ability to reconstruct the history of escape, but fortunately for posterity, Douglass opened up about his route to freedom in his final autobiography, published eighteen years after slavery had been abolished. In 1893 he revealed that he had been involved in fugitive escape "long before I left the South," helping others to escape by sea from Baltimore. In the end he revealed, through his widely circulated writings and his well-attended lectures, a waterfront experience that shaped his own freedom struggle and no doubt inspired many others.[3]

EARLY LIFE

Frederick Augustus Washington Bailey was born in February 1818, probably in the cabin of his grandmother, Betsey Bailey, who lived near Tuckahoe Creek, Talbot County, Maryland. She was a skilled fisherwoman, adept at extracting protein for her family from the waterways of the region. His mother was an enslaved woman named Harriet Bailey; his father was likely her white enslaver, Aaron Anthony, a sailor who eventually rose to be the captain of a large sloop, the *Sally Lloyd*, owned by the wealthy Colonel Edward Lloyd.

All of Fred's male enslavers followed maritime trades. At age eight, he was sent to labor for Anthony's relatives Sophia and Hugh Auld, the latter of whom was a shipwright working in Baltimore's Fell's Point. A year later, he was transferred as property to Lucretia Auld, Captain Anthony's daughter and the wife of Hugh's brother Thomas, the captain of another of Colonel Lloyd's sloops. Douglass spent nine and a half formative years in the bustling port of Baltimore. Water was never far from his person, thoughts, and dreams.[4]

Fred learned about the power of ships and the sea as a child. He recalled the excitement felt by the workers on Colonel Lloyd's plantation when his cousin, sailor Tom Bailey, returned from Baltimore to spin magical yarns about the voyage. Tom was two or three years older than Fred and served as cabin boy aboard the *Sally Lloyd*, then captained by Thomas Auld and manned by enslaved workers named Peter, Isaac, Rich, and Jake: their work on the vessel was considered "privileged." Every time Tom came home from a voyage to the big city, Fred recalled, "he was always a sort of hero amongst us." Fred's maritime dream began with a sailor's storytelling.[5]

Tom was not, however, "fluent in speech"; he "stuttered immoderately." But he nonetheless told riveting tales. Any time Fred pointed out something of note on the plantation—pillars, paintings, the "Great House itself"—Tom had always "seen something at Baltimore far exceeding, both in beauty and strength, the object which I pointed out to him." Nothing compared to what the sailor saw in the big city, including things Fred could hardly imagine: firecrackers, church bells, soldiers, markets teeming with people, and shop windows jammed with appealing things for sale. On one occasion Tom bought a trumpet for six pence and brought it home for all to admire. He had also seen a new marvel called the steamboat as well as grand tall ships three or four times larger than the *Sally Lloyd*. The young sailor's tales captured Fred's curiosity and imagination.[6]

A big day finally came when Fred was eight years old: he had his first memorable personal encounter with ships, sailing, and ports. Dispatched to live with Hugh and Sophia Auld, he sailed on the *Sally Lloyd* down the Miles River and into Chesapeake Bay with a cargo of sheep, first to Annapolis, then to Baltimore. Once the wind filled the sails of the sloop, Fred "walked aft, and gave to Colonel Lloyd's plantation what I hoped would be the last look." He then walked forward and "placed myself in the bows of the sloop." He spent the rest of the voyage spellbound as he beheld new sights, "looking ahead, interesting myself in what was in the distance rather than in things nearby or behind."[7]

BALTIMORE'S WATERFRONT

Baltimore was a brave new world, and thanks to Cousin Tom, Fred knew something about it before he arrived. Fred stepped off the *Sally Lloyd* into one of the most dynamic port cities in the young United States. He would work among the motley crew at Fell's Point, the epicenter of the port-city economy. Fred quickly recognized that the port city offered him opportunities that were inconceivable in the plantation society he had left behind. "Going to live at Baltimore," he wrote, "laid the foundation, and opened the gateway, to all my subsequent prosperity."[8]

One day in 1830 on Water's Wharf, located on the very tip of Fell's Point, Fred saw two Irish sailors unloading a shipment of stone from a scow, a flat-bottomed barge. He decided to lend a hand—as much as a twelve-year-old could in lifting heavy cargo—even though the sailors had not asked for his help. He saw the need, joined in, and got to work, perhaps hoping for two bits in thanks. When the three had finished unloading the stone, the men pulled him aside, away from the bustle of the dock, to speak with him privately. One asked the boy a series of questions—most pressingly, was he a slave and would that be his lifelong fate? Fred answered that he was indeed a slave and would be "for life." The "good Irishman," Fred later recalled, shrugged his shoulders "and seemed deeply affected by the statement." The Irish tar replied, "it was a pity so fine a little fellow as myself should be a slave for life." At this point the other seaman joined in with strong opinions of his own: "They both had much to say about the matter, and expressed the deepest sympathy with me, and the most decided hatred of slavery." Fred had offered the solidarity of help with common work and received a different kind of solidarity in return.[9]

The Irish sailors soon took the conversation in an even more subversive direction: "They went so far as to tell me that I ought to run away, and go to the north; that I should find friends there, and that I would be as free as anybody." Another life was possible. Despite his tender years, Fred already knew enough to be wary. He pretended neither to understand nor to be interested in their proposal, for he feared that the sailors might entrap him—that is, encourage him to escape, kidnap him, and then either sell him or return him to his enslaver for a reward. These perfectly rational fears shadowed his mind even though he felt that these men "were honest and meant me no ill." Despite the fierce fights that would go on between Black and Irish workers on the waterfront of Baltimore and other ports for decades to come, Fred continued, as he grew older and as he rewrote his autobiography, to believe that the Irish sailors were sincere in their convictions and concerns.[10]

The sympathetic suggestions of two seafaring Irish strangers would have a powerful long-term effect on Fred's life. Even though he did not immediately embrace their tip that he should abscond—he was, after all, too young to strike out on his own—he "nevertheless remembered their advice, and from that time I resolved to run away."

He looked forward to the moment when he would "escape to the north," to find the friends and freedom promised by the sailors. He continued to reflect on the issue they raised, his fate of being enslaved for life; that, he realized, "was the saddest thought." He resolved not to accept it. He was already thinking ahead to the mechanics of escape: "I wished to learn how to write, before going, as I might have occasion to write my own pass." The sailors had nonetheless given him a great gift, "the hope of freedom," and moreover had even foreshadowed how he might someday achieve "the liberty for which my heart panted."

The process of learning to write commenced quickly in a nearby part of the waterfront: Durgin and Bailey's shipyard, also on Fell's Point. Fred had been taught the rudiments of reading by Sophia Auld, soon after he first arrived in Baltimore in March 1826. But those lessons ended abruptly when her husband Hugh learned of the instruction and commanded his tenderhearted wife to desist immediately: "It would forever unfit him to be a slave," he said. Sophia complied, and Fred was crushed. He would have to find other ways to continue his education.[11]

At the shipyard Fred noticed that after the sawyers hewed the timber for the hull of a ship under construction, the ship carpenters would write in red chalk (called "ocher") on the lumber "the name of that part of the ship for which it was intended." The notation informed the shipwrights of how they had judged the grain of the wood and where it would best serve the vessel. Any piece of wood intended for the larboard side of the vessel would be chalked with an "L." A piece for the starboard was marked "S." Larboard-side forward would be designated "L. F.," larboard aft "L. A." The same applied to the starboard: "S. F." and "S. A."[12]

The simple code was useful to Fred. He memorized the four letters, and when the shipyard workers broke for dinner, he copied them repeatedly to master their form. He would then find white boys in the shipyard or beyond who knew how to write and would challenge them by saying that he could write as well as they could. The other boys knew that he was enslaved and was therefore forbidden to learn how to write, so they would answer, Fred recalled, "I don't believe you. Let me see you try it." He would then carefully write the four letters he had learned and say, "Beat that." Whatever the boys wrote in reply, he noted the letters and studied them, slowly adding to his stock of knowledge. Years later he wrote with no small pride, "In this way I got a good many lessons in writing, which it is quite possible I should never have gotten in any other way." Instead of pen and ink he used a lump of ocher that he had no doubt pilfered from a shipwright. Instead of a copybook, he used pavement, a brick wall, or a board fence: "With these, I learned mainly how to write." The original foundation of an eloquent career as a writer was a carpenter's notation on ship lumber, from which Fred built the hull of his own literacy. Six years later Fred would write his own counterfeit pass to escape bondage by taking to the water.[13]

BREAKING THE SLAVE BREAKER

In March 1833 Fred's enslaver, Thomas Auld, had a falling out with his brother Hugh and summoned Fred back from Baltimore to St. Michaels on the Eastern Shore. Having lived in the port city for seven years, Fred was deeply disappointed to be forced back to the plantation, not least because his avowed escape would be more difficult to achieve from there. He took another maritime passage, this time on the sloop *Amanda*, into a new phase of life. Fred used his time on the water to good effect, studying how steamboats out of Baltimore steered a course toward Philadelphia. He discovered that when they reached North Point, they went up Chesapeake Bay "in a north-easterly direction." Already thinking strategically at the age of fifteen, he "deemed this knowledge of the utmost importance." As he stood there on the deck of the sloop gazing at the steamers, his "determination to run away was again revived."[14]

Things did not go well with "Master Thomas," whom Fred considered cowardly and cruel. Auld starved his workers and used a heavy cowskin whip to rip flesh from their backs. Yet Fred retained a defiant edge. "My city life," Auld scolded him, "had had a very pernicious effect upon me. It had almost ruined me for every good purpose, and fitted me for every thing which was bad." On January 1, 1834, after nine months of strife, Auld hired Fred out for a year to Edward Covey, a vicious, mean-spirited small farmer who had a reputation for "breaking" rebellious slaves. Fred would soon be sixteen years old. His growing political will landed him in Covey's bloody grasp.[15]

Fred had never worked as a field hand, so he had a lot to learn. His inexperience gave Covey the pretext to whip him frequently, which he did, about once a week for the first six months. Fred's back was constantly raw and sore. "Work, work, work" was the order each day with Covey: "The longest days were too short for him, and the shortest nights too long for him." The young man who had been "somewhat unmanageable" when he first arrived was, as he himself admitted, eventually "tamed." After half a year of beatings, "Mr. Covey," Fred remembered ruefully, "succeeded in breaking me. I was broken in body, soul, and spirit."[16]

Covey's farm lay west of St. Michaels, near Chesapeake Bay. On Sundays Fred would walk all alone to the water's edge for peace and quiet, spiritual escape, and reflection. As he gazed on the "broad bosom" of the Bay he saw that it "was ever white with sails from every quarter of the habitable globe." His time in Baltimore had helped him to understand the internationalism of seafaring life, how the mobility of the watercraft and their workers connected the world through commerce. The vessels' freedom of movement both fascinated and tormented him. He stood on the banks "and traced, with saddened heart and tearful eye, the countless number of sails moving off to the mighty ocean. The sight of these always affected [him] powerfully." Free men, he thought, might look upon those "beautiful vessels, robed in purest white," with delight. But to him they were "so many shrouded ghosts, to terrify and torment me with thoughts of my wretched condition." The sight of the ships moved him to urgent, intimate conversations with God: "with no audience but the Almighty, I would pour out my soul's complaint, in my rude way, with an apostrophe to the moving multitude of ships."[17]

Fred then turned from addressing God to speaking directly to the ships themselves. In his autobiography of 1845, *Narrative of the Life of Frederick Douglass*, he penned some of the most anguished and poetic lines ever written over the two centuries of the abolitionist movement:

> You are loosed from your moorings, and are free; I am fast in my chains, and am a slave! You move merrily before the gentle gale, and I sadly before the bloody whip! You are freedom's swift-winged angels, that fly round the world; I am confined in bands of iron! O that I were free! O, that I were on one of your gallant decks, and under your protecting wing! Alas! betwixt me and you, the turbid waters roll. Go on, go on. O that I could also go! Could I but swim! If I could fly! O, why was I born a man, of whom to make a brute. The glad ship is gone; she hides in the dim distance. I am left in the hottest hell of unending slavery. O God, save me! God, deliver me! Let me be free! Is there any God? Why am I a slave?

By juxtaposing his own miserable immobility, standing on the shore "fast in [his] chains," to the ship's freedom to "fly round the world," Fred created the ship as an object of desire and a symbol of a hopeful future. The free wind moved the ship; "the whip moved the bondman." If only he could get aboard one of "freedom's swift-winged angels," take protection under its wing, and cross the "turbid waters"— that was his dream. He asked God to deliver him, but soon he realized that he must deliver himself.[18]

Fred's decision became an invocation and a creed: "I will take to
the water. This very bay shall yet bear me into freedom." He recalled
that the steamboats "steered in a north-east course from North Point."
Then he laid out an embryonic plan of escape: "I will do the same;
and when I get to the head of the bay, I will turn my canoe adrift, and
walk straight through Delaware into Pennsylvania." He swore, "Let
but the first opportunity offer, and, come what will, I am off." He
consoled himself with the knowledge, "There is a better day coming."[19]

The day of glory would not come soon. Meanwhile, Fred still had
to deal with Edward Covey. After a particularly severe beating, Fred
walked seven miles to Thomas Auld to protest his abusive treatment.
He arrived covered in blood from head to toe, but Auld refused to
protect him, ordering him back to Covey's farm early the next morning. Arriving around nine, Fred saw Covey coming toward him with
a cowhide lash, so he ran into the woods and hid until Covey finally
relented. Fred wrote, "I spent that day mostly in the woods, having
the alternative before me,—to go home and be whipped to death, or
stay in the woods and be starved to death." Given a root by his friend
Sandy Jenkins for protection, he returned to Covey's farm. The moment of truth came two days later.[20]

When Covey showed up in the barn with a rope, determined to tie
Fred up to administer a ferocious whipping, the young man suddenly
"resolved to fight." Where the spirit to resist came from in that moment, he did not know. He grabbed Covey by the throat, dug in his
fingernails, and drew blood. The "n———-breaker" was astonished
and "trembled like a leaf." He called other enslaved people to assist
him. A man named Hughes tried to help subdue Fred but a swift,
hard kick to the ribs took him out of the fray, sapping Covey's courage further. A gasping Covey asked Fred if "[he] meant to persist in
[his] resistance." Fred answered, "I told him I did, come what might;
that he had used me like a brute for six months, and that I was determined to be used so no longer." The fight went on for two hours until
the bloodied Covey stood down. For the remaining six months of his

yearlong hiring out, Covey "never laid the weight of his finger upon me in anger." The victory over Covey was another turning point in Fred's life: "My long-crushed spirit rose, cowardice departed, bold defiance took its place." He would never be whipped again—and he would run away.[21]

FIRST ATTEMPT

After being hired out in 1835 to a planter named William Freeland, Fred began to plan in earnest for "a final struggle" to escape from bondage. He understood that the effort would likely have one of three outcomes, two of which were not happy. First, he might die. He envisaged "grim death" in "the most horrid shapes," whether by starvation or perhaps cannibalism, his body being ripped apart by bloodhounds, drowning in Chesapeake Bay, or getting shot and killed by slave catchers. He was willing to accept these risks. Second, he might be recaptured and sold to the Deep South, probably to work in the cotton fields of Alabama, where his prospects of ever gaining his freedom would be almost zero. This would have been the worst fate of all—to be trapped in the living death of slavery for the rest of his days. Fred made clear that he would "prefer death to hopeless bondage." Only the third option, a successful escape, offered the life he wanted. Not quite seventeen years old, he began the year thinking that 1835 "should decide my fate one way or the other."[22]

Fred took awhile to get organized. In early 1836 he began to plan a maritime escape for himself and four comrades, but all of them were wracked with doubt. Looking at the big picture, the map of slavery and freedom, "We could see no spot, this side of the ocean, where we could be free." He knew that the British had begun to abolish slavery in 1833, but he and his fellow conspirators "knew nothing about Canada." They knew little more about the Northern states a hundred miles away. They had learned a bit about New York, probably from sailors, but that knowledge had a dark side: the city had strong commercial ties to the South and feral packs of slave catchers sniffed around the docks every day. If they went there, they might be "forever harassed with the frightful liability of being returned to slavery—with the certainty of being treated tenfold worse than before." As Fred surveyed the danger points on the escape route, he saw that "at every gate through which we were to pass, we saw a watchman—at every ferry a guard—on every bridge a sentinel—and in every wood a patrol." What abolitionists called the "Slave Power" was armed and vigilant.

The five brave men nevertheless continued their planning. Fred had recruited only those he trusted deeply to join the dangerous enterprise: two uncles, Henry Bailey and Charles Roberts, and two friends who were brothers, John and Henry Harris. The group chose a maritime escape because it provided greater cover than a landed route, on which anyone with a white face "could stop us, and subject us to examination." On the water, they would encounter fewer white people and look less like runaways. They would present themselves as fishermen or as belonging to any of the other occupations routinely pursued by Black workers, both enslaved and free, on Chesapeake Bay. Fred would use his hard-won literacy skills to write passes for every member of the group, which would increase their chances of getting away.[23]

The next step would be to find a large canoe—they already had their eyes on one owned by a local planter named William Hambleton. They would make their break on the Saturday night before Easter, taking advantage of the looser discipline and greater freedom of movement permitted by the holiday. Pushing off from Eastern Bay, the men would "paddle directly up the Chesapeake Bay," about seventy miles. Once they reached land somewhere near Havre de Grace or Charlestown, they would "turn our canoe adrift" and follow "the north star" by foot until they got beyond the state border of Maryland into Pennsylvania. The plan got very murky at this point, and the risk of recapture would have been great. Fred understood this and noted, "It was truly a matter of life and death with us."

In the days before their departure, Fred spent a lot of time encouraging himself and his comrades, all of whom were filled with dread. He was busy "explaining every difficulty, removing every doubt, dispelling every fear, and inspiring all with the firmness indispensable to success in our undertaking." It was truly now or never, he insisted to the group: "if we did not intend to move now, we had as well fold our arms, sit down, and acknowledge ourselves fit only to be slaves." The five men pledged themselves to each other one last time and dispersed back to their plantations, making ready for the big day: Saturday, April 2, 1836.

Fred passed a sleepless Friday night. Even though he was only eighteen years old, he was the ringleader of the escape, and he felt a special responsibility for the safety of all. He arose early, as usual, and went to work in the field, spreading manure, when an ominous portent of betrayal swept over him. The horn sounded for the workers to return from the field for breakfast. Fred went, not because he was hungry, but to convey the impression that this workday was routine like all others. He soon saw four white men riding on horses toward the farm, with two bound Black men walking behind them. Someone, probably former coconspirator Sandy Jenkins, had betrayed them. William Hambleton galloped up, asked for William Freeland, and met him in the barn. Three constables arrived, joining Hambleton and Freeland in urgent conversation. Freeland summoned Fred, whose wrists the constables immediately lashed. The white men then tied up John Harris and sought to do the same to his brother Henry, who defied them. The constables drew their pistols and threatened to shoot him. Henry taunted them to do so: "You can't kill me but once." Nine white men mobbed Henry and subdued him with a hail of punches, overpowering him and tying him up. During the commotion Fred managed to slip his self-written pass into a nearby fire, destroying evidence of their plan. William Freeland's mother soon emerged from the house to scream at Fred, "You devil! You yellow devil! it was you that put it into the heads of Henry and John to run away." During the fifteen-mile trek to the stone jail in Easton, Fred quietly urged Henry to eat his pass and to "own nothing" when interrogated.

Under close questioning, all the arrested men denied their intention to run away. They expected to be sold to the Deep South, yet they held out hope that they might be sold together. "Our greatest concern was about separation," Fred recalled later. The Easton jailor sent them to separate cells to limit their ability to coordinate their stories. Within twenty minutes local predators had sensed blood in the water: "a swarm of slave traders . . . flocked into jail to look at us," assessing their value and taunting the prisoners by asking "Ah, my boys! we have got you, haven't we?" They promised to "take the devil out of us in a very little while, if we were only in their hands."

A few days later Hambleton and Freeland arrived at the jail to take the other prisoners home, leaving Fred all alone. Fred thought he had seen his friends and relatives for the last time. Their departure "caused me more pain than any thing else in the whole transaction." Fred also figured that he, as the leader of the failed escape, would be sold away as an example to everyone on the Freeland and Hambleton plantations. The joy Fred had anticipated in a successful escape only a few days earlier was replaced with "the utmost despair." A week later Fred's enslaver, Captain Auld, arrived at the jail, removing the young man and vowing to sell him to a gentleman he knew in Alabama. That plan somehow never came to fruition, so Auld opted instead to send him back to his brother Hugh in Baltimore, where Fred would now learn a craft on the waterfront. His maritime dream of freedom not only remained alive; it grew stronger. The prospects of success in running away, he knew, were "tenfold greater from the city than from the country."

BACK TO THE DOCKS

Fred had been absent from the waterfront for more than three years, and he would soon discover that things had changed. He remembered Fell's Point at a time when shipyard laborers Black and white "worked side by side, and no one seemed to see any impropriety in it." Most of the Black workers were free people of color who had occupied their positions for years as carpenters, caulkers, coopers, and in many other maritime occupations. Yet by April 1836 the composition of the waterfront working class had begun to change. Many of the increasing thousands of European immigrants arriving in the port of Baltimore sought both skilled and unskilled jobs along the docks. The Irish would engage in fierce competition for waterfront work. Tensions were rising as Fred returned to Fell's Point "to learn a trade."[24]

Shipwright Hugh Auld hired Fred out to one of the city's biggest shipbuilders, William Gardner, who would apprentice the young man to a caulker—Fred would become a maritime artisan. But the plan soon fell victim to a big hubbub that engulfed the shipyard: Gardner procured contracts to build "two large man-of-war brigs" for the government of Mexico, which required him to mobilize a team of seventy-five carpenters to build the vessels under deadline. As energy surged around the shipyard, Fred discovered that his first job would not be to learn how to caulk after all, but rather to serve as a helper to these master craftsmen: "Their word was to be my law." Fred suddenly felt he "needed a dozen pair of hands" as he might be called to do a dozen different things "in the space of a single minute." Sometimes three or four voices barked at him at once.

Fred would learn the labors of shipbuilding the hard way. The sawyer commanded, "Fred, come help saw off the end of this timber," or "Fred, come help me to cant this timber here," by which he meant to square the timber into a beam, usually ten to fourteen feet long. The shipbuilder yelled, "Fred, come carry this timber yonder," likely referring to planks chalked "L. A." or "S. F." to indicate where on the ship they would go. Another command was "Fred, bring that roller here," to put a pulley in place for lifting timber. "Come, come! move, move! and bowse this timber forward," to haul the timber by tackle. "Fred, go get a fresh can of water" to steam the timber to fit the curvature of the hull; "I say, Fred, bear a hand, and get up a fire as quick as lightning under that steam-box." Fred scrambled to fetch the shipwright's tools: "Fred, go quick, and get the crowbar," or "Fred, go to the blacksmith's shop, and get a new punch" to insert pins and bolts. "Hurra, Fred! run and bring me a cold chisel," to cut metal. Some of the carpenters attached racist curses to their demands: "I say, darky, blast your eyes, why don't you heat up some pitch?" Or "Halloo, n——! come, turn this grindstone." Others were outright threats: "Come here! Go there! Hold on where you are! Damn you, if you move, I'll knock your brains out!" It was not easy to serve seventy-five overseers yet somehow Fred did it for eight frenetic months.

The simmering threat of racial violence soon became real. Using the leverage they had in the rush to finish the two big brigs, the white workers organized a strike against the many free Black workers in the shipyard. "All at once," Fred recalled, "the white carpenters knocked off, and said they would not work with free colored workmen." They claimed that "if free colored carpenters were encouraged, they would soon take the trade into their own hands, and poor white men would be thrown out of employment." They vowed "to put a stop to it." They broke off, "swearing they would work no longer, unless [Gardner] would discharge his black carpenters."

The strike did not immediately affect Fred, who was still enslaved, but white apprentices took on the attitudes of the master carpenters and began to consider it "degrading to them to work with me." They began to "put on airs" around Fred and to complain, as they had heard the men do, "about the 'n——s' taking the country, saying we all

ought to be killed." The white boys began to hector Fred and occasionally struck out at him. In the aftermath of his fight with Edward
Covey, Fred had taken a personal oath that whenever a white man hit
him, he would hit back "regardless of consequences." He did not lack
courage. He felt he could whip the whole lot of them if he could fight
them one at a time: "While I kept them from combining, I succeeded
very well." But soon the gang came at him from all directions, "armed
with sticks, stones, and heavy handspikes"—wooden bars used to
turn a ship's capstan or windlass. While Fred fought off the one who
ran at him wielding half a brick, another ran up behind him and hit
him over the head with a handspike, stunning him and laying him
out, whereupon they all jumped on him, "beating [him] with their
fists."

Fifty white ship carpenters watched the uneven fight and cheered
the white boys on. Some of them cried, "Kill the damned n——! Kill
him! kill him! He struck a white person." Fred knew that "to strike a
white man is death by Lynch law," and that was all too quickly be-
coming the law in Gardner's shipyard. White supremacy, in short,
was advancing. Not one of the fifty white carpenters said a "friendly
word" on Fred's behalf.

As the crowd cheered his knockdown, Fred lay on the ground,
covering up and taking punishment for a while to gather his strength
to fight back. He rose to his hands and knees: "Just as I did that, one
of their number gave me, with his heavy boot, a powerful kick in the
left eye. My eyeball seemed to have burst." The boys retreated when
they saw the swelling about the eye. Fred picked up the handspike
and went after them, until some of the carpenters interfered and re-
strained him. Fred knew that his only chance to survive now was to
run. "I succeeded in getting away without an additional blow, and
barely so." The lesson he drew from the fight was that "it was impossible to stand my hand against so many."[25]

Hugh and Sophia Auld were sympathetic, tending to his wounds
until he was "restored to health." His eyeball had not burst after all,

so he was able to recover his eyesight. Meantime, Hugh complained directly to Gardner about the attack but got no satisfaction. He then arranged for Fred to be hired at Walter Price's shipyard, where he himself was a foreman. Now the instruction in caulking would begin in earnest. Fred got the essential tools and was soon immersed in the arts and mysteries of the craft.

Fred did not record who trained him as a caulker. But we know what kind of person likely taught him the trade, as his apprenticeship began at a historic moment: the Association of Black Caulkers, an early African American benefit society, had begun to form along the docks. Black workers had dominated the trade since 1822, when nineteen of the twenty caulkers in the city directory were free people of color. In the coming years Black caulkers threatened strikes, achieved collective bargaining with the shipyard owners, and won consistently higher wages, sometimes as much as $1.75 per day ($58 in 2024). Fred's consciousness of wages and exploitation would continue to grow as he learned his craft among the best organized and most politically conscious workers on the waterfront.[26]

Fred was a fast learner and was soon "able to command the highest wages given to the most experienced calkers" in the city. His independence on the job expanded: he lined up his jobs and collected the money he earned, six to seven and occasionally as much as nine dollars a week. He was now, he explained, "of some importance to my master." Fred's life grew easier, more comfortable. But he was still rankled by having to give his money to his enslaver. *Why?* he asked. "Not because he earned it,—not because he had any hand in earning it,—not because I owed it to him,—nor because he possessed the slightest shadow of a right to it; but solely because he had the power to compel me to give it up."

Every Saturday night the same drama played out. Hugh carefully counted out the money Fred had earned, dollar by dollar. He would then, Fred recalled, "look me in the face," searching "my heart as well as my pocket, and reproachfully ask me, 'Is that all?'—implying that I had, perhaps, kept back part of my wages." In those weeks when Fred forked over a larger than usual amount of money, Auld would award his conscientious worker with "a sixpence or a shilling." He expected the action to elicit gratitude but in fact it provoked the opposite feeling, reinforcing Fred's belief that he was entitled to his entire earnings. Fred understood that the pittance made Hugh feel like "a pretty honorable robber, after all!"

By the early months of 1838 Fred had grown restless and "was ever on the look-out for means of escape." Finding none that were reliable and therefore safe enough, he decided to seek the half freedom of hiring out his own time and labor on the waterfront, which would permit him to make enough money to eventually abscond. He raised the issue with Thomas Auld, who by this time knew Fred well. Auld saw through the request and refused it, saying that it was yet "another stratagem by which to escape." He added that if Fred ever did leave him, he would hunt him to the ends of the earth. "I could go nowhere but he could catch me," Fred recalled Auld threatening. "I might be assured he should spare no pains in his efforts to recapture me."

Two months later Fred took the same request to Thomas's brother Hugh, with whom he lived in Baltimore and who was, for all practical purposes, the main authority in his life. He did not tell him that Thomas had already emphatically rejected the proposal. When Fred suggested that he be allowed to hire himself out, Hugh "gazed at me in amazement," but he did not say no immediately. He thought the matter over and eventually came around, dictating these terms: Fred would pay him three dollars at the end of each week and would also pay for his own caulking tools, room and board, and clothing. Fred would have to pay his weekly charge "rain or shine"—and caulkers could not work when it rained. Fred considered it "a hard bargain," but he took it. After four months the arrangement came to an end when one week Fred did not fork over his earnings on time. Hugh blew up and embraced his brother's view: "The next thing he should know of, I would be running away." The revocation of the self-hire arrangement would make the prediction come true.

THE ESCAPE

The time had come. Fred scheduled his date of escape three weeks in the future: he would "take out" on September 3, 1838. He worked assiduously to give his enslaver the appearance of normalcy up until his chosen date. He even worked extra hard and brought home more money than usual. As he did so he battled the same fears he felt during his previous escape planning two and a half years earlier. These were now magnified by the certainty that if he failed, his fate would surely be exile to the Deep South, "beyond the means of escape." He had been lucky after the previous failed escape, and he knew it. He also fretted over separating himself from "a circle of honest and warm hearted friends." Such attachments, he knew, were what kept thousands of other enslaved people from absconding. These were "the strongest obstacles to my running away."[27]

Despite the docks and their thousands of waterfront workers as potential allies, Baltimore was not an easy city to escape. William Still, agent of the Vigilant Committee who supported hundreds of fugitives arriving in Philadelphia, noted that Baltimore was "one of the most difficult places in the South for even free colored people to get away from, much more for slaves." All people of color traveling in North-bound vessels or trains were subjected to stringent regulations— personal examinations, daytime boarding only, and frequently renewed, expensive-to-purchase "free papers" featuring the signatures of well-known officials. All turnpikes headed northward out of the city, Fred noted, were "beset with kidnappers, a class of men who watched the newspapers for advertisements for runaway slaves, making their living by the accursed reward of slave hunting."[28]

In this dangerous context Fred prepared to depart, deciding that he would go by train on the first leg of his journey. He and his free bride-to-be Anna Murray pooled their resources to buy his ticket. He decided the best disguise on the day of departure would be to dress like a seaman: "In my clothing I was rigged out in sailor style. I had on a red shirt and a tarpaulin hat and black cravat, tied in sailor fashion, carelessly and loosely about my neck." The hundreds of Black sailors who came into and out of Baltimore year-round would be his cover. He could walk the sailor's distinctive walk and he could talk the talk: "My knowledge of ships and sailors' talk came much to my assistance, for I knew a ship from stem to stern, and from keelson to cross-trees, and could talk sailor like an 'old salt.'"[29]

This engraving by Ephraim W. Bouvé shows Frederick Douglass dressed as a sailor, walking and talking his way to freedom as an "old salt" in 1838.

The next step was to acquire convincing identification. Fred had been planning for years to use his painfully acquired skills of literacy to write his own free paper, but when the critical moment of escape arrived, he decided that he needed a document more recognizably authentic. Once again, he drew on his waterfront connections: he had a friend named Stanley who possessed a seaman's protection certificate that identified him as "a free American sailor." The free Black man of the sea took no small risk in lending his certificate to Fred, for if the operation failed, both men would suffer serious consequences. The paper was emblazoned with the American eagle, "which at once gave it the appearance of an authorized document." The only drawback was that Fred did not look like Stanley, who was significantly darker in complexion. Fred would try to prevent the careful inspection of his document if possible. He would make his way to freedom under a new name, "Stanley."

To escape the scrutiny of agents at the railroad station, Fred arranged with another friend, drayman Isaac Rolles, to bring his baggage to the train at the precise moment of departure, allowing Fred to jump, bag in hand, onto a crowded car "when the train was already in motion." He was counting on his ability to act the part of a sailor and on the pervasive "kind feeling which prevailed in Baltimore and other seaports at the time, towards 'those who go down to the sea in ships.'" Ever since the War of 1812, "Free trade and sailors' rights" had been a popular slogan.

A moment of truth arrived when a white conductor entered "the Negro car to collect tickets and examine the papers of his black passengers." Full of inner turmoil but outwardly "calm and self-possessed" as a cosmopolitan man of the waterfront might be, Fred realized that his future would depend on this encounter. Fred noted that the conductor was "somewhat harsh in tone and peremptory in manner" in dealing with other Black passengers in the car. His demeanor changed when he approached the young sailor: "Seeing that I did not readily produce my free papers, as the other colored persons in the car had done, he said to me in a friendly contrast with that observed towards the others, 'I suppose you have your free papers?'" Fred replied, "No, sir; I never carry my free papers to sea with me," implying that he had just returned from a voyage. The conductor then said, "But you have something to show that you are a free man, have you not?" Fred answered with bright confidence, "Yes, sir . . . I have a paper with the American eagle on it, that will carry me round the world." He then drew the protection certificate from his deep sailor's pocket: "The merest glance at the paper satisfied him, and he took my fare and went on about his business." Had the conductor looked closely, he would have seen that Fred did not resemble the man described in the document and would have arrested him on the spot, dragged him off the train at the next station, and put him on a southbound train back to Baltimore's city jail, where dozens of runaways were routinely incarcerated.

But Fred was not yet out of danger. He was still in a slave state and could be arrested at any moment. He spied on the train "several persons who would have known me in any other clothes." Perhaps too well-known around the waterfront for his own good, Fred feared these people might still recognize him in "my sailor 'rig,' and report me to the conductor." The train was moving at a high speed, but the time dragged slowly: "Minutes were hours, and hours were days during this part of my flight." He no doubt pulled his broad-brimmed tarpaulin hat as far down over his face as he could.

When the train reached Havre de Grace, Maryland, everyone had to cross the Susquehanna River by ferry as there was no bridge. This transit posed new dangers, brought on, oddly enough, by his sailor's clothing. A young Black ferry worker by the name of Nichols took an inordinate interest in Fred, "asking me dangerous questions as to where I was going, and when I was coming back, etc." The fugitive wished the curious man would just mind his own business. He extricated himself from his new and "inconvenient acquaintance" as quickly as "I could decently do so, and went to another part of the boat."

Passing from Maryland to Delaware, another slave state, the level of danger remained high. As travelers edged closer to the free state of Pennsylvania, slave catchers stepped up policing. "The border lines between slavery and freedom," Fred observed, "were the dangerous ones, for the fugitives." He experienced two more scares. After he disembarked the ferry and boarded another train, he caught sight of someone else he knew, a Captain McGowan, on whose revenue cutter he had worked recently at Price's shipyard. McGowan was seated on a different train with a direct sight line to Fred. Fortunately, he did not look up, and the trains soon sped off in different directions. But then another familiar face appeared in his very own car—a German blacksmith he knew well from the waterfront. The man stared at

Fred "very intently," and seemed to recognize him, but apparently, he "had no heart to betray me." The last point of peril, and the one Fred dreaded most, was Wilmington, where he had to exit the train and board a steamboat. Here was a danger point where he might be examined, discovered, and arrested. Yet he strolled coolly onto the vessel without difficulty. He arrived in Philadelphia, inquired of a "colored man" how to get to New York, went to the Willow Street depot, and took the night train to the big city. "Stanley," the jauntily dressed sailor, reached his destination after a nerve-racking twenty-four hours spent on three trains, a ferry, and a steamer. His heart beat "anxiously" and "noisily" all the way.

NEW YORK

Once Fred reached the waterfront of New York, he experienced a deep, churning torrent of emotion that overwhelmed his own eloquent rhetorical powers. "I have been frequently asked how I felt when I found myself in a free State. I have never been able to answer the question with any satisfaction to myself." The first feeling was excitement, the "highest" he had ever experienced. Up to that point in his life, he wrote, "I had been dragging a heavy chain, with a huge block attached to it, cumbering my every motion. I had felt myself doomed to drag this chain and this block through life." Suddenly it was gone. "I WAS A FREEMAN, and the voice of peace and joy thrilled my heart."[30]

But the flush of excitement upon arriving in New York was rapidly replaced by "a feeling of great insecurity" based on abject fear. Fred understood all too well that he could be captured at any moment and returned to "all the tortures of slavery." Loneliness, he recalled, "overcame me." He had willingly torn himself from the only people and places he had ever known. Here he was, in America's largest and most dynamic city, "in the midst of thousands, and yet a perfect stranger;

without home and without friends." Many of these people were "my own brethren—children of a common Father, and yet I dared not to unfold to any one of them my sad condition." The docks swarmed with people, and he was terrified of all of them:

> I was afraid to speak to any one for fear of speaking to the wrong one, and thereby falling into the hands of money-loving kidnappers, whose business it was to lie in wait for the panting fugitive, as the ferocious beasts of the forest lie in wait for their prey. The motto which I adopted when I started from slavery was this—"Trust no man!" I saw in every white man an enemy, and in almost every colored man cause for distrust.

Fred was momentarily overwhelmed, not just by the omnipresence of slave catchers, but by his own extreme vulnerability, having, as he put it, no "home or friends," no "money or credit," no shelter, and no food. He was "in total darkness as to what to do, where to go, or where to stay." This, he emphasized, was the situation that every "toil-worn and whip-scarred fugitive slave" faced when arriving in a northern port.

Fortunately, he knew his way around the waterfront, and he was still dressed as a sailor, which helped him to blend in. He spent a few days wandering around the docks, trying to figure out his next steps. At night he tucked away himself in an empty barrel on the wharf to sleep, something destitute sailors had done for decades. Then he got lucky: he spied someone he knew well, Allender's Jake, a Black sailor who had previously escaped Baltimore, renamed himself William Dixon, and now sailed out of New York. He conveyed to Fred sage advice: be careful and keep moving. The city was full of white Southerners and slave catchers, as well as members of the Black community who were paid snitches. He should not tell anyone he was a runaway. Fred recalled him adding, "I must not think of going either on the wharves to work, or to a [sailor's] boarding-house to board; and, worse

still, this same Jake told me it was not in his power to help me." Dixon
was even a little fearful that Fred might be part of a plot to recapture
him. He disappeared quickly into the dockside crowd, leaving Fred
wiser but more anxious than ever. His mood now bordered on despair.[31]

Fred now felt he had to find an honest man who could help him.
He got lucky again. A sailor named Stuart (or Stewart) spotted Fred
in his sailor's outfit standing across the street from his "humble home"
on Centre Street in lower Manhattan. Perhaps the young man's
down-on-his-luck posture beckoned him. Fred saw the sailor coming
toward him from across the street and made a friendly, engaging re-
mark, which led to a conversation. Stuart turned out to be "warm-
hearted and generous, and he listened to my story with a brother's
interest." Against Dixon's advice, Fred told him "I was running for
my freedom" and knew not where to go. He explained that he was
hungry and almost broke. He felt it was unsafe to seek work in the
shipyards, for this was the first place his enslaver would look for him.
Stuart offered solidarity. He took Fred into his home and sheltered
him overnight. The first thing the next morning he went in search of
sailor-abolitionist David Ruggles, the leader of the New York Vigilance Committee, the organization formed three years earlier to fight
slave catchers and assist fugitives. Thanks to his seafaring brothers,
Dixon, Stuart, and Ruggles, Fred was not alone after all.[32]

Ruggles, who lived only five blocks away at the corner of Lispenard and Church streets, received Fred with great warmth and understanding. At that time Ruggles was engaged in a high-profile
courtroom battle with New Orleans enslaver John Darg over a runaway named Thomas Hughes. He was involved with several other
fugitives as well, many of them veterans of the waterfront in one way
or another. Part of an entire network of abolitionists, Ruggles offered
safety to Fred, who later gratefully observed, his "vigilance, kindness,
and perseverance, I shall never forget." He remembered Ruggles as "a

whole-souled man, fully imbued with a love of his afflicted and hunted people."

Fred spent a momentous week on Lispenard Street, during which time he embraced his freedom by taking a new name, Fred Johnson. Ruggles helped him to summon Anna Murray from Baltimore and to engage the Reverend James W. C. Pennington, who, like Fred, was a self-emancipated man from Maryland, to marry the young couple. Ruggles agreed with William Dixon that it was unsafe for Fred to stay in New York; he would send him farther along the maritime freedom circuit to a safer destination. As soon as Ruggles learned that Fred was a caulker, "he promptly decided that the best place for me was in New Bedford." He explained that "many ships for whaling voyages were fitted out there, and that I might there find work at my trade and make a good living."[33]

NEW BEDFORD

Fred's journey showed that maritime marronage usually had several passages. Knowing, thanks to David Ruggles and other Black sailors, that slave catchers infested the docks of New York, he and his new wife soon headed farther north, boarding a steamboat, the *John W. Richmond*, for Newport, Rhode Island, and from there taking a coach on to what would be their final destination for the next three years: on September 18, 1838, they arrived in New Bedford, Massachusetts. They chose the destination for three related reasons: it was a port city with a maritime sector that offered jobs to workers like Fred; it had a strong free Black community committed to the American revolutionary principle of self-defense; and its residents included abolitionists, Black and white, who wielded significant political and economic power.[34]

Welcomed into the home of Black abolitionists Nathan and Polly

Johnson, Fred celebrated by taking a third new name, one for each of his passages toward freedom. Fred Bailey had become Stanley the Sailor in Baltimore, Fred Johnson in New York, and now Fred Douglass in New Bedford. (Nathan explained that eighteen Johnsons already lived in the free Black community of New Bedford, and that Fred should pick a more distinctive last name.) Selecting a name from Sir Walter Scott's novel *Lady of the Lake*—a name formed from the Gaelic words *dubh ghlais*, which mean "dark water"—and adding an extra *s* for distinction, Fred was ready to stride into a new "life of freedom." Even his new name expressed a maritime identity.

Yet the Massachusetts port proved not to be the paradise it had seemed from a distance, as Fred learned after completing his first job and seeking employment in his hard-won craft of caulking. The trade was organized differently in New Bedford than in Baltimore, where free Black workers controlled large parts of it through their own benefit society. To his surprise Fred encountered strong "prejudice against color" up north: white caulkers threatened to walk off the job if any shipwright hired him. Fred was therefore unable to get work in the trade at which he had excelled down South. (This situation, he wrote later, was soon reversed by "anti-slavery effort," but too late to help the Baltimore caulker, who had moved on to Rochester, New York, by that time.) Fred thus threw off his caulker's clothing and sought any kind of work he could get—sawing wood, shoveling coal, or rolling casks. No labor was "too hard" nor "too dirty" for this young, strong, determined waterfront worker.[35]

Soon after arriving in New Bedford, Fred began to participate in the political life of the community. He assisted runaways, most of whom had arrived by sea. He discovered the American Anti-Slavery Society's newspaper *The Liberator*, which set his soul afire. He joyfully realized that he could join a movement against slavery. He began to speak in public, first as an "exhorter" in the small local African Methodist Episcopal Zion Church, then before the Bristol County Anti-Slavery Society. On August 11, 1841, he spoke at an antislavery convention in nearby Nantucket, where he was "discovered" by several eminent abolitionists in attendance. This "poor . . . labourer," as abolitionist Ellis Gray Loring called him, could "produce great effect" for the antislavery movement. William Lloyd Garrison later wrote, "I think I never hated slavery so intensely as at that moment" when he sat there listening to Fred tell his life story. His maritime dream realized, the young man of many names and much waterfront experience commenced a gilded fifty-year career as abolition's greatest orator. He "took to the water" and cast a bright light on its role in the freedom struggle.[36]

Fred's background of maritime labor stayed with him throughout his life. During the 1840s, he argued that labor was a key to Black progress. In 1850 he helped to found the unprecedented but short-lived American League of Colored Laborers, established to improve the conditions of Black workers. The maritime milieu of Fell's Point, writes historian David Blight, was Fred's "school" where he learned "deep lessons about the natural struggle between labor and capital" that informed his outlook for the rest of his life.[37]

The waterfront created America's greatest abolitionist—its most powerful orator, its most eloquent writer, and its most profound example of the political and intellectual power of fugitivity. Fred spent a lifetime realizing his maritime dream. Formed by his work in Fell's Point and brandishing the literacy he gained in its shipyards, he was an organic intellectual of the docks. He looked, walked, and talked like an "old salt" as he made his way to freedom. He traveled by sea and launched his career as a militant and an agitator in maritime New England, New Bedford, and Nantucket, after which American abolitionism would be forever changed. He crisscrossed the Atlantic to connect, unify, and strengthen the international antislavery movement. He always acknowledged "the invisible agency" of resistance—in this case, a diverse, mobile, and ever-changing body of maritime workers who over many years helped him to conceive, and eventually to achieve, his own freedom and that of countless others.

Chapter 4

Harriet Jacobs on a "Dark and Troubled Sea"

The saga of Harriet Jacobs, who bravely took to sea in June 1842, illuminates the special challenges women faced in slavery and in their efforts to escape it. Her enslaver, Dr. James Norcom of Edenton, North Carolina, subjected her to years of sexual innuendo, threat, and outright terror, developing what can only be described as a predatory sexual obsession with Harriet from the time she was fourteen years old. Harriet's efforts to ward off his advances took many forms and enlisted the assistance of numerous family and community members over a period of fifteen years. Norcom's efforts to reenslave her after she escaped continued until the day he died in November 1850. Harriet's victory over this vicious man was one of the great triumphs in the history of resistance to slavery. Maritime marronage made it possible.[1]

It is well known that Harriet, author of the abolitionist classic *Incidents in the Life of a Slave Girl* (1861), grew up in the port town of Edenton and escaped slavery by sea. What has been less appreciated is that she came from a maritime family. Her three uncles were sailors, two of whom themselves escaped slavery by sea, one of them three times. One reason why these crucial facts are little known is that Harriet did not mention any of her uncles by their real names in her memoir: "I have concealed the names of places, and given persons fictitious names," she wrote. All three men, however, loom large in her brother John's two shorter, less guarded autobiographies, published in Sydney, Australia, in 1855 and in London in 1861. Most important, these familial sailors shaped Harriet's ability to imagine, plan, and execute her own successful escape.[2]

Harriet was born in 1813 to enslaved parents Delilah Horniblow, a domestic worker, and Elijah Knox, the best house carpenter in the region. Harriet described both as "mulattoes." The couple had a second child, John, two years later. Harriet's mother passed away when she was six, whereupon she was taken into the home of enslaver Margaret Horniblow, who would teach her to spell, read, write, and sew. Harriet lived much of her early life under the care of her grandmother, Molly Horniblow, an enterprising and powerful woman who was respected throughout Edenton. Margaret Horniblow died six years later, deeding Harriet to Mary Matilda Norcom, the three-year-old daughter of Dr. James Norcom, into whose household Harriet now moved. Harriet's father Elijah passed away the following year, but not before imparting a fierce hatred of slavery to both of his children. Harriet's life, like so many others, was for many years determined by the premature death of her parents and the division of human "property" among ruling-class heirs.[3]

LIFE IN A SMALL PORT TOWN

Harriet's life was shaped by the ebb and flow of the struggle against slavery in Edenton, throughout North Carolina and nearby Virginia, and up and down the Atlantic coast. Because of the state's many sounds, rivers, swamps, and extensive coastline, North Carolina legislators were among the first in the new American nation to pass laws against maritime runaways. A 1784 law noted that enslavers in the

Cape Fear region had been "greatly injured by masters of vessels carrying slaves and servants out of the said port" and therefore required shipmasters to post securities against potential losses. The way the economy worked facilitated escape. Enslaved workers in North Carolina went aboard Northern-owned vessels in geographically dispersed, hard-to-police locations to work and sometimes to trade, both legally and illegally, thereby making social connections that would help them to stow away. During Harriet's lifetime, the state passed several laws to limit the access of enslaved people to ships to prevent escape by sea, but these were rarely enforced.[4]

Harriet's childhood was filled with the stories of local runaways who took refuge in the dense growth of Cabarrus's Pocosin, the main swamp of her native region, about forty miles south of the Great Dismal Swamp, the greatest site of marronage in North America at the time. Here fugitives armed themselves and built camps from which they conducted midnight raids on Edenton's farms and plantations. They fought pitched gun battles with patrols sent to root them out. Harriet knew the stories of runaways whose flesh had been torn from the bone by dogs and of a woman who, after being captured and returned to her so-called owner, was shot through the head. The region, bounded and crisscrossed by waterways of all kinds, had a long history of escape by sea.[5]

Like all other Southern ports, Edenton received an electric jolt when sailors began to smuggle David Walker's *Appeal* up and down the eastern seaboard beginning in 1829. North Carolina governor John Owen dispatched a warning to all maritime counties and passed a package of new repressive legislation "to prevent the circulation of seditious publications" and create additional punishment for "the harbouring or maintaining runaway slaves," two subversive acts that went together, as David Walker knew. In September 1830 the *Edenton Gazette* railed against radical publications and the "emissaries"—sailors—who "have been dispersed, *for some time*, throughout the Southern States, for the purpose of disseminating false principles and infusing the poison of discontent." The "free colored people of the North," that is Black sailors, were conspiring and "exciting insurrection" in the South.[6]

Those fears materialized in the charismatic figure of Nat Turner, who in 1831 led what was perhaps the greatest slave rebellion in US history in Southampton County, Virginia. The uprising caused a "great commotion" in Edenton, which was only fifty miles south. Harriet wrote about the terror visited upon Edenton's Black population in the aftermath of the revolt. She professed to have known nothing of local collaboration, but it is likely that Turner had sympathizers if not outright supporters in and around Edenton. In any case, David Walker and Nat Turner inaugurated a fierce decade-long Atlantic cycle of resistance to slavery that served as a fiery backdrop to Harriet's own search for freedom. From Boston to Virginia and North Carolina, to Jamaica and Cuba, resistance from below exploded repeatedly throughout the 1830s.[7]

UNCLE JOSEPH

Harriet's closest family members waged their own struggle against slavery. Her Uncle Joseph Horniblow, the youngest of her grandmother's five children, was more like a brother to Harriet than an uncle, since they were close in age and upbringing. Joseph grew into "a tall, handsome lad, strongly and gracefully made, and with a spirit too bold and daring for a slave." He came to Harriet one day in 1828 and announced that he was sailing away to the North. His enslaver, Josiah Collins, a member of one of the richest families in town, had attempted to whip him. Joseph refused the lash and fought back, throwing Collins to the ground. He then ran away but knew that he now faced a fearsome public thrashing if caught. Joseph would become, as far as we know, the family's first maritime runaway—and in the end a shining example for Harriet.[8]

When Joseph came to say goodbye to Harriet, she tried to talk him out of leaving, warning him first about the poverty and hardship he would face, and the violent horrors that would rain down upon him if recaptured. He replied, "we are dogs here; foot-balls, cattle, every thing that's mean. No, I will not stay. Let them bring me back. We don't die but once." He was willing to risk his life for freedom. Harriet escalated the debate by saying that he would break the heart of his mother, her grandmother, the beloved Molly Horniblow, "a woman of a high spirit" and the family matriarch who had recently gained her own freedom. But Harriet saw that Joseph's jaw was set and his mind made up. He was going no matter what she said. The nineteen-year-old man said farewell and turned toward the docks.[9]

Joseph was a skilled sailor himself, like so many of the youth who grew up in Edenton on Albemarle Sound, fifty miles from the Atlantic Ocean. Black watermen were everywhere on the North Carolina coast. Joseph quickly, and with apparent ease, got himself on board a packet vessel bound for New York before his enslaver could find him. But after a few days at sea, he ran into bad luck, or more precisely a bad storm, which sent the captain of his vessel into the nearest port to ride out the high winds and waves. Once ashore the captain happened to see a runaway slave advertisement that described Joseph perfectly, quickly clapped the young runaway in chains, and proceeded on to New York, planning to take him back to Edenton on the return voyage. Joseph somehow managed to get out of his chains, throw them overboard, and escape the vessel. Yet his freedom in New York was short-lived. He was recaptured by a Mr. Skinner and slapped into a heavier set of chains. His captors would accept the challenge to bring him back to Edenton.[10]

Harriet recalled the day of his return vividly. The proud fugitive was paraded through the streets on the way to the jail. "His face was ghastly pale, yet full of determination," remembered Harriet. Joseph turned to one of the sailors close by and asked him to take a message to his mother: she must not meet him. He feared that "the sight of her distress would take from him all self-control." The sailor relayed the message to Molly, who could not stay away but did shield herself from Joseph's view near the jail. Family members were not officially allowed to visit him, but a friendly jailor opened the door to a moving midnight reunion. "The moon had just risen and cast an uncertain light through the bars of the window," recalled Harriet. The only sounds for a time were the jangling of Joseph's chains and sounds of muffled sobs. Joseph quietly asked Molly to forgive him for the suffering he had caused her. She replied that she could not blame him for seeking freedom. He added that he had contemplated suicide by throwing himself into the river as he was being recaptured in New York, but thoughts of her had changed his mind. Molly asked Joseph if he also thought of God at that moment. Harriet "saw his face grow fierce in the moonlight." Joseph answered, "No, I did not think of him. When a man is hunted like a wild beast he forgets there is a God, a heaven. He forgets every thing in his struggle to get beyond the reach of the bloodhounds."

Josiah Collins, meanwhile, had vowed to make an example of Joseph to the other enslaved people on his plantation. If Joseph would not repent and return to the plantation in utter subservient disgrace, Collins would sell him, for as a little as a dollar, he swore, just to be rid of him and his subversive example. For three months Joseph refused to submit, which resulted in increasingly heavy punishment. He was now confined to a dark dungeon, chained to other prisoners, and soon covered with vermin. His mother urged him to beg Collins's pardon; Joseph refused. After three more months of stalemate Collins sold him to a slave trader, who quickly saw what Harriet had long known: the man's temperament raged against enslavement. As a condition of sale, the soul seller was required to take Joseph out of the state of North Carolina. He soon departed Edenton's jail, bound for New Orleans, trailed by a throng of people crying for mercy, no one louder than his mother.

The family lost touch with Joseph completely, although Molly wrote to someone she knew in New Orleans to purchase her son's freedom and return him to Edenton. The attempt failed. Joseph was now 1,500 miles away by sea. Yet in only a matter of months he was drawing closer again. He had made another break for freedom by water. As Harriet later learned, "one morning, long before day," Joseph turned up missing at his new enslaver's home in New Orleans. Having gotten aboard a ship, he was soon "riding over the blue billows, bound for Baltimore."

Joseph's ability to get aboard the vessel had been based in part on his light complexion. The captain who hired him apparently had no suspicion that his "white face" belonged to someone enslaved or else he would have turned him over to Baltimore port authorities as a runaway as soon as the voyage was completed. Joseph had signed on as a member of the crew and worked his way to Baltimore. The voyage itself was a difficult one, however, as Joseph grew sick and worried that he would never make it back to a "free land." Slavery was still legal in Maryland, so he would have to travel on to New York. In these circumstances he apparently did think of God. Harriet wrote, "how he prayed that he might live to get one breath of free air."[11]

Joseph disembarked in Baltimore, but he was too weak to continue the journey to New York. He spent three weeks trying to recover his strength. He began to take walks around the city, careful to stay on small streets and byways. On one of them he heard terrifying words called out to him: "Halloo, [Joseph], my boy! what are you doing *here*?" He wanted to run but his trembling legs would not carry him. He turned to face the man who greeted him; it was Daniel McDowell, his enslaver's next-door neighbor in Edenton, a Northern man who had married a Southern woman and was now the so-called owner of "a goodly number of slaves." McDowell saw that Joseph looked shocked and sickly: he exclaimed, "you look like a ghost." The surprises had only just begun. McDowell then stated, "Never mind [Joseph], I am not going to touch you." He told him, "You may go on your way rejoicing." He even offered to tell his grandmother Molly back at home that he had seen him. Then he gave helpful advice about the "nearest and safest route to New York" and suggested that he "get out of this place plaguy quick, for there are several gentlemen here from our town." The man then walked away with Joseph's astonished but undying gratitude. A chance meeting with a sympathetic slaveholder in the port of Baltimore was the first way Harriet and Molly learned that Joseph was not only alive but free once again.

The full dramatic story of Joseph's second escape by sea would reach home weeks later, through a maritime encounter. Harriet's other seafaring uncle, Mark Ramsey, happened to run into Joseph on the waterfront of New York. The fugitive brother still looked sick, and his clothes were ragged. He had been obliged to sell his better apparel to pay his living expenses in Baltimore. Still, he had no regrets, sickness be damned: "If I die now," he exclaimed to Mark, "thank God, I shall die a freeman!"

Mark brought up an urgent issue with his brother. Their mother, Molly, had mortgaged her home and was ready to use the money to buy Joseph's freedom. "No, never!" the rebel growled in response. He was already free and would never give his former enslaver "one red cent." Nor would he impose on his mother, who needed the money to free other members of the family, including Mark, Harriet, and her children, born in 1828 and 1833. He was resolute, and he had not yet secured his freedom in any case. New York, after all, was seething with what Harriet called "human bloodhounds," slave catchers. Joseph felt he could only be free by going "beyond the reach of the stars and stripes of America," as Harriet's brother John later explained. "Unwilling to trust his liberty any longer in the hands of a professed Christian," he sought freedom "in another hemisphere." His distrust of hypocritical Christians apparently steered him away from Great Britain, even though the antislavery movement was much stronger there than in the US and progressing toward full abolition in the British empire. He planned to sail instead to the Mediterranean and "to seek safety among the Turks," likely as a convert to Islam. Joseph told Mark that he had to make a third passage over the seas.[12]

Before parting, Joseph urged Mark to desert his ship and "stay and work with him, till they earned enough to buy those at home." Mark declined, saying that it would kill Molly if he were to desert her now. Joseph relented in his request: "You have been a comfort to her, and I have been a trouble." Mark furnished Joseph with clothes "and gave him what money he had." The brothers faced each other and said a tearful goodbye. Joseph's last words to his family were, "I part with all my kindred." As Harriet related with a piercing sadness, "And so it proved. We never heard from him again."

When Mark arrived back in Edenton, he told Molly, "Mother, [Joseph] is free! I have seen him in New York." The old woman dropped to her knees and began to pray: "God be praised! Let us thank him." She then asked Mark to tell her every single word Joseph had spoken. He told her the whole story, omitting only "how sick and pale her darling looked," for this would serve no useful purpose and create only pain and worry. Molly, Mark, and Harriet sat together in the happy knowledge that Joseph was free. They would henceforth "prove to the world that they could take care of themselves, as they had long taken care of others." Their concluding, triumphant thought for the evening was, "He that is willing to be a slave, let him be a slave." It was not a fate the family was *willing* to accept. Harriet and her brother John were so moved by their uncle's freedom story, they both resolved to name one of their own children after brave Uncle Joseph. Both did so, transmitting the cherished memory of the long-gone seafarer to the next generation.

UNCLES AND BROTHER

Uncle Mark Ramsey also played a key role in the lives of both Harriet and John. Working as a steward on a packet line vessel sailing regularly from Edenton to New York, he had opportunities to jump ship, but he never seized them. His mother Molly eventually bought his freedom, as Joseph had suggested she should, which allowed Mark to continue at sea as a free worker. After he gained his freedom, the enslaver of Harriet's little brother John wanted Mark to serve as security in case the young man, who was then in jail, should run away. By this he meant, if John absconded, the so-called owner would have the right to claim Mark as his property. After the enslaver proposed this arrangement, Mark visited John in jail and offered his body as a guarantee. John shot back, "I promptly told him no; that I wanted my liberty; that I would make good the first opportunity to secure it; that he might do as he pleased; but, God being my helper, I would die a free man." The youth sounded a lot like Uncle Joseph. He did not want Uncle Mark to lose his freedom, which he thought he inevitably would. John and Mark therefore declined the enslaver's offer. Even more crucially, it was Uncle Mark, not a fictional free Black man named Peter who appeared in *Incidents in the Life of a Slave Girl*, who worked everything out for Harriet to escape by sea in 1842. John quoted Harriet as writing to him that it was Mark who "made arrangements with the captain of a vessel running between New York and Edenton, for my passage to the former port." The reference to the ship's oscillation from New York to Edenton shows that this, too, was a packet vessel, on which Mark had a trusted comrade. Mark had kept a careful watch along the Edenton waterfront for years awaiting the right opportunity.[13]

A third uncle, Stephen, was also a "seafaring man," enslaved to the master of the vessel on which he sailed. He had "had several chances to make escape from slavery, yet he had returned on every voyage" because of his attachment to his wife of twenty years, Harriet's aunt Betty, her mother's twin sister, who also lived in Edenton. Stephen also played a significant role in Harriet's move toward the waterfront, and he would pay a price for his involvement. After Harriet sailed away, Dr. James Norcom punished Aunt Betty, whom he also enslaved, in retaliation. Knowing that Stephen had likely played a role in Harriet's escape, he suddenly and strictly prohibited Betty from seeing him, thereby breaking what nephew John considered to be the "only tie that bound my uncle to slavery." After this wicked man had desecrated "a union holy in the sight of God," Stephen decided he would no "longer submit to the yoke." On the very next voyage he emancipated himself from bondage by jumping ship. As far as we know he, like Joseph, was never seen in Edenton again.[14]

All three uncles gained their freedom on the sea either directly or indirectly, a lesson that was not lost on either Harriet or her little brother. John too would escape slavery by sea, after a complicated experience of travel and negotiation. His enslaver, Samuel Tredwell Sawyer, was elected to the United States House of Representatives in 1837. Despite Sawyer's fear that John would try to escape, he nonetheless took the young man with him the following year to Washington, DC, and on other travels to Chicago, Buffalo, Niagara Falls, and even Canada, where John tried to get a Seamen's Protection Certificate to use as a freedom paper. Canada, where slavery had been abolished in 1834, was tempting, but John did not consider it the right time to run. He waited until he went with Sawyer on a business trip to New York, where John had "friends from home" (many of them no doubt maritime maroons) in the free Black community. John deserted his enslaver after leaving him a letter written for him by one of those friends: "Sir—I have left you, not to return; when I have got settled, I will give you further satisfaction. No longer yours, John S. Jacob."

Off to the maritime circuit he went: he sailed immediately for Providence, Rhode Island, then to New Bedford, Massachusetts, the "Gibraltar" of maritime runaways, where he quickly signed onto a whaling ship for a three-and-a-half-year voyage. He later went on a long tour on the abolitionist circuit as a speaker with fellow seafarer Jonathan Walker, the white ship captain whose effort to carry seven African Americans out of slavery in Florida to freedom by sea in 1844 had resulted in his capture, conviction, and the branding of "S. S." (for "slave stealer") into his right hand. The sea was in the blood of the Horniblow-Jacobs family.[15]

THE WOMAN'S WAR

Once she had escaped and began in the 1850s to write her memoir, Harriet assumed the name Linda Brent as she addressed "the women of the North." Her experience of bondage in North Carolina was not typical of enslaved people across the South, as she herself explained in vivid detail:

> I was never cruelly over-worked; I was never lacerated with the whip from head to foot; I was never so beaten and bruised that I could not turn from one side to the other; I never had my heel-strings cut to prevent my running away; I was never chained to a log and forced to drag it about, while I toiled in the fields from morning till night; I was never branded with hot iron, or torn by bloodhounds.

Harriet had witnessed these horrors visited upon others and dutifully recorded them in her book as an act of solidarity. She worked during the enslaved portion of her life as a domestic and a seamstress. She added that she "had always been kindly treated, and tenderly cared for"—until, that is, she "came into the hands" of Dr. James Norcom.

Norcom's war against Harriet was a long, unrelenting, vulgar campaign of sexual harassment, waged by a man of property and power some thirty-five years older than his intended victim. A graduate of the University of Pennsylvania Medical School in 1797, he owned a fine home in town, several farms, and around fifty human beings, although he always seemed to be short on cash. He was a serial predator: Harriet estimated that he had already raped enough enslaved women in and around Edenton to produce eleven children, two of them by her tormented older sister. The principle that underlay his sexual terror, Harriet recalled, was the very foundation of slavery: "He told me I was his property; that I must be subject to his will in all things." He held a razor to her throat to try to force her submission, but she risked death and held firm. His sexual advances were accompanied by threats that "he would kill me, if I was not as silent as the grave." Norcom tried in numerous ways to isolate and rape Harriet, but he never succeeded.[16]

Harriet's greatest protector was her grandmother Molly, who had purchased her own freedom by this time. Molly had made money selling baked goods and was beloved by many people in Edenton, Black and white. Even though Molly had been enslaved, Harriet explained, Norcom "was afraid of her." In a small town where everyone knew everyone else, the enslaver "dreaded her scorching rebukes." Unintended protection also came from Norcom's wife, Mary Matilda Horniblow Norcom, who, like many Southern wives, reserved a special hatred for the young African American women who attracted the lecherous gaze of her husband. Her own threats of murder required Dr. Norcom to place Harriet in her grandmother's home for a time.

In 1829, in an act of self-defense, Harriet initiated a secret relationship with Samuel Tredwell Sawyer, a single, white, rather aristocratic lawyer and politician who lived on her block. Later that same year she had a son by Sawyer, named Joseph for her uncle, and four years later, a daughter, Louisa. The relationship with Sawyer filled Harriet with "sorrow and shame," but not remorse: "I know what I did, and I did it with deliberate calculation." She also did it in a spirit of revenge: "I knew nothing would enrage Dr. [Norcom] so much as to know that I favored another; and it was something to triumph over my tyrant even in that small way." She also considered Sawyer as a means of escape from Norcom: he was a man of wealth who might purchase her and her children.[17]

Norcom's "restless, craving, vicious nature" remained unchanged. He roved around the house "day and night, seeking whom to devour," and continued to focus his obscene energies on young Harriet. "O, how I despised him!" she recalled. To remove Harriet from the eyesight of his wife and to separate her from her protective family, Norcom began in 1835 to "build a small house for me, in a secluded place, four miles away from the town." Harriet swore she would never set foot in it. "I had rather live and die in jail, than drag on, from day to day, through such a living death" of endless rape. She would do anything to defeat his design. "What *could* I do?" she wondered. "I thought and thought, till I became desperate, and made a plunge into the abyss." She ran away. To explain her decision to abscond she reached back to the American Revolution and to many slave revolts thereafter: "'Give me liberty, or give me death,' was my motto."

Norcom exploded with rage. He launched a desperate search all around the region, offering a reward to encourage others to catch and return Harriet. In a local advertisement, he described Harriet as "an intelligent, bright, mulatto girl," twenty-one years old, five-foot-four, with "dark eyes, and black hair inclined to curl; but it can be made straight." She had "a decayed spot on a front tooth." She "can read and write and in all probability will try to get to the Free States." Norcom then threatened that anyone who harbored or employed her—meaning sailors—would suffer "under penalty of the law." He promised a reward of $300 (more than $10,000 in 2024). The ad he placed in the *American Beacon* newspaper in Norfolk, Virginia, added several new details: "She speaks easily and fluently, and has an agreeable carriage and address." He noted her skill as a seamstress, which allowed her to "dress well . . . in the prevailing fashion." She might even appear "tricked out in gay and fashionable finery." He wanted everyone to know that she "absconded from the plantation of my son without any known cause or provocation."[18]

FIRST ESCAPE

Harriet took refuge in the home of a friend but knew that she would be discovered if she stayed there long. A week later, when a search party got close, she flew from the house and hid in the woods for twenty-four hours. Meanwhile, her grandmother Molly had found an unlikely source of help in a desperate time: a friend of hers, Martha Blount, a white woman who owned slaves and whose husband was a slave trader. As a personal favor to Molly, she was willing to hide Harriet away in a small room, but only with the understanding that the arrangement be kept under the strictest secrecy: "If such a thing should become known, it would ruin me and my family." Harriet and Molly eagerly promised. Norcom would never imagine the home of a slave trader as refuge for a runaway. Little did he know, Harriet could watch him from her window as he walked to his office every day: "I felt a gleam of satisfaction when I saw him."[19]

The infuriated Norcom pressured Harriet by sending her aunt Betty; her brother John; and both of her children, Joseph and Louisa, to jail, with the added threat that if she did not return, he would sell them out of the region. He assumed that the "common wind," the clandestine communication network of the enslaved, would get the news to Harriet, and indeed it did. Meanwhile Norcom, who knew that Harriet's best chance of escape was aboard a packet boat to New York, sailed northward to try to find her. In New York he mobilized a posse of "fleshmongers," or slave catchers, who were, her brother John recalled, "sticking their unwanted faces in every colored man's door, on account of my sister." Of course, he failed to find her because Harriet was hiding near him in Edenton. Norcom also imprisoned Uncle Mark, even though he had no charges to bring against him, and on another occasion, he threatened to "butcher" John, who later observed, "I had seen too much of his cruelty to doubt his purpose."[20]

With the runaway advertisements, payments to slave catchers, and a trip to New York, Norcom had gone to considerable expense, and meantime the costs of keeping Harriet's family members in jail were mounting. In this moment of crisis Harriet and Molly came up with a brilliant idea. They encouraged Sawyer to employ a slave trader secretly and send him to Norcom to purchase John, Joseph, and Louisa. Norcom hesitated but finally accepted the offer. Sawyer took John into his own household and placed the children with Molly. "My master had power and law on his side," concluded Harriet; "I had a determined will. There is might in each." Her might, carefully and strategically deployed, won the day, at least regarding her children, who were now safe. The outwitted Norcom erupted once again in impotent rage.[21]

FROM THE DOCKS TO THE SWAMP

Harriet's situation remained precarious. The fear of discovery became so intense in 1835, Uncle Mark advised Harriet to leave the slave trader's house and head with him immediately toward the waterfront. She had no idea where she was going, nor for how long. In preparation for moving to the "free parts" of the country, her aunt Betty had brought her "a suit of sailor's clothes,—jacket, trousers, and tarpaulin hat," the same outfit in which Frederick Douglass had escaped. The moment required disguise. Harriet's aunt also helped her to apply charcoal to her light-skinned face. She then gave her "a small bundle, saying I might need it where I was going." Her final instructions were, "Put your hands in your pockets, and walk ricketty, like de sailors." She referred to the distinctive wide-legged, side-to-side gait of sailors, whose manner of walking preserved their balance on the rolling decks of ships at sea. Mark and Betty dressed Harriet as they did because sailors were a common sight in a port town such as Edenton and almost the only type of person who would routinely be a stranger, unknown to small-town dwellers, who were accustomed to recognizing everyone who walked the streets. Harriet noted that she "lived in a town where all the inhabitants knew each other." The very trait of the town that provided a degree of protection against Norcom now made it harder to escape.[22]

Edenton elites like Norcom had devised a rigorous system for policing the local waterfront. The sovereignty of the individual enslavers was complemented by the swollen powers of the town constable, who assisted in the buying and selling of slaves and publicly flogged anyone who resisted. As the town's whipper-in-chief, he hired out his services at fifty cents per flogging to enslavers who needed additional disciplinary violence. He patrolled the streets at night: "If he found any slave out after nine o'clock, he could whip him as much as he liked." That, according to Harriet, "was a privilege to be coveted" by a white man who was not usually a slaveholder himself. The constable also had a special charge to deal with runaways. As Harriet noted of the constable when she described her first disappearance, "every vessel northward bound was thoroughly examined, and the law against harboring fugitives was read to all on board." Later that night "a watch was set over the town." The constable, who could halt all vessels from the leaving the port to recover a fugitive, was the enslaver's last line of defense against escape by sea.

Edenton's sailortown was called Cheapside—an area on Broad Street between Water and West King, and a block south onto what was called the Wharf. Here sailors Black and white found food, drink, and accommodations for their time in port. The area bustled and buzzed as people were bought and sold in the market. Molly knew the area well, as she shopped there for produce for Horniblow's Tavern and sold her own round wheat-flour biscuits, called hardtack—known for their ability to last long voyages—to captains, stewards, and sailors. Runaways frequented Cheapside to sell stolen items to the "dram-shop gentry on the wharf, that are suffered to vend their articles at an unseasonable hour of the night, and on the Sabbath." The money from such sales might be used to pay a mariner for a spot on an outward-bound vessel. The town's constable and his night watch kept a close eye on Cheapside, knowing that this was where runaways were most likely to negotiate their way out.[23]

As Harriet headed off toward Cheapside, she felt exhilarated to be outside, breathing fresh air and hearing human voices above a whisper. She walked with Uncle Mark, who told her not to worry: "I've got a dagger, and no man shall take you from me, unless he passes over my dead body." They encountered several people she knew, "but they did not recognize me in my disguise." They walked the two blocks from her mother's house to the wharf, where they met Uncle Stephen, who took her and Mark into his boat and "rowed out to a vessel not far distant, and hoisted me on board." This was likely a sloop, a small multipurpose vessel often used on Carolina coasts. The three of them went aboard, whereupon Harriet asked "what they proposed to do with me." The plan was to remain on board until near dawn, when the men would take her to a place called Snaky Swamp. Meantime, Uncle Mark prepared a temporary hiding place for Harriet aboard the vessel. Harriet noted that, "If the vessel had been bound north, it would have been of no avail to me, for it would certainly have been searched."

Around four in the morning, Harriet and her two uncles climbed down into the boat and commenced rowing three miles to the swamp. Harriet was not happy about the destination, especially since she had suffered a serious bite by a venomous snake a couple of years earlier. "But I was in no situation to choose," she added, and gratefully accepted what her uncles could do for her. It was still dark when the boat arrived at Snaky Swamp. Mark landed first, machete in hand. He slashed a path "through bamboos and briers of all descriptions" and created a seat deep in the swamp. He then returned to the boat, took Harriet in his arms, and carried her through the lush vegetation. By the time they arrived both were "covered with hundreds of mosquitos." Within an hour Harriet considered herself "a pitiful sight to behold." As the sun came up, Harriet began to see what the swamp was named for—snakes "larger than any I had ever seen," many of them probably poisonous water moccasins, also called cottonmouths. She shuddered as she and Mark used sticks to club and push snakes away from them. Toward the end of a long day Mark and Harriet, "fearful of losing our way back to the boat," moved back toward the entrance of the swamp. They soon heard a "low whistle" from Stephen, the agreed-upon signal, as well as the plashing of his oars in the water. They boarded the boat in haste and went back to the vessel to spend a second night. Harriet was in poor shape: the heat and humidity of the swamp, the mosquitoes, and the "constant terror of snakes" had made her sick. She spent a "wretched night" running a fever and had barely fallen asleep when she was awakened to return to the swamp. Harriet steeled her courage by reminding herself that the "large, venomous snakes were less dreadful to my imagination than the white men in that community called civilized." This time Mark brought tobacco to burn to keep the mosquitoes away, but the smoke only added to Harriet's feeling of illness. At the end of the day, they returned to the vessel. Mark saw that Harriet was at a breaking point and "declared I should go home that night, if the devil himself was on patrol."

The following morning the two uncles and their niece boarded the boat once again and rowed back to Edenton harbor. Wearing her sailor clothes and with her face freshly blackened, Harriet went with Mark "boldly through the streets," back to Grandmother Molly's house. Once again Harriet passed several people she knew, at least one of them intimately: "The father of my children [Samuel Tredwell Sawyer] came so near that I brushed against his arm; but he had no idea who it was." Mark added, ominously and sadly, "You must make the most of this walk . . . for you may not have another very soon." Harriet had "performed" in her role as a sailor to her aunt's satisfaction. After a stressful but successful test run on the docks and at sea, Harriet was entering a new phase of life.

THE ATTIC

Uncle Mark knew whereof he spoke. He had been secretly constructing a concealed trap door at Molly's house, connecting a storeroom through a cupboard to a garret above—a small, dark, airless attic room where Harriet would, astonishingly, spend the next six years and eleven months as she hid from Norcom and his vicious pack of slave catchers. Norcom would make two more trips to New York in search of Harriet. Molly and Mark became convinced that she might be safe hiding right under his nose. Harriet herself had doubts: "They told me a place of concealment had been provided for me at my grand-mother's. I could not imagine how it was possible to hide me in her house, every nook and corner of which was known to the [Norcom] family. They told me to wait and see."[24]

The garret was nine feet long, seven feet wide, and three feet high, which meant that Harriet could not stand up in it. "The air was stifling; the darkness total," she recalled. The room was scorching hot in the summer, drafty and cold in the winter. The roof leaked. Rats and mice scurried around in the dark. Harriet was "deprived of light and air, and with no space to move my limbs." To get any exercise at all, Harriet was forced to crawl around the room. Over time her arms and legs grew numb, and at one point she lost the power of speech from weakness and isolation. She became delirious. She overheard that her grandmother had grown seriously ill, which required a home visit from none other than Dr. Norcom. The miniature prison was a chamber of horrors as her brother John captured in verse years later:

> Dark and gloomy in the captive's cell
> No light of day e'er entered there
> The feelings of a broken heart no one can tell,
> It sickens, it weakens, it sinks in despair.

Harriet fought the despair. She made peace with her harsh new cir-cumstances. She used a gimlet to pierce small holes in the wall, which allowed her to get a little air and see outside. In a cruel coincidence, the first person she saw was her mortal enemy, the would-be rapist James Norcom, walking down the street. She was eventually able to let in enough light to read the Bible and sew. When a family member passed food up through the trapdoor, she could whisper about local news in the dark. After considerable time she was able to come down into the storeroom to stretch and move her limbs. The greatest consolation was that she could hear the voices of her children, who were living in the same house.

Everyone seemed to believe that Harriet was in New York, which was just what she wanted. With the help of Uncle Mark and other sailors, she waged a clever campaign of deception. Harriet began to write letters to Norcom, but she needed information to make them sound authentic. She asked her uncle for a copy of a New York newspaper to find the names of streets and other details to add to her letter. Mark had half a page of the *New York Herald*, a notoriously racist paper that in Harriet's words "systematically abuses the colored people." She made it serve her own purpose of resistance. Once she had found what she needed in the newspaper and written the letter, Harriet now needed a courier, so she went back to Uncle Mark, hoping that he could find a "trustworthy seafaring person" to carry her letter to New York. Mark replied that "he knew one that he would trust with his own life to the ends of the world." The sailor took the letter to the post office in New York and mailed it back to Edenton from there. Harriet continued to write letters pretending to be in various other places, from New York to Boston to Canada, sending each one by sailor courier to be mailed from that place. The trick worked. Norcom became convinced that Harriet was not in Edenton and gave up trying to find her locally.

FINAL ESCAPE

After almost seven years, Harriet and her family prepared for the final escape. She had already hatched several plans for running away, but her grandmother opposed each one. Harriet finally "determined to steer for the North Star at all hazards" and again Uncle Mark the sailor opened the way. He came to her one day and announced, "Your day has come." For years he and Uncle Stephen had quietly scoured the waterfront for safe opportunities for escape. Mark had finally found her a reliable passage by ship and gave Harriet two weeks to decide if she wanted to go. He added that "such a good chance might never occur again." Mark also promised to convince Molly of the necessity of escape, and this he was able to do.[25]

The day of the planned escape arrived, but suddenly everything was postponed as "the vessel was unexpectedly detained several days," probably in a previous port of call. Meanwhile Harriet and Molly learned of the murder of a local runaway named James, whose mother Charity was a longtime family friend. Molly was beside herself, convinced that "a similar fate" awaited Harriet. "She sobbed, and groaned, and entreated me not to go," prompting her granddaughter to relent and forego her planned escape. Uncle Mark was disappointed, telling Harriet that it would be a long time before another such opportunity would present itself. Harriet proposed that a friend named Fanny be allowed to take her place. Fanny had gone into hiding after her enslaver sold all four of her little girls to a slave trader. Mark made the arrangements and led Fanny, "half dead with fright," aboard the vessel. She was taken aboard to a small cabin, an "accommodation [that] had been purchased at a price that would pay for a voyage to England."[26]

For the next two days the vessel lay stalled in the harbor by contrary winds. By the third day, Molly was terrified that the escape would be discovered and everyone, including Mark, would suffer terribly, by torture and perhaps death. In going to meet Harriet inside her own home, Molly accidentally left open a door, through which walked a neighbor named Jenny, a woman known for her loose tongue. She apparently caught sight of Harriet. Suddenly everything was at risk. Upset with herself over her careless mistake, Molly declared to Harriet, "The boat ain't gone yet. Get ready immediately, and go with Fanny. I ain't got another word to say against it now; for there's no telling what may happen this day." Uncle Mark agreed and went immediately to the wharf, only to discover that "the wind had shifted, and the vessel was slowly beating down stream." Mark hired two boatmen to row him out to the vessel as quickly as they could. Captain James A. Wright saw them coming and at a distance thought that the light-skinned Mark was a white man coming after Fanny, the runaway on board. He ordered the hoisting of sails to get away, but Mark managed to catch up and go aboard. Referring to Fanny, Wright explained, "Why, the woman's here already; and I've put her where you or the devil would have a tough job to find her." Mark countered that he wanted to bring another woman aboard, a proposition to which the captain agreed after receiving a second payment. He and the vessel would wait at a designated spot until evening.

Harriet, meanwhile, was excited—and terrified. She said a tearful goodbye to her son Joseph, promising that he would join her one day soon in the "Free States." He promised to tell no one where his mother had gone. (Louisa had already been sent to Brooklyn by her biological father.) Molly soon showed up with a small bag of money, which she insisted Harriet take in case she fell sick and ended up in the New York poorhouse. Molly, Harriet, and Joseph knelt in prayer, and soon the time to depart had arrived.

Harriet did not explain in her memoir how she got from her grandmother's house to the wharf, perhaps because she could not remember: the sudden, unexpected departure put her brain in a "whirl." She likely donned her sailor's slops again, especially since they worked so well the last time. Leaving her grandmother's house at dusk, she met Uncle Mark in the street feeling "faint in body, but strong of purpose." She did not look back at the place where she had spent her entire life. When they got to the wharf, a rowboat was ready. She boarded and soon the boat swiftly "glided over the water." One of the sailors said to her, "Don't be down-hearted, madam. We will take you safely to your husband." Harriet did not understand his meaning but assumed it was based on something the captain had told him. She thanked him in response and added with typical Southern politeness, "I hoped we should have pleasant weather."

After ascending the vessel's ladder, Harriet boarded and met Wright, "an elderly man, with a pleasant countenance," captain of the *Skewarky*. Mark apparently did not go aboard. Wright escorted Harriet "to a little box of a cabin," wherein sat her friend Fanny, who was astonished to see her. She blurted out, "Can this be *you*? or is it your ghost?" The women embraced and began to sob. Wright overheard the loud crying and came to the cabin to remind the women "that for his safety, as well as our own, it would be prudent for us not to attract any attention." He added that anytime another ship was nearby, they should stay in their cabin, "but at other times, he had no objection to our being on deck." He promised to keep a good lookout and assured the women that they would be in no danger. He had told the crew that both women were on their way to meet their husbands in Philadelphia. Harriet noted, "We thanked him, and promised to observe carefully all the directions he gave us."

THE VOYAGE

Harriet and Fanny now talked in hushed tones in their small cabin, exchanging terrifying stories about their respective secret hideouts while awaiting escape. Fanny understandably "dwelt on the agony of separation from all her children on that dreadful auction day." Harriet, full of sympathy, explained, "We have the same sorrows." But Fanny quickly corrected her: "No . . . you are going to see your children soon, and there is no hope that I shall ever even hear from mine." Despite their sadness, both women felt happy to have a companion for the dangerous journey ahead.[27]

The vessel got under way, but the beginning of the voyage was agonizingly slow. The "wind was against us." Harriet and Fanny would not have minded such doldrums had they been farther out at sea, where there were "miles of water between us and our enemies," but they were still in sight of Edenton and therefore suffered "constant apprehension that the constables would come on board" to search for runaways, as they often did. Harriet also felt ill at ease with the captain and his men. Even though her uncles were sailors, she declared herself "an entire stranger to that class of people," by which she probably meant white seamen. She had heard that "sailors were rough, and sometimes cruel." She knew only Fanny on board the ship and trusted no one else: "We were so completely in their power, that if they were bad men, our situation would be dreadful." She also worried that Captain Wright, already paid, might now seek to make more money by returning the runaways "to those who claimed us as property." Fanny, however, did not share Harriet's distrust. She explained that she was afraid when she first came aboard the vessel, but that for the three days the vessel lay at anchor awaiting departure, "nobody had betrayed her, or treated her otherwise than kindly." Harriet took comfort in the news.

The vessel's route had likely been worked out in advance by Uncle Mark and Captain Wright as the least dangerous: there would be no other ports of call or transfer points and no exposure to Atlantic storms or swells. The *Skewarky* would sail southward and eastward through the Albemarle Sound, north up the Pasquotank River to the Dismal Swamp Canal, which had been dug in 1805 and deepened in 1829. The vessel would then enter the Elizabeth River, pass Norfolk, sail into Hampton Roads, then veer eastward into Chesapeake Bay. The schooner sailed the two hundred miles north up the bay to the Chesapeake and Delaware Canal (opened 1829), onto the Delaware River, and finally to the docks of Philadelphia.[28]

Harriet's first night as a free woman was memorable: "I shall never forget that night. The balmy air of spring was so refreshing!" She delighted in sailing up historic Chesapeake Bay. The entire passage was suffused with beauty, not least because she had been cooped up in her grandmother's attic for almost seven years! "O, the beautiful sun-shine! the exhilarating breeze! and I could enjoy them without fear or restraint." Thinking back on her time in the garret, she observed that she "had never realized what grand things air and sunlight are till I had been deprived of them."

Early in the voyage Captain Wright gestured westward toward Snaky Swamp as they sailed past. He knew that this was a place in-habited by fugitives: there, he pointed out, "is a slave territory that defies all the laws," a space for outlaws. Harriet instantly recalled "the terrible days I had spent there" with mosquitoes buzzing around her head and snakes slithering at her feet. The memory "made me feel very dismal," but the feeling diminished with every nautical mile she sailed away from the swamp.

The voyage of the *Skewarky* was quick and uneventful, a ten-day journey to Philadelphia. Wright advised Harriet and Fanny that they would dock in port late at night, and that it would be better to disem-bark "in broad daylight" as that was "the best way to avoid suspicion." Feeling fearful, Harriet replied, "You know best. But will you stay on board and protect us?" He saw that she was suspicious and said "he was sorry, now that he had brought us to the end of our voyage, to find I had so little confidence in him." Harriet thought to herself, "Ah, if he had ever been a slave he would have known how difficult it was to trust a white man." He told the women they could sleep soundly through the night, without fear; he would guarantee their protection. At the end of the voyage, Harriet was convinced, claim-ing that Captain Wright, "Southerner as he was," had treated Fanny and herself as he would have treated "white ladies" on a fully legal passage. Uncle Mark had chosen well. The captain "could not have treated us more respectfully." He proved to be a man of his word.

Harriet was up on deck before dawn, eager to see the "free soil" on which they would land. "We watched the reddening sky, and saw the great orb come up slowly out of the water, as it seemed. Soon the waves began to sparkle, and every thing caught the beautiful glow." Before the women lay the City of Brotherly Love, which to them was a beautiful but daunting "city of strangers." Harriet and Fanny stared deeply into each other's teary eyes. Their voyage had brought them to freedom. They had "left dear ties behind us; ties cruelly sundered by the demon Slavery." They had escaped from bondage but at a price: they were now "alone in the world."

PHILADELPHIA

During the third week of June 1842, the *Skewarky* anchored a short distance from the Philadelphia docks. Harriet and Fanny boarded a small boat and were rowed ashore. Waiting for them was a free Black man named Jeremiah Durham, a carter on the waterfront who worked with the Philadelphia Vigilant Committee, the abolitionist group founded in August 1837 by local African American activists Robert Purvis—a merchant—and James Forten—a sailmaker—to assist runaways. Concerned for her safety, Harriet asked where she might find veils and gloves for herself and Fanny. She made the purchase and returned to Durham, who also happened to be the minister at the Mother Bethel African Methodist Episcopal Church. He took her hand and explained that she would be staying with him and his family nearby. Fanny apparently would stay with another waterfront worker who was a friend and neighbor of Durham.[29]

At this point the sailors who had originally filled Harriet with fear and dread approached to say goodbye to her and Fanny and to wish them well. Harriet took their rope-hardened hands into her own and thanked them: "I shook their hardy hands, with tears in my eyes." They had proved to be neither rough nor cruel. "They had all been kind to us, and they had rendered us a greater service than they could possibly conceive of." She also expressed her gratitude to Captain

Wright and begged his assistance to convey messages to friends and family at home. He promised he would deliver them on his next voyage.[30]

Harriet thus entered the free Black community of Philadelphia, nineteen thousand strong and an anchor of the maritime network that made her escape possible. As it happened, she already knew some of its members. She told Durham that she would like to seek out "friends . . . from my native town," most of whom would have been maritime fugitives themselves. Durham promised to help her find them. When she entered the Durham home, she encountered a family that "had comforted other weary hearts," that is, the hunted fugitives who arrived on previous ships seeking the comforts of solidarity and sustenance.

Later that same day Mrs. Durham knocked on Harriet's door to say that an unnamed abolitionist, likely Purvis, Forten, or another member of the Vigilant Committee, would like to meet with her, "to inquire into my plans, and to offer assistance, if needed." The man offered to pay Harriet's way to New York, but she declined, saying that "my grandmother had given me sufficient to pay my expenses to the end of my journey." She continued to take pride in her independent family. The man offered to provide someone to travel with her and Fanny by train to New York. "I gladly accepted the proposition," admitted Harriet, "for I had a dread of meeting slaveholders, and some dread also of railroads. I had never entered a railroad car in my life, and it seemed to me quite an important event."[31]

Harriet stayed in the Durham home for five days and continued to be fascinated by the activity of the waterfront. One morning she was awakened at daylight by the sounds of the market women outside her window: "I heard women crying fresh fish, berries, radishes, and various other things." She got up, got dressed, and "sat at the window to watch that unknown tide of life" as it ebbed and flowed from sea to shore and back again. At that moment, "Philadelphia seemed to be a wonderfully great place."

Had all this happened because Uncle Mark Ramsey had worked with the Vigilance Committees of New York and Philadelphia? He did, after all, make regular trips aboard a packet vessel to New York just as the city's Vigilance Committee was increasingly active along the waterfront assisting sailaways. He would have spent a fair amount of time in the city between voyages, staying near the docks, perhaps at William Powell's Colored Sailors Home, a Black Atlantic crossroads of news and abolitionism located near New York's East River in lower Manhattan. Ramsey also sailed to Philadelphia. It seems certain that Ramsey made the arrangements that resulted in an opportunity so safe that it "might never occur again." The Philadelphia Vigilant Committee was certainly well prepared to receive Harriet (and Fanny), suggesting that they knew about the arrival in advance.[32]

NEW YORK

Lymas Johnson, a free Black porter on the waterfront and a member of the Vigilant Committee, escorted Harriet and Fanny to the train bound for New York. The fugitives took their seats among the "people, apparently of all nations," amid the smells of cigar smoke and whiskey and the sounds of "coarse jokes and ribald songs." On arrival Harriet sought out the people from her small hometown who lived in the free Black community of New York; they, too, had no doubt escaped Edenton by sea, some of them perhaps with Uncle Mark. She soon went on to Boston and then to New Bedford, Massachusetts, looking for her brother John. He was away at sea, whaling in the Pacific, so she returned to New York and secured work as a domestic in the household of magazine writer Nathaniel Parker Willis and his wife Mary Stace Willis.[33]

A few months later, as she stood at the window one bright morning holding the Willis baby, she saw a young sailor, "closely observing every house as he passed." It was her brother John, returned from his long Pacific whaling voyage. She safely put down the baby, "flew down stairs, opened the front door, beckoned to the sailor, and in less than a minute I was clasped in my brother's arms. How much we had to tell each other! How we laughed, and how we cried, over each other's adventures!" This was the first of three happy family reunions over the next year as Harriet also reunited with son Joseph and daughter Louisa. She had realized her goal of getting herself and those closest to her to a "free land."[34]

FREEDOM

Harriet spent nine years trying to escape the Norcom family's efforts to reclaim her as a slave, retreating four times to Boston, where a strong abolitionist movement made slave catchers skittish. Harriet gained her freedom in February 1852 when her new employer, Cornelia Grinnell Willis, bought her out of bondage, without her knowledge or approval, from James Norcom's daughter, Mary Matilda Norcom. Harriet was relieved but felt degraded by the transaction. When a "gentleman" said "It's true; I have seen the bill of sale," Harriet responded with fury:

> "The bill of sale!" Those words struck me like a blow. So I was *sold* at last! A human being *sold* in the free city of New York! The bill of sale is on record, and future generations will learn from it that women were articles of traffic in New York, late in the nineteenth century of the Christian religion. It may hereafter prove a useful document to antiquaries, who are seeking to measure the progress of civilization in the United States. I well know the value of that bit of paper; but much as I love freedom, I do not like to look upon it. I am deeply grateful to the generous friend who procured it, but I despise the miscreant who demanded payment for what never rightfully belonged to him or his.

Formal freedom, when it finally came, was bittersweet.[35]

As a woman, Harriet Jacobs escaped slavery against heavy odds. As a teenager she fought "the war of [her] life" against a powerful, lascivious enslaver for years before she could even contemplate getting away. She figured out how to free herself and her children. She disguised herself as a sailor and made her way to the docks of a small town without being recognized. She navigated the hypermasculine waterfront. She traveled 350 miles from Edenton to Philadelphia, which would have been almost impossible by land. Her escape required extraordinary head-work to overcome these obstacles. Her only real hope for freedom was to secure passage aboard a safe ship.

Harriet's three seafaring uncles opened the way, and Harriet herself helped to continue the maritime tradition of labor. Her brother became a sailor, as did her son Joseph, named for the heroic uncle who escaped bondage three times. John and young Joseph both sailed on whalers. Her sailor uncles originally inspired and then carefully piloted Harriet to a freedom ship. It is no wonder that in the final words of her memoir, Harriet compared her own life in slavery to "a dark and troubled sea," invoking the Middle Passage of dreaded memory. Her family had helped her to navigate that sea, to freedom, with supreme skill, will, and daring.[36]

Chapter 5

Jonathan Walker's
Branded Hand

onathan Walker was "the man with the branded hand." An official of the government of Florida burned the initials "S. S.,"
for "slave stealer," into his right palm after the sailor-abolitionist
attempted to help seven African American men escape slavery by sea
from Pensacola in 1844. John Greenleaf Whittier soon wrote a poem
to immortalize Jonathan's punishment; he reinterpreted the letters to
mean "slave savior"—a symbol of honor. The lines of the poem were
soon set to music and sung in abolitionist meetings around the nation. A daguerreotypist created an image of Jonathan's branded hand,
which became a centerpiece of antislavery iconography. Northern
crowds flocked to see Jonathan's scarred hand as he toured the abolitionist lecture circuit for four years after he got out of jail. The story
of a federal official branding Jonathan was scandalous—a gruesome
sign of the oppressive "Slave Power" and the corrupt Southern government abolitionists railed against. Jonathan gained fame as an abolitionist martyr and raised maritime marronage to national and
international visibility.[1]

Jonathan's life as a maritime abolitionist was a story about hands,
and not only because of the branding. As the youngest of four boys

and one of seven children in his Massachusetts family, Jonathan had no patrimony with which to sustain himself, and in this proletarian condition he was exactly like tens of thousands of others who went to sea: he had only the labor of his hands to sell to make a living. Sailors had hands like leather mitts from hauling ropes at sea, which might have made the branding less painful than it would have been for softer, more privileged hands. As it happened, Jonathan's other hand had experienced trauma too: it was described as "lame" after he was shot in the wrist by a gang of robbers while sailing the coast of Mexico in 1836. But perhaps the most important meaning of Jonathan's hand was captured by the Reverend Frank Edward Kittredge, the sailor's friend and pastor, who noted in his funeral oration of 1878 that his was "a hand which never harmed a human being, but was ever ready to succor the needy, the friendless and the outcast." Jonathan described his own calling simply: "*to deliver the oppressed from the hands of the oppressor.*" This he would do by sea.[2]

Jonathan described his maritime adventures in his book, *Trial and Imprisonment of Jonathan Walker, at Pensacola, Florida, for Aiding Slaves to Escape from Bondage, with an Appendix, Containing a Sketch of His Life*, which was published by the American Anti-Slavery Society in Boston in 1845, the same year as Frederick Douglass's *Narrative of the Life*. A collection of legal documents, newspaper articles, correspondence, autobiography, a jail journal, and his own narrative of events, Jonathan's book proved to be popular and went through four more editions in the nineteenth century, republished in 1846, 1848, 1850, and finally in 1870. Jonathan sold four to five thousand copies himself as he spoke on the abolitionist lecture circuit, but the profits were too little to cover the most basic living expenses for his wife and nine children. His goal in writing the book was not only to narrate his own capture, trial, and punishment, but to lay bare for Northern readers the bloody realities of slavery. He was one of a relatively small number of white Northern abolitionists who knew Southern slave society intimately. He had spent twenty years sailing around and living in the South. He put his knowledge at the service of those seeking emancipation.[3]

THE MAKING OF A SAILOR-ABOLITIONIST

Jonathan's account of his ordeal, from the attempted escape, through the arrest, the branding, and release from prison, also contained a "sketch" of his own life. He presented himself as a man well traveled, worldly, wise, and lucky, for, like most who sailed the high seas, he had faced down death on numerous occasions. He defended the common sailor against the "active agents" of the demonic fallen angel "Beelzebub"—merchants, captains, officers, crimps, card sharks, and tavern-keepers, all of whom preyed on him and his brother tars. He indicted slavery as one of "the highest wrongs and crimes that ever were invented by the enemy of man." The peculiar institution was poisonous to family, community, and nation.[4]

Born in Harwich, Massachusetts, on Nantucket Sound, in 1799, Jonathan was a fifth-generation New Englander. An element of religious radicalism ran through his family history and predisposed him to abolitionism. He was descended from the Puritan radical Stephen Hopkins, who along with Roger Williams and Anne Hutchinson had rocked the earliest Puritan settlements with their antinomian views: they obeyed the "higher law" of conscience rather than the laws that Puritan elites made for their own protection. Some of Jonathan's ideas—his opposition to war and his belief in absolute spiritual equality—had Quaker roots. He named his last child George Fox Walker, after the seventeenth-century founder of Quakerism.[5]

The greatest source of radicalism in Jonathan's life was his work experience as a sailor. He went to sea at eighteen, signing on for long voyages and working with seamen from all over the world, from the frigid waters of Russia to the "burning vertical sun" of the tropics. He trusted multiethnic sailors with his life day after day, embracing the seafaring tradition of solidarity that enhanced survival in a dangerous line of work. Mutual work and care among sailors changed the human heart. Jonathan was proud to say that "of all classes of men, none possess more open or greater hearts than do the sailors; or are so ready to run any risk or make any sacrifice in aid of their suffering fellow-beings." Jonathan expanded the practice of solidarity from fellow sailors to all of laboring humanity.[6]

Some of the catastrophes Jonathan suffered at sea fueled this expansion in unexpected ways. Early in his seafaring life he somehow got separated from his shipmates on an island in the Indian Ocean, eight thousand miles from home. He found himself "sweating out a violent fever," probably caused by malaria, for twenty-one days in a thatched bamboo hut. He survived thanks to "the kindness of those [villagers] whom I never saw before." Years later, when he was attacked in the Gulf of Mexico and shot through the wrist, he staggered, weak from the loss of blood, to a small village of Indigenous people at the mouth of the Rio del Norte in Texas. Once again, the "charity of strangers" saved his life. He swore that he would ever after do "unto others as I would they should do unto me, if I were in their condition." The golden rule, embodied by the poor around the world, would become a central theme of his abolitionist life.[7]

Jonathan used his wide-ranging labors at sea to educate himself about slavery. He recalled that beginning in 1822, when he was twenty-three years old, "on all occasions which presented, I tried to inform myself of its mode of operation, and have, in several of the slave states, scrutinized it in the parlor and in the kitchen, in the cottage and in the field, in the city and in the country." He sailed into ports, coasted up and down rivers, and visited plantations; he worked and talked with both enslavers and enslaved people. He did the headwork of an abolitionist. As a man whose "country was the world," he came to oppose slavery everywhere it existed and despised everything it represented. Jonathan's abolitionism combined the egalitarian traditions of radical Christianity, seafaring, and Indigenous hospitality in a potent mix.[8]

A BEACON FOR RUNAWAYS

When Jonathan arrived in Pensacola with his family in early 1837, he settled into a city that had a long-established "tradition of slave flight." The slave code of the federal territory of Florida had seventy regulations to govern the practice of slavery; twenty-seven of them concerned runaways. Between 1820 and 1860 hundreds of runaways from New Orleans and Mobile, as well as from rural Alabama, Mississippi, and Georgia, "aimed for Pensacola," a large proportion of them escaping by sea through interracial networks of people, including sailors, who showed the very solidarity Jonathan described and embodied. For decades the port city had been a beacon of freedom, a fact that Jonathan understood and had probably acted on in moving there in the first place.[9]

Located at the edge of the booming cotton economy of the lower South, Pensacola, a bustling port of three thousand people, featured a protected harbor and a big, busy naval base operated by the United States government, by far the biggest employer in the region. The port's nautical complex included the Navy Yard as well as granite wharves, a floating dry dock, brick warehouses, and barracks for the multiracial crews of naval vessels. A surgeon remarked on the rough equality that characterized social relations aboard the ships that docked in Pensacola: "The white and colored seamen messed together . . . and there seemed to be an entire absence of prejudice against the blacks as messmates among the crew." The Navy Yard employed a mix of formally free and enslaved workers, a significant number of whom had hired themselves out for a year at a time and thereby escaped the close surveillance of their enslavers.[10]

A dynamic, mobile international proletariat worked Pensacola's docks and ships. A missionary passing through in 1850 noted that the port's workers came from "almost every part of the known world." They were "Philadelphians, New Yorkers, Baltimoreans, Scotch, Irish, Dutch, Swedes, Danes, Norwegians, Spaniards, French, Portuguese, English, [mixed race] Creoles, and Africans, [who] mingle here promiscuously together." As in all other Atlantic ports, these workers met, drank, sang, and danced in grogshops, subverting the increasingly rigid racial codes of Southern society. They would translate the organized interracial cooperation of work into other projects of their own such as escaping slavery by sea.[11]

During his six years in Pensacola, Jonathan learned about the runaway tradition and decided, over time, that it was his moral responsibility to become part of it, an attitude for which he became well-known in both the Black and white communities. As he wrote in a book he published for children in 1846, "I knew many instances, when I lived at the south, when people would go into the woods and swamps with their hounds and guns to hunt runaway slaves; and not unfrequently, the poor fugitives are shot badly, their flesh is torn in pieces by savage bloodhounds, and they are left in the woods to die." The extreme torture and violence of slavery moved him to solidarity—and haunted him for the rest of his life. He observed of the enslaved that freedom was "their right" and he would help them to gain it if he could.[12]

Jonathan applied his abolitionist principles to daily life, even though this was a dangerous thing to do in Pensacola. He set white tongues wagging when he invited Black workers into his home, where he associated with them "on terms of equality and intimacy" and treated them with "great brotherly affection." He showed them the hospitality of meals, "seating them with him at his table while his daughters (half-grown girls) awaited on the table." Over dinner he exhorted all to seek racial equality, "preach[ing] to the Negroes . . . that they were just as good as he was." He described the difference of color as something ephemeral and insignificant: it was a "mere shadow." This was the stuff of scandal in a slave society.[13]

In 1840 Jonathan came to the assistance of a Black seaman named William Cook, a twenty-five-year-old from Virginia who had worked as a cook aboard the schooner *Mary Ellen* before being thrown in jail as a fugitive by Pensacola authorities. Cook insisted that he was free and had merely left his free papers with his captain. His pleas were to no avail: the local jailor held Cook for a year, then forced him to work in the Navy Yard as an indentured servant to pay off his inflated fines and fees. When Cook fell ill, Jonathan took him into his home and restored his health by treating him with "botanic medicines." Jonathan then "advised him to go on board of a vessel and leave the place" as quickly as possible. Cook was unable to do this immediately, but he did escape eventually, probably with Jonathan's assistance.[14]

Around the same time Jonathan made another foray into the maritime circuit of escape. A writer for the *Pensacola Gazette* reported in 1844 that "three or four years ago" Jonathan "was suspected of tampering with the Negroes and of being accessory to the concealment on board of a vessel and the escape of two slaves." Jonathan himself confirmed this involvement after the Civil War when he explained to his pastor that during the late 1830s and early 1840s he had built a small vessel and engaged in the coasting trade from New Orleans to Pensacola, all the while assisting slaves, perhaps many of them, who came aboard "in obtaining their freedom."[15]

"NO WHITE ASSOCIATES"

Jonathan returned with his family to Massachusetts in 1843, but in the fall of that year he sailed back to the Gulf of Mexico, working in Mobile for several months as a boatbuilder. He returned to Pensacola on June 4, 1844, arriving in a whaleboat he had apparently built himself. According to a local official, he had no apparent "business" in town at that time. He may have revealed his secret plans when he rented a room from a "quatroon" or "colored woman," whose property extended from town all the way down to waterfront, which allowed Jonathan to pull his vessel up onto the shore, under some shady trees, where he intended to work on it—and to plot. The unnamed woman was likely a free "Creole," a mixed-race person of French or Spanish ancestry. When Jonathan noted later, during his trial and imprisonment, that most of the Creoles in town were sympathetic to his plight, he probably referred to the woman and others. It was later noted that "Walker was seen frequently during his recent sojourn here in close conversation with Negro men. He took lodgings with a quatroon woman and had no white associates during his stay." Over the next two weeks he and seven would-be freemen plotted their escape.[16]

Throughout his life Jonathan always insisted that the initiative for the mass escape came directly from enslaved people themselves, from below. The "colored woman" may have worked as a go-between. Jonathan did not recruit the men to escape, but he had already decided that he would assist anyone who appealed to him for help. The word of Jonathan's willingness apparently spread out from his rented room discreetly, among networks of kinship and trust, as suggested by the group who ended up joining him on the boat: six of the seven were two sets of brothers, two named Scott and four named Johnson. All had heard stories about how Jonathan transgressed the South's racial boundaries. Having "previously ascertained his anti-slavery proclivities," they took encouragement and approached him.

By all accounts, including Jonathan's, Silas Scott, a man who was described in a runaway advertisement as "about 5 feet 2 inches in height, very muscular, and considerably bow-legged," was the first to approach him about the escape. Scott had a scar on his face and a recent wound on his right hand, caused by a sickle. Jonathan maintained that he did not know Scott at the time, but the men shared maritime experience, as Scott worked as a fisherman. Scott asked Jonathan, "Did you ever think how sweet our freedom would be to us?" Scott then drew upon knowledge of American history to try to convince Jonathan to assist in the escape: "Do you know that if we had the privilege of fighting for it as the revolutionary fathers had, how gladly we would avail ourselves of this blessed opportunity?" The stranger in search of kindness made a winning argument even if Jonathan did not require persuading.[17]

A man named Charles Johnson, who clearly had previous ties to Jonathan, also played a major role in the escape. Someone said of Johnson, "This boy was with Walker, lying under the trees in the lot where he was working on his boat, nearly all of the day," soon after Jonathan had arrived in town. The men apparently plotted in a leisurely, relaxed way. A writer in the *Pensacola Gazette* reported that Jonathan and Charles, who was described as "an excellent labourer," had worked together, probably at the Navy Yard, and that they shared another bond: they had attended the same "ranting, shouting" interracial church characterized by a subversive religious and political "enthusiasm." Jonathan likely knew several of the other men from common work at the local Navy Yard and railroad. In any case, the eight conspirators shared some level of familiarity and trust. Jonathan acknowledged past connections in 1846 when he wrote, "some slaves with whom I was acquainted, wanted to come away with me." He told the men "he would share the risk with them." "By God's help," he solemnly intoned as they came to agreement, "I will do my best to assist you to a land of freedom."[18]

The goal of the runaways was apparently to get to a Northern port, most likely Philadelphia, New York, or Boston, and perhaps seek the assistance of a local Vigilance Committee once there. Jonathan knew of the Boston committee that had formed in 1841 to help fugitives reach freedom, and he very likely knew of the other two that had formed earlier. Getting to the North was revealed as part of the eventual plan when the enslavers found that all the fugitives took winter clothes with them on the sea journey. This was not the apparel to be worn while sailing in the sweltering summer heat of the Gulf of Mexico or the Caribbean Sea.[19]

In planning their sea route, the men had to be cautious: Jonathan's small boat could sail the Gulf, especially if they hugged the shoreline, but it was too frail to withstand the stronger currents and turbulent waves of the Atlantic. Jonathan observed that his boat could carry up to ten men "in good weather, and when the sea was not very rough." He apparently suggested to Scott and Johnson that they aim for the Bahama islands, where the British had fully abolished slavery six years earlier. Once there, it would be possible to catch a ride on a vessel bound for a port in the Northern United States if the runaways so desired. The men agreed and planned to meet in the middle of the night of June 22, "on the shore south of the city."

Jonathan immediately set about readying the vessel and gathering supplies for the voyage. Having grown up in Cape Cod and worked as a boatbuilder in and around New Bedford, both places located in the very heart of the New England whaling industry during its glory years, Jonathan would have known almost all there was to know about a whaleboat. Whaleboats were lightweight but sturdy, built of small oak frames and planked with rot-resistant cedar. They were quick in the water and easily propelled by oar or paddle, which would have been especially valuable to people trying to escape bondage as quickly as possible. The whaleboat, in short, was a fast, sturdy vessel. Jonathan had chosen the vehicle of escape well.[20]

Jonathan made an additional sail for the boat, probably a large jib because the whaleboat's shape lends itself to fore and aft rigged sails. He also acquired two additional oars and paddles. He used his carpentry skills to install "cross-pieces [of wood] for rowers to brace their feet against," knowing that rowing would enhance their speedy escape. He built "watertight boxes to fit in the bow and stern and under thwarts" to load with either ballast or extra water. He bought two barrels of bread, 120 pounds of pork and bacon, a keg of molasses, a wheel of cheese, a compass, and a binnacle lantern. He added a barrel and a demijohn of water, knowing that this would not be enough and that they would have to go ashore for water "every few days" throughout the voyage. They simply did not have enough room on the boat for big, bulky water casks. Jonathan also brought aboard two harpoons for turtling as well as a gun and ammunition, probably to hunt for food. Preparations went well until a couple of days before the intended departure, when Jonathan began to feel sick.[21]

THE VOYAGE AND THE CAPTURE

The men pushed off in the early morning hours of Saturday, June 22, 1844, no doubt churning with fear and excitement. Some of the freedom seekers had been spotted making their way toward the rendezvous. Silas and Harry Scott were out at around eleven at night, "passing down a street toward the Navy Yard." Leonard Johnson apparently lived at the Navy Yard in the barracks for workers; he was up and around well before daybreak. Once everyone had come aboard, Jonathan began the voyage with a feint to throw off anyone who might be watching. He originally sailed westward before cutting back to the east toward Florida and the Bahamas. But he and his shipmates quickly ran into hard luck and bad weather, as Jonathan recalled: for the first week they faced "strong headwinds with frequent squalls, and rain." As the drenched men rowed onward, Jonathan grew sicker day by day. The weather finally improved, but the sun soon scorched the men in the open vessel. Six days into the voyage Jonathan "pitched forward senseless to the bottom of the boat," likely suffering from a combination of malaria, dehydration, and what he later described as "sun stroke." When he recovered consciousness, he was delirious and could no longer manage the vessel. He later wrote to his wife that at this moment in the voyage he was sure he was going to die.[22]

The men sailed and rowed onward as Jonathan began to recover, although he remained weak. Their plan was to stay close to the shore: "They coasted it all the way around, running day and night, closing in and running by the land at nightfall, and standing further out during the day." They went ashore every few days to dry their clothes, cook their food, and replenish their water supply, fighting swarms of mosquitoes at every stop. They passed St. Andrews Harbor on June 26, St. Joseph Bay the following day, and St. George Sound June 28–29. They traveled roughly fifty miles a day, much of it by rowing. By July 2 the winds had improved and Jonathan was feeling a bit better, although he was still having trouble breathing. Yet he found the spirit to encourage his comrades, saying at one point, "Four days more, my lads . . . and I will have you safe beneath the British flag."[23]

After two long and troubled weeks at sea, at daybreak on July 8 Jonathan spotted two sloops bearing toward them. When Captain Richard Roberts of the *Eliza Catherine* got close enough, he saw the seven Black men and assumed that they were runaways, although he kept the thought to himself. He pretended to aid the men in the smaller vessel, saying he would tow them and their boat to Cape Florida, where they were bound. The mate of the *Eliza Catherine* came alongside and tied a rope to the whaleboat, inviting the men to come aboard the sloop. Jonathan knew it was a trap and urged the men not to go, but he was too exhausted to resist. It was too late: four had already clambered aboard. Jonathan himself finally joined Roberts aboard the sloop as the vessel got under sail for Key West, the nearest location of the United States government in the federal territory of Florida. Jonathan later observed that Roberts "had no right whatever to interfere with us," which was true because the United States law of slavery did not apply to the high seas. But the legality of the capture did not matter to the authorities when, on July 9, Roberts took Jonathan and the seven sailaways ashore at Key West. The local US constable arrested them, carried them before a magistrate, and threw them in jail. Jonathan freely admitted that he was an abolitionist and that they were escaping slavery, as a man who thought he had done nothing wrong might logically do. His declaration inspired great hostility. Preparations were soon under way to return the group to Pensacola to face charges. Roberts would collect a $1,700 reward ($67,000 in 2024), almost two-thirds of the money for Jonathan alone.[24]

Four days later Jonathan was carried aboard a government steamship, the *General Taylor*, commanded by a man named Ferrand, who had no use for abolitionists. (Jonathan's seven shipmates—and his boat—would return a few days later aboard the *Reform*.) Ferrand unceremoniously tossed the still-weak Jonathan, manacled "in double irons, both hands and feet," into the burning hot hold of the steamer amid "rubbish and filth." Jonathan later joked that Ferrand had "indulged me in a steam bath" and attached manacles and shackles insuring that "I should neither dance nor play the fiddle," as sailors customarily did. After six days at sea the *General Taylor* arrived in Pensacola late in the evening on Thursday, July 18, 1844. What began as a maritime passage to freedom ended as the opposite: Jonathan went to jail as his seven shipmates returned to bondage.[25]

Jonathan and his comrades had been defeated by bad luck, and they knew it. Had Jonathan not gotten sick they would have made it to the Bahamas. They would have saved time by "running more direct courses," docking in the Bahamas after ten to twelve days at sea, he estimated, several days before they were taken. Even if they had not saved such time, had they arrived at the place of capture half an hour earlier or later, they would have missed Captain Roberts and the *Eliza Catherine* altogether. As Jonathan ruefully recalled, "In about one day more, if we had not fallen in with an enemy, we should have been out of their way altogether." His seven shipmates would have been free at last.[26]

A MURDEROUS MOB

On July 19 Pensacola deputy sheriff James Gonzales met the *General Taylor* in a small boat and took Jonathan aboard, rowing him eight miles through a rainstorm to the port's main wharves. Undeterred by the cloudburst, a large, agitated, jeering crowd had "thronged the streets and sidewalks," awaiting the return of the now-chained "slave stealer." In his own narrative of events Jonathan downplayed the animosity of the crowd toward him when he came ashore, but other evidence suggests that hostility ran high. Jonathan admitted later that he had received "the sneers and scoffs of the popular rabble," surely referring to this moment. He also admitted to Reverend Kittredge that he "would have been lynched by the frenzied crowd" at the docks but for the protection of the deputy, who drew his revolver and kept "the infuriated mob at bay." Fellow abolitionist Parker Pillsbury, who knew Jonathan well and had heard his stories of escape and capture, agreed: if not for the deputy's protection, Jonathan "would have been murdered by the exasperated crowd" at the wharf.[27]

Jonathan was taken first to Pensacola's courthouse on the west side of Palafox Street, directly up from the wharves, then to the "Spanish jail," a two-story "plain brick building," located at the corner of Alcaniz Street, near Calaboza Square, where he would spend the next eleven months incarcerated as a political prisoner. The building itself was eighteen by thirty-six feet with two rooms on each floor. Upstairs lived city marshal and jailor Francis Torward, his wife Maria, and their six children, along with their enslaved cook Joaquina and her six-month-old son. Torward secured Jonathan to the jail cell wall by "a large ring bolt" attached to a twenty-two-pound iron chain. Around Jonathan's ankle was riveted a five-pound shackle. His feet and legs were so swollen that the irons were "partly buried under the flesh." Moreover, the prisoner was still sick, suffering from malaria—headaches, stomach pain, aching bones, and "violent chills and fevers." His cell had no bed, no table, and no chair, although he did eventually get some straw for bedding. One small, barred window offered the only glimmer against darkness.[28]

Robert C. Caldwell, the local enslaver from whom Silas Scott, Harry Scott, and Moses Johnson had sailed away, soon paid Jonathan a visit in jail, not to confront him in anger but rather to seek his favor: he wanted to acquire Jonathan's whaleboat, which had just been brought to dock from the *Reform*. Jonathan agreed to let him have it if he would promise not to whip Silas, Harry, and Moses for absconding. Caldwell consented to the deal and apparently kept his word. Jonathan's other worldly possessions, which had been taken aboard the *Eliza Catherine* by Captain Roberts, had been lost or, more likely, stolen, including his small, valued chest of "botanic medicines," the tools he used as a boatwright, and a spyglass. Once the prisoner had given away the boat to protect his shipmates, he was now entirely "destitute of property."[29]

On July 28, Jonathan's other comrades, Charles, Philip, and Leonard Johnson, and Anthony Catlett joined him in jail. (Silas Scott, Harry Scott, and Moses Johnson had been released directly to Caldwell.) These four had no legal rights and therefore, unlike Jonathan, had no scheduled hearing before the magistrate. Instead, their enslavers had sent them directly to Torward, who was not only the jailor but the town whipper, charging seventy-five cents ($30 in 2024) to administer a flogging. In this instance he delivered to each fugitive fifty blows with a wooden "paddle-whip," followed by multiple lashes from a cowhide whip. Jonathan heard every crack, gasp, and cry.

After six weeks in jail, Jonathan experienced a new and especially intimate moment of horror. One of his seven shipmates, Silas Scott, the man who had first approached him about the collective escape, was accused of theft and thrown into jail in the room next door. The accusation by the vindictive George Willis may have come from lingering anger about Scott's leadership in the escape. Scott now faced fierce punishment, which he was unwilling to accept. He had somehow managed to smuggle into jail with him a razor, which he used to cut open his throat and belly. He expired a couple of hours later. The item he was accused of stealing was soon found, having been misplaced by another person. Jonathan was subsequently moved into the adjoining room, where he lived amid the heart's blood of his shipmate's suicide.[30]

"A GLORIOUS TRIAL"

On November 14, 1844, Jonathan's grim jailhouse existence was interrupted by his trial for "slave stealing." In phase one of trial, the judge and jury tried Jonathan, whom they described as a "laborer," for the theft of Silas Scott, Anthony Catlett, Moses Johnson, and Charles Johnson and the loss of their labor to their enslavers. A large, buzzing crowd filled the courtroom. Anticipating the event, Jonathan's friend back in Massachusetts, Elkanah Nickerson Jr., wrote him in a letter: "My dear brother, you have a glorious trial; make a right use of it." A trial about slave escape in a place like Florida was inevitably high political drama.[31]

Yet Jonathan was not one for drama. His courtroom presence was humble, calm, cooperative, and confident. He was polite, even generous, toward his tormentors. He felt that some townspeople, perhaps even some of the jurors, had sympathy for him, partly out of personal acquaintance, partly, he hoped, because they shared his ideas about slavery. Moreover, he was certain in his heart that even though he had broken the law, he was entirely free of guilt, for his conscience told him so. John M'Kinlay, editor of the *Pensacola Gazette*, reported hearing Jonathan say "he had done nothing wrong, and that he would do the same thing again if he had the opportunity." Jonathan was accordingly nonchalant about the charges. In his view, what had happened was simple and straightforward: seven men who wanted to leave Pensacola, which they had every right to do, had asked to board his vessel and go away with him. He agreed to take them, and he felt complete moral justification in doing so, let the law be damned.[32]

The jury, which included several enslavers, disagreed. After consulting for only thirty minutes, they found Jonathan guilty of "stealing" ringleader Silas Scott and sentenced Jonathan "to be branded on the right hand with the letters SS." The court would treat Jonathan like a slave, degrading him through a practice normally reserved for those held in bondage. The jury took another two to three hours to return a second guilty verdict on the other three cases, sentencing Jonathan to serve fifteen days in jail (he had already served four months), to stand in the town pillory for one hour, and to pay a fine of $150 ($6,000 in 2024). He would of course be remanded to jail because he was indigent and could not pay the fine. The second set of punishments to which Jonathan was sentenced was relatively mild considering the seriousness of the "crime."[33]

At ten in the morning, two days later, Deputy Sheriff Gonzales arrived at the jail to take Jonathan to receive his punishments. Jonathan would normally have walked to the pillory with his wide, rolling sailor's gait. At six feet, he was considered sturdy and tremendously strong from a life of hard labor at sea. Now Jonathan was rail thin, weakened by illness and the four months he had already spent chained in jail. Not long ago "almost a skeleton"—he quipped that the mosquitoes in his jail cell had no flesh to feast on—he had trouble walking on his own.[34]

A sizeable crowd had gathered at the pillory, located in front of the courthouse, to observe the public humiliation. Jonathan bent over and Gonzales locked his head between the two blocks of wood carved out to fit around his neck. The sun blazed above. The deputy took mercy on Jonathan, placing a handkerchief on his head to protect him from the sun. In the run-up to the event, Jonathan's greatest enemy, the big slaveholder George Willis, whom he described as a "haughty, overbearing and cruel man," tried to bribe some local boys to pelt Jonathan's head with rotten eggs, but none of them would take his money. Willis would therefore administer the insult himself. He removed the handkerchief and splattered the eggs on the top of his head. A young boy cried out "Shame!" angering Willis, who tried to get him arrested but failed. Several others present responded with what Jonathan described as "a burst of indignation." He had some sympathizers after all.[35]

After an hour Gonzales escorted Jonathan to the courtroom for the branding of his hand. Court authorities had encountered unexpected difficulties carrying out the sentence, which required the forging of a special branding iron. They approached a local blacksmith, who replied to the request with anger barely tempered by politeness: "No, sir," he insisted, "I make branding irons to brand horses, mules and cattle with; but to burn into the flesh of a fellow man,—by the living God I will not." A second blacksmith agreed to make the iron but refused to heat it up for application to Jonathan's hand. He swore that "there was but one fire in the universe fit to heat an iron for such a use": those flames, everyone knew, roared in hell. These metalworkers probably knew Jonathan; indeed, they may have worked with him in the Navy shipyard. The court officers would have to heat the instrument of torture themselves.[36]

Jonathan knew well the man who would wield the brand: Ebenezer Dorr IV, a Northerner from Maine, who had married into a slaveholding Southern family and been appointed United States marshal of the western district of the territory of Florida. Jonathan entered the prisoner's box, where Dorr began to tie his right hand to the front railing. Jonathan objected, explaining that there was no need to restrain his hand as he would "hold still." Dorr refused the offer. He wanted to make sure everything went as planned, so he tied the hand tightly, in full view of the crowd that assembled in the courtroom to witness the grisly punishment. It was no common thing for a white man to be branded in the antebellum United States.

Dorr took the red-hot branding iron and applied it to the ball of Jonathan's right hand for fifteen to twenty seconds. Jonathan described the moment: when the brand hit the flesh, "It made a spattering noise, like a handful of salt in the fire, as the skin seared and gave way to the hot iron." Some of the people in attendance recoiled in horror from the shocking sight and sound, but George Willis, who claimed ownership of three of the men who had sailed with Jonathan toward freedom, "feasted his eyes upon it, apparently with great delight." Although the pain was severe, Jonathan absorbed the torture without complaining, resisting, flinching, or crying out. After the branding Jonathan was escorted back to his jail cell.

After his trial and conviction, Pensacola authorities branded Jonathan Walker's hand with "S. S." for "slave stealer." He served eleven months in jail as a political prisoner.

Phase two of the trial, concerning the "theft" of the three remaining men, Harry Scott and Philip and Leonard Johnson, took place six months later, on May 9, 1845, by which time abolitionist groups were trying to free Jonathan from jail. The authorities hoped to extend Jonathan's incarceration, but the members of the jury had other ideas. For the "detestable" crime of "slave stealing," the jury found Jonathan guilty but imposed only a light fine of $5 per case ($200 in 2024),

which could be paid off easily with funds raised by Northern abolitionists. Jonathan called their finding against him a "mild and humane verdict." His decision to appeal to the finer feelings of the jury
had paid off.

THE MOTLEY CREW IN JAIL

Jonathan spent nearly a year "caged up . . . as a strange animal" in the
Pensacola jail. It was a brutal yet instructive experience, allowing Jonathan to observe and learn a great deal more about the sadistic es-
sence of slavery. What made the biggest impression on him was the
casual, deeply pervasive violence of slave society. He later observed
that bondage required enslavers to "surround the accursed system with
cow-hides, gags, and thumbscrews; with chains, prisons, and starvation; with edge-tools, halter and buck shot; with branding irons,
muskets, and blood hounds' teeth." He saw the hardware of bondage
used daily on people of all colors.[37]

Pensacola's jail was a violent place and a busy one. More than a
hundred prisoners passed through during Jonathan's eleven months
behind bars. One was a Native American fugitive who had escaped
slavery in Alabama only to be arrested in Pensacola. Jonathan noted,
"I frequently saw and talked with this man," but he did not say what
they discussed. When he wrote about the encounter in 1846, he used
it to preface his view that "the Indians have always been wickedly and
cruelly treated by the white Americans, ever since they have had the
power to do it." He went on to denounce the role of the United States
in the Seminole Wars in central Florida and added mournfully that
he "saw some of the Indians on board the steamboats while being
transported from their homes to the far west," a maritime "trail of
tears." He concluded with a plea for solidarity for Native Americans,
a "greatly abused class of our fellow-men."[38]

Jonathan also met a lot of fellow sailors in jail. They cycled through for a variety of reasons, as he noted in his diary. Many had deserted either naval or merchant ships, taking what Jonathan and other sailors called "French leave." One seaman was sent to jail for dereliction of duty, "not being down to the boat on time to go on board." Two more were brought in for drunkenness and fighting, no uncommon practices among sailors. Two from the brig *Hazard* found themselves in jail on Christmas Day for mutiny; they had "refused to do duty on board."[39]

Many sailors also came to visit Jonathan as he lay in chains, not to see how this "animal" called an abolitionist looked, but rather to express "their active and manifest sympathies" and "to see in what way they could contribute to my comfort, or ameliorate my condition." An old shipmate from New York remitted $25 (almost a thousand dollars in 2024). Other sailors, many of them "entire strangers," cheerfully opened their purses to him, enabling him to buy food to supplement the meager fare offered by the jailor. Yet another mariner had apparently witnessed the branding of Jonathan's hand and showed up at the jail to donate money and to express "his sympathy in my behalf," Jonathan recalled. A boatswain from the steamship *General Taylor*, the vessel that transported Jonathan from Key West to Pensacola, "made me a present of a pair of blankets." Had the two men met on Jonathan's voyage back to Pensacola, the boatswain powerless under the circumstances to help his brother tar? The sense of solidarity among sailors was strong.[40]

The majority of people Jonathan met in jail were enslaved individuals, who, like the sailors, were locked up for a variety of reasons—staying out too late, attempting to "steal fruit," or simply "not doing enough work." The common theme of most jailings was resistance. Many of the prisoners were runaways or, if younger, "truants." On August 12, 1844, noted Jonathan, "A fugitive slave man [was] caught and committed." Ten days later he was "taken out" and returned to his enslaver in Alabama. Several were jailed for other practices of resistance. Torward gave one enslaved man ten blows for "disobedience."

An enslaved woman was jailed when she tried to "defend herself when about to be whipped by her mistress"; this affront earned twenty-four blows with the paddle and another dozen with the cowhide whip. Another "colored woman" (who may have been free) fought back against a naval officer who had tried to flog her; she went to jail for her daring. Jonathan took a special interest in an enslaved man who was jailed on January 10, 1845, after leaving town to be with his wife and children over Christmas—and staying away too long because he fell sick. His angry enslaver tried to sell the man in both New Orleans and Mobile, but he proved "too old to meet with a ready sale." Back in Pensacola, the man was given a brutal beating—twenty-four blows with the paddle and another thirty with the cowhide whip—in order "to gratify his drunken mistress," observed Jonathan.[41]

Jonathan's term of eleven months in a Southern jail confirmed and deepened his abolitionist views of slavery and indeed radicalized them. He personally had been tortured by the "Slave Power," which increased his sensitivity and sympathy for others who had it worse. The insults of his case continued right up to the moment of his release, when he discovered that he was being charged "rent" for occupying his jail cell. In the end he (or more precisely his abolitionist supporters) paid $600 (almost $24,000 in 2024) in fines and fees for his liberation. The payment paled in comparison to the public humiliation of standing in the pillory and the violent branding of his hand. Jonathan walked out of jail a free man on June 16, 1845.

THE POLITICAL AFTERLIFE
OF ESCAPE BY SEA

After Jonathan's conviction in November 1844, it took a couple of weeks for the news to make its way back to Boston. William Lloyd Garrison fumed over the treatment of his fellow abolitionist by the proslavery government of Florida and immediately began to publicize the case in *The Liberator*, beginning December 6, 1844. Other antislavery newspapers followed suit, as outcries and appeals for money to free Jonathan circulated widely. Sailors carried the news of Jonathan's ordeal across the Atlantic, reaching no less a person than the grand old man of British abolition, the eighty-four-year-old Thomas Clarkson. The British and Foreign Anti-Slavery Society wrote a letter in support of Jonathan and in condemnation of the Florida authorities, who in turn howled against the "vicious fanaticism" of "foreign incendiaries."[42]

The men who ran the government of Florida soon did more than howl. After juries awarded Jonathan lenient punishments, the governor of Florida, John Branch, commissioned a review of the law against "slave stealing" in Florida, to be undertaken by I. Ferguson Jr. and Walker Anderson, the U.S. attorney for West Florida who prosecuted Jonathan. The report recommended a new law against "negro-stealing" as not merely a crime against property but a "species of treason against the State—a direct assault upon the very existence of our institutions." After Florida gained statehood in March 1845, its legislature enacted the death penalty for anyone caught assisting runaways. This might have been called the "Jonathan Walker law." The history Jonathan and his seven shipmates made from below produced a fierce counterattack from above.[43]

The actions taken by Jonathan and his comrades also underlined the failure of the local system of policing the docks and the motley crew—a fact that did not go unnoticed by John M'Kinlay and his staff at the *Pensacola Gazette*. Where, they wanted to know, were the police and patrols that were supposed to keep their eyes peeled for subversion on the waterfront? How was it that "numbers of negroes can prowl unmolested" along the docks at all hours of the night? Where were the officers paid by the town government to make sure that "no negro is at large after bell ring?" The newspaper demanded that the mayor and his alderman take up these issues and implement serious reforms.[44]

Jonathan left jail in a terrible state of health. A fellow abolitionist noted that he could no longer withstand hardships and that his "constitution is broken." Another explained that he had "a constitution much impaired by great exposure, repeated sickness, and severe treatment, the dependence and wants of a large family, and bills he cannot meet." He returned to a "rough and humble cabin" in Plymouth, Massachusetts, where he soon began to house runaways who had escaped by sea. Sadly, he was too poor to be able to do this for very long and had to help the fugitives along to the homes of others who had greater means to care for them.[45]

Jonathan left jail weak in body and poor in material goods, but by the summer of 1845 he was a celebrity. On July 24, 1845, more than a thousand people showed up in Lyceum Hall, Boston, to hear him speak and, perhaps more important, to see his branded hand. He joined the abolitionist lecture circuit, speaking with Frederick Douglass in New Bedford, a leading port for runaways where both men had lived and worked earlier in their lives. Over the next four years Jonathan was constantly in motion, speaking in more than a hundred towns in New England and New York. For many of these events he joined forces with John S. Jacobs, the brother of Harriet and a seaman recently returned from a long whaling voyage. Jonathan denounced Southern slavery and addressed his fellow workers about complicity and liberation: "You, my working friends," he explained, must understand that the "chain which you have been helping to secure on the limbs of the southern chattled slaves, has its other end fastened upon your own."[46]

Jonathan's fame reached a new peak in late summer 1845, when John Greenleaf Whittier published "The Branded Hand" to celebrate his heroism and to make him a martyr for the antislavery campaign. "Welcome home again, brave seaman!" began the poem. Whittier knew that Jonathan's work life as a sailor had been crucial to his radicalism: "In thy lone and long night watches, sky above and wave below, / Thou did'st learn a higher wisdom than the babbling school-men know." He alluded to Jonathan's antinomianism when he referred to the higher law that God had written, not in Southern Black Codes but on "the great heart of humanity." But what interested the poet most of all was the hand.[47]

"Is the tyrant's brand upon thee?" asked Whittier. Cheering Jonathan for his "front of calm endurance" against "the fiery shafts of pain," Whittier drew on Christian martyrology as he likened Jonathan and his branding to Jesus and the stigmata. His poem transformed the scarred marks of shame into a symbol to rally abolitionists everywhere now and ever after:

> Why, that brand is highest honor—than its traces never yet
> Upon old armorial hatchments was a prouder blazon set;
> And thy unborn generations, as they tread our rocky strand,
> Shall tell with pride the story of their father's branded hand!

The sailor's hardened, branded hand, according to Whittier, must become a standard, a flag, to inspire freedom seekers and at the same time to send a fearsome message to the "tyrants of the slave-land" who "shall tremble at that sign." When Whittier's poem was adapted to song, the branded hand achieved even wider circulation. Rochester schoolteacher Julia Wilbur saw Jonathan and heard the song in March 1848: "Whoever heard that singing I think can never forget the 'Branded Hand.' It was very beautiful indeed, both in sentiment + execution."[48]

After Whittier published the poem and abolitionists sang the song in churches and political meetings, Jonathan's scarred, disembodied hand became an eerie symbol of the abolitionist movement, appearing in books, magazines, newspapers, and broadsides. It became a holy symbol of the antislavery cause. Thousands turned out to Jonathan's lectures to hear his story and to witness his marks of torture.

Many saw him as a Christian martyr. He referred to his scars as the satanic "mark of the beast."[49]

Frederick Douglass recalled Jonathan's electrifying effect on mostly white antislavery audiences: "I well remember the sensation produced by the exhibition of his branded hand. It was one of the few atrocities of slavery that roused the justice and humanity of the North to a death struggle with slavery." It was easy, Douglass claimed, to see in Jonathan's "simple, honest face" that Southern instruments of torture could leave "no trace of infamy." The seaman's "example of self-sacrifice nerved us all to more heroic endeavor in behalf of the slave." Jonathan was an inspiration within and beyond the movement. Yet the popular fascination with his hand betrayed a racial subtext: Northern audiences in a republic based on slavery were shocked that a white man had been branded.[50]

Amid civil war in 1864 Jonathan ventured south to work as a teacher among the recently emancipated people. In the same year he reunited with his old friend, the Black sailor-abolitionist William P. Powell, whom he had probably met through the Methodist missionary group the American Seamen's Friend Society. The year before his death—May Day 1878—it was reported that he was "living in extreme poverty in a forlorn shanty" in Michigan. He remained utterly committed to radical principles. He wrote in his children's book, "I have suffered a great deal myself for the slaves, and am willing to suffer more if I can do anything for their emancipation."[51]

Final words about Jonathan Walker belong to Frederick Douglass, another who knew the maritime system of escape intimately. In 1878 he reflected on his late comrade's life:

> Yes, I knew Jonathan Walker, and knew him well; knew him to love him and to honor him as a true man, a friend to humanity, a brave but noiseless lover of liberty, not only for himself but for all men; one who possessed the qualities of a hero and martyr, and was ready to take any risks to his own safety and personal ease to save his fellow-men from slavery.

Douglass understood the centrality of Jonathan's maritime experience to his militant abolitionism: "It was on the free, dashing billows of the Atlantic, when the voices of nature spoke to his soul with the grandest emphasis of love and truth; and responsive to those voices, as well as to those of his own heart, he welcomed the panting fugitives from slavery to the safety of his own deck,—though in doing so he exposed himself to stocks, prison, branding irons, and it might have been to death." Douglass knew that Jonathan had almost died on the freedom voyage, and that he was willing to make the ultimate sacrifice for the antislavery cause. Everything he did, he did with quiet, courageous, and unshakeable dignity and resolve.[52]

Douglass also compared Jonathan to John Brown and the other great martyrs of the abolitionist movement. The sailor belonged in memory alongside Brown and other "notable men who suffered at the hands of the slave power" such as the murdered Elijah P. Lovejoy and Abraham Lincoln. The reference to Brown also contained a more literal truth: Jonathan was a forerunner of Brown in the development of aggressive, militant, direct-action abolitionism. Jonathan wondered, "When did tyrants, as a class, ever repent, of their own accord, of their usurpations, and take their station among their vassals or their slaves? And is it not a home-born truth, that They who would be free, Themselves must strike the first blow?" Deeply convinced of the truth of their cause, both Walker and Brown ventured boldly into the South, taking radical action to make real the promises of freedom.[53]

But Douglass knew perfectly well that despite his celebrity, Jonathan would not be as well remembered as his exalted company. He offered a reason why: Jonathan "was one who felt satisfied with the applause of his own soul. What he attempted was not intended to attract public notice." It was, rather, meant to secure freedom for those entitled to it. Douglass concluded that the "true-hearted" humble sailor "is not less entitled to grateful memory than the most honored of them all." Jonathan Walker's escape, trial, imprisonment, and most of all his branding, made him one of abolition's best-known figures during the late 1840s. His actions brought the long, secretive history of escape by sea to national and international attention. The sailor's hand, hard from labor and mutilated by the "Slave Power," became a central symbol of the struggle against slavery.[54]

Chapter 6

William P. Powell
and Solidarity at Sea

The word traveled quickly from the docks at the end of New York's Roosevelt Street, a mere block and a half to the Colored Sailors Home at 61 Cherry Street. On the morning of June 27, 1847, Black dockworkers boarded the Brazilian barque *Lembrança* to unload coffee. They discovered three enslaved people aboard the vessel: two men, a sailor and a cook, and a woman who cared for the wife and children of the captain. The dockworkers knew that New York had abolished slavery twenty years earlier and that the principle had been established in law to free enslaved people who traveled to the state. They also knew where to go with the news.[1]

The keeper of the Colored Sailors Home, Black abolitionist William P. Powell, received the message and rushed to the docks. He brashly boarded the ship to look around, pretending to be the New York merchant to whom the Brazilian cargo had been shipped. As a former sailor, he knew his way around a ship. He strolled around, examining the rigging, the windlass, and the pumps as a merchant curious about the quality of his shipper might wish to do. As he inspected the coffee beans, he saw "two able-bodied Africans," both in their early twenties and dressed in blue nankeen, hoisting bags out of the hold.

Standing just forward of the cook's galley, he saw one of the Africans coming along the starboard side of the windlass. "I asked him," recalled William, "in the Portuguese language if he were a slave?" (Years earlier, the cosmopolitan William had sailed to, and spent time in, Brazil.) The man replied affirmatively. William then asked if there were any other enslaved people aboard the ship. The man again said yes: a man and a woman. William then "told him he was no longer a slave," and that he and his friends "were free, according to law." William urged him to go to back to work and to "say nothing." The three "should be free before sunset."

The news leapt from dock to dock like wildfire. A crowd of Black workers, with a few white abolitionists, gathered at the Roosevelt Street dock and contemplated an armed rescue. William left the ship and contacted Louis Napoleon, an African American porter who played a key role in assisting fugitives in New York, and asked him to apply to a judge for a writ of habeas corpus, something Napoleon was well practiced at doing. Two hours later José da Costa, José da Rocha, and Maria da Costa stood in front of Judge Charles P. Daley, who remanded them back to the captain of the *Lembrança*. The captain, who was also their enslaver, had maintained that the men were members of the crew and that their status was protected by the laws of Brazil, whose consul he summoned to bolster the claim. Two New York city policemen returned the men to the ship and shackled them together to prevent their escape. Dockers and sailors jeered and protested. Meanwhile abolitionist attorneys John Jay II and John Hopper rushed to defend the enslaved men, seeking a second habeas writ, and raising various points of law. After several days of legal wrangling and pending an appeal to the state Supreme Court, the enslaved Africans ended up in New York's Eldridge Street jail.[2]

The African cook to whom William spoke was not José da Costa, as his enslaver claimed, but rather Mahommah Gardo Baquaqua, born

The Eldridge Street jail in New York City housed many maritime fugitives, including Mahommah G. Baquaqua before his liberation by abolitionists in 1847.

in city of Djougou (in the northern part of what is now the Republic of Benin). He had been enslaved and transported to Ouidah in the Kingdom of Dahomey, forced onto a slaver, shipped to Pernambuco, Brazil, then on to Rio de Janeiro. His enslaver shipped him as the cook of the *Lembrança* for a sixty-day voyage to New York. Baquaqua had been seeking his freedom long before he met William. Like the New York dockworkers, he knew that slavery had been abolished in New York; this, he thought, was a "happy land" where he might gain his freedom. It is fortunate that William knew Portuguese because Baquaqua knew only one word of English, "F-r-e-e," which an English sailor taught him on the passage to Manhattan.[3]

The morning after they were incarcerated, Baquaqua and the other man were nowhere to be found. They had disappeared from their cell overnight. The city was abuzz with curiosity, but none of the newspapers could explain the mystery. Again, William was the man in the know. Years later he told the tale. A fellow abolitionist had recently been locked up for debt. Someone got a message to him that he must

AN INTERESTING NARRATIVE.
BIOGRAPHY
OF
MAHOMMAH G. BAQUAQUA,
A NATIVE OF ZOOGOO, IN THE INTERIOR OF AFRICA
(A Convert to Christianity.)
WITH A DESCRIPTION OF THAT PART OF THE WORLD;
INCLUDING THE
Manners and Customs of the Inhabitants,

BY SAMUEL MOORE, ESQ.

MAHOMMAH G. BAQUAQUA.

DETROIT:
1854.

After William P. Powell helped him to gain his freedom in 1847, Mahommah G. Baquaqua joined the antislavery movement and wrote an autobiography published in 1854.

help to liberate the two African prisoners, so the abolitionist sat down with their prison guard and a bottle of brandy. After a few hours the guard fell asleep, "dead drunk," with the cell keys under his pillow. The abolitionist gently took the keys, unlocked the prisoners, let the men out of their cells, and returned the keys to their rightful place. The next morning the hungover guard had no idea what had happened, nor did anyone else outside a small circle of conspirators. He suggested that perhaps the men had escaped through an underground sewer.

William and other abolitionists were waiting in a coach outside the jail. They whisked the men in and sped off to Boston, where they arrived the next morning. Boston abolitionists then took over and completed an international circuit of maritime escape by placing the fugitives aboard a ship bound for Haiti, where they would be beyond the reach of American slaveholder law once and for all. Dockworkers and sailors had connected wharves and ships over thousands of nautical miles from Rio to New York, Boston, and Cap-Haitien.[4]

William P. Powell was a crucial although little-known figure on the receiving end of the Atlantic circuit of escape. He assisted many hundreds who traveled to freedom by sea from 1832 through the end of the Civil War. Joining the American Anti-Slavery Society in Boston in 1833, he was a loyal comrade of William Lloyd Garrison. As a committed abolitionist he shared the lecture podium at antislavery events with Frederick Douglass, John S. Jacobs, and Jonathan Walker. The world of maritime escape was intimate, but not always harmonious. In 1851 William wrote a maritime skit in which an "old salt" (himself) fiercely criticized "green hand" Fred (Douglass) as they worked together on the good ship *Abolition* on a voyage toward "human rights."[5]

Having sailed the Atlantic and the Pacific himself and lived close to the dockworkers and sailors of New Bedford and New York as the proprietor of boardinghouses for Black sailors, William was the quintessential waterfront intellectual and activist. He was a leader of the free Black community in both ports for decades: he had come up from the bottom, earned the respect of his peers, and played a guiding role in abolitionist and labor organizations. Combining the struggle against slavery with advocacy on behalf of Black seamen, William promoted maritime solidarity in the broadest sense throughout his life. He made the Colored Sailors Home a new kind of abolitionist organization, where the struggles of enslaved and free workers intersected and enriched each other.[6]

CLASS TRAINING

William P. Powell was born free in New York in 1807 to an enslaved man, Edward Powell, who was "held a slave for life by the laws of New York," and a free Native American woman whose name has been lost to posterity. When William applied for a passport in 1849, he described himself as a man "of mulatto color, but of Indian extraction." He had already married a Native American woman and described one of his daughters as a "lineal" descendent of the Abenaki people of Plymouth, Massachusetts. In the census of 1870, William and two of his children were listed as "mulatto," while his wife and seven other children were denoted as "Indian." Even though he identified throughout his activist life as Black, it would be more accurate to call his origins Afro-Indigenous.[7]

William's education began with "the commonest rudiments of school marms, and ignorant pedigogue tutors." At age thirteen he apprenticed to a shoemaker and added an "F.R.C."—First Rate Cobbler— to his credentials. Dissatisfied, he joined the "Sons of Vulcan," where the sparks of the blacksmith's forge quickly destroyed his clothes, making him an "F.R.S."—Fellow of the Ragged Society. Thwarted by the prejudice of the white masters of the anvil, he turned to the waterfront and entered a line of work that is "happily open to all, rich or poor, high or low, black or white," and soon obtained another degree, "C.D.L.": Common Dock Laborer. Soon thereafter, around the age of twenty, he joined the "Sons of Neptune," among whom he became a "First Rate Sailor." William's alma mater was "the University of Negro Slavery," which awarded him a "N.B.N." degree, which stood for Nothing but a Negro. William concluded that he got, not a "classical education," but extensive "class training."[8]

William first went to sea in 1829, sailing to the Antilles in the Caribbean. His initial voyage was a profound experience, revealing to him the truth expressed by his contemporary fellow sailor Herman Melville: "As everyone knows, meditation and water are wedded for ever." Thus began William's "philosophic toil of life" as a worker-intellectual. His labor at sea prompted lifelong "sober reflection." Awed by the Atlantic Ocean's sublime combination of fury and beauty, he delved deeply into the issues of his day.[9]

William soon "obtained a roving commission" and traveled the world. During his five years at sea, he acquired the sailor's ethos of solidarity, born and bred in a dangerous environment that required workers to entrust their lives to each other daily, and the cosmopolitanism that developed from working with shipmates who came, as he described them, "from every tribe under heaven." His time at sea would shape his worldview and guide him like the North Star for the rest of his life. The deep-sea sailing ship would be his most formative school.[10]

One enduring lesson William learned at sea was how the "generous" and "free-hearted" sailor was exploited and oppressed: though not technically enslaved, the seaman "was looked upon only as an article of merchandise" to be bought and sold internationally "from his ship to a rum-selling boarding-house—to the brothel and those sinks of pollution, where he is exchanged for what he is worth, until, like a depreciated currency, he is shipped at a discount to some foreign port, and passed off as current coin." The sailor's labor was a commodity, a kind of currency exchanged on a global labor market. Degradation and immiseration were built into his line of work. And yet the seaman connected the world and provided the "common necessaries of life."[11]

In 1828 William moved to New Bedford, Massachusetts, the Fugitive's Gibraltar and a central place in the maritime struggle to escape bondage. A year later Boston waterfront slopseller David Walker published his *Appeal*, calling on sailors to carry the revolutionary word to enslaved people around the Atlantic. Walker's manifesto electrified Black workers up and down the Atlantic coast, some of whom would have known him personally through their travels. William soon got involved in antislavery activism and at the same time took an interest in the temperance movement. He was proud that Black sailors had circulated *Walker's Appeal*.[12]

William and many other Black seamen worked in the transoceanic industry for which New Bedford was famous worldwide: whaling. Thinking back to one of his voyages, William recalled "climbing up to the top gallant cross trees of a whale ship, there to sit two hours every day during a two years' cruise, watching the ripple of every wave, to detect the movements of monster whales." He also remembered how whaling vessels became engines of education. Aboard the vessel came "unlettered," ignorant men who nonetheless had a fierce "thirst . . . for mental cultivation." The forecastle was transformed into a "schoolroom" where educated sailors taught their less-privileged mates reading, writing, arithmetic, and even navigation. William was surely talking about himself when he made these remarks.[13]

William settled in New Bedford and made the port his home. In 1832 he married Mercy O. Haskins, an eighteen-year-old woman who traced her matrilineal genealogy among the Abenaki peoples of Massachusetts back eight generations. Two years later William and Mercy opened a boardinghouse for Black seamen at 109–111 Ray Street, placing their first advertisement for the establishment in the *New Bedford Mercury* on June 9, 1837. (Frederick and Anna Douglass would live at 111 Ray Street in 1841, after William and Mercy had moved to New York.) William began what would prove to be a life-long endeavor: to provide food, shelter, clothing, and comfort to Black sailors and at the same time to fight those he and other sailors called "landsharks"—the crimps, crooks, tavern-keepers, and land-lords who preyed upon sailors in port. By September 1837 William had moved to 94 North Water Street and announced a new name: the Seamen's Temperance Boarding House and Shipping Office. William would now connect sailors to captains and merchants he felt would treat them fairly, benefitting the men and himself as a ship-ping agent. For the next thirty years his boardinghouses would serve as shape-up halls for maritime workers.[14]

William's twin lifelong engagements—maritime escape and the struggles of Black sailors—began in New Bedford. He was much more outspoken about the latter than the former for an obvious rea-son: the work of helping people to escape bondage by sea was illegal and therefore clandestine. Only later in life did William freely discuss the subject. In 1874, after he had moved to San Francisco and taken a position at the African American newspaper the *Elevator*, William spoke at a public memorial to honor his recently deceased friend and abolitionist comrade Lewis Berry, who had worked with him in New Bedford on the "silent, secret, mysterious road" of maritime escape.

William first met Berry in 1832, when both were working on the New Bedford waterfront. The relationship endured and strengthened after William opened his safe house for runaways. He would quietly continue the work until slavery was abolished. William named Berry, ten other men, and himself as the "scar-worn old guards" who "controlled the road running from the extreme South" by safe ships to places of refuge in New Bedford, Nantucket, and Boston. These brave men "delivered the fugitive passengers with safety, security, and dispatch to the land of freedom."[15]

NEW YORK'S EAST RIVER DOCKS, 1839

William left no record to indicate why he decided to move to New York in late 1839, but the port's rising economic power and its large and growing number of Black seamen likely attracted him. He no doubt received encouragement from the American Seamen's Friend Society (ASFS), a Methodist missionary group established in 1828, to move to New York to open a Colored Sailors Home. The ASFS had opened a home at 190 Cherry Street two years earlier, but white racial prejudice apparently kept Black sailors away. William might also have seen an opportunity to expand his antislavery activism, which indeed he did immediately, helping to found the Garrisonian Manhattan Anti-Slavery Society in October 1840. New York's big fleet of ships going to and from Southern ports would allow him to assist many more seaborne fugitives. William and Mercy moved to New York and opened a boardinghouse at 70 John Street, near Gold Street, about six blocks from the East River wharves.[16]

William placed the first advertisement for the new establishment in the *Colored American* on December 7, 1840. With the assistance of the ASFS, William appealed to "Cooks, Stewards, and Seamen"— the only positions Black seafarers could usually get within the racialized shipboard division of labor—to stay at the new boardinghouse.

From the beginning William worked as a broker to secure work for sailors on outward-bound vessels in New York. His advertisement promised those "who come to this house will have their choice of ships, and the highest wages." He was so confident in his ability to find well-paid work, he added that for anyone "not satisfied after remaining twenty-four hours, no charge will be made."[17]

Over the next quarter century William's Colored Sailors Home (CSH) would occupy five different buildings, all on the Lower East Side of Manhattan near the East River docks. William apparently did not care for the first location on John Street, for he stayed there only six months, moving closer to the river's edge at 61 Cherry Street, down the street from the larger sailors home. William operated the CSH with both success and significant financial difficulty at this location for nine years. On May 1, 1849, he moved to 330 Pearl Street and remained there until he sailed with his family to Liverpool

two years later to educate his four oldest sons. Fellow abolitionist Albro Lyons took over the home and ran it for several more years, moving to a smaller building on Vandewater Street before finally giving up the project. After William returned to New York in late 1861 amid the Civil War, he opened a new home at 2

The Colored Sailors Home, operated by Black sailor-abolitionist William P. Powell at 330 Pearl Street in Manhattan's Lower East Side, was a busy depot for seaborne fugitives.

Dover Street and operated it for nine more years through numerous ups and downs, including a vicious racist attack during the Draft Riots of July 1863.[18]

"THE REFUGE"

Late at night a Black sailor with a runaway in hand stepped guardedly off a ship docked at Corlears Hook on the East River. Based on a tip from a shipmate, he made his way to William P. Powell's Colored Sailors Home. What kind of place did the seaman and the fugitive encounter?[19]

On entering the building, the visitors would have encountered William himself, an always-present, hands-on proprietor. He must have been a rather imposing man, for a physical presence would have been required to handle the tough characters of the waterfront, including the slave catchers who sniffed around the quarters. William lived in the building along with the members of his family, all of whom pitched in with their labor. A boardinghouse of fifteen rooms and forty to seventy boarders at any one time required endless cooking, cleaning, and laundry service, as well as maintenance by painters, carpenters, masons, whitewashers, and other craftsmen, although William did a fair amount of the work himself. He also hired those he called "servants," to whom he paid wages, including a "runner" to help with business communications around town. The combination of family, staff, and boarders made the CSH a busy place.

If the visitors needed clothing, as many sailors and almost all fugitives did, William would have gone to the stockroom for sailor's attire—shirts, pants, vests, stockings, and caps, most of which had been donated by women's benevolent organizations or the Marine Industrial Society (along with quilts, sheets, pillowcases, and towels). William might then have directed the visitors to a bedroom, which featured beds and mattresses rather than the bunks more commonly found in boardinghouses. Each bedroom held four or five sailors—crowded by modern standards but spacious by comparison to a ship's forecastle. William would also have offered the visitors a hot or cold bath in a specially designed bathroom, inquiring about the men's health and offering medical assistance if required. He took pride in the small number of his residents who ended up in the hospital or the cemetery.

After the visitors had rested up, William would have given them a full tour of the home, especially its drawing, dining, and living rooms. He would have explained the daily schedule: breakfast at eight, dinner at one, and tea at six. All boarders were invited to attend the prayer services the proprietor led every Wednesday evening and Sunday morning, although many of the sailors declined to do so. William's favorite part of the tour would have been to show the new boarders his well-stocked library. He hoped his residents would read the Bible and the library's many abolitionist books and pamphlets. He would have introduced the visitors to the home's weekly social and political program of lectures and discussions on the issues of the day, especially the movement against slavery so dear to William's heart. William wanted the sailors to converse with each other and to learn; self-improvement was a major theme of the home. William would also have explained the moderate fees of boarding at the home, adding that there would be no cost to anyone who was truly destitute. Those who could afford to pay should do so; most seamen could and did. No one, neither sailor nor fugitive, would be turned away.[20]

William would offer to assist the boarders in various ways, perhaps most importantly by helping them to find a ship. He promised good jobs with fair treatment, and he was apparently adept at providing both. He assisted most boarders in signing onto merchant or naval vessels. William also helped the seamen, who were known as wild and profligate binge spenders when in port, to manage their money. Some of their wages he was willing to deposit on their behalf into the

Seamen's Savings Bank. He noted in a report that he had also routed $5,000 in wages to the sailors' "aged parents and families." The CSH was in some ways a miniature welfare state.

The visitors would have seen that most of the boarders were Black sailors; it was the Colored Sailors Home after all. But the home was not reserved exclusively for people of color. William frequently advertised the place as simply a "Seamen's Home" without designation of race and wrote in a report of 1863 that he had taken in a "white orphan boy" and "a white man, 2d mate sick and destitute with his family." When Philadelphia abolitionist Robert Purvis visited the home in 1849, he recommended that all Black and unprejudiced white sailors make the place their "Head quarters," as indeed some did. William also invited "friends of the slave"—that is, abolitionists of any color— to patronize the establishment whenever they visited New York.[21]

William would have made clear to the visitors the nature of his home by specifying precisely what it was *not*: a place of "profanity, drunkenness, vile books, cards, lewd songs, gambling, mischief, and mutiny," or so claimed the Methodist missionaries of the American Seamen's Friend Society, with which William was affiliated. That is to say, the CSH was dramatically unlike most sailor's boardinghouses, which featured bars, prostitutes, card games, swearing, fights, and boisterous disorder of all kinds. William clearly shared some of the values of middle-class moral reformers who sought to "improve" the rougher aspects of working-class culture. William might have repeated to his visitors a declared goal of the home: "To make the *sailor* a better *man*, and the *man* a better *sailor*." In case anyone should forget the ethos of the home, its rules were, according to visitors, "conspicuously printed" on the wall of the main room in "large letters": no swearing; no intoxicating drinks; no smoking in the bedrooms; no gambling. Everything was to be orderly, neat, quiet, cheerful, and studious.[22]

It would have been clear to the visitors, even if William had not said a word, that the Colored Sailors Home was the perfect place to hide a fugitive. The doors of the home swung open at all hours of day and night for people of color who were constantly coming and going to the nearby wharves and ships. The home had a high degree of transiency: the average stay by a boarder, William noted in one of his reports, was four days. Any fugitive who arrived looking tired, beaten down, and dressed in rags after a trying voyage would have looked no different from many of the destitute seamen who routinely entered the home. Once inside and under the care of the proprietor, the fugitive would, like all the other boarders, get shelter, food, and clothing, for little or no money. The home was literally a "refuge," a "house of mercy," as William called it, a place where both sailors and sailaways could recover their health and prepare for the next voyage. The runaway would walk out the door indistinguishable from the other 2,500–3,000 Black seamen who worked in the city. Disguised by poverty on arrival and in new seafaring attire on departure, fugitives could use their new contacts to get aboard vessels for the next part of their escape. William could also get jobs for those many who already had seafaring skills. The Black sailor and the fugitive had certainly arrived at the right place.[23]

When Frederick Douglass visited the Colored Sailors Home in 1848, he called it "an Oasis in the desert, when compared with the many houses where seamen usually congregate." He was impressed by the "excellent Library and other reading-room facilities," and he commented on the conversations that transpired over meals and during free time: the sailors discussed "various questions incidental to the elevation of man." At this establishment, a place of enlightenment, he concluded, "the Banner of Reform floats conspicuous." Other visiting abolitionists made similar remarks.[24]

The very existence of the home was a victory for Black sailors. From the moment William first established the Colored Sailors Home in late 1839, he faced stiff, sometimes "violent opposition" from "the wicked designs of unprincipled men," conmen, sharps, thugs, and hard-fisted gentlemen, Black and white, who owned competing establishments. William battled crimps, pimps, alehouse keepers, landlords, and other boardinghouse proprietors—all of them, in his view, enemies of the common seaman. These landsharks used a variety of weapons, from alcohol and debt to trickery, intimidation, and violence to bilk the sailor of his wages or his money advance on a coming voyage. Sometimes William's fight was physical. On more than one occasion he was forced to "rescue [sailors] in the street from the hands" of crimps.[25]

William also battled merchants and shipowners because he regarded the "whole system of shipping sailors" as "wrong and oppressive." Sailors suffered downright "robbery!" He fought against "the abuses of many shipping offices," some of which, he noted, "extort fabulous sums for the poor privilege of signing shipping articles." At times William despaired that he was losing the battle and might have to close the boardinghouse. Yet he survived the war over maritime labor and continued the struggle to "reconstruct the shipping interest on the principle of equal and exact justice for the sailor." This commitment made him popular among waterfront workers.[26]

A NEW KIND OF SLAVERY

Between September and November 1846 William published a series of eight articles in the *National Anti-Slavery Standard* under the title "The Character and Condition of Colored Seamen." William showed how Black seafarers, the group most deeply involved in assisting enslaved people to escape by sea, were now the targets of unrelenting repression by ruling elites in each port city in every Southern state. What William called "the great anti-slavery war" raged around and through the Black seafarer, which is why he wrote the articles for an antislavery newspaper. He went on the attack against "the Southern States and their Northern apologists," many of whom lived in New York.[27]

William understood why Black seamen were considered so dangerous in Southern ports. Their very presence as free people was subversive: they embodied precisely what abolition and emancipation had to offer—and what enslavers most feared. As one white ship captain explained, Black workers who disembarked from Northern ships into Southern ports were thought to be carriers of "contamination" and fomenters of "insurrection" or "servile war." These charges were based on fear, but they were not fanciful, for sailors Black and white had circulated David Walker's *Appeal* along the docks, spawning several Negro Seamen Acts after 1829. A closely related concern was the solidarity Black sailors would, and did, show to those who wished to escape bondage by sea. It was not lost on freedom seekers that some of these Black sailors had themselves been maritime maroons. According to Southern politicians, many disturbances of the social order in Southern ports originated "in the agency of colored seamen of Northern vessels."[28]

William learned about the Negro Seamen Act through Black sailors like John H. Slate of Connecticut, who had shipped out of Boston as steward on the *Gulnare* for New Orleans. Local authorities took him off the vessel and tossed him in jail. Unable to produce a document to prove his freedom, Slate was forced to work on a chain gang for four and half years, digging graves in the public cemetery. He slept on a "naked plank floor" and had naught to eat but stinking food. When Slate finally staggered through the door of Colored Sailors Home "destitute and crippled," William saw that "the iron shackle" he wore on his ankle while in prison had "chafed the FLESH off to the BONE." Once strong and vital, the sailor was now "a mere skeleton." The very sight of the man, the proprietor wrote, "made my heart sick." William expressed his rage through scripture—"Shall I not visit for these things, saith the Lord, shall not my soul be avenged on such a nation as this?" (Jeremiah 5:29)—and by writing in militant defense of Slate and his brother tars.[29]

William's attack on the Negro Seamen Acts came from all angles—

historical, political, legal, and economic. The acts were in the first instance based on a denial of the role Black sailors had played in winning American independence and in defending the nation in the War of 1812. By failing to acknowledge those contributions, "historians have not done us justice," wrote William, hence "I am compelled to draw my own conclusions." He would rewrite history, from below. The political and legal arguments were, first, that the acts violated the spirit of the American Revolution and the principles of republican government and, second, they were unconstitutional because they transgressed the fundamental rights of American citizens. The acts also damaged the American economy because Black seamen played such an outsize role in maritime trade. William calculated that in 1846 some 6,000 Black sailors worked in the national merchant shipping industry, 2,200 of them based in New York, while another 1,400 toiled in the navy. They had a sizeable presence on whaling and riverine vessels too.[30]

Sailors in the free Black community of Boston had led the way in the struggle against the Negro Seamen Acts. William first took up the issue in New York in 1841 as part of a wider movement. On behalf of the Manhattan Anti-Slavery Society, he drafted a set of resolutions, soon to be affirmed in a public meeting, declaring the laws to be unconstitutional. He then served on a committee to gather signatures for a petition to be submitted to Congress on the issue. In 1842, 222 New York seamen petitioned Congress for protection of their rights as citizens. The petition had no doubt been written by William and the signatures gathered at the Colored Seamen Home. William would remain a steadfast critic of the Negro Seamen Acts through the outbreak of Civil War.[31]

One of William's main purposes in his series of articles was to explain the Negro Seamen Acts to his readers. Toward this end, he published several sections of the laws of South Carolina and Louisiana and made clear that the worst offenders were the city authorities of Charleston, Savannah, Mobile, and New Orleans. Black sailors were arrested as soon as their vessel arrived in port and held in jail until the vessel was unloaded, reloaded, and ready to return to its Northern port of origin. Merchant captains were responsible for redeeming their Black workers by paying their jail fees, which of course some of them refused to do, thereby shifting the expense to the sailors and extending the sentence indefinitely. Sailors usually had no money and, once in jail, no means to acquire any. William also noted how merchant captains connived with local officials to escape wage payments after a crew member was arrested.[32]

William emphasized that one of the biggest problems faced by free Black sailors in Southern ports was proving their status through some kind of free paper. As the proprietor of a boardinghouse William would have officially witnessed numerous seamen's protection certificates. (His concern with free papers helps to explain why he became New York's first Black notary public later in life.) Paper mildewed and turned to pulp at sea, and in any case some police were known to rip essential documents to pieces.

William also detailed the horrific conditions the sailors faced in Southern jails. He cited the stories of ten men who had been held without charge for extended periods of time. He noted that some prisoners were eventually "enslaved for life." In New Orleans they were dispatched from the "police prison" several miles downriver to "the Balize" (the lighthouse and quarantine station), where they worked on pilot boats like "galley slaves." One sailor told William he had counted sixty-eight imprisoned sailors at one facility. William estimated the number of Black seamen who had been imprisoned for only "the crime of color," breaking down the numbers by port: New Orleans, 420; Charleston, 240; Savannah and Mobile, 204 each; an additional hundred in Cuba, bringing the total to 1,168. This was almost one in five of all Black workers in the merchant shipping industry.[33]

William based his arguments on what he had learned through the yarns by which working people communicated subversive bodies of knowledge over vast maritime spaces. William had heard seamen like Slate "tell the tales of their perilous adventures"—tales that were not included in the history books and unknown to the bourgeois public. Over the previous seventeen years, William had talked with hundreds of seamen on ships, on the waterfront, and in the boardinghouse, asking them about their experiences, analyzing what he learned, and drawing his own conclusions. He estimated that one-third to one-half of all Black sailors discharged from naval vessels stayed at his boardinghouse. He explained his method of gathering evidence: he always sought out "the most intelligent of the crew, either white or coloured men, of undoubted veracity, who have kindly furnished me with all the necessary information." His account of the Negro Seamen Acts was based on "the testimony of seamen who have suffered imprisonment" for various lengths of time. He got crucial information by word of mouth: when seaman William H. Davis returned from a voyage to Charleston, he told William that he shared the city jail with seventy other Black seamen. The oral histories he gathered fed his indictment of the Negro Seamen Acts.[34]

William acquired what he called an "experimental knowledge" from his years working at sea and in the boardinghouse. He supplemented his own experience and the many stories he heard by studying the shipping lists of New York, to get a sense of the numbers of vessels and workers required to sail them. If his goal was to learn all he could about the working world of the Black sailor in the antebellum era, the experiment was hugely successful. William may have known more about Black maritime labor than any other person alive because of his experience, strategic position on the waterfront, willingness to listen, and political will to learn. Sailors not only trusted and talked to William about the conditions of their working lives, they counted on him for solidarity and support when they ran into trouble. William did all he could to help. His articles on "The Character and Condition of Colored Seamen" revealed how closely he followed social and political trends of the docks. He was a genuinely organic intellectual of the Black maritime proletariat. He knew that the more he helped Black workers who sailed to Southern ports, the more likely they would be to strike a blow against slavery by bringing fugitives back north with them.[35]

CRISIS: FROM NEW YORK TO LIVERPOOL

William carried on his work in the world of maritime escape quietly, of clandestine necessity, but his visibility rose as soon as President Millard Fillmore signed the Fugitive Slave Act into law on September 18, 1850. The New York Vigilance Committee, which had assisted four hundred fugitives over the previous fifteen months, now prepared to meet the "red-mouthed" human bloodhounds who raced toward the city. The free Black community mobilized quickly, William leading the way. In his eleven years fighting the exploitation of enslaved and maritime waged laborers in New York, he had built a strong base of support among Black workers. As a key member of the all–African American Committee of Thirteen, created to deal with the Fugitive Slave Act crisis, his leadership was well-earned.[36]

Two thousand people, two-thirds of them women of color, met at the Zion Chapel on Church Street on Tuesday, October 1, 1850. William was chosen to preside and give the opening address on the new crisis. Engaging an angry crowd with fiery eloquence, William asked, "Shall the blood-thirsty slaveholder be permitted by this unrighteous law to come into our domiciles, or workshops, or the places where we labor, and carry off our wives and children, our fathers and mothers, and ourselves, without a struggle"? The crowd roared back, "No, no." William reminded his audience of Crispus Attucks, the part-Black, part–Natick Indian sailor who led a motley mob into a street battle against British redcoats in 1770, who was shot and killed for his daring and became the first martyr in the struggle for American independence. William urged his people to don the mantle of revolution and to resist the new unjust law "unto death," like Attucks in the Boston Massacre, if need be.[37]

William informed the audience that the previous day he had paid a visit to New York City mayor Caleb Woodhull to find out precisely how much protection he planned to offer the free Black community against kidnappers. William took along with him a gang of seamen recruited from the Colored Sailors Home to reinforce the militant resolve of his fellow citizens. Mayor Woodhull apparently pondered the issue for a few days, then replied with an important assurance: he had "forbidden the Policemen or any other officer of the Corporation from assisting the slaveholder in returning slaves under the late act of Congress; but as to what course the free colored people ought to pursue in the event of seizure, not having read the Fugitive Law he was unable to say."[38]

The meeting at Zion Chapel affirmed fourteen resolutions that William had likely drafted. Black citizens "utterly repudiated" the Fugitive Slave Law, pledged to resist tyranny, and declared their support for fugitives, whom they advised to fly to freedom in another country or "to arm themselves with the surest and most deadly weapons" to fight to the end. The resolutions also created a "secret committee" that would assist all fugitives in escaping to Canada or Great Britain. William, who pledged that he "will not obey the law," would be a leading member.[39]

Four days later, on October 5, William was once again the opening speaker before what was, at the time, the largest demonstration the Black community had ever held in New York. "Several thousand" flocked to City Hall Park to celebrate the recently won freedom of James Hamlet, who had been arrested under the terms of the Fugitive Slave Law and returned to Virginia before the free Black community of New York bought his freedom (for $800, or $30,000 in 2024) and restored him to his family in Brooklyn. William welcomed Hamlet, thirty years old and "dressed as a laborer," to the stand, adding the truthful but dissonant note that the man had been freed "not by the irresistible genius of universal emancipation, but by the irresistible genius of the almighty dollar." William then shook Hamlet by the hand to a deafening roar from the crowd. Many were "sobbing and shedding tears." They would soon bear Hamlet away on their shoulders.

As William explained, the Fugitive Slave Act "declared war" on the entire free Back community and put all its members at risk of kidnapping. This new, ominous reality no doubt hung like a dark cloud over William's own head, for by 1850 he had a large family: his wife Mercy, age thirty-six; sons William Jr., Edward, Sylvester, and Isaiah, ages sixteen, fourteen, twelve, and eight; daughters Mary and Sarah, ages ten and five; and baby Samuel, just a year old. William was probably most worried about the older boys, but perhaps he feared for himself too. After all, slave catchers had tried to hustle David Ruggles aboard a ship and sell him into slavery back in the early days of the Vigilance Committee. William had lots of enemies who might try the same trick.

William identified strongly with enslaved people who had run away, as he later revealed in a letter to abolitionist Maria Weston Chapman. Although technically free, he considered himself "a poor despised outcast," an "outlawed American negro." He would soon be "driven from my country for no 'color of crime' but the 'crime of color.'" The sources of these feelings included not only slavery but its foul offspring, what William denounced as "negro hate," or racism. He was acutely conscious of how America's racial atmosphere poisoned his children's prospects for the future.[40]

On November 27, 1851, William and his entire family took their own passage on the maritime freedom circuit, sailing across the Atlantic to Liverpool. None of them were enslaved, but that did not mean that they were not at risk. Before he departed, William wrote a letter to the New York State legislature, revealing his keen sense of history and his own attachment to his country, both of which prefaced a demand for reparations—money to finance his family's emigration. If the state would subsidize the American Colonization Society to remove free African Americans to Liberia, an enterprise

William detested, why not pay his family's way to Liverpool? The state refused, but William had made his point.[41]

Upon arrival in Liverpool, William stuck close to the waterfront, going to work as a shipping clerk for Bushell and Company. He had likely lined up this position a few months earlier when he toured the United Kingdom. (At that time, he wrote William Lloyd Garrison that the Tower of London "should be razed to the ground, its treasures given to the poor, and the land divided among the landless as a homestead.") William secured educational training for his four oldest sons: one as a physician, two as engineers, and the youngest as a cooper on the docks. William also opened yet another boardinghouse for Black sailors and joined the British antislavery movement, staying in touch all the while with abolitionists based in the United States and doing what he could to assist their movement from afar.[42]

Before he left New York, William made certain that the Colored Sailors Home was in good hands and would survive as an institution dedicated to both antislavery and working-class principles. In 1849 Albro Lyons, another African American man of the waterfront (like David Walker, he sold clothing to sailors), began to work as William's assistant at the home. A convinced and experienced abolitionist, Albro took over the operation of the home on William's departure, eventually moving it to a new but nearby location at 20 Vandewater Street. Lyons's daughter Maritcha later estimated that during his time as proprietor he and his wife Mary housed and assisted around one thousand fugitives at the CSH, almost all of whom would have likely arrived by sea:

> Father's connection with the underground railroad brought many strange faces to our house, for it was semi-public and persons could go in and out without attracting special attention. Under mother's vigilant eye, refugees were kept long enough to be fed and to have disguises changed and be met by those prepared to speed them on in the journey toward the North Star.

Maritcha aptly emphasized the female labor required to make the underground work. She and the other children "were taught then to neither see, hear nor talk about the affairs in which grown ups were concerned."[43]

Meanwhile William remained active in the Atlantic world of maritime escape, as sailaways regularly arrived in Liverpool on cotton ships from Southern ports and New York. He took fugitives into his home as he had done in New Bedford and New York. He wrote humorously to *The Liberator,* "I have met several thousand dollars' worth of slave property, walking on two legs" in Britain. In 1853 alone, he assisted five maritime escapees from Maryland, Virginia, Georgia, and Louisiana. He played an especially important role in securing the freedom of a young French-speaking woman named Josephine, who departed New Orleans as a secret stowaway aboard the *Asterion* bound for Liverpool, only to be discovered between bales of cotton two days out by the ship's Black boatswain. He cared for her for the next three weeks, but she grew sick, suffered greatly, almost died at one point, and was unable to walk when she arrived in Liverpool. A customs officer found her as he searched the forecastle for contraband tobacco, the "socking" seamen considered to be their customary right as a supplement to the money wage. William housed and protected the fugitive, who told him that she escaped "for the benefit of her health, which has been so indifferent for the last twenty-three years that Dr. Liberty advised her to cross the water and visit England." William also noted that the young woman had, since her arrival, become a member of his family.[44]

With his sons educated and the war against slavery now taking a military form, William brought his family back to New Bedford, then to New York, in late summer 1861. One of his first actions was to find a vacant building at 2 Dover Street in his old neighborhood, the Lower East Side of Manhattan, and to open a new Colored Sailors Home. He aptly named it the Globe Hotel in honor of its cosmopolitan seafaring clientele. William remained involved with runaways, assisting four men who had escaped "rebel masters" and made their way into the US Navy before arriving in New York and turning up at the Colored Sailors Home in need of clothing, shelter, food, and comfort.[45]

A NEW SOLIDARITY

The solidarity practiced among Black sailors and self-emancipated fugitives soon took a new form at the Colored Sailors Home. In late 1862 twenty residents of the CSH convened to form a new kind of organization among themselves. Over several months they talked about the need for a society dedicated to "mutual relief" for each other and their families as well as their own "moral and social elevation." They formed the American Seamen's Protective Union Association (ASPUA), a combination of an older benevolent society and a new trade union—the first Black trade union and the first seamen's union of any kind in the history of the United States.[46]

The Reverend Amos Beman, an African American minister from New Haven who hid runaways in his church basement, attended one of the early meetings in which the "sons of the ocean" discussed their plans. He noted that the men ranged in seafaring experience from green hands to old salts; some had spent a year or two at sea, while others counted twenty years or more. A primary topic, on which William held forth at some length, was "the importance of Union among our seamen" as a means by which "their condition might be improved, and their welfare secured." Beman was present at the Colored Sailors Home when the men decided to draw up a constitution.[47]

No copy of the ASPUA constitution has survived, but the certificate of incorporation awarded by the State of New York has; it is dated June 16, 1863. The organization had seventeen trustees, a mixture of

sailors and dockworkers, along with William and a few others, including leading merchants and ministers from the Black community.
Membership in the organization was restricted to "seamen, cooks,
and stewards," the only positions on ships Black mariners were likely
to get. By April 1863 the union had grown to seventy members who
gathered every Wednesday evening at the CSH. William knew that
it would not be easy to build a union among such highly mobile workers; he and the rank and file faced a "Herculean task." Yet he was
confident that the time would come when the members of the American Seamen's Protective Union Association "would meet the *ills of the
earth*," which he himself had been addressing for decades.[48]

Over a quarter century, Powell and his colleague Albro Lyons held
open the doors of the Colored Sailors Home at all hours of day and
night to freedom seekers arriving in New York from throughout the
South, almost all of them by sea. If Maritcha Lyons was correct in
estimating that her father assisted roughly a thousand fugitives, William would have helped even more, probably another 1,500, making
the total number assisted 2,500—a hundred a year, or two or three
escapees a week, between 1839 and 1865. William made sure that at
the Colored Sailors Home, a simple communism could be found: "not
only shipwrecked destitute sailors, but also the flying fugitive slave
always found shelter, food, and raiment without money and without
price."[49]

William P. Powell believed strongly in the power and strategic importance of autonomous Black organization. Even though he was a
devoted activist in the interracial Garrisonian American Anti-Slavery
Society, he pioneered the Colored Sailors Home as an independent
base from which to build a movement that would assist both Black
sailors and fugitives, two agents of subversive change. William's two
causes were inseparable in his view because Black sailors helped to
transport fugitives, who, once free, frequently became sailors them-

selves. Free laborer or slave laborer, it did not matter to William; both deserved solidarity. Like his friend and fellow sailor-abolitionist Jonathan Walker, William believed that anyone who fastened a chain on his brother or sister's ankle might as well attach the other end around his own neck. The working class would advance only by overcoming its own internal hierarchies. Solidarity meant removing all shackles.[50]

Chapter 7

Boston's War on
the Waterfront

In the early nineteenth century, the port of Boston fed New England's booming industrial revolution. As a center of transport, communication, and industry, the city was often called the Hub. In 1830 Boston merchants imported roughly seven hundred thousand bales of cotton; by 1860 that number had swelled to more than five million, a sevenfold increase required to stock the clattering textile mills that dotted the city and its hinterlands. Roughly three thousand ships and more than twenty thousand sailors handled the city's trade. In 1850 Boston boasted the largest fishing industry and the second-largest vessel tonnage in the nation after New York. Among its population of 135,000 people, maritime workers loomed large, playing a central role in both the economy and the growing abolitionist movement.[1]

A key to maritime escapes was Boston's free Black community, modest in size at 2,300 members in 1860 but well organized and active. It served as a bedrock of the local abolitionist movement. Many of its members were maritime escapees themselves and attended the Fugitive Slave Church located on Southac (Philips) Street, a center of subversive activity. Many free African Americans lived and worked

on the waterfront as sailors, dockworkers, and laborers. They were a
cosmopolitan motley crew, hailing not only from the American South
but also from Cuba, West Africa, Amsterdam, and India, among other
far-flung places. The free Black community independently established
one of the nation's first antislavery organizations, the Massachusetts
General Colored Association, in 1826. In 1833 the organization would
be incorporated into William Lloyd Garrison's New England Anti-
Slavery Society. Garrison first published *The Liberator* in 1831, which
brought Black and white abolitionists closer together. Although most
Black Bostonians disagreed with Garrison's nonviolent, apolitical, "moral
suasion" approach to abolition, they nonetheless respected him, supported his causes, and even provided him with personal bodyguards
on numerous occasions. One result of the alliance was to make Boston the national epicenter of abolitionist activity from the 1830s to
the outbreak of Civil War in 1861.[2]

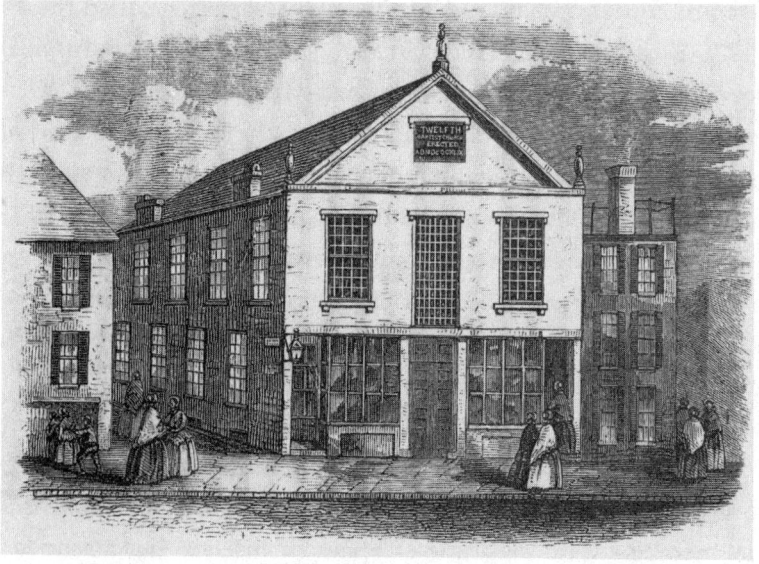

The Twelfth Baptist Church in Boston, the Fugitive Slave Church, was
led by abolitionist leader Reverend Leonard Grimes.

Maritime escapees helped the city to achieve its leading role in the national antislavery movement. Abolitionism in Boston advanced through seven high-profile, fiercely controversial cases involving maritime runaways between 1836 and 1854. Along the way it developed crucial new tactics, publications, legislation, and organizations, all suffused with an ever more militant spirit. Those who stowed away in Boston-bound ships did much to renew the city's reputation as the birthplace of American liberty. They also inflamed Southern hatred of abolitionism and accelerated the movement toward war.

ELIZA SMALL AND POLLY ANN BATES, 1836

The first big political event sparked by maritime runaways in Boston was a decidedly female affair from start to finish. It began in Baltimore when two African American women, Eliza Small and Polly Ann Bates, got aboard the brig *Chickasaw* with forged passes. When they arrived in Boston on Saturday, July 30, 1836, their captain, Henry Eldridge, docked at a wharf, then moved back offshore and anchored, arousing the suspicion of four Black waterfront workers, who climbed into a boat to row out and investigate. Matthew Turner, a policeman representing Baltimore enslaver and Maryland state senator John B. Morris, boarded the vessel, discovered the women, and declared them to be fugitives. He asked Captain Eldridge to hold them until he returned with an arrest warrant. The Black workers tried to board the *Chickasaw* to find out what was going on, but Captain Eldridge repeatedly drove them off. They rowed their boat around the brig and saw the women "making signals of distress to them from the cabin windows." A Black member of *Chickasaw*'s crew also signaled to the men in the boat. One of the Black workers in the rowboat, sailor Samuel H. Adams, returned to shore and secured a writ of habeas corpus.[3]

After two nights in the Leverett Street jail the women appeared before Chief Justice Lemuel Shaw of the Massachusetts Supreme Judicial Court on August 1, in a room crowded with African Americans, mostly women, and a dozen white abolitionists, half of them members of the Boston Female Anti-Slavery Society. Judge Shaw ruled that Captain Eldridge had no right to turn his vessel into a prison and quickly discharged the women, all the while expecting Turner to request a new and immediate arrest under the Fugitive Slave Law of 1793.

Before the new arrest could be made, however, someone in the courtroom cried out, "Go! Go!" The women in the audience "spring from their seats in every direction," surged forward, seized Small and Bates, and rushed them toward the exit. Two courtroom officers tried to control the crowd and recapture the fugitives as Judge Shaw himself struggled to hold the main door closed, all to no avail. An older African American cleaning woman "of great size" wrapped one of the officers in an embrace and, according to an eyewitness, "effectually prevented his interference with the fugitives." The female rioters triumphantly carried Small and Bates out onto School Street, into a crowd of several hundred more Black protesters. Some of those who had led the liberation shed their shawls and bonnets, which Small and Bates donned in disguise. The fugitives hopped into a waiting carriage and sped away.[4]

The women's successful direct action caused a national stir. The *Boston Courier* denounced the rescue. The *Charleston Courier* called it "one of the most outrageous and disgraceful proceedings as ever witnessed in any Court." The *Richmond Enquirer* complained of "the mortifying spectacle . . . of seeing *women*, those who enjoy the reputation of being considered decent and respectable, and of possessing a modicum of modesty and delicacy with which nature is supposed to endow their sex, in the midst of a *melee*, and participating in the affray, we hope, for the credit of Boston, will never again be witnessed here."[5]

The boldness of the rescue also shocked white abolitionists. The women's attorney, Samuel E. Sewall, later wrote, "I am sorry for the disorderly proceedings of the colored people," while *The Liberator* expressed, on behalf of Garrison and the New England Anti-Slavery Society, "deep regret" and "decided disapprobation" of the "ignorant" actors. By 1852 *The Liberator* had caught up with the mass action from below and remembered it differently: Black abolitionist Charles B. Ray called the event something "sacredly cherished and committed to posterity." The event stood in marked contrast to Boston's anti-abolition riot of October 1835, when a crowd of "gentlemen of property and standing" mockingly dragged William Lloyd Garrison through the streets with a noose around his neck.[6]

Once freed from the captain, the sheriff, and the judge, the women continued their escape through maritime circuits by sailing from Boston on to Halifax, Nova Scotia. They were never recaptured. Two female maritime fugitives, assisted by Black men who worked in the port, and in the end rescued by their Black working-class sisters in the courtroom, thus precipitated one of the first major legal confrontations over slavery and secured an early victory for the abolitionist movement. A Boston newspaper editor was left to ask, "Where is the fat, burley wench—the dusky amazon—who took such an active part in the rescue—aiding, abetting, and encouraging, by muscular strength and inflammatory language?" Southerners in Maryland and Virginia burned with rage over the successful escape, threatening to lynch Sewall should he ever venture South. In September 1836 a naval officer from Baltimore, Lt. George Adams, came to Sewall's Boston office with a cowhide whip and "applied it eight or nine times" to the attorney's back in retribution for his interference with "the *property* of strangers."[7]

JOHN TORRENCE, 1841

A group of sailors secretly guided John Torrence aboard the *Wellington*, a Boston-based schooner docked in New Bern, North Carolina, in mid-May 1841. Torrence had probably met the sailors in grogshops along his hometown's waterfront. A writer for the local newspaper, the *Newbern Spectator*, complained that John "kept the worst company, gambled with the idle, and became the abettor of thieves and the receiver of stolen goods." This common class description inevitably referred to sailors, who routinely consorted with the enslaved in port cities to drink, dance, sing, gamble, and exchange goods within the second economy. Many freedom seekers forged relationships in such settings that would get them aboard a ship.[8]

John was an intelligent man, twenty-four years of age, a skilled, enslaved shoemaker who could read, write, and "calculate figures with much accuracy." He was also at the time heartbroken. He had worked long hours making shoes into the middle of the night, assisted by his friends, to make enough money to purchase the freedom of his wife Mariah, who, once freed, moved to Philadelphia. He was now desperate to join her there. His motive for escape was love. Sailors hid John aboard the vessel, which soon sailed for Boston. His "tale of his sufferings" had touched their hearts.[9]

Four days out, a passenger on the *Wellington* discovered John hidden away and reported him to Captain James Higgins, who made regular voyages between Boston and New Bern with his brother and mate, Benjamin Higgins. Master and mate knew that John would be trouble. They could be charged with kidnapping, which might result in fines (up to $1,000), prison (up to ten years), and banishment from North Carolina ports, a serious punishment for a regular trader. Captain Higgins decided that they would stop off in Norfolk en route to Boston and drop John into jail. Higgins would send a message back to shipping authorities in New Bern and arrange for another vessel to return John there. But his sailors had other ideas. They defied the order to sail the ship to Norfolk. In the words of abolitionist Charles T. Torrey, who apparently spoke to some of the seamen after they arrived in Boston, "the whole-hearted sailors refused to be made instruments of such oppression and threatened a mutiny. Whereupon they continued their voyage to Boston."[10]

When the *Wellington* docked at Long Wharf, near 83 Commercial Street, in Boston late in the evening of Monday, May 24, Captain Higgins faced a delicate situation. He did not know what to do with John. He needed the counsel of his employers and no doubt an attorney. Higgins worried about the loyalty of his crew, who remained mutinous—and apparently committed to John's freedom. The captain told a fellow mariner soon after he arrived in Boston that "he feared his men might get into a mutiny and attempt to escape, and if they should he wished to prevent their reaching the slave." Higgins also knew that the free Black/abolitionist community of Boston had a history of armed rescues; Polly Bates and Eliza Small had been liberated not long before. Higgins tried to hide the news that he had arrived in port with a fugitive aboard his vessel.[11]

John promptly intensified the struggle by jumping overboard into Boston Harbor and trying to swim ashore. The sailors may have helped him. The Higgins brothers called to a nearby boat full of men for assistance, screaming "Catch him!" and offering a reward if they would bring him back to the schooner. John countered by offering a bigger reward if the men would help him to shore, shouting frantically: "I am a slave! for God's sake let me have my liberty; let me go on shore!" The men in the boat apparently did not believe him and likely thought instead that he was a member of the crew trying to desert his ship, a more common occurrence in Boston. They brought John back aboard, whereupon Captain Higgins placed him in double irons, confined him in the cabin, and stationed guards armed with guns and knives outside. An eyewitness later claimed that Higgins "placed a large quantity of powder under the deck, and swore that he would blow the vessel up, if a rescue should be attempted."[12]

Word of John's arrival slowly made its way around the docks, probably through Black dockworkers who always kept eyes peeled for fugitives on incoming vessels. Reverend Torrey, an abolitionist who had split with William Lloyd Garrison and the Massachusetts Anti-Slavery Society by seeking more aggressive and political resistance to slavery, filed a complaint in the police court of Boston that once John got into the water, he became a resident of Boston and subject to its laws. The Higgins brothers had therefore kidnapped him. The court did not certify Torrey's complaint until Saturday, May 29, and by then Captain Higgins and John were long gone, having quickly and silently departed Boston Harbor on the morning of Thursday, May 27. Benjamin Higgins remained behind to face the mounting storm. Torrey soon had him arrested in his hometown of Eastham and returned to Boston to face charges of kidnapping.

John was on his way back to North Carolina, but the "great excitement" that would grip Boston had just begun. After the vessel had departed but before his arrest, Benjamin Higgins knew he was in trouble, so he began to ask abolitionists if they would like to purchase John's freedom. That would get him off the hook. He even attended an abolitionist meeting to float the idea. Some thought Higgins was properly remorseful and acting now "from pure motives and from sympathy for [John's] condition," but Torrey and other antislavery activists did not trust him; they thought he was trying to defraud them, hoping to gather money that would go into his own pocket, not to John's liberation. Nothing came of the proposal to purchase John's freedom.[13]

Yet something new and important did emerge from the agitation of John's freedom struggle. Abolitionists—including a "quite numerous" group of "colored citizens"—met on June 4 to create a new kind of organization: the Boston Vigilance Committee, dedicated "to protect the liberties of persons alleged to be slaves, and to rescue from bondage persons of color who are entitled to be free." The premise was radical: people were only "alleged to be slaves," and everyone was "entitled to be free." Anyone who showed up on a vessel seeking freedom would be fought for.[14]

The meeting began with a discussion of maritime fugitives, pre-

Frederick Douglass, a maritime artisan and a man of
the waterfront, escaped bondage in Baltimore in 1838.
A fellow abolitionist called him "majestic in his wrath."

Harriet Jacobs escaped her lecherous
enslaver, Dr. James Norcom, in Edenton,
North Carolina, in 1842, with the inspiration
and assistance of three uncles, all sailors.

Market women, this one painted by Thomas
Waterman Wood in 1858, boarded vessels to
sell food to sailors, gather intelligence about
fugitives, and assist in their rescue.

New York's Hudson River docks were a vast and chaotic workplace, offering freedom to fugitives and posing problems of control for merchants and police.

Despite the racist caricature, this image expressed an important truth about seafaring in the mid-nineteenth century: roughly one sailor in six was Black.

STEAMER
ROANOKE

Steamships such as the *Roanoke* carried fugitives to Philadelphia and New York as they transformed shipping and travel in the middle of the nineteenth century.

The bustling docks on the Lower East Side of Manhattan were a place where sailors, dockworkers, porters, draymen, and market women assisted fugitives arriving from the South.

The Suriname escapee pictured here shows how many fugitives
used small watercraft, escaped to a remote swamp, and
lived on the commons until getting aboard a ship.

Harriet's brother John S. Jacobs escaped slavery by sea
and went on to become a lifelong sailor. He holds a copy
of William Lloyd Garrison's *The Liberator* in 1848.

Sailor-abolitionist Jonathan Walker of Massachusetts tried to help seven people escape slavery in Pensacola, Florida, in 1844. They were caught and punished.

Jonathan Walker's hand, branded "SS" for "slave stealer"
after a failed maritime escape with seven enslaved people
in 1844, became a symbol of the abolitionist movement.

The Plot Exploded!

JOHN H. PEARSON

AND THE

BLOODHOUNDS!

The **VIGILANCE COMMITTEE** give their fellow citizens to understand that they have for several days known the plan by which this unhappy man, Thomas Sims, an alleged fugitive from Georgia, is to be dragged back from the soil of Massachusetts,

WITHOUT A TRIAL!

Without a particle of anything which any other Court but ours would dignify with the name of evidence, against the **MASSACHUSETTS PRESUMPTION THAT EVERY MAN WHO TREADS HER SOIL IS A FREEMAN.**
He is to be delivered by armed soldiers, in violation of the Massachusetts Statute of 1843, on board

THE BRIG ACORN,

Now lying at the foot of **LONG WHARF, HENRY COOMBS, of Barnstable, Master,** CEPHAS I. AMES, Mate, the wretch who boasted in open Court of his brutal treatment of Sims on the voyage North, and has since said on the deck of his own vessel, that he only WISHED to have that damned nigger to take back with him, and expected to have him, too.
This will probably be done by the Revenue Cutter, under the guns of the Navy Yard ; or by the Military insulting the streets of Boston with their presence.
THIS IS THE PLOT A Boston Merchant volunteers his services not only as Slave-Catcher, but as SLAVE-CARRIER FOR HIS SOUTHERN CUSTOMERS.

THIS IS THE PLOT!

Be not misled by the reports circulated by the Marshal and his friends, for the purpose of deceiving the public that "this man would be taken to New York by railroad." Should this exposure lead the Slave-Hunters to CHANGE THEIR PLANS, WE SHALL ANNOUNCE THEM AS SOON AS DISCOVERED. OUR WISH IS THAT THE LARGEST NUMBER OF THE GOOD PEOPLE OF THE COMMONWEALTH MAY BE PRESENT TO WITNESS THIS INFAMOUS MOCKERY OF LAW, AND THIS CROWNING DISGRACE TO THE SOIL OF MASSACHUSETTS.

Boston abolitionists shamed "merchant prince" John H. Pearson, a wealthy trader with the South, for his role in sending maritime fugitive Thomas Sims back to slavery in 1851.

INSPECTOR'S CERTIFICATE.

I hereby Certify that the *Schoo Bell of Gloucester* whereof *T Dunton* is Master, has been duly inspected by me, this *11* day of   185*6* as provided for by the Law of Virginia, passed March 18th, 1856, constituting me an Inspector to prevent the escape of Slaves from this State.

Signed, *Wm J Clark*

Inspector.

No *206*

ATTESTE, *J J Simkins*

The hundreds of fugitives who boarded northern-bound vessels prompted the legislators of Virginia to pass and enforce a ship inspection law in 1856. It failed.

Over almost half a century of antislavery activism, Wilmington
Quaker Thomas Garrett helped more than 2,700 fugitives
to freedom, shipping many of them on to Philadelphia.

Abolitionist William Still of the Vigilant Committee of Philadelphia took down the life stories of more than nine hundred escapees, many of them seaborne, during the 1850s.

eminently John, who was on everyone's mind, and a fugitive named Peter, who had escaped aboard a British vessel in Savannah, Georgia, only to be discovered in Boston and returned to bondage before abolitionists could do anything about it. The founders of the Vigilance Committee drew inspiration from the waterfront struggles and from a new organization of the same name that had recently been established in New York. The Boston Vigilance Committee grew up to answer the cries of fugitives like John and Peter.

Meanwhile the police court referred John's case to the Suffolk County Grand Jury, which took testimony and considered the charge of kidnapping. The jury decided that state and federal laws protecting private property overrode a Massachusetts law of 1784 that made kidnapping in the state illegal. On June 9 the grand jury discharged Higgins, prompting Torrey to write a scathing denunciation, published in *The Liberator.* He castigated the jurors for forsaking the law:

> Monstrous! What is this but a proclamation that the
> laws of Massachusetts shall yield to those of North
> Carolina, whenever the two conflict? Worse still, it says
> that whenever southern slavery and Northern FREEDOM
> conflict, the latter shall bow down in slavish subjection!

Torrey lamented that John had been "returned to his tyrant" in North Carolina. He had lost his bid for freedom, but his determined action, made possible by the solidarity of sailors, continued to roil Boston. The Vigilance Committee had been founded, with its own officers, procedures, and a resolution that it would be independent of all other antislavery organizations. The founders acknowledged that most escapees from slavery arrived by sea and proposed cooperation throughout maritime New England: "Resolved, we invite the friends of liberty in all these seaport towns, especially which have commercial intercourse with the slaveholding states and countries, to cooperate with us, by correspondence and in all other suitable ways."[15]

GEORGE AND REBECCA LATIMER, 1842

The young married couple George and Rebecca Latimer boarded a steamship in Norfolk, Virginia, bound for Boston, on October 4, 1842. Eleven days later their enslavers placed advertisements in the *Norfolk Beacon* to try to recover them, offering a $50 reward for each. James B. Gray described George as young, "about 22 years of age," five feet three or four, compact and strong of body, "bright yellow" (light-skinned) in complexion, and "rather silent and slow spoken" in affect. Rebecca was a little younger at age twenty, with a "good countenance, bland voice," and a confident demeanor: she was "self-possessed and easy in her manners when addressed." The "dark mulatto or copper colored" woman was almost eight months pregnant. Rebecca's enslaver, Mary D. Sayer, signaled some knowledge of their destination and mode of escape when she wrote in Rebecca's ad, "She will in all probability endeavor to reach some one of the free States. All persons are hereby cautioned against harboring said slave, and masters of vessels from carrying her from this port." Her warning came too late, as Norfolk's waterfront workers had already made the escape possible. Both enslavers knew that the docks of Norfolk opened the way to freedom. Little could they have known, however, that the maritime escape of the Latimers would become a national controversy, inflaming relations between North and South and strengthening organization, communication, and political mobilization in abolition's strongest base, Boston.[16]

George's decision to run had been a long time in the making. He had, in a sense, been born into the Norfolk waterfront and its opportunities for escape: his white father, Mitchell Latimer, worked as a stonemason at the Norfolk Naval Shipyard. George himself had worked as a drayman along the docks. "I have thought frequently of running away even when I was a little boy," he recalled. His eye for the main chance grew sharper in the tippling house where James B.

Gray sold liquor to, and bought stolen goods from, Black workers. George also had the advantage of being hired out to various businesses by the age of sixteen, increasing his freedom to escape surveillance, move around the city, and make and save money. Gray, a young businessman who purchased George in 1839, turned out to be a violent tyrant. He was prone to fighting, and he beat George with "a stick and cowhides," fortifying the bondman's will to run. In 1840 George made his first escape attempt, almost certainly by sea (sheer topography made Norfolk hard to leave by land), but he was caught before he got to Baltimore. Gray later wrote that the effort was "almost successful." In terms of its outcome for George, Rebecca, and the abolitionist movement, the second attempt would be "successful" beyond anyone's wildest dreams.[17]

Like many fugitives, George Latimer did not reveal precisely how he escaped by sea as long as he thought anyone else might follow in his wake. He waited until late in life, at age seventy-five in 1894, when he dictated a short autobiography to a friend. He explained that he and Rebecca hid themselves "under the fore-peak" of the steamer, in the forward extremity of the hold, where they lay "on stone ballast in the darkness for nine weary hours." They were likely assisted by a Black steward, cook, or sailor, but George made it clear that not all the sailors would have welcomed their presence on the vessel. From their hiding place George and Rebecca "could peek through the cracks of the partition into the barroom of the vessel, where men who would have gladly captured us were drinking." When the steamship stopped at Frenchtown, Maryland, a new danger flashed before George's eyes—he spotted a man who knew him, having sold liquor to his former enslaver for the saloon in which George had worked. Dressed at the time in a floppy Quaker hat, the fugitive pulled it down over his eyes and passed the man undetected. At this point his strategy of escape changed from hiding below deck to acting the part of a white gentleman traveling with Rebecca as his "servant" (i.e., slave) on first-class tickets he had managed to buy with his savings in

Norfolk. The ruse worked: George and Rebecca safely arrived in Boston October 7, 1842.[18]

On the very same day the Latimers arrived in Boston a new peril confronted them: someone recognized George. This was bad luck, but it was not entirely accidental. Deep connections between the Northern and Southern economies meant that many Southern elites had business partners and agents in Philadelphia, New York, and Boston, where cotton and other commodities were routinely shipped. Latimer encountered William R. Carpenter, once James B. Gray's employee, who quickly notified his former boss that his wayward property had just stepped off the ship in Boston. Gray in turn rushed to Boston, arriving on October 18, to seize George and Rebecca and return them to bondage in Norfolk. Boston constable and jailor Nathaniel Coolidge, privately retained by Gray as his agent, arrested George on a trumped-up charge of larceny, fearing that a mob would form and rescue the fugitive if the real reason for his capture had been known. Rebecca managed to escape arrest and was hidden away in the homes of various free Black residents of the city, one of them on High Street. Mary D. Sayer apparently never tried to recover her.[19]

The news of George's arrest circulated quickly, with electric effect: by the following day, October 19, more than three hundred people of color had assembled at the courthouse to make sure that Gray did not try to smuggle George back to the wharf, carry him aboard a vessel, and secretly return him to bondage in Norfolk. The mobilized Black community remained vigilant: they deputed fifteen to twenty of their number to watch the building, all night, armed and ready to rescue George if possible or necessary. Attorney Sewall visited George in jail and told him to "scream and raise an outcry" if anyone tried to remove him to the docks. If he made a ruckus, Sewall explained, "the negroes would rescue him."[20]

Antislavery activists Black and white mobilized around the Latimer case. They made threats against jailor Coolidge for serving as Gray's agent, prompting him to resign because of "the prejudice the abolitionists were creating against him." They had Gray arrested for slander. They held rallies in Boston and nearby towns (Abington, Lynn, New Bedford, Northampton, Salem, Springfield, and Worcester) to keep up the pressure on state and local government officials. They organized a massive petition drive demanding freedom for George and new laws to protect fugitives. Meanwhile they negotiated behind the scenes to gain the fugitive's freedom by purchase. Amid all the commotion James B. Gray feared that he could not "find a place strong enough" to protect Latimer from his would-be rescuers, so he quietly accepted a low offer of $400, which was said to be less than half of his expenses. At ten at night on Friday, November 18, after six weeks of intense agitation, Latimer became a free man.[21]

Watching from a distance, the enslavers of George's native Norfolk erupted in fury. In 1843 they produced a document of protest entitled *Proceedings of the Citizens of the Borough of Norfolk, on the Boston Outrage, in the Case of the Runaway Slave George Latimer*. Rehearsing the details of the case alongside supporting documents, they raged against the "negroes" and "abolitionists" of Boston and against the inadequacies of the Fugitive Slave Law of 1793. Their ambitions for the protest were lofty. They sent a copy of the pamphlet to every member of the United States Congress; to the governor of every state; to all members of the Virginia legislature; and to the editors of every newspaper in the nation, with the request to all that their report be circulated and published. The document can be read as a fierce early demand for what would be passed as the federal Fugitive Slave Law of 1850.[22]

George and Rebecca Latimer's maritime escape, and the broad agitation it spawned, created three main innovations and advances within the abolitionist movement in Boston. First, the Black community founded a new organization, the New England Freedom Association, its avowed purpose "to extend a helping hand to all who may bid adieu to whips and chains, and by the welcome light of the North Star, reach a haven where they can be protected from the grasp of the man-stealer." Led entirely by the Black community and funded largely by the Black churches, the Freedom Association met in the African Meeting House to provide food, clothing, and shelter to fugitives, prefiguring the revival of the Boston Vigilance Committee in 1846, but in some ways surpassing it: two of the Freedom Association's twelve officers were women.[23]

A second innovation resulting from the Latimer struggle was a new publication, a twice- or thrice-weekly newspaper entitled the *Latimer Journal, and North Star*, which first appeared in print November 11, 1842, when Latimer was still incarcerated in the Leverett Street jail, also known as the "Boston barracoon." It continued until May 10, 1843, and achieved a broad circulation of twenty thousand copies. Its pages featured correspondence, legal opinion, poetry, songs, and an irreverent skewering of Boston authorities by an anonymous writer who imagined the urban procession that would carry Latimer to the docks, onto a ship, and back into slavery in Virginia. Latimer's enslaver, James B. Gray, is declared the "King of Boston" and the city jail is transformed into his Bastille. The mayor and alderman march bareheaded and barefooted with ropes around their necks, prisoners of the Norfolk enslaver. Boston merchants proceed "with their eyes bandaged with cotton, and their mouths stopped with sugar and tobacco." Latimer himself, heavily chained, is escorted by a guard of orators who read the Declaration of Independence. At the end of the procession, the mayor kneels and offers his neck "to the august foot of His Imperial Majesty," the representative of the "Slave Power."[24]

White abolitionists had clearly made progress since they stood by and watched the free Black community liberate Eliza Small and Polly Ann Bates in the "Abolition Riot" of 1836, but reservations about direct action remained: the editors officially discouraged "all intemperate and violent measures, even for the rescue of our citizens from enslavement," but at the same time they published a song with the refrain, "Boston boys! Boston boys! Rescue the slave!" They also provided "A voice from the cell," allowing Latimer to "tell his own story!" The mass movement in the streets and courthouses would continue to lead—and educate—the abolitionist vanguard for several more years.[25]

The third innovation had a long-lasting and far-reaching impact. George and Rebecca inspired a massive petitioning campaign, in which they and their fellow abolitionists gathered sixty-five thousand signatures from 205 Massachusetts towns demanding new laws to protect fugitives. The sheaves of paper bearing the signatures weighed 150 pounds, stretched for more than half a mile, and required six men to carry them on their shoulders into the Massachusetts state legislature. The result was the Personal Liberty Act, passed March 24, 1843, making it illegal for state employees to assist slave catchers or to hold fugitives in any building owned or operated by the state. This was the third set of such laws (after Pennsylvania and New York) that would be passed in the North as abolitionists fought Southern planters and their slave catchers up to the outbreak of Civil War. A man and woman who sneaked aboard a steamship five months earlier had helped to increase the organizational, communications, legislative, and political impact of the abolitionist movement, and to make Boston the city Southern enslavers despised more than any other in the nation.[26]

GEORGE, 1846

The "bright, intelligent mulatto youth" named George traveled two thousand miles by sea, from New Orleans to Boston, one of the longest trips ever taken on the maritime circuit of freedom. He had apparently heard of Boston and its antislavery reputation before seeing the name of the city painted on the *Ottoman,* a packet ship that carried mail, passengers, and freight on a regular schedule between the two cities. He got to know the captain and the crew of the vessel when he came "to sell milk on board." He was quickly regarded as a "favorite": "every man, from the captain to the cabin-boy" joked around with him. It is not clear whether any of the sailors urged him to sail away with them, but at the very least he took encouragement from their friendly interactions. He decided to stow away on the vessel, departing New Orleans on August 10, 1846.[27]

Some abolitionists and newspaper writers called the fugitive "Joe" or "Joseph"; many used no name at all. But two sailors from the *Ottoman* who had spent a month with him on the voyage from New Orleans called him "George" in their testimony before Boston's grand jury. It seems likely that he is the same George whose enslaver, Charles Moore, explained in a runaway ad that the "mulatto boy" had escaped the evening of August 7, shortly before the *Ottoman* set sail. Moore listed the young man's age as twenty-four; a Boston newspaper said he was twenty-five. George resided in New Orleans at 24 Front Levee, from whence he could see the bales of cotton piled up on the nearby docks and the masts of the ships ready to receive them. He lived near the sailors to whom he would sell his milk. Moore thought George had help in getting away. He offered a higher reward for evidence that might convict the "person or persons who are suspected of concealing him."[28]

George boarded the *Ottoman*, crept down into the forward part of the hold, and hid among the cargo, which probably included bales of cotton bound for the mills and markets of New England. He took bread and water for sustenance. The usual August heat in New Orleans was almost unbearable in the dark, airless, stifling space below the main deck of the brig, so George peeled off his clothes. The voyage to Boston would be a test of endurance. Did he bring enough food and water? Would he perish of dehydration or some other malady? Ships could be hothouses for disease. The only certainty was his will to be free.

A week into the voyage George was "discovered," likely by sailors who were checking to see if cargo had shifted as waves rolled and tossed the vessel. George immediately "begged the sailors who found

him," some of whom he knew, "not to betray him to the captain, for
he had rather die than be discovered before he got to Boston." Even if
George snuck aboard with no one's foreknowledge, he no doubt
hoped the sailors would help him once they got out to sea. Maybe
someone snitched. Maybe George got hungry or thirsty and left the
hold to dip into the ship's provisions and got caught in the process. In
any case, the *Ottoman* was a vessel of modest size, on which it would
have been hard for a stowaway to remain undetected for a month.

Captain James W. Hannum jerked George out of the hold; he was
undoubtedly in a foul mood to find a runaway on his vessel. The "discovery" meant trouble—with his employer and shipowner, John H.
Pearson, a "merchant prince" of Boston, and even more worryingly
with the businessmen, governmental officials, and enslavers of New
Orleans. Previous examples of successful escape by sea loomed large
in everyone's memory. Hundreds of runaway advertisements in the
Daily Picayune contained the same threat: "Masters of vessels and
steamboats are cautioned not to employ or carry off said negro, as the
law will be rigidly enforced." The law invoked by the enslavers levied
fines and a prison sentence for captains convicted of concealing and
carrying away fugitives. Guilty shipmasters would also be excluded
from conducting future business in the port of New Orleans.[29]

A full week into the voyage, Hannum decided that the *Ottoman*
was too far from New Orleans to turn back and return George to his
so-called owner. He told George that he would place him aboard any
ship the *Ottoman* should pass that was headed toward his home port.
Hannum immediately dispatched a man to the masthead to keep an
eye out, but the sailor spied no such ship. Over the remaining three
weeks of the voyage, George would eat and sleep with the crew as
Hannum pondered his course of action once they reached Boston.
There was no doubt in his mind that George should be sent back, but
that decision would ultimately lie with Pearson, whose fortune depended on his line of packet ships trading between Boston and New
Orleans.[30]

What transpired subsequently between George and the crew is not known. Perhaps they remained friendly and kept joking. Perhaps Hannum kept them apart. Dr. Samuel Gridley Howe later argued, before a packed crowd of six thousand people in the largest event ever held in Faneuil Hall up to that time, that the sailors of the *Ottoman* had nothing to do with George's return to slavery. Howe asked, "Can we suppose that sailors, so proverbial for their generous nature, could have been, of their own accord, the instruments of sending the poor fellow back?" He concluded, "I, for one, will not believe it."[31]

Hannum was an experienced seafaring man who had heard the stories of fugitives and their maritime escapes to Boston and other ports. He likely knew of the case of George and Rebecca Latimer that had rocked the city only four years earlier. He knew that he would face serious trouble when he arrived in port with a fugitive whom he intended to send back into bondage. He devised a strategy to get George off his ship and onto another one bound for New Orleans as quickly and quietly as possible. Above all else he had to keep the news of George from the free Black/abolitionist communities of Boston.[32]

Every action Hannum took from the time he arrived at the Boston lighthouse revealed his strategy of secrecy and evasion as well as the fear that occasioned it. When he sailed into Boston harbor at two in the morning on September 7, he removed George under the cover of darkness to a pilot boat, the *Sylph*, as sailor John Smith, who was "then at the wheel" of the *Ottoman*, later testified to Boston's grand jury. Hannum asked the *Sylph*'s captain, a man named Fowler, to hold George on the vessel while he went ashore to consult with Pearson. Hannum clearly did not trust the sailors on his own ship in his absence. Another pilot captain came aboard the *Sylph* and advised Fowler "to let the mulatto go," to which Fowler answered, "he had promised Hannum to keep him till the evening."

In his talk about the fugitive slave case, Samuel Gridley Howe not only exonerated the sailors of responsibility for George's fate, he directly blamed Captain Hannum and the "rich and *respectable* owners" as the disgraceful cause of return, whereupon members of the Faneuil Hall crowd shouted raucous cries of "Shame" and "Let us know the name of the owner." "John H. Pearson and Company," Howe announced boldly, which brought forth louder cries of "Shame." Pearson, one of the wealthiest inhabitants of Boston, was apparently in the crowd. According to one report, "no look of trouble clouded his face" during the denunciation.[33]

When Hannum got to the merchant's office on Long Wharf, Pearson quickly confirmed the captain's own preferred solution. To avoid the loss of future business, they must send George back to his owner immediately. He added specific instructions about how this would happen. Another of Pearson's vessels, the barque *Niagara*, was departing Boston for New Orleans the following morning. All Hannum had to do was protect George from Boston's motley crew of antislavery militants for twenty-four hours. This task would prove harder than either man imagined.[34]

Hannum returned with three other men to the *Sylph* and took George into his own boat, the *Warren*, and headed for Spectacle Island, keeping his distance from Boston. He dared not get too close to the docks where he would customarily anchor lest the dockworkers and sailors start snooping around and discover his secret passenger, just as they had done in the Small/Bates case. Hannum was sagging under the strain of the situation, so he went to the Spectacle Island hotel, or more specifically to its bar, to imbibe "a drop of consolation." He met there a local man named William C. Reed, to whom he lied about what he and his mates were up to: "They said they had been down fishing, were caught in a squall, and spent the night at Light House Island." The real squall was yet to come.

George saw an opening and bolted from the hotel in a desperate effort to escape Hannum and save his dream of freedom. Demonstrating that he was no stranger to sailing, he jumped into the *Warren*, set sail, and made for South Boston Point as quickly as the wind and probably a pair of oars would carry him. Hannum realized immediately that the young man had given him the slip, so he jumped into another boat and set off in hot pursuit. George was all alone and did not know where he was going, so he got ashore in South Boston as quickly as he could and took off, running through the cornfields and climbing over fences, trying with all his might to escape Hannum and his boatmates, who were only a few minutes behind. The chase went on for two miles, after which George had reached the South Boston bridge, where Hannum caught up and seized him.

George made a ruckus, attracting the attention of workers and residents. Hannum grew nervous as a crowd began to form around him. He quickly resorted to two more lies, explaining to the assembled that George was a member of his crew (Black sailors were common, so the lie was plausible) and that he was apprehending him because he was a thief: he had stolen something aboard the ship. As Hannum and his gang marched George back to the Point, a suspicious "crowd of men and boys" followed them. At just that moment a friend of Hannum arrived with a team of horses and a wagon, taking George on board, and separating him from the crowd that might have saved him. Hannum and his gang hurried George back to the shore at a gallop and forced him aboard the recovered boat, the *Warren*.[35]

Hannum sailed back to Spectator Island, but he kept the *Warren*—and more crucially, George—"off in the channel" at sea to prevent another escape attempt. He sent one of his sailors ashore, probably for food and drink. But that sailor, once on land, promptly gave away their enterprise to William C. Reed, perhaps hoping to save George: pointing to the vessel offshore, he said, "the mulatto is in her, and he was a runaway slave whom Hannum was going to send back." The sympathetic Reed immediately set sail for Boston "to give information to the police." Both Reed and the people of South Boston would now circulate the news of George's presence offshore.

In response, Hannum changed his location again, trying to make it harder for the now-alerted citizens to find the young man he called "the darkey." Yet Hannum encountered a new problem as he waited to dispose of George: he and the small crew on the pilot boat were low on food and water. He dispatched some sailors to Boston to buy provisions "while we remained hid in the gullies of the rocks" offshore. When the men went ashore they bought gin and crackers, but soon their identity was discovered. Hotly pursued by an angry mob, they ran back to the docks and escaped. After their return to the *Warren*, Hannum sailed north to Point Shirley, where George spent his last night near Boston "tied hand and foot" in the bottom of the boat.[36]

The next morning Hannum set sail again, this time for Little Brewster Island, where he would meet Pearson's vessel, the barque *Niagara*, bound for New Orleans. By this time, the Boston police had been alerted, the abolitionists had gotten mobilized, and a habeas corpus petition for George had been granted by Judge Samuel Hubbard. A search party that included an armed "motley crew of whites and blacks" and two constables boarded a small steamer called the *Lincoln* and took to sea. One of its leaders was John S. Jacobs, a former fugitive from Edenton, North Carolina, who had returned from a three-year voyage on a whaling cruise, and a militant who would later be associated with John Brown.[37]

Hannum placed George aboard the *Niagara*, then he boarded a fast-sailing pilot boat called the *Vision* himself just as the *Lincoln* came into sight. To distract the pursuing party, he sailed in one direction as the *Niagara* sailed in another. Thinking that they were in search of a pilot boat rather than a barque, the skipper of the *Lincoln* followed the *Vision*. Hannum described the angry, mostly African American men who pursued him: "Bayonets glistened in all parts of the boat; darkies were there of every hue, crying out, 'Run him down,' 'Fire into him.'" When the constables finally went aboard the *Vision*, armed with the habeas writ, they searched the vessel high and low only to discover that Hannum had outwitted them. The captain said, "he had brought the man on the Ottoman—had now got rid of him, and was glad of it," but added, in one last effort at deception, "that he did not go in the Niagara." The *Lincoln* took off after the *Niagara* anyway, but it was too late and gave up the chase after a few miles. Hannum smugly reported later that they were forced to do so because some of the abolitionists got seasick. The captain of the *Niagara* eventually delivered George to his owner, whereupon the fugitive disappeared once again into the bloody maw of the "Slave Power."[38]

Popular agitation and Hannum's related troubles were far from over. Abolitionists had placed a $100 reward ($3,900 in 2024 dollars) on the captain's head. Rumors circulated that he returned George to collect the reward. Northern newspapers railed against the "kidnapper captain" while Southern newspapers defended him. A warrant had been issued "on the ground that he had forcibly carried off the man contrary to law," and indeed on September 22 the police arrested Hannum and incarcerated him in the Leverett Street jail, the very place where runaway George Latimer had been held four years earlier before he was liberated. On his way to jail, Hannum wrote to the New Orleans *Daily Picayune* expressing his disbelief over the "lavish abuse" he had suffered, all because of a "vagabond drunken negro." Casting himself as a victim of injustice, "sorely hunted and tracked by those cursed bloodhounds, the abolitionists," he appealed "to the South . . . to save me from fine and imprisonment" in his home state. It may not have been a good idea to use abolitionist rhetoric about slave-trackers and bloodhounds to make his plea. There is no evidence that Southerners did anything to help him.[39]

Boston abolitionists conducted interviews as evidence against Hannum and presented them to the Boston grand jury, but its members declined to pursue the charges of kidnapping. It is not clear how long Hannum stayed in jail, but he was back at sea in nine months, perhaps earlier. He apparently never returned to New Orleans, no doubt out of fear because he had been labeled a "slave stealer," even though he had dutifully returned George to Moore. With Pearson's help he changed his shipping routes, sailing primarily to Charleston, South

Carolina, and Savannah, Georgia, over the next few years. He and Pearson continued their "commercial intercourse with the ports of the slave-holding States" as well as what abolitionists denounced as their "constant participation in the support of slavery." That intercourse and support from Boston would grow more vexed in coming years, partly because of the events of 1846.[40]

The forces of antislavery lost the battle over George's freedom, but in the end it was a productive defeat. The struggle strengthened and advanced the abolitionist movement as new ideas and initiatives bubbled up from the agitation. The public meeting of six thousand citizens held at Faneuil Hall on September 24 affirmed seven resolutions, two of which were practical. The first was the demand that Hannum and Pearson must disavow what they had done and "make all the reparation in their power" by freeing and bringing George back. The public shaming of the supporters of slavery would remain an important tactic until the Civil War. The second was reconstructing a Boston Committee of Vigilance, the radical direct-action antislavery organization that had already been established, to good effect, in New York in 1835, Philadelphia in 1837, and in its earlier form in Boston in 1841.[41]

The Vigilance Committee vowed to be better prepared for the next round of runaways and revised its mission statement, which was originally to "give comfort and help to any fugitive slaves who may be thrown upon our hospitality, and to strive to secure for them the rights and privileges which we claim for ourselves." The language of the declared objective was condescending, as runaways like George were not "thrown," as if by some supernatural power, upon the shores of Boston; they arrived by dangerous, conscious choice. Since Hannum had cleverly bypassed and outmaneuvered the antislavery networks of communication, the Vigilance Committee henceforward would attempt to expand its reach by offering $100 for the "earliest information concerning any alleged slave, held secreted here for the purpose of being carried away against his will." It would always remain vigilant against the slave-hunter, the "common enemy of mankind."[42]

Maritime fugitives continued to arrive in Boston Harbor. The Vigilance Committee provided them with cash, clothes, shelter, legal assistance, and jobs. The main agent of the committee, John W. Browne, kept records of nineteen people he assisted immediately following the struggle over George's freedom, from November 30, 1846, to April 13, 1847. During these four and a half months it is likely that as many fugitives or more went directly to the free Black community for aid rather than through the committee, so the records understate the number of those who arrived. Browne noted the means of travel by which eight of the nineteen fugitives arrived in Boston; seven of them came by sea. Some of them had maritime work experience.[43]

Joshua Holmes, who had captained a local steamship in his native North Carolina, arrived on a steamer from Charleston. Joseph Johnson, a sailor from New Bern, North Carolina, came north in the schooner *Erma & Julia*, likely working his way to freedom. Oysterman Joshua Davis traveled from Norfolk on a schooner, all the while "not known to any person on board, except to a colored man." Edward Ross escaped by sea from the Eastern Shore of Maryland to New York. Levin Walker got from Norfolk to New York on a packet boat like the *Ottoman*. George Langdon jumped from a train carrying him to Georgia, splashing down into Virginia's Great Dismal Swamp. He lived there with two other runaways for eighteen months and took some buckshot in the back before getting aboard a schooner loaded with shingles, probably in Norfolk, for New York. John Armstrong left Baltimore in a packet ship to Brandywine, Delaware, near Philadelphia. His wooden leg apparently did not hinder his escape.

George, whose quest for freedom failed, at least in the short run, was but one among many who arrived by sea in Boston Harbor, seeking "sanctuary" and a "haven of the oppressed." As the national debate about George and his fate unfolded in 1846, the Philadelphia *Public Ledger* commented disapprovingly on the runaway's bold action when he hid himself in the hold of the *Ottoman*: "The slave had no right to convert the vessel into an 'underground railroad.'" Yet this is precisely what George and many hundreds of others before and after him did, seizing a right in action and forcing people in Boston and around the country to take sides. National polarization would intensify in the 1850s.[44]

SHADRACH MINKINS, 1850–51

Like many fugitives, Shadrach Minkins was a man of many names. The uncertainty of naming among people of African descent began, of course, with the deliberate, violent stripping of identity in the Atlantic slave trade and the New World plantation system. Slave ship captains and planters forced alien names on millions of people as they tried to separate them from their ancestors and their history. The vexed issue of naming was compounded whenever someone decided to leave slavery behind and seek a better life. A new name not only symbolized the change but also made the runaway harder to track down, capture, and return to bondage. The fugitive in question had been known by combinations of three first names—Frederick, Sherwood, or Shadrach—and three last names: Wilkins, Jenkins, or Minkins. After his successful escape by sea from Norfolk to Boston in 1850, many people would come to know his ensuing struggle as the "Shadrach case," perhaps because the Biblical Shadrach had, with Meshach and Abednego, escaped the trial of faith in the fiery furnace. The name aptly summarized what the fugitive would go through. He would walk through fire—on water—to freedom.[45]

As one of the first cases prosecuted under the auspices of the new federal Fugitive Slave Law, passed by Congress and signed into law on September 18, 1850, Shadrach Minkins's battle for freedom took on special meaning across the nation. Boston had been the epicenter of the antislavery movement since the 1830s, its activists leading a blistering attack on the southern "Slave Power" year after year. The previous mobilizations to shelter and protect runaways discussed previously had heightened the antagonism. Southern enslavers were therefore eager for a test case of the new law that would defeat, or better yet, humiliate, their abolitionist enemies in New England.

An emergency meeting of Boston's Black community at the African Meeting House soon after the passage of the Fugitive Slave Law resulted in a resolution adapted from words written by Lord Byron about the Greek War of Independence (1821–29): "They who would be free, themselves must strike the first blow." Antislavery militants were learning that rebels like Minkins made history from below, around the world, through popular direct action. Another resolution at the same meeting called for the creation of a new abolitionist organization, the League of Freedom, the main purpose of which would be to "rescue and protect the slave, at every hazard." The resolution specifically identified the agents of rescue and protection—"actors, and not speakers merely . . . men of over-alls—men of the wharf—who could do heavy work in the hour of difficulty." The call honored the role dockworkers and sailors had played in previous struggles as it engaged them for a new battle against enslavers and their recently expanded federal powers.[46]

Four months before the Black community of Boston honored its own waterfront workers for struggles past and future, Shadrach Minkins was scheming with their counterparts on the docks of Norfolk, Virginia. His ability to plot was enhanced by having grown up on the waterfront, where almost all workers were Black. He himself labored at the Eagle Tavern on Market Square, near the crossroads where enslaved people were sold at auction and ferries entered and departed the port. Like many other escapees he had the advantage of being hired out by his enslaver, which enhanced his freedom of movement. Minkins's biographer, Gary Collison, notes that the young man was, like Frederick Douglass, inspired by the "great white sails" that dotted the waterscape near the port. In May 1850 he found a vessel to carry him to Boston, likely arriving in Boston "penniless, ragged, lonely, homeless, helpless, hungry, and forlorn," as the Reverend J. W. Loguen described his own state as a fugitive two decades earlier.[47]

All seemed to go well for Minkins in Boston. He found community right away among the substantial number of self-emancipated people from Norfolk who had already escaped to Boston by sea. He expanded his sense of belonging by joining the Reverend Leonard Grimes's Fugitive Slave Church, where his fellow runaways offered mutual aid. And he found a job, working as a waiter at the Cornhill Coffee House. Yet he soon discovered that his place of work had a serious drawback: it was frequented by Southern gentlemen when they traveled to Boston to meet with their business partners in the cotton trade.

When Congress passed the Fugitive Slave Law, everything changed, and not only for Minkins. The law launched what maritime escapee Harriet Jacobs described as a new "reign of terror" against the free Black communities of the North. Fearing arrest, some four hundred Black residents of Boston—roughly 20 percent of the free Black population—quickly took off for Canada, many of them by sea to Halifax, Nova Scotia, and St. John's, Newfoundland, where they sought the protection of Great Britain, which had abolished slavery in 1838. The Fugitive Slave Church suddenly lost a third of its membership. Hundreds of other African Americans in turn sailed into Boston from New York, where the dangers of being captured were even greater. Abolitionist Theodore Parker estimated in 1852 that several hundred free people of color had fled Boston. Like many others, Minkins stayed, trusting in the power of the Black/abolitionist communities to protect him.[48]

On October 14, more than five thousand people gathered in Faneuil Hall to discuss the emergency the new law had created. Frederick Douglass, who had traveled five hundred miles to attend the meeting, delivered an address, "Do Not Send Back the Fugitive," in which he recounted the history of Elizabeth Blakeley, who withstood three fumigations of her freedom ship in Wilmington, North Carolina, resolving to die rather than return to slavery. Would the assembled crowd allow the slave hunters to return this woman to bondage? The audience roared no. A little later Douglass would famously say, "The only way to make the Fugitive Slave Law a dead letter, is to make half a dozen or more dead kidnappers." The comment did not sit well with the pacificist white abolitionists allied with William Lloyd Garrison, but it resonated with the Black community, who armed themselves in readiness.[49]

Minkins watched as the Fugitive Slave Law drama played out before his eyes, when Willis H. Hughes arrived from Macon, Georgia, in late October 1850 to recapture William and Ellen Craft, a runaway couple now sheltered in Boston. The Crafts had traveled more than a thousand miles over land to reach Boston, Ellen passing as white, the darker-skinned William pretending to be her servant. Once they landed in Boston, William was no one's servant. As his pastor Theodore Parker noted, "He walked the streets boldly; but the kidnappers did not dare touch him," not least because he was well armed, with both pistols and a poniard, a long, lightweight thrusting knife. The Crafts may have arrived over land, but in the end they would secure their freedom by sea: they sailed to Halifax, Nova Scotia, where they boarded the *Cambria*, bound for Liverpool. Boston's abolitionists cleverly secured a victory against the "Slave Power" and the Northern supporters of the Fugitive Slave Law.[50]

Like hundreds of other runaways living in Boston, Minkins must have wondered whether he might be next. On February 12, 1851, a man named John Caphart arrived from Norfolk to capture the fugitive and return him to his enslaver, John DeBree. Caphart was exactly the kind of man the Black community was expecting: he was a slave trader, a jailor, a debt collector, a slave catcher, and an arm for hire as a whipper of rebellious bondmen and women. (He charged fifty cents per whipping and bragged that he never declined a business opportunity.) The abolitionist press created and circulated a broadside warning about Caphart, describing him as lean, lanky, and "*ugly*, not only in form and feature, but expression." Caphart appealed to federal officials in Boston for a warrant to arrest Minkins and received it two days later. On February 15 the slave catcher and group of federal deputy officers arrested Minkins at his place of work.[51]

Unable to jail Minkins because of the Personal Liberty Law passed in the aftermath of the successful defense of the Latimers, Caphart and the federal agents took the fugitive to the courthouse and locked him in the jury room. News of the arrest coursed through the city and soon hundreds of people, Black and white, surrounded the courthouse. Six attorneys volunteered to assist Minkins, seeking a delay of three days to allow them time to prepare their defense. The growing crowd outside was not willing to wait. Twenty African American men, many of them clad in "oil cloth jackets," "rubber coats," "tar-paulin hats," and "sou'wester caps,"—that is to say, dockers and sailors—burst through the courthouse doors, physically grabbed Minkins, and rushed him outside to a waiting carriage. The maritime liberators even gave Minkins a sou'wester hat, which he pulled down over his face as he escaped to freedom. The maritime militants had defied and defeated the Fugitive Slave Law, rescuing Minkins based on a "writ of Deliverance issued under the Higher Law." As they exited, the crowd took the US marshal's "sword of justice" for good measure.[52]

The successful escape of Minkins caused the greatest Southern uproar yet about a liberated fugitive. Editors of Southern newspapers bellowed forth their rage and indignation and pronounced both the new Fugitive Slave Law and the federal government abject failures. Kentucky senator Henry Clay railed in the Senate against "the government of blacks" who "possess no part . . . in our political system." Secretary of state and strong supporter of the Fugitive Slave Law Daniel Webster was embarrassed and furious about the triumphant rescue of Minkins from a courtroom in his native New England. The liberators even captured the attention of the president himself: Millard Fillmore wrote an angry proclamation against "sundry lawless persons, principally persons of color, [who] combined and confederated together, for the purpose of opposing by force, the execution of the laws of the United States." The defenders, in his view, were guilty of treason. The anger of the defeated was compounded when Boston juries refused to convict any of the ten people who had been arrested for assisting Minkins's escape.[53]

The poor and lowly maritime fugitive Shadrach Minkins had commanded the full attention of some of the most powerful people in the nation. Liberated by maritime workers who were ready, as charged by the League of Freedom, for "heavy work in the hour of difficulty," he made his escape to Canada, where he would live out the rest of his life. His supporters exulted. Theodore Parker compared one great waterfront event to another: the freeing of Shadrach Minkins was "the noblest deed done in Boston since the destruction of the tea in 1773." Meantime the Southern and federal foes of Minkins and Parker loudly pledged themselves to fight harder and use more resources in the next struggle in Boston. The urgent desire to teach the abolitionists a lesson had resulted in yet another humiliation, but the battle was far from over.[54]

THOMAS SIMS, 1851

Thomas Sims hid himself among bales of upland cotton aboard two-hundred-ton brig, the *M. and J. C. Gilmore*, docked in Savannah in February 1851. He almost made it to Boston without being discovered. On March 6, in sight of the lighthouse on Little Brewster Island, a mere nine miles from the city, the mate of *Gilmore*, a rough character named Cephas Ames, carried a lantern in the forecastle, where a disembodied voice emanating from a dark corner asked if they had arrived. Startled, Ames recovered quickly, grabbed the runaway by the nose, and pulled him out of the shadows as he rained down curses and punches on his head. He then dragged Sims off to the captain of the vessel, Kimball Eldridge, saying he had found "a prize."[55]

Sims was accustomed to living by his wits, so he had a good story at the ready. He explained to Captain Eldridge that his real name was Joseph Santinna (or Santana) and that he was born in St. Augustine, Florida, to an enslaved woman and a Spanish father, who had freed him when he was six months old. Threatened with reenslavement in Florida, he had fled to Savannah and given his "free papers" to a Morris Porter for safekeeping. He was now on his way to Boston, where his mother and his sister lived.[56]

Unmoved by either the origin story or the pending family reunion, the captain incarcerated Sims in the ship's run (toward the stern, beneath the waterline), exposing the fugitive's thinly clad body to the early March cold. Eldridge would go ashore to arrange to send Sims back to Savannah. Later in the day Ames found that Sims was "most frozen," so he moved him to one of the vessel's cabins and locked him in. Sims, however, had hidden on his person a pocketknife, which he used in the middle of the night to unscrew the door's lock and escape. He jumped into the ship's boat and rowed furiously to South Boston, where he probably got a tip from a sailor about where to hide out. He took up lodging at the Colored Seamen's Boarding House at 153 Ann Street in the North End, in the city's so-called Black Sea, where he would have many defenders. Sims apparently reveled in nightlife— drinking, gambling, and carousing. A policeman who knew him claimed that he was something of a card shark.[57]

Sims had been in Boston only four weeks when slave hunter John B. Bacon arrived in town on behalf of Savannah rice planter James Potter. Sims had written to a relative back home and made the mistake of including a return address. Bacon applied for and received an arrest warrant from federal commissioner George T. Curtis under the auspices of the Fugitive Slave Law. Bacon took to the streets with a gang of ruffians, including two Boston policemen, to search for the young man. When they found him, they moved in for the capture, announcing to bystanders that Sims was being arrested for stealing a watch, to prevent the sympathy they might have felt for a runaway being captured and returned to bondage. Sims fought back. He pulled a knife and stabbed the leg of Bacon's fellow slave catcher, the despised Asa O. Butman. Subdued and being carried away, Sims yelled to the onlooking crowd, "I am in the hands of kidnappers!" The word of his capture spread quickly around the city. The Vigilance Committee mobilized immediately, dispatching a team of attorneys to defend him, posting broadside warnings about kidnappers around the city, and organizing meetings.[58]

Mindful of the rescue of Shadrach Minkins only two months earlier, Boston's officials watched with high anxiety as hundreds of angry protesters, Black and white, surrounded the courthouse, now called Boston's "slave-pen," where Sims was incarcerated. City leaders called out Boston's entire police force and added hundreds of other special guards for security. Women in the crowd scolded the police. Black men screamed at the guards in protest, and several got arrested for it. Authorities barricaded and wrapped chains around the courthouse to prevent mass entry. The door to the jury room where Sims was held was locked and double barred. Dozens of guards stood outside the door armed with swords, firearms, and bludgeons. This was more than protection against protesters; this was war.[59]

On the morning of Friday, April 11, a pack of armed guards stood at the courthouse entrance when it opened. Inside, two armed soldiers stood on each side of Sims and five more immediately behind him, a total of nine to prevent a rescue. Federal commissioner Curtis heard evidence to prove that Sims was the property of Potter and that he should be returned to Savannah. A witness named Edward Barnett recalled having seen Sims ten months earlier in Savannah at a "fancy dress ball," in which the runaway "was there in the character of a sailor," dressed in the very clothing he probably used for his escape. Abolitionist attorneys Robert Rantoul Jr., Charles G. Loring, and Samuel E. Sewall argued that the Fugitive Slave Law was unconstitutional, to no avail. As Curtis prepared to give his verdict, Sims blurted out in the courtroom, "I will not go back to Slavery. Give me a knife, and when the Commissioner declares me a slave I will stab myself in the heart, and die before his eyes! I will not be a slave."[60]

Abolitionists tried every conceivable tactic, filing endless legal motions in one court after another as well as appealing to the state legislature. The Vigilance Committee tried to disrupt the plan to return Sims to slavery by posting a broadside around the city with the headline "The Plot Exploded! John H. Pearson & the Bloodhounds." The daring Thomas Wentworth Higginson hatched a scheme in which Sims would jump out of his third-floor window onto mattresses below, but the escape was foiled when the fugitive's captors barred the windows. Sailor-abolitionist Austin Bearse floated the idea of a piratical attack on the vessel that would carry Sims back to Savannah, but it was rejected as likely to fail. Abolitionists collected and offered money to Potter to buy Sims's freedom. Nothing worked. Curtis ruled that Sims was indeed Potter's property and that he should be returned to his so-called owner immediately.[61]

For the eight-block march from the courthouse where Sims was imprisoned down State Street to the waiting ship at Long Wharf, Mayor John P. Bigelow mobilized three hundred armed men, and a hundred each of the city guard, the New England Guards, and the Boston Light Guards. Another 250 federal troops were placed on alert at the city navy yard. A private army of several hundred more, called the Sims Brigade, had been called into existence and funded by the 1,500 "wealthy and respectable citizens-merchants, bankers, and others" who had volunteered to assist the city marshal in returning Sims to slavery. The mobilization of military firepower against Sims and his allies was unprecedented.[62]

Preparations to transport Sims to the ship began in the early morning hours of Saturday, April 12. Policemen, each equipped with a double-edged "mariner's cutlass," trained for an hour before various guards joined them to fetch Sims from the courthouse. Sims emerged with tears flowing down his cheeks, but he walked to his fate unbowed, like a martyr, one person noted. He was surrounded by guards standing shoulder to shoulder, several columns thick, and marched in formation toward Long Wharf. A hundred angry abolitionists, Black and white, followed the train, hissing "shame" as they went. The defense of the Fugitive Slave Law would take place as the city lay sleeping. City authorities opted for safety, not courage. The extensive military preparations revealed how militant abolitionism had advanced over the previous fifteen years and that armed rescues were widely feared.[63]

Walking down King Street toward Long Wharf, the procession of soldiers and the prisoner passed the spot where British soldiers in 1770 had shot and killed Crispus Attucks. Abolitionist John Greenleaf Whittier recorded the passing in verse:

> The first drawn blood of Freedom's veins
> Gushed where ye tread;
> Lo! through the dusk the martyr-stains
> Blush darkly red!

Another moment in Boston's revolutionary history suggested itself as the armed marchers stepped onto Long Wharf, where in 1773 sailors and other patriots, disguised as Native Americans, destroyed casks of British tea before flinging them overboard into a chilly Boston Harbor.

It is not clear what young Thomas Sims may have known about these maritime events of Boston's past, but the militant abolitionists following the solemn train knew a great deal. The Black community of Boston had celebrated Crispus Attucks year after year, forming social clubs and holding days of remembrance in his honor. One of the protesters bellowed out to the "minions of slavery" surrounding Sims to take note of "the holy spot over which they were now treading." The reenslavement of Sims disgraced the memory of the Boston Massacre and the Boston Tea Party.[64]

Waiting ahead on the wharf to receive Sims was the brig *Acorn*, whose owner was well-known and much despised by abolitionists— John H. Pearson, the very merchant who had sent the sailaway George back to bitter bondage in 1846. In fear of a direct-action rescue and to expedite the departure, the steamship *Hornet* was ready to tow the *Acorn* out to sea. When the prisoner went aboard, abolitionists called out, "Sims, preach Liberty to the Slaves!" They alluded to the Biblical Jubilee, an idea central to Black liberation theology that forecast the end of slavery and the return of land to the oppressed. The last words Sims spoke before he was forced back to bondage were a question: "And this is Massachusetts liberty?" He went below and soon embarked on a new Middle Passage.[65]

DEPARTURE OF THE BRIG ACORN FROM BOSTON HARBOR WITH SIMS ON BOARD.

Maritime fugitive Thomas Sims from Savannah, Georgia, was carried back into bondage aboard the Boston vessel *Acorn* after the Fugitive Slave Law was passed in 1850.

The Reverend Theodore Parker, who was among the protesters, remembered Sims's words when he gave a sermon on the first anniversary of the rendition, appealing to his fellow Bostonians and their proud revolutionary history. At one point in the sermon, Parker dramatically held up the coat Thomas Sims had been wearing the night he was arrested. "Here," Parker announced, is a "trophy" of the event. He held up before the congregation a garment that bore the signs of a fierce struggle. One sleeve had been ripped off. The coat was "torn to tatters." Parker paused for effect, then thundered an answer to the question Sims had posed on the deck of the *Acorn*: "And this is Massachusetts liberty!"[66]

When Sims returned to Georgia, James Potter jailed him for three months, during which time he grew sick and almost died. Potter released him from confinement to protect his investment. Sims recovered his health and returned to his trade of laying bricks. Sims later forced Potter to sell him by threatening to make it better known in Savannah and beyond that he was the man who "had been to Boston." Potter had refused to sell Sims to abolitionists, but now he relented, putting the young man up for sale first locally, then in Charleston, South Carolina, but in neither place did anyone want to buy a famous fugitive. Resistance was contagious, after all. Sims was eventually sold to someone in New Orleans, then to a new unsuspecting enslaver in Vicksburg, Mississippi. When the Civil War broke out, Sims took to the water again to run away, this time with his new wife, child, and three other armed men, all of whom escaped in a dugout canoe on the Mississippi River. He returned to Boston as a free man to speak in May 1863, "with complete self-possession and self-confidence," to a thousand citizens about his ordeal. After an address of an hour and three quarters, in which he narrated his maritime adventures old and new, abolitionist Wendell Phillips handed to Sims his ripped and battered coat.[67]

ANTHONY BURNS, 1854

Anthony Burns took a long and crooked path to Roberts's Wharf on the James River in Richmond, Virginia, where he found a friendly sailor and a vessel that would carry him to freedom. Born in 1834 in Stafford County, not far from the Potomac River, he was the youngest of his mother's thirteen children. Burns showed independence and political will from an early age, refusing at age nine to continue with the first of four captors to whom he had been hired out by his enslaver, Charles F. Suttle. Burns sought not only a better situation but also the anonymity that came with a frequent change of enslavers, which, he reasoned, would make it harder to identify and recapture him when he made his inevitable move to run away—another decision he had made in his youth. When he got to Richmond, Burns struck a deal with the man to whom he was hired out and finally gained almost full control of his own time.[68]

Burns went to work on the waterfront. According to his contemporary nineteenth-century biographer, Boston abolitionist Charles Emery Stevens, he labored "in daily sight of those northern keels that seemed to him a part of the very soil of freedom." The big, broad-chested twenty-year-old worked as a stevedore, unloading the cargoes of guano that would fertilize Virginia's plantation fields and the coal that would power Richmond's tobacco factories. Every day on the docks he worked and talked with Northern seamen, "whose birthright was in a free land, and whose language to the slave had no smack of the whip." It was these "kindhearted sailors [who] . . . did not hesitate to urge him on to flight." Burns befriended a sailor, and soon the two men were "on the most confidential terms." Burns brought up "his aspirations for freedom." The sympathetic sailor offered to help, and together they began to plot an escape. "Plainly," Burns had concluded, "the time was at hand, when, if ever, he was to achieve his freedom."[69]

One evening in early February 1854 Burns gathered some belongings and lay down to sleep dressed in four layers of clothing, the outer of which was "the coarse garb in which he performed his daily toil." He awoke an hour before dawn and walked a mile to the wharves, appearing just as he did every morning when he went to work. He boarded the vessel of his "sailor-friend" and slipped into a concealed place that had been prepared for him in advance. His departure delayed by a day, Burns eventually fell asleep, waking up ten or fifteen miles down the James River with the vessel under full sail. The passage to Norfolk was rough: Burns got seasick as he lay in the cramped, dark hold. The usual ten-to-fourteen-day sail from Norfolk to Boston took three weeks, during which time Burns ate whatever bread and water his friend was able to smuggle to him. By the time he arrived he had lost the use of his right arm from lying on one side for so much of the voyage, "his feet were frozen stiff in his boots," and his body was bruised from the rolling of the ship.

The vessel reached Boston's wharves on a gray early March morning. Neither the ship's captain nor any crew member except his friend had known that he was aboard. He disembarked without notice on ship or shore, "assum[ed] the air of a seaman," and made his way to the Colored Seamen's Boarding House. After a short period of recovery, he sought work on the waterfront and secured a position as cook aboard a mud-scow, a heavy vessel used to dredge the harbor. There was only one problem with his plan: Burns's skills as a cook left something to be desired. He "was unable to make his bread rise" and was fired within a week. Had he been able to keep this job he might never have been found by the slave hunter soon on his trail.

Burns found work in a used clothing shop owned and operated by Black abolitionist Coffin Pitts, who allowed the young runaway to board in his home, located on Joy Street on the north side of Beacon Hill. On his way home from work on May 24, Burns felt a hand on his shoulder and heard someone command, "Stop, stop!" The hand belonged to the dreaded slave catcher Asa O. Butman, who bore the scar of Thomas Sims's knife and was now employed by Suttle. Burns did not recognize Butman and demanded to know why he was being arrested. The slave catcher lied to him and more pointedly to the quickly gathering crowd, saying, as Burns himself recalled, "You are the fellow who broke into a silversmith's shop the other night." At this point six or seven men waiting nearby rushed to Butman's assistance, surrounded Burns, grabbed him, and carried him "like a dead person," his feet never touching the ground, to the courthouse, where federal marshal Watson Freeman hurried the prisoner up to the jury room on the third floor, the very place where Shadrach Minkins and Thomas Sims had been sequestered after their arrests. When the silversmith did not show up to press charges, everyone realized that Burns had been arrested as a fugitive.[70]

The Black community and the Vigilance Committee exploded into action, both debating whether to pursue an armed rescue or a more peaceful protest. After a big meeting held at Faneuil Hall, which featured antinomian declarations that "wicked laws"—epitomized by the Fugitive Slave Law—must not be obeyed, a mixed-race group of ten to twelve men, led by Thomas Wentworth Higginson, attempted to force their way into the courthouse but were repelled by superior strength, Higginson getting a "sabre cut across the chin" and eight or nine of the men getting arrested. In the melee someone stabbed federal deputy James Batchelder in the abdomen and within a few hours he had bled to death. The defenders of the courthouse carried the day, the protesters withdrew, and the crowd outside dispersed.[71]

The hearing on the Burns case, as well as the outcome, paralleled what had happened to Thomas Sims. The courtroom was jammed to capacity as thousands of people milled around outside. Abolitionist attorneys tried one tactic after another, all without success. They had found ten people, mostly workers, Black and white, who testified that they had seen Burns at work in Boston two to three weeks before he was said to have gone missing in Richmond. Even before federal commissioner Edward G. Loring announced that Burns would be taken back to bondage in Virginia, local authorities had begun to expand their military force beyond the mobilization around the Sims rendition three years earlier. They called out the entire city police, a

Amid a massive military force assembled to prevent a rescue by fifty thousand protesters, maritime fugitive Anthony Burns was transported back to slavery in Virginia in 1854.

federal marshal's civic posse of 125 specially deputized guards, two companies of cavalry, an artillery battalion, and four platoons of United States Marines. A dissonant note within the mobilization was sounded when Boston police captain Joseph K. Hayes resigned his position rather than participate in the rendition of Burns. Loring ruled on June 2, 1854, that Burns would be marched to a ship and carried back to bondage in Virginia.[72]

As many as fifty thousand people gathered to watch the concluding act of the maritime drama, the march of Burns a mere six hundred yards from the courthouse to the docks. The route would not be identical to the one walked by Thomas Sims, because the owner of Long Wharf refused this time around to allow his property to be used to return a free man to slavery. Protesters had arrived from all around Boston, including six or seven hundred from the "machine-shops and factories" of Worcester, all bitterly hostile to the enforcement of the Fugitive Slave Law. Boston citizens draped their windows in black as they mourned the day. Bells tolled solemnly throughout the city. A black coffin was passed through the crowd in what was described as the "Funeral of Liberty." People groaned and hissed at the authorities as the train passed. Some of the soldiers "hang[ed] their heads with shame." Scuffles broke out between the guards and the crowd, resulting in multiple injuries and arrests.[73]

The massive military force escorted Burns to the dock, placing him aboard a small steamboat, the *John Taylor*, rented by the United States government. The vessel departed the wharf rapidly and carried the prisoner to a federal revenue cutter offshore, the *Morris*, which would take him back to Richmond. Surrounded by armed guards on the vessel, Burns later reported that "no one looked kindly upon him but the sailors that manned the vessel." After an eight-day voyage, Burns arrived in Norfolk, where an angry mob followed him to the local jail. He went back to sea the following day and soon arrived in Richmond, where Suttle incarcerated him in a six-by-eight-foot cell in Robert Lumpkin's dreaded and infamous jail. His jailors did all they could to segregate Burns from other prisoners, fearing the "infection" of freedom. After four months Suttle grew weary of the man "who had excited such commotion throughout the country."

Suttle decided to sell Burns to a slave trader named David McDaniel of Rocky Mount, North Carolina. The new enslaver had to smuggle Burns out of town in the dead of night to avoid a mob bent on terror. In the end Burns was saved by the Reverend Leonard Grimes of the Fugitive Slave Church, who raised money to purchase his freedom from McDaniel. In March 1855 Burns made a triumphant return to Boston, where he spoke with flair to a large crowd.[74]

FACE-TO-FACE WITH THE "SLAVE POWER"

Between 1836 and 1854, seven high-profile cases involving nine maritime fugitives agitated the city of Boston. In four of the cases, the
fugitives achieved their objective of emancipation. Extralegal direct
action, largely initiated and carried out by the Black community, especially its waterfront workers, freed Eliza Small, Polly Ann Bates,
Rebecca Latimer, and Shadrach Minkins. Boston abolitionists, led by
Leonard Grimes of the Fugitive Slave Church, liberated two runaways, George Latimer and Anthony Burns, using ransom money.
The movement lost three of these people to bondage: slavers took
John Torrence back to New Bern, George to New Orleans, and
Thomas Sims to Savannah. Sims successfully ran away again on his
own, without the assistance of the abolitionist/free Black community
of Boston. Seven of the nine who boarded vessels in their bold, dangerous bids ended up free.[75]

These cases of maritime escape demonstrate how the docks and
waters of port cities had become zones of struggle where proslavery
and antislavery actors consciously planned, strategized, and fought it
out. They also reveal the elite political and economic pressure fugitives
and abolitionists were up against—the interests of wealthy merchants,
the so-called Cotton Whigs, and ship captains in the transnational
circuits of trade, labor, and capital accumulation they managed. By
sailing out of Southern ports into Boston Harbor, sailaways activated
a lot of powerful people who sought to reverse their self-emancipation,
but they also mobilized supporters who grew stronger as a movement
over time. The actions of maritime escape rippled across the city of
Boston with amplified effect. Writing in 1854, Mary E. Blanchard,
the daughter of former Boston mayor Benjamin Seaver, noted that
since the passage of the Fugitive Slave Law in 1850, "many who
would have assisted on the return of the slave will be glad to assist
now in his escape." She noted that some local abolitionists were ready

to tar and feather enslaver Charles F. Suttle and that her aunt Emily was ready to "help do it." Mary's brother B. F. added, "there has been the most wonderful change in public sentiment on the subject of slavery."[76]

At the same time, sailaways helped to educate white abolitionists during these years, advancing a more radical vision of why slavery must end and how it might happen. Attorney Samuel E. Sewall and publisher/activist William Lloyd Garrison regretted the first armed rescue, but they and their white colleagues eventually caught up with the initiatives from below. Over two decades they watched maritime runaways and the agitation they produced advance the antislavery movement in one crucial way after another—in tactics, strategy, organization, communication, legislation (the Personal Liberty Acts of 1843), and the degree and strength of popular participation in the antislavery movement. What began as several dozen African American women rescuing Small and Bates from a courtroom ended as a crowd of tens of thousands angrily protesting the rendition of Anthony Burns. Slave catchers, fearful that working-class people in the streets of Boston would protect the fugitive, routinely lied about why they were making an arrest. Direct action involving waterfront fugitives, moreover, stimulated organization—the formation of the Vigilance Committee (1841), the New England Freedom Association (1842–43), the League of Freedom (1850), and the Boston Anti-Man-Hunting League (1854), which threatened to capture slave catchers and hold them hostage. As the Fugitive Slave Law criminalized the cooperation of runaways and the Black/abolitionist community, it triggered a dialectical response, which included new forms of solidarity, one of which was armed struggle.[77]

Even though Southern enslavers and their federal allies won the day and sent John Torrence, George, Thomas Sims, and Anthony Burns back to bondage, these defeats contained within them victories for enslaved people, the free Black community, sailors, dockers, and abolitionists. Increasingly broad-based resistance made the cost of rendition fatally high. In 1851 it cost $20,000 ($700,000 in 2024) to return Sims to Savannah and vastly more, as much as $40,000 ($1.4 million in 2024), to send Burns back to Virginia three years later. This was not an economically viable way to return fugitives to Southern enslavers, and both Sims and Burns ended up gaining their freedom anyway. Perhaps the clearest sign of victory was something that did not happen: the rendition of Burns in 1854 would be the last effort to enforce the Fugitive Slave Act in Massachusetts.[78]

Maritime fugitives brought Northern abolitionists face-to-face with Southern slavery. Runaways from Maryland, North Carolina, Virginia, Georgia, and Louisiana made the abstract "Slave Power" concrete. Real people, with real needs to escape slavery, arrived in Boston in ragged clothes, hungry and thirsty after long, trying voyages. Other people—washerwomen, sailors, "Men of the Wharf"—helped them as they were chased furiously by villainous slave catchers, police, judges, and enslavers. The big dramas of slavery and abolition played out vividly in the streets and courtrooms of Boston. Bondage was suddenly a living, pulsing, gasping matter of life and death.[79]

Against the victories won by the Black/abolitionist community, the South's defenders of slavery spewed flaming invective. The strongest impact of the Burns case was felt in the South. The same point could be made about all seven cases, whose progression produced increasingly extreme denunciations of "wicked abolitionists" nationwide. What Senator Charles Sumner of Massachusetts had denounced in 1848 as "an unhallowed union . . . between the cotton-planters and flesh-mongers of Louisiana and Mississippi and the cotton-spinners and traffickers of New England,—between the lords of the lash and the lords of the loom," had been challenged and, in specific cases, defeated. National polarization and eventually crisis continued apace.[80]

Chapter 8

Sea Routes to Philadelphia and New York in the 1850s

B oston may have been the hottest bed of abolitionism among the port cities in the 1850s, but the truth remains that more maritime fugitives sailed or steamed their way to Philadelphia and New York. These ports lay geographically closer to the Southern states, which made them easier to reach. Human engineering also played a part: the fourteen-mile-long Chesapeake and Delaware Canal, which bisected the Delmarva Peninsula and connected Chesapeake Bay to the Delaware River, opened to maritime traffic in October 1829, dramatically reducing travel time from the ports of Maryland, Virginia, and Washington, DC, to Philadelphia and Wilmington, Delaware. In 1850 alone almost thirteen thousand ships took passage through the canal, carrying timber, lumber, grain, flour—and fugitives. Philadelphia and New York also dominated American shipbuilding at midcentury. As the number of ships and tonnage of cargo that connected North and South expanded, voyages grew more regular and predictable, especially with the rise of the industrial steamship, which by the late 1840s had become central to many commercial routes. Infrastructural and economic change thus expanded the range of available choices to escape bondage.[1]

During the 1850s, after the passage of the Fugitive Slave Act, the nature of escape by sea to Philadelphia and New York took a new form. Several ship captains—William B. Baylis, James Fountain, William H. Lambdin, and others—worked with the Vigilance Committees to bring escapees northward on more regular voyages, creating a steadier, more reliable system of escape. This regularization contained within it a process of commercialization as most of these captains began to charge runaways a fee for their passage. The new phase in the history of escape by sea was also accompanied by changes in ship technology: these captains often constructed secret compartments in the holds of their vessels to hide the fugitives. Meanwhile, escape by assistance from below, in which sailors, stewards, cooks, and chambermaids helped the enslaved to board vessels without the knowledge or consent of the ship's officers, continued apace. But there can be no doubt that a new kind of maritime escape organized from above—what we might call a "business of escape"—emerged in the 1850s and successfully moved hundreds of men, women, and children by sea to the Northern ports. This was a distinctive feature of the circuit of escape that led to Philadelphia and New York.[2]

This chapter traces the sea routes of fugitives to Philadelphia and New York from North Carolina, Virginia, and Maryland during the 1850s. Fugitives enlisted captains, sailors, ships, and abolitionist organizations to their cause to create a circuit of movement and liberation that would withstand the tests of intensified violence from enslavers and new policing initiatives along the waterfront. Records secretly kept by abolitionists permit both a human and a statistical portrait of maritime escape. Newspapers North and South endlessly publicized the high drama of escape by sea, making direct actions against bondage more consequential than ever across the nation as the United States veered toward bloody Civil War.

FROM WILMINGTON TO PHILADELPHIA AND NEW YORK

Only fifteen miles from the border of Maryland in one direction and ten miles from Marcus Hook—located in the free state of Pennsylvania—in the other, the port of Wilmington, Delaware, was a strategic site for fugitive transit to Philadelphia and New York. The key figure in the Delaware River circuit was Quaker abolitionist Thomas Garrett. Originally trained as a blacksmith and possessing a stout, powerful physical presence, the fearless Garrett befriended and worked closely with Harriet Tubman and many other Black activists. In 1868, after slavery had been abolished, he observed: "I have not felt at liberty to keep any written word of Harriet's or my own labors, except in numbering those I have aided." After a court case in 1848, in which he lost thousands of dollars to Maryland slaveholders who successfully prosecuted him for harboring and assisting runaways, he defiantly announced that he had already assisted 1,400 fugitives and would redouble his efforts in the future. By 1863 the number had indeed almost doubled to 2,700 as he "forwarded" escapees northward. William Still and Sydney Howard Gay documented many of them, as they kept detailed records in the 1850s. The legislature of the state of Maryland acknowledged Garrett's centrality to the highly successful network in 1860, when it offered a $10,000 bounty for the abolitionist's arrest.[3]

Garrett worked with a group of white ship captains who routinely brought fugitives from Virginia and North Carolina to Wilmington. The three most visible captains in this operation, James Fountain, William B. Baylis, and William H. Lambdin, were all based in Wilmington. Garrett linked these captains, their ships, and the fugitives they carried to free Black maritime workers and the Philadelphia and New York Vigilance Committees, establishing one of the most productive circuits of maritime marronage.[4]

James Watson Fountain was a short, stout, rough, and rugged sea-faring man. His shining moment as a direct-action abolitionist came in November 1855 as his schooner lay at the wharf in Norfolk. Dockers had loaded it with wheat, an export of rising importance in Virginia during the 1850s. Fountain had been assisting fugitives in Norfolk for a while, so perhaps he had aroused suspicions. When word got out that a significant number of enslaved people had gone missing all at once, the mayor of the city, Ezra T. Summers, led "a posse of officers with axes and long spears" to Fountain's vessel and angrily demanded to come aboard. To both Fountain and the fugitives, he was danger personified.[5]

According to William Still, who recounted the tale he had heard from fugitives and likely from Fountain himself, the "fearless commander received his Honor very coolly," even though twenty-one men and women lay hidden in a secret compartment he had constructed below deck. The mayor announced his intention to search the vessel for the runaways, to which Fountain replied, "Very well . . . here I am and this is my boat, go ahead and search." Knowing something of the techniques of escape, Summers ordered his deputies to "spear the wheat thoroughly," which they did, "with alacrity." Disappointed that "the spears brought neither blood nor groans," he ordered one of his men to start chopping up the deck of the vessel to see what, or who, might be hidden below. Fountain stood by, fully composed, "wearing an air of utter indifference." After a time, Fountain seized the moment, announcing to the mayor, "Now if you want to search, give me the axe, and then point out the spot you want opened and I will open it for you very quick." To give emphasis to his words he raised the axe and brought it down violently on the deck, sending splinters flying in all directions. The mayor and his minions were startled, indeed frightened, by the blow, and after a second, even more explosive hack, "they looked as though it was time for them to retire." A few minutes later "they actually gave up the search and left the boat without finding a soul." Fountain soon set sail for Wilming-

ton, where "the twenty-one," as they were called, were assisted by
Garrett and sent on to Still in Philadelphia and Gay in New York.
Several of them then traveled on to New Bedford and Boston. Foun-
tain's bluff made possible a legendary mass escape.[6]

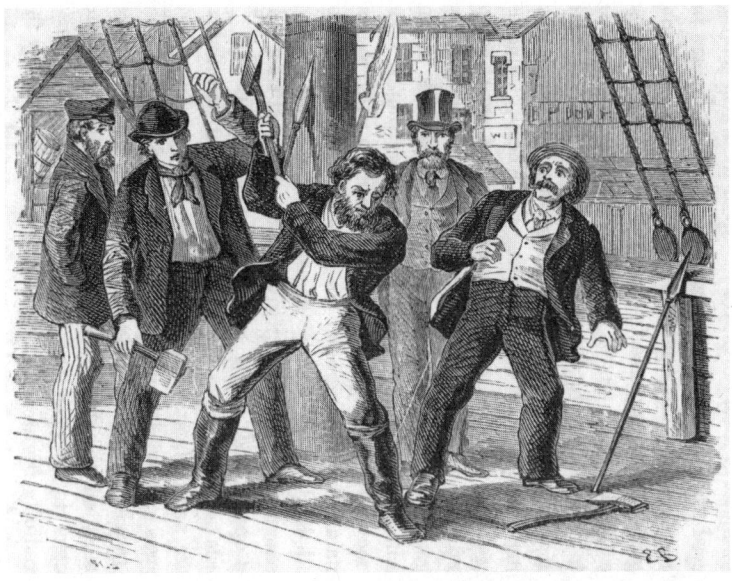

Captain James Fountain helped the mayor of Norfolk look for fugitives
aboard his ship but ended up scaring him away by hacking his own deck
with an axe.

Still provides documentation that Fountain carried fifty-seven
people (fifty-four of whom are named) from Norfolk, Portsmouth,
and several ports in North Carolina to Wilmington and Philadelphia
between June 1855 and November 1857, but of course the number of
fugitives he transported was no doubt greater and the timespan of his
efforts much longer. Fountain family lore had it that the captain had
assisted more than a thousand. Fountain sometimes charged fugitives
for the voyage, no doubt because he thought the risks he ran justified
the payment. Fountain's daughter Liz recalled that he was also paid
in gold by Quakers for ferrying fugitives to northern freedom.[7]

Another Wilmington-based ship captain involved in assisting people to escape by sea was William H. Lambdin, who in the 1850s lived with his wife and small child at 607 Orange Street, about eight blocks from the river. The "intelligent young captain," as Garrett called him, took an unusual path to the sea. Born around 1829, he worked at the *Delaware Gazette* for a time, and as postmaster and merchant in Smyrna, Delaware, before going to sea. He apparently had the means to purchase his own vessel. Lambdin was known for his conscience, intellect, and "progressive mind"; he was something of a free thinker. An acquaintance wrote, "He does nothing but work and study."[8]

Captain William H. Lambdin carried many to freedom in the 1850s, until he was caught, convicted, and sent to prison in Virginia in 1856. Note the sailor's broken nose.

Lambdin sailed the Chesapeake Bay and the Atlantic coast, bringing back to Wilmington both commodities and fugitives. He was a significant part of Garrett's network. In November 1855 Lambdin picked up three women and two men in a planned escape aboard the schooner *Mary Ann Elizabeth*. Eager to get out of Norfolk and avoid detection, Lambdin set sail into a storm that proved to be a hurricane. High winds and waves broke the vessel up and drove it ashore only a few miles from Norfolk, near Cape Henry. Everyone on board survived the wreck. Lambdin sought assistance from a nearby resident and ended up in the hands of a local official, who assumed, correctly, that the African Americans with him were fugitives. He threw the whole lot in jail and the following day carried the group back to Norfolk, where Lambdin gave the authorities the only excuse available to him—that he and his mate were "astonished" to discover the fugitives aboard their vessel. The Norfolk judge and jury would have none of it and pointed to additional incriminating evidence: Lambdin had on his person $125 in gold that had been paid to him by the fugitives for their passage. The captain admitted to the governor that he was "anti-Slavery in [his] sentiments" and was sentenced to seven to ten years in the Virginia State Penitentiary.[9]

Captain William B. Baylis was a man of the sea, and he looked the part. Described as "a low, but not thickly set man, quite muscular, about forty-five years of age," he possessed "a rather frank, sailor-like appearance." Years of work at sea had "bronzed his complexion and hardened his features to some degree." He had taken to the sea by 1854, following his brother Samuel's banishment by port authorities in Petersburg, Virginia, for "tampering" with enslaved people. Baylis sailed the Chesapeake and its tributary rivers, taking aboard fugitives from Richmond, Petersburg, Portsmouth, and Norfolk. He was part of an extensive network of pilots, Black and white, enslaved and free. Like Fountain and Lambdin, Baylis was based in Wilmington and worked closely with Thomas Garrett and William Still. His last attempted voyage was in May 1858 when he was captured in the James River, convicted, and sent, like Lambdin, to the Virginia State Penitentiary.[10]

Baylis was perhaps the most entrepreneurial, and certainly the most mercenary, of the Wilmington-based captains, routinely charging fugitives $50 to $100 ($1,750–$3,500 in 2024) for northward passage. William Still, who received many of his passengers, noted that Baylis "would bring any kind of freight that would pay the most." Baylis felt that, given the risk, "it was no more than fair to charge for his services," although he occasionally brought fugitives for free. He was highly successful in his actions, wrote Still: "Quite a number of passengers at different times availed themselves of his accommodations and thus succeeded in reaching Canada."[11]

Baylis, like Fountain, was a man of considerable daring. In January 1855 he carried to freedom two enslaved brothers, Joseph and Robert Robinson, from Richmond. One of their enslavers, George E. Sadler, owned an oyster bar; the other, Robert Slater, was a slave trader. On his way to the docks Richard reappropriated some of the filthy lucre of the trade in human flesh, roughly $1,500 ($54,000 in 2024), to finance their trip. Baylis packed away both men, along with a woman named Emma Brown from Petersburg, "in a very private hole of his boat" and carried them to the Philadelphia Vigilance Committee. All three went on to Canada, where the Robinsons wrote taunting letters to Sadler and Slater, describing their "good times," delicious food, and "very choice wines and brandies," all beyond the reach of the "Slave Power." When Baylis returned to Richmond, he audaciously visited Sadler's oyster bar and asked about the escape that he had engineered. Sadler pulled out the letter and read it aloud, adding furious curses, threats, and the offer of $2,000 ($72,000 in 2024) to anyone who would bring the defiant fugitives back. William Still noted that all the while, Baylis "was good at concealing his feelings, and obviously managed to avoid suspicion." He would make several more freedom voyages to Richmond.[12]

Sometimes the Wilmington-based captains cooperated when they found themselves in the same Southern port. In an interview with a reporter in 1879, Baylis recalled an occasion in 1856 or 1857 when he and Captain Fountain were both docked in Petersburg. Three port officials came aboard Baylis's vessel, the *Keziah*, and informed Baylis that they planned to inspect Fountain's vessel next. Baylis knew that Fountain had already taken some fugitives aboard, so he told the officials that he had to go ashore to make a purchase, leaving them with his mate. He then took the vessel's boat and "rowed in a circuitous route" to Fountain's schooner to inform him of the coming raid. Baylis returned to his vessel to entertain the inspectors with drink and song. When Fountain heard a signal song, he knew that "all was well" and that he should slip anchor, raise a sail, and ease out to sea, which he did, with his illegal passengers, undetected.[13]

As Captains Baylis, Fountain, and Lambdin organized escape by sea "from above" in new, more commercial ways during the 1850s, the autonomous tried-and-true methods of escape from below continued unabated, as initiatives in Richmond demonstrated. Workers found berths for a young couple named Jeremiah and Julia Smith on a steamer—berths that were "not known to the officers of the boat." "One of the colored women running as cook or chambermaid" stowed banjo player Miles Robinson away in the place where she might best be able to protect him, in "one of the closets where the pots and other cooking utensils belonged." Blacksmith Henry Johnson, "being down about the wharfes" one day in November 1856, encountered the cook of a vessel who "asked him if he would not like his freedom." Henry said yes and "was taken on board stowed away and cared for by his friend." The Smiths went on to Philadelphia, Robinson to Boston, and Johnson to New York.[14]

PHILADELPHIA

One of the most remarkable documents in the long, bloody annals of the struggle against slavery was created by African American abolitionist William Still, who interviewed runaways on behalf of the Philadelphia Vigilance Committee as a prelude to providing them with material aid—food, clothing, shelter, money, and transport to destinations beyond the reach of their enslavers. Between 1852 and 1860 Still listened sympathetically as hundreds of escapees filed through his office, narrating the stories of their lives under bondage, from the violence they had suffered in the past to their dreams of the

future. Still's Journal C and his book *The Underground Railroad*, published in 1872, provide the single richest portrait of antebellum fugitives ever created.[15]

Still documented the lives of 930 runaways, most of whom arrived
"in a very sad plight—in tattered garments, hungry, sick, and penniless," their cheap clothing worn out by years of slaving away on the
plantation. Some bore scars caused by the whip or the bullets fired at
them on previous escapes. Others carried the fresh wounds of their
most recent fight for self-liberation. Still interviewed some people
who were exultant at their freedom, joyous beyond words, and others
who trembled in terror of recapture. A few were gifted, exuberant
storytellers, others distrustful and taciturn. Quite a few were ill, exhausted, hungry, and beaten down, but never without hope. Still listened with tender concern and took notes from men and women,
young and old. These fugitives educated Still and indeed the entire
American abolitionist movement about the grim realities of the "Slave
Power."[16]

Yet Still imposed limits on what he was willing or able to say about
the fugitives. He considered some of their stories of cruelty "too re-
volting to be published," especially, it would seem, the underrepre-
sented accounts of sexual abuse, although he did describe Nancy
Grantham's escape by sea from Richmond to avoid the "evil designs"
and "brutal purposes" of a lecherous enslaver. Still also held back information because even as late as 1872 he thought it could be dangerous: "It might not be prudent even now, to give the names of persons
still living in the South, who assisted their fellow-men in the dark
days of Slavery." What Still did record remains, however, a treasure
trove for the study of slavery, resistance, and abolition.[17]

The social profile of the 930 runaways reveals that they were
mostly men, who made up almost three quarters of the total (72.7
percent). Women comprised a little less than one in five (18.6 percent), while children, who usually escaped with their mothers, were
almost one in ten (8.7 percent). The runaways who made it to Phila-

delphia were mostly young, in their twenties, fit and strong, which made it easier to withstand the rigors of escape. Some came from the skilled crafts: Elias Jasper, who escaped aboard Captain Baylis's schooner in 1855, knew the trades of "rope-making, carpentering, engineering, and photographing." A few had mastered the crafts of blacksmithing or shipbuilding, but most had been common laborers in port or plantation. A minority had defied the laws of the South and learned to read. A substantial number had been hired out by their enslavers, which gave them some degree of autonomy, freedom of movement, and access to money.[18]

Most runaways had begun their journey northward in Maryland or Virginia, the slave states closest to Philadelphia, linked by roads, trains, and ships, which were especially important given the geographical prominence of Chesapeake Bay to both states. Half of all fugitives (51.1 percent) came from Maryland, where, after the expansion of wheat production in the eighteenth century, labor demands had declined and hiring out had become more common. The percentage of runaways coming from Maryland also increased over time, suggesting that as resistance rose, the system of slavery on "the middle ground" began to collapse in the late 1850s. Around three in ten escapees (29 percent) originated in Virginia, many of them from Norfolk and Richmond. A smattering of runaways came from Delaware; Washington, DC; and coastal North Carolina; and even smaller numbers from Georgia, Alabama, and Louisiana.[19]

For many of the runaways, Still recorded exactly how they escaped. A modest number arrived in Philadelphia by train, some of them in disguise, which included passing as white. Charlotte Giles and Harriet Eglin boarded a train in Baltimore in 1856 dressed for "mourning, with heavy black veils." Even though one of their enslavers searched the car, they successfully "wept" their way to freedom. A few arrived by horse, hidden away in wagons or carriages. In March 1857 Abram Harris showed up in Still's office having traveled by foot without a guide for nine frigid days and nights, with nothing to eat for the last three days. He had been forced to leave behind his fifty-year-old companion, George Weems, who succumbed to hunger and frostbite and later passed away. Every one of these runaways risked not only sickness and death but also arrest and imprisonment on almost every mile of their landed journey through the South, where law empowered every white person to stop and arrest anyone suspected of being a runaway.

Still's notations made it abundantly clear that the most common—and the most important—means of transportation to freedom was the ship. For the 283 people whose means of escape he noted, two-thirds (191 total, 67.4 percent of the recorded) did not so much run away from bondage as sail, steam, or row away from it, depending on the kind of vessel they boarded in their home port. Arrivals by sea were thus more than twice as common as all other noted means of travel combined. Still offers hard data and statistical proof of the centrality of maritime escape to the misnamed Underground Railroad.[20]

People made their way to freedom on all kinds of vessels, from the smallest self-constructed raft to the largest industrial steamship. Stebney Swan armed himself with a broadax and a hatchet before embarking with four comrades from Portsmouth on a skiff, a small, shallow, flat-bottomed open boat with sharp bow and square stern, in October 1857. Brothers Anthony and Albert Brown escaped from Tanner's Creek in Norfolk on "one of their master's small oyster-boats, which was pretty-well rigged with sails." Many African Americans in Maryland and Virginia worked on the water and drew on their maritime knowledge in the urgent moment of escape. Many seeking to escape the "prison house" of bondage found hiding places aboard steamships, which were large, complex vessels with many nooks and crannies. Thanks largely to Black steward John Minkins, the steamer *City of Richmond* brought runaways from Richmond, Petersburg, Portsmouth, and Norfolk to Philadelphia on at least thirteen voyages between August 1853 and November 1854, each time carrying someone who was usually hidden near the scorching hot boiler in the engine room. The steamer *Pennsylvania* made at least six voyages with fugitives in 1854 and 1855. Runaways James Mercer, John Clayton, and William H. Gilliam all "endured frightful torment when they were secreted in a dark space very near the ship's boiler and coal bin. The heat and dust nearly suffocated them on several occasions and they survived by taking turns breathing fresh air through a little hole in a nearby wall." Almost a quarter of those who arrived in Philadelphia by sea had hitched rides on a steamboat.

Most people reached Philadelphia on an old-fashioned sailing ship, usually the nimble, speedy, versatile two-masted vessel called the schooner, which could have a carrying capacity as small as thirty tons or as large as two hundred tons or more. Captain Baylis skippered a smaller schooner, while Fountain's vessel in 1855 must have been much larger since he was able to carry away as many as twenty-one fugitives at once. The larger the schooner, the bigger the hold and the greater the ability of a ship carpenter to create hidden compartments that inspectors would have trouble finding. This was a key to Fountain's success. Roughly two in five (42.4 percent) of the runaways stepping off a vessel in Philadelphia disembarked from schooners, which were common to all Atlantic trading circuits, especially up and down the North American coast.[21]

Working in the aftermath of the passage of the Fugitive Slave Act in September 1850, Still preferred to send those who arrived in Philadelphia on to Canada rather than risk local recapture, as he wrote to fellow abolitionist James Miller McKim in 1858: "Far better will it be for them in Canada this winter where they can procure a plenty of work, than it would be in Pa., where labor will be scarce and hands plenty with the usual amount of dread & danger hanging over the head of the Fugitive." Many who traveled on to Canada continued their escape by sea, either along the Atlantic coast or via the Great Lakes after a landed passage.[22]

NEW YORK

How the blue highway worked was illuminated in another remarkable document much like Still's Journal C: abolitionist Sydney Howard Gay, the editor of the *National Anti-Slavery Standard*, recorded
information about two hundred fugitives he assisted in 1855 and
1856. His "Record of Fugitives" represents but a fragment of the work
he did with free Black porter and dockside militant Louis Napoleon
in assisting hundreds, if not thousands, of fugitives in New York during the 1840s and 1850s, as sailors on New York–based vessels continued to bring freedom seekers to port in defiance of the Fugitive
Slave Act of 1850.[23]

Born in Massachusetts, Gay failed as a merchant and land specu-
lator before finding his life's calling as a journalist and editor committed to the cause of abolition. A follower of William Lloyd Garrison,
he assumed the editorship of the *National Anti-Slavery Standard* in
1844 and held the position until 1858, during which time he was a
leading figure in organizing fugitive escapes to New York, although
his was only one of five such groups in the city. (The others, all connected, were the American and Foreign Anti-Slavery Society, organized by the Tappan brothers; the African American Committee of
Thirteen; the Vigilance Committee; and William P. Powell's Colored Sailors Home.) Gay's office functioned as a receiving depot for
runaways, welcoming and assisting fugitives and sending them on to
Albany, Syracuse, New Bedford, and Boston. After 1850, many went
to safer destinations in Canada, continuing their maritime journey on
barges up the Hudson River, canal boats on the Champlain and Erie
Canals, and watercraft on the Atlantic coast.[24]

The heart and soul of Gay's operation was Louis Napoleon. Born
free in 1800 to a Jewish father and an enslaved African American
mother around 1800, he went work in his twenties to help fugitives.
The gregarious Napoleon was always in motion; indeed, his job as a

porter, moving cargo along the waterfront, required constant movement and a deep knowledge of the city. One of Gay's entries in the "Record of Fugitives" illustrated how things worked: "A coloured man by y[e] name of Jackson employed on one of y steamers to N.Y. gave [James Russell] a passage here, + put him in Napoleon's hands." Napoleon "found" runaways aboard ships; he met them in the middle of the night, at the 3:00 a.m. train from Philadelphia, or wherever they arrived in the city; he sheltered them in his own home; and he often traveled with them as they left New York in search of a freer, more secure life. Napoleon signed his name with an *X*, but this did not prevent him from securing from judges one writ of habeas corpus after another to free fugitives who were incarcerated in jails or on ships. Napoleon's certificate of death in 1881 listed his occupation as "Under Ground R.R. Agt." Legend had it that over thirty-seven years he had assisted three thousand runaways, many of them in collaboration with Gay.[25]

The two hundred people who passed through Gay's office consisted of 124 men, 46 women, and 30 children. Women made up 23 percent of the adult escapees arriving in New York and 18.8 percent of the adult maritime fugitives, both figures similar to those recorded by Still and likewise comparable to the 20 percent usually suggested for female runaways across the nation in the antebellum era. Several women pulled off near-miraculous escapes. Harriet Shepherd managed to get out of Chestertown, Maryland, with five children between the ages of three and seventeen in late October 1855. Sophia Gray escaped Portsmouth, Virginia, aboard a schooner with her two children during the summer of 1856. She followed her sister-in-law Phyllis Galt, who had absconded several months earlier among "the twenty-one." Sophia herself was hired out by her enslaver and therefore did not live with her children, but as she explained to Gay, "they were sometimes permitted to visit her," hence "she had no difficulty in getting off with them to y vessel."[26]

Like Still, Gay interviewed the fugitives as a prelude to offering

The biggest maritime escape of the antebellum era happened in 1855, when twenty-one men, women, and children escaped from Norfolk with Captain James Fountain.

assistance—usually money for food, shelter, and transportation—and he too was inconsistent in the amount and quality of the information he recorded. Some of his entries are brief: "James Johnson of Deer Creek, Md. William Rambley, master, left on Friday y 4th inst. His master had threatened to sell him." How Johnson ended up standing before Gay in his lower Manhattan office was not specified, and indeed roughly a third of Gay's entries in the "Record of Fugitives" are similar.[27]

At times, however, Gay grew fascinated with the story he was hearing and transcribed abundant details of the escape. Such was the case when a man appeared before him named Charles, about forty-five years of age, "but seeming much older," who arrived in the office from Richmond "in a state of great trepidation." Charles explained to Gay that "he has had a hard life + long wished to be free, + has tried to run away before." One day on the docks some sailors promised Charles that "they would conceal him on board if he would help load y vessel." Charles took the offer and did the work. The sailors hid him in the hold, giving him hardtack biscuit and a barrel of water. All went well until eight days into the voyage when the ship hit rough seas. Charles got seasick and started to retch loudly, attracting the unwelcome attention of the captain, who brought him up on deck and whipped him to make him disclose who had concealed him on board. Charles took the lash, protected the sailors, and all the while "denied that any one had any knowledge of his being there."[28]

When the vessel arrived in New York, the captain told Charles that he would return him to Richmond on his next voyage, but meanwhile the runaway should get to work to pay his fare. When the captain dispatched him on an errand to the market, Charles "fell in with a coloured man," probably a sailor, who encouraged him to return to the vessel to get his clothes—and run. Charles did just that and was almost off the ship with "his bundles" when the mate of the ship spotted him and asked what he was doing. Charles thought quickly under pressure and said that the clothes belonged to some sailors who had been discharged from the ship. The mate took the clothes from Charles and threw them onto the wharf, where Charles and his new friend later retrieved them and escaped. The friend might also have told him where he could find assistance. Charles nervously appeared before Gay, told his story in convincing detail, and off to Albany he went.

A woman named Winny Petty also told Gay a compelling tale. When a Norfolk enslaver brought a "spectulater," or domestic slave trader, to inspect her and her three-and-a-half-year-old daughter, Winny "was sure that she was sold." Winny's husband had already escaped Norfolk by sea the previous fall. Rumor had it that she would soon follow, as indeed she planned to do. The moment the two men left the room she grabbed her child and fled to a house outside of town where she knew she could take refuge. She and the child went under the house, through a trapdoor "covered by a piece of carpet." Inside they found "a place a few feet square had been excavated by y slave who lived there, for y concealment of fugitives." The space had a bed but no window and no other source of light or ventilation except the trapdoor. For the next five months Winny and her child were fed "at y expense of a soc[iet]y among y slaves, organized to aid persons in her circumstances." Even so, "they Suffered extreemly from the dampness & cold," including frostbite. Meantime Winny's husband Peter engaged Captain Fountain to pick her and the child up on a future voyage to Norfolk and to bring them north. The husband had found work in New Bedford, to which port Gay arranged to send Winny and her little girl.[29]

Gay also found that surprising facts popped up in the narratives of escape. Henry Chadborn hid himself aboard the schooner *Sarah Elizabeth* out of Richmond in early 1856. One day out on the voyage he emerged from his hiding place and "showed himself" to Captain Hosskiss. He explained to Gay that he was "well treated by y capt. + was put on shore." Not long afterward Sarah Bellons learned at the last minute of an opportunity to get aboard a freedom ship in Norfolk. When she got to the place of rendezvous, she "was surprised to find so many companions in y place of concealment provided for them," highlighting once again the superior organization and capacity of the maritime system of escape in Norfolk.[30]

Gay also learned of the importance of patience among the fugitives. Albert Hennison, who worked as a porter on the docks of Richmond, had "wished and tried for 18 yrs. to escape, but had never had y opp[ortunit]y" until the cook of a schooner offered, for fifty dollars, to hide him away in the vessel's "state room." Gay also learned, like Still, that runaways lived for months as maroons in the Great Dismal Swamp awaiting a ship from a port in North Carolina or Virginia. Charles Thompson, considered by Gay to be "the leader" of a company of seven men from the maritime region of North Carolina and Virginia near Norfolk, was "engaged for a year past" in plotting their collective escape by sea.[31]

Gay's "Record of Fugitives" confirms that the patterns found in Philadelphia also apply in New York. Three-quarters of the two hundred people who showed up in Gay's office had escaped from Maryland (eighty-one) and Virginia (sixty-six). Other fugitives originated in North Carolina (fifteen), Delaware (eleven), and Washington, DC (seven). Three from Kentucky had already been brought east by their enslavers to Baltimore and Philadelphia before making their escapes. Only a few individuals came from either South Carolina or Georgia. None came from the Deep South states of Louisiana, Mississippi, or Alabama, which, apart from New Orleans and Mobile, sent few vessels to New York. Gay did not record an origin for eight runaways. Abolitionist James Miller McKim wrote in 1857 that fugitives flocked to New York from border states and "all along the Atlantic seaboard."[32]

Of the sixty-nine men, women, and children Gay identified as having arrived by sea, he noted the type of vessel on which almost three-quarters of them made their escapes. (For the other quarter he wrote something generic such "sail boat" or "vessel.") Nine fugitives arrived on steamships that usually came from Richmond. The largest portion of sailaways arrived on schooners, which were seagoing workhorses in the regular packet voyages between New York and all major Southern ports. A substantial number of the fugitives arrived with Fountain or Baylis after stopping off in Wilmington or Philadelphia. All twenty-nine maritime runaways from Norfolk and its vicinity arrived by sea, primarily because of the economic linkages the port had with New York and the number of ships that sailed between the two cities. Gay did not provide the means of escape for Norfolk natives Harriet Taylor or her three children, but other sources demonstrate that they departed Norfolk on a schooner.[33]

Gay's "Record of Fugitives" shows that a majority of those who passed through his New York office (51.5 percent) had escaped by sea. Here, too, the ship was the most important means of escape during 1855 and 1856, and surely in most other years as well. The proportion of people arriving by sea was undoubtedly significantly higher in New Bedford and Boston, which were two and three hundred miles farther north and therefore significantly harder to reach by land. For many of the maritime runaways, the passage to New York was simply the first on a longer voyage. Gay helped to dispatch a substantial number of the escapees by vessel up the Hudson River to Albany and up the Atlantic coast to ports farther north. The record books of Still and Gay make it clear that 1855 to 1856 was a peak period for the arrival of fugitives by sea.[34]

VIRGINIA STRIKES BACK

As national tensions around slavery soared, the ruling class of Virginia took bold action against maritime maroons in 1856. In recent years enslavers had seen hundreds of enslaved people disappear from their plantations and workshops, hidden away on northbound vessels by the combined power of fugitives; ship captains like Fountain, Baylis, and Lambdin; and assorted sailors, dockworkers, cooks, and stewards. Virginia planter and Civil War firebrand Edmund Ruffin, himself affected by frequent escapes from his plantation on the James River, identified sailors as "abolition agents" in and around Norfolk, which in 1855 alone "lost about one hundred slaves, of the most valuable description, all of which were doubtless forwarded by Northern agents, and taken off in Northern vessels." He also noted that along the Potomac River "property in slaves is there of such uncertain tenure, as to be of but little value." Richmond too had suffered many losses, as Ruffin knew from personal experience.[35]

Clarissa Davis exemplified Virginia's trend. She fled Portsmouth, Virginia, in May 1854 aboard the steamship *City of Richmond*. Dressed in "male attire," she followed in the wake of her two brothers who had already escaped by sea to New Bedford. When the time came to make her break for the ship, she prayed for rain to keep people who might recognize her off the streets. She got her wish, "in torrents." A white pilot named William Bagnall and the steamboat's unnamed steward (perhaps John Minkins), whom she already knew, hid her in a box on board the vessel and directed her to William Still and the Vigilance

Committee in Philadelphia. She took a second voyage to meet her brothers in New Bedford and later engineered the escape of other family members to join them. This mobile maritime family reunion was exactly what the new Virginia law was meant to eliminate.[36]

Clandestine chain migrations such as the one involving the Davis family caused petitions to pour into the state legislature from officials in Virginia's maritime counties, which were hemorrhaging workers. Elected officials in Norfolk, who had complained bitterly about escape by sea for three decades, were now joined by petitioners from Elizabeth City County, north of Hampton Roads, and Princess Anne County on Virginia's Atlantic coast, east of Norfolk. These maritime localities requested legislation to arm ship pilots with state power to search vessels and to arrest captains, sailors, and fugitives. Virginia House delegate Dr. Francis Mallory, an enslaver, former naval officer, and agent of the US Navy in Norfolk, proposed new legislation in early 1856 aimed specifically at Northern-owned vessels operating in Virginia. Fifteen years earlier, a law aimed at fugitives on New York ships had failed.[37]

Virginia's legislators passed "An Act Providing Additional Protection for the Slave Property of Citizens of this Commonwealth" on March 17, 1856. The bill's primary purpose was policing—to crack down on ships, captains, sailors, dockers, and especially would-be sailaways. The bill was perhaps the single greatest legislative evidence of the power of maritime escape, which the government of Virginia was now prepared to spend significant time, money, and labor to combat. An ambitious initiative from above sought to crush a many-headed resistance from below.

Governor Henry A. Wise appointed his friend Dr. Jesse J. Simkins of Northampton County, located at the southern end of the Delmarva Peninsula, as the chief inspector of vessels. Simkins based his operation in Norfolk, the epicenter of escape by sea, and presided over a large and geographically expansive network of officers, police, and spies. He would at the same time keep track of all local pilots, their vessels, and their crew members, not least because some pilots were African American and presumed to be sympathetic to fugitives. Simkins appointed twelve river inspectors, showing that the problem was geographically widespread throughout Virginia. The law also appointed thirty-five pilots as inspectors, who boarded trading vessels, conducted searches, and issued certificates to those who harbored no runaways, clearing the way for homeward passage to the North. Inspectors earned five dollars for each inspection, to be paid by the captain of the outward-bound vessel. Any captain who attempted to leave Virginia waters without a certificate would be fined $500. The certificate itself would have to be obtained within twelve hours of departure to limit the amount of time a runaway might have to steal aboard.

Over the next five years the new pilot police, as they were called, generated massive data about thirteen thousand outbound voyages by Northern vessels—a documentary monument to the prevalence and power of escaping slavery by sea during the 1850s. The chief inspector wrote quarterly reports to the governor in ledger booklets and bound volumes, listing each inspected vessel by name, owner, home port, trade route, commodity, captain, and number of crew members. The vessels inspected were overwhelmingly schooners, carrying mostly coal and timber, sailed by crews of four to eight men. If someone was taken aboard such a vessel of modest size as a stowaway, everyone on board would have almost certainly known about it. Even though the law specified that the inspection be carried out along twelve rivers and across the Chesapeake Bay, the reports concern traffic only from the Potomac, York, and Rappahannock Rivers, along with Hampton Roads, which included vessels from Norfolk and Richmond.[38]

Governor Wise expected resistance to the new law, so he armed the pilots with muskets and cannon, to be used against any vessel that refused to heave to for inspection. He also awarded pilots the even greater power to command local militias if necessary. The law al-

The legislature of Virginia empowered "Port Police" in 1856 to search for maritime escapees by inspecting all Northern-bound vessels. The effort failed.

lowed counties located on Chesapeake Bay to enact a "fugitive slave tax" to be used to support a "police patrol" for the recapture of runaways. When a fugitive was discovered aboard a ship, inspectors could "arrest all persons on board." Virginia legislators understood that many escapes took place without the knowledge of the captain. A negligent inspector who allowed a vessel to leave Virginia's waters without scrutiny would be subject to stiff penalties. Fearing corruption or noncompliance with the law, state authorities policed the maritime police.[39]

The new initiative by the government of Virginia to inspect all

Northern ships quickly generated what Chief Inspector Simkins denounced as "obstruction." On Sunday, April 6, 1856, less than a
month after the new law had been implemented, a deputed Virginia
pilot suspected the New York–based schooner *Maryland* of carrying
concealed fugitives and boarded the homeward-bound vessel at Hampton Roads. The vessel had loaded coal at Alexandria, where, according to a newspaper correspondent, a group of Northern captains had
plotted to undermine, indeed nullify, the new law. Captain Speight of
the *Maryland* refused the request to search his vessel, so the pilot
sailed away to Elizabeth City for reinforcements, bringing back a
group of armed militia members who made the first arrests under the
new law. The pilot took charge of the schooner and carried the captain and eight crew members to Norfolk, where a magistrate threw
them in jail. He then searched the vessel for runaways and found
none. Captain Speight paid a fine and after a few days resumed his
voyage. The owners of the vessel vowed to test the constitutionality
of the new law but apparently never did so. Freedom seekers bound
for New York and Philadelphia in 1858 and 1859 would continue to
test the law in their own ways, demonstrating that ship captains like
Speight were not the only key to escape.[40]

RESISTANCE CONTINUES

In late May 1858 William H. Thompson, a free nineteen-year-old
African American ship cook, worked alongside an enslaved man
named Ned, loading 150 cords of high-quality pinewood onto the
Francis French, a New Jersey–based vessel anchored on Chuckatuck
Creek in Isle of Wight County, off the James River, which feeds into
Chesapeake Bay. William and Ned talked as they worked. Ned explained that his brother Anthony, also enslaved, was being mistreated
by his enslaver, James Scott of Smithfield. Ned apparently painted a
vivid picture of the abuse. Thompson later explained that Ned's ac-

count "so worked upon his feelings" that he was moved a day or two later to lead Anthony into the forecastle of the *Francis French*, where he raised some loose planks on the deck; helped him into a dark, snug space below; and covered the planks with several barrels of supplies to hide the point of entry. The vessel must have passed inspection and prepared to set sail for New York on May 26, but contrary winds delayed its departure.[41]

Meanwhile James Scott discovered that Anthony had gone missing and suspected that he was stowed away aboard the *Francis French*. Scott quickly sailed to Norfolk to meet with his brother-in-law, Mayor F. F. Ferguson, to explain his loss of "a valuable negro" and to seek his assistance. Ferguson in turn mobilized William Parker, the new chief inspector under the law of 1856, as well as several other officials, including two pilots. The party chartered a tugboat and took off after the *Francis French* at one in the morning. They caught up with the vessel the following day around noon, boarded, found Anthony, and brought him and the entire crew back to the Norfolk jail.

The actions taken by William, Ned, and Anthony enraged the leaders and populace of Norfolk, who on the very day that the culprits were thrown in jail assembled for a mass meeting in Ashland Hall, attended—according to the *Norfolk Argus*—by "many of our most respectable and intelligent citizens" amid Norfolk's largest public meeting ever. Infuriated by the latest in a long line of maritime escapes, they poured out their wrath on a man named Willett Mott, who formerly sailed a packet ship from New York and had now settled in Norfolk, and on shipowner William Dannenburg. Both men, the citizens insisted, were helping runaways escape by sea. Mott had the nerve to express sympathy for the men recently arrested, using "expressions which no man from the North should be permitted to use in a Southern State." The citizens promised to tar and feather both Mott and Dannenburg unless they left town within twenty-four hours and promised never to return. Mott went into hiding while Dannenburg boarded a departing vessel the following morning. The meeting also targeted free Black men Edmund White and George Washington, who were "acting in concert with the Abolitionists of the North, and ought to be driven hence." Moreover, they vowed to create a record of all free Blacks living in the city and to mimic the abolitionists in forming their own "Vigalance Committee," not to assist but rather to prevent flight, with twenty-five members in each ward of the city to be mobilized for the police action.[42]

At a legal hearing a few days later, Captain Thomas F. Loveland and the other white members of the *Francis French* all insisted that they had no idea that Anthony was on the vessel. But they did not stop there. They used the courtroom as a stage to pledge their undying loyalty to the South and its way of life. A Southern character witness for Loveland announced that the captain and crew had "defended our rights against the Black Republicans, and were ready to do so to the last extremity." Moreover, if the Union were to divide, Loveland would, he declared, move to the South to take up residence among "gentlemen." Another person implicated in the shoreside part of the plot, Barney Kayton, "declared his innocence, and said he was born in the South, and raised in the South and would assist in putting a rope around the necks of every negro stealer in the land." The courtroom audience burst into applause. Everyone seemed to agree, wrote an eyewitness, the white men were not "slave stealers."[43]

William H. Thompson then stepped forward to take full responsibility for Anthony's presence on the *Francois French*, confirming that neither Loveland nor any other members of the crew knew anything about it. Thompson understood that "slave stealing" was a serious crime in Virginia and that his admission would send him to prison. He also knew that the law of 1856 allowed the government of Virginia to fine Loveland $500 and confiscate his vessel. William turned to the captain and apologized for causing so much "suffering and loss." If the Black cook thought his truthfulness and remorse would "work upon the feelings" of the court, he was mistaken. The judge sentenced him to ten years in prison for the solidarity he showed to Anthony and sent him away to Richmond to serve his time. White solidarity carried the day.[44]

"THE MOST INTENSELY EXCITING EVENT"

The biggest capture of a captain assisting fugitives to freedom happened simultaneously with the seizure and condemnation of the *Francis French*. On Monday, May 31, 1858, in Petersburg, Virginia, Captain William B. Baylis loaded 1,200 bushels of wheat into his small, low schooner, the *Keziah*, which had a regular crew of only two, Baylis and his mate Joseph Simkins. Local men on the docks watched Baylis closely because his brother had been suspected of involvement with runaways two years earlier on a voyage aboard the same vessel; he had been warned off and told never to return. The reputation of the *Keziah* along the waterfront was the "ground-work" for close surveillance, but nothing seemed untoward, and the vessel was allowed "to pass down the [Appomattox] river without interference," bound for Philadelphia and its Vigilance Committee.[45]

Enslaver and former mayor Andrew Kevan had heard that his bondman John Bull had been seen "loitering about the city wharf" shortly before the *Keziah* weighed anchor. Kevan and three others in search of wayward workers enlisted Captain Butts of the local police, got a search warrant, and chartered a side-wheel steam tug, the *W. W. Townes*, for a midnight pursuit. They caught up with the *Keziah* at Minge's Reach, twenty-six miles beyond City Point at the confluence of the James and Appomattox Rivers. They went aboard and announced their mission. Baylis and Simkins immediately denied that they had any fugitives aboard, but the search, "after considerable difficulty," proved them wrong. The men from Petersburg went into the captain's cabin, where they found a trapdoor, beneath which sat a woman named Sarah, dressed in the male attire that allowed her to board the ship unnoticed; she was "stowed away in the midst of a lot

of bacon." Making their way through a warren of specially constructed subdivisions in the hold, they then discovered the men, one
by one, "secreted in the wheat." Baylis, Simkins, and every newly
found fugitive protested that each person the authorities discovered
was the very last one. When all five fugitives had been taken into
custody, the captain of the steamer took the schooner in tow and
headed back toward Petersburg, stopping off at City Point to telegraph the news ahead that the "slave stealers" had been caught and
would arrive in the early evening.[46]

An angry crowd began to gather at the docks two hours before the
prisoners arrived, screaming for "tar and feathers, hanging, ducking,
lashing, burning, and every conceivable method of retributive Judge
Lynch" for the "kidnappers," according to a reporter for the Petersburg *Daily Express*. When the vessel anchored at the docks, a large
body of police received Baylis and Simkins and escorted them off the
wharf. A mob of two thousand men—almost half of the town's white
male population—surged forward quickly, shouting at Baylis, "hang
him" and "kill him." According to an eyewitness, "the throng pressed
in from all sides" to capture the prisoners and nearly succeeded in
prying Simkins from the clutches of Officer Butts: "Blows were
struck at him, lunges made for his throat and all sorts of attempts to
drag him into the mob followed without cessation." The police and
some "law-abiding citizens" waged battle against the mob and eventually regained control, placing Baylis, Simkins, and the recaptured
fugitives in jail. The police then established a special watch to guard
against a rumored attack on the jail overnight. The following day the
Express began its coverage of the return of Baylis, Simkins, and the
runaways by saying, "Our city was yesterday evening the theatre of
the most intensely exciting event that has ever transpired within its
limits from the earliest to the latest period of its history." The event
had almost resulted in lynchings, the preferred remedy of many white
citizens.

The following day, as people gathered at the docks to take guided tours of the *Keziah*, another mob formed at the courthouse in hopes of a second chance to get at the race traitors Baylis and Simkins. Overnight Butts and other city authorities had interrogated the runaways and learned more about the plot. Baylis had recruited the five, one by one, in the central marketplace near the docks, with the help of an unnamed local white abolitionist who served as a go-between. Baylis asked each fugitive for $50 for the passage, but he accepted less: John Bull paid the full $50, while Joe Mayo paid $48, Gilbert $40, and William $34. Sarah paid nothing at all, but promised her labor, agreeing to work in the Baylis household as a domestic. It turned out that Mayo had a life savings of more than $100. Gilbert had an astonishing $500 "in gold, silver, and notes" (more than $18,000 in 2024), which he had saved over twenty-seven years of "pig raising." What was perhaps more worrying to the authorities was that maritime communications had enabled the plan of escape to reach many hundreds of miles. Joe Mayo was on his way to New York to meet his wife, while John Bull looked ahead to a job as a waiter that had been arranged for him in Toronto "through the influence of some of his old friends," likely earlier maritime escapees. If the sheriff hoped to expose the secret organization behind the escape, he failed. The five fugitives divulged nothing.[47]

Baylis himself seemed resigned to his impending conviction, foregoing an attorney to send all his money to his family back in Delaware. Simkins, on the other hand, maintained that he had no idea that the five fugitives were on board, although it was later suggested that he and another man by the name of Valentine had been involved in maritime marronage for some time. In sentencing Baylis, Judge Nash of the Petersburg Circuit Court declared that "this is not your first offense, as the interior construction of your vessel would seem to indicate that it had been built for that purpose." The judge fined Baylis $500 and ordered that the *Keziah*, valued at $800, be sold at auction. The judge also gave Baylis an eight-year term for each runaway he assisted, forty years in all. He joined William H. Lambdin and

William H. Thompson in the Virginia State Penitentiary, where he was likely to spend the rest of his life.[48]

Word of Baylis's arrest floated on the "common wind." Philadelphia abolitionist Lucretia Mott wrote to a friend in June 1858, "Don't you pity poor Captn Bailyss—a lifelong incarceration—unless emancip'n be achieved. It is too great a risk for any to run." She added that she and others were raising funds on the captain's behalf: "We are just issuing circulars for more money, so as to make a fresh onslaught." The news also made its way to Canada: former fugitive John Henry Hill, who five years earlier had literally fought his way off Richmond's auction block with a knife before securing secret passage on a steamer to Philadelphia, wrote to William Still: "I have just heard that our friend Capt. B[aylis] have being taken Prisoner in Virginia with slaves on board of his vessel. I h[e]ard this about an hour ago. the Person told me of this said he read it in the newspaper, if this be so it is awfull. You will be so kind as to send me some information. Send me one of the Virginia Papers. Poor fellow if they have got him, I am sorry, sorry to my heart." Hill had not escaped with Baylis but rather on the steamship *City of Richmond*; he must have known the captain through a clandestine network that linked Virginia, Philadelphia, and Canada.[49]

The Virginia law and its subsequent vessel seizures commanded the attention of abolitionists from Wilmington to Philadelphia, New York, and Boston. In response to the act, militant New England sailor-abolitionist Austin Bearse built a small, fast vessel called the *Wild Pigeon* and proposed to the Boston Vigilance Committee that he sail the vessel to Virginia to make piratical attacks against the state's pilot boats, rescue any fugitives who had been seized, and bring them to freedom in Boston. Bearse eventually gave up on this John Brown–like direct action because Boston's "coasting captains would not join me in the enterprise." He sold the *Wild Pigeon* and returned the money that had been advanced by the Boston Vigilance Committee.

But like the ocean itself, the sea-based struggle for freedom rolled on evermore.[50]

A SPACE TOO VAST

Did the Virginia law of 1856 provide "Additional Protection for the Slave Property of Citizens of this Commonwealth" as its title promised? Did it successfully criminalize the cooperation of seafaring people and freedom seekers bound for Philadelphia and New York? As early as March 1857, a year after the law was passed, Chief Inspector William Parker thought so. He wanted his patron, Governor Henry A. Wise, to think so too. He wrote, "The inspectors have been faithful in the discharge of their duties, and the operation of this new law has been beneficial to an almost incalculable extent. The escape of slaves from tide water Virginia to the north has now become very rare. Soon, the grievance will cease to exist."[51]

Parker spoke too glibly, too soon. Captains Fountain and Baylis defied the intensified surveillance and continued to ferry people to freedom. Some of their escapes took place right under the noses of the new maritime police in Norfolk. The two biggest successes after the passage of the act, the capture of the *Francis French* and the *Keziah* in 1858, happened after what must have been failed inspections. Both vessels had left the docks and were making their way out to sea when suspicious enslavers persuaded local authorities to commandeer steamboats and head after them to recover fugitives. Curiously, Parker's thick, data-filled reports to the governor did not include evidence on how many fugitives he had actually captured.[52]

On the eve of civil war Parker might have pointed to a slight increase in the small number of seafaring men captured and imprisoned in the Virginia State Penitentiary, as enumerated by the United States Census of 1860. The list included Lambdin, age thirty-one, and Baylis, age forty-nine, both from Delaware; Thompson, age twenty-one (New Jersey); white sailor A. Cottingham, age fifty-two (Maryland); and Black ship cook Lot Munday, age thirty-seven, and Black seaman Cato Ricketts, age thirty-three (both from New Jersey). Samuel A. Smith, who had helped Henry "Box" Brown to freedom in 1849 before being caught and imprisoned after a failed escape, served his term and emerged in 1857 to speak about the conditions of life for those convicted of harboring and "carrying off slaves," "advising slaves to run," and "Negro stealing" in Virginia. Smith had been "kept *heavily chained* in a cell four feet by eight feet in dimensions" and was stabbed five times by "a bribed assassin." Small wonder that Captain Robert Lee, who ferried people to freedom in a small skiff, died in the same prison. (The fugitives captured in the late 1850s would not have been imprisoned but rather returned to their sovereign enslavers, so it is impossible to know how many of them were recaptured.) It is unclear how many people were incarcerated specifically because of the inspection act, but we know that Lambdin ended up in prison because of a shipwreck, and Baylis and Thompson because of post-inspection pursuit by enslavers. That leaves only three who might have been ensnared by the inspection practices of the law of 1856.[53]

The Virginia law, in sum, did not find many offenders nor did it make maritime escapes "very rare," much less cause them to "cease to exist." But it does seem to have had a minor impact on the transit of fugitives to Philadelphia, as noticed by William Still. Looking back from the vantage point of 1872, Still thought that by late 1858 "the Underground Rail Road business was not very brisk. A disaster on the road, resulting in the capture of one or two captains, tended to damp the ardor of some who wanted to come, as well as that of sympathizers." He referred to Baylis, Lambdin, and the chilling effect of their arrests.[54]

Still added, however, that "the road was not idle"; nor were the maritime channels, far from it. From the moment the law passed through the end of their recordkeeping for year 1856, Still received another thirty-eight fugitives who arrived by sea in Philadelphia, while Gay received forty in New York. These arrivals represented 95.2 percent and 85.1 percent respectively of the year's total arrivals for each city. Such figures do not suggest an immediate decline in escapes. The following year, 1857, Still met and interviewed more runaways (206) than in any previous year. Chief Inspector Parker was wrong. The maritime pipeline to Philadelphia and New York continued to operate, perhaps even more cleverly than in the past.[55]

It is not hard to see why the effects of the law were limited. Sheer geography was the most powerful reason. The vastness of the Chesapeake Bay—4,479 square miles of water—not to mention the additional mileage added by the Potomac, Rappahannock, York, Appomattox, and James Rivers, among several others—simply overwhelmed the thirty-five pilots charged to inspect all ships with only six vessels. The pilots could not possibly police so many ships over so vast a space. Nor were they equal to the rising will of the enslaved people of Virginia to resist and escape. To put the same point another way, the forces of freedom were stronger than the forces of surveillance and repression in Virginia in 1856.[56]

From Clarissa Davis and her brothers to the unnamed chambermaid on a steamship and the young sailor William H. Thompson, to Captains James Fountain and William B. Baylis, to abolitionists Louis Napoleon, Sydney Howard Gay, and William Still, in that order—these people helped push the United States to Civil War. They created deep and sustained conflict over the Fugitive Slave Act of 1850 and the Virginia inspection law of 1856. Their pressure from below showed that "law" could not solve the issues of the day. Throughout the 1850s they made the sea routes from Virginia and Maryland to Philadelphia and New York profitable in ways never intended by Southern enslavers or Northern merchants: they turned Atlantic waterways into sites of struggle and freedom. Some of the effects of the maritime system of escape in the 1850s were indirect, when, for example, the African American militant Shields Green helped John Brown attack the armory at Harpers Ferry on October 16, 1859, in a dramatic effort to detonate insurrections across the slave South. The raid carried out by Brown and Green is widely regarded as a turning point toward war. Behind it, in the case of Green, lay a personal freedom struggle, which was relayed by Anne Brown Adams, John Brown's daughter, after the Civil War. Green had told her of his escape from slavery in Charleston, South Carolina, years earlier. He was "stowed away by one of the hands" in a "sailing vessel loaded with cotton." He was one of thousands for whom one act of resistance sparked many more.[57]

Epilogue

The Middle Passage
to Freedom

The Middle Passage was a haunting, and defining, chapter in the history of the African diaspora, as slave ships carried millions of souls across the Atlantic Ocean from West Africa to the slave societies of the Americas. Over nearly four centuries, those trapped on the floating dungeons experienced merciless violence, abject terror, and unimaginable suffering. Every morning slave ship captains enacted a ghoulish ritual aboard their ships: they ordered sailors to retrieve the bodies of the dead from the lower deck and to cast them overboard to the sharks that trailed the slavers across the ocean. I documented this grim shipboard reality in *The Slave Ship: A Human History*, published in 2007.[1]

Freedom Ship is a hopeful sequel to that work, bringing this awful history full circle by showing how thousands of the descendants of those forced aboard slave ships emancipated themselves and in so doing transformed the ship and the sea, against dangerous odds, into spaces of freedom. Every successful escape story told in this book represents a victory of head-work—intelligence, strategy, and planning—over brute oppressive force. Indeed, one of the joys of writing this book is that it allowed me to spend time with so many deeply courageous people who risked life and limb to escape bondage and to fight back against the hideous social system it spawned. What impressed me again and again about the escapees was their indestructible determination to be free. In the end, this book is a study of political will.

For all the violence, blood, and death of the Middle Passage, it too was a place of creative action and agency. The resistance to slavery chronicled in this book was in some ways a continuation of practices that began on the slave ships, where enslaved people fought back under extreme circumstances in every way they could imagine. They waged endless hunger strikes, rose in insurrection, and "ran away" by jumping over the rails of the ship into the ocean. They built systems of fictive kinship to protect themselves against the violence that surrounded them. They formed a culture of resistance aboard the slave ships; carried it ashore in their hearts, minds, and memories; and reformulated it for plantation society. Escaping that society by sea was an innovation, but at the same time it was a return to a previous phase of seaborne struggle. The voyage out of slavery began with the voyage into slavery.

THE MARITIME ORIGINS OF CIVIL WAR

What we have come to call the Underground Railroad had its origins on the waterfront. By the time the phrase had been invented in the late 1830s, enslaved people had been escaping bondage, by land and by sea, for almost two centuries. But only in the late 1830s did the collective action of runaways prompt the formation of durable new organizations dedicated to providing regular, dependable mutual aid. Fugitives began to arrive in significant numbers on merchant ships returning to their Northern home ports after voyages to the South. By taking death-defying risks, getting aboard these vessels, and arriving in New York, Philadelphia, New Bedford, and Boston, fugitives forced reactions from many quarters—their own enslavers, of course, but also merchants, political authorities, police, and perhaps most important of all, abolitionists, who organized during the 1830s to help escapees in new and permanent ways. Fugitives met Northern abolitionists in ports that were centers of economic power, where merchant princes and rising industrialists steered the nation into a new global system of capitalism. These ports also boasted dozens of newspapers and magazines, including abolitionist publications such as *The Liberator* and the *National Anti-Slavery Standard*, which trumpeted the dramas of stowaways to the nation. Fugitives made port cities into both combat zones against bondage and places of refuge: the majority of fugitives who made it to a Northern port would never be recaptured.[2]

It is now widely accepted that the intensifying struggle over fugitives helped to cause the Civil War, even though the system of maritime escape has remained largely invisible amid the consensus. It was evident, however, to a formerly enslaved man named Ellis Bennett, who had lived in South Carolina and Virginia and in 1937 recalled the political importance of vessel searches for runaways: "What caused the war was white folk searching Yankee vessels when they came in the harbor. The [Southern] white man went on the boat just looking [around]. He'd [find a fugitive and] say 'N——, get out of here!' He'd see the n—— running away and he'd kill him. The Yankees got mad." The Yankees did indeed get mad, and the fight over maritime escape escalated during the 1850s.[3]

Free Black communities in the Northern ports played a central, often independent role in protecting and organizing on behalf of those who had escaped bondage. They took the fugitives into their homes and led the way in forming new organizations. Former sailor David Ruggles drew on his dockside connections and Black maritime workers to establish the first Vigilance Committee in New York on November 20, 1835. The Philadelphia Vigilant Committee followed in 1837. Free Blacks in Boston formed the Fugitive Slave Church in 1840 and, working with white abolitionists, a Vigilance Committee of their own in 1841 after a fierce fight over a maritime fugitive from

New Orleans named George. In 1842–43 the Black community of Boston formed the New England Freedom Association, prompted by the initiative of runaways: "Fugitives are constantly presenting themselves for assistance which we are at times unable to afford." By the early 1840s all major port cities boasted organizations devoted to providing material solidarity for maritime maroons. Escaping and resisting slavery by seaborne flight helped to expand and elevate the abolitionist movement to a national level.[4]

Having witnessed the ebbs and flows of the struggle against slavery waged at sea, we may now propose a periodization of its history. The first of four phases began in the late 1820s with an unusual confluence of historical forces: America's expansion of seaborne trade; a surge of antislavery radicalism from below; and the rapid early growth of the abolitionist movement. Escaping slavery, by land and by sea, acquired a new political charge after David Walker wrote his *Appeal* in 1829, Nat Turner led a rebellion in 1831, and William Lloyd Garrison founded *The Liberator* in the same year. The option of seaborne escape expanded as greater numbers of Northern ships, many of them employing Black seamen, sailed into Southern ports. Subversive networks of maritime communication—the "common wind"—beckoned even more fugitives who recognized new opportunities, accepted deadly risks, and "took out" over the waters in unprecedented numbers. The main achievement in this phase was the formation of a new kind of abolitionist organization, the Vigilance Committee, which increased the likelihood that flight would be successful.[5]

Phase two, from 1836 to 1843, witnessed a major escalation of the battle between fugitives and enslavers and between North and South. Maritime escapees caused fierce and lasting interstate conflict over how the law would deal with fugitives. Would those who arrived in free states—in New York after it abolished slavery in 1827, for example—be subject to the laws of Southern states, which demanded that the sailors who helped them be returned for punishment? Or had those fugitives gained their freedom as soon as they reached the free harbor of a Northern port? Abolitionist Charles T. Torrey demanded to know in 1841 whether the legal clash over maritime escapes would result in free Northern states bowing down to the South in "slavish subjection."[6]

Beginning in May 1837 the governors of Georgia and Maine fought a five-year battle over these questions. An enslaved man named Atticus had stowed away aboard the schooner *Susan* and sailed from Savannah to East Thomaston, Maine, with the assistance of mariners Daniel Philbrook and Edward Kelleran. Atticus himself was recaptured, but Georgia's political leaders insisted that Philbrook and Kelleran face rendition and punishment for "slave stealing." Three successive governors of Maine refused the request. Georgia, supported by the legislatures of South Carolina and Alabama, threatened to secede from the union. As ships and fugitives crossed state lines, the debate about maritime marronage expanded nationally.[7]

At the same time, New York's governor William H. Seward engaged in three similar clashes, with the officials of Louisiana, Georgia, and Virginia, all over maritime fugitives and their seafaring helpers. He waged a protracted legal and political battle with successive governors of Virginia beginning in 1839, when an enslaved ship carpenter named Isaac sailed to New York with the assistance of three Black sailors. Virginia demanded that the sailors be returned to stand trial for "slave stealing," but Seward refused, saying that the men had broken no law in the state of New York. Virginia escalated the battle by threatening secession and appealing to other Southern states for support: South Carolina, Georgia, Louisiana, Maryland, and Missouri joined the fray. Seward and New York legislators counterattacked by passing personal liberty laws that protected fugitives and their accomplices and made their return to the South more difficult, if not impossible. Massachusetts passed similar laws after it battled Virginia over maritime fugitives from Norfolk named George and Rebecca Latimer in 1842 and 1843. In response, the citizens of Norfolk demanded federal legislation that prefigured the Fugitive Slave

Act of 1850. Personal liberty laws, along with the formation of new Vigilance Committees in Philadelphia and Boston, were major achievements of maritime fugitives and their supporters between 1836 and 1843. This was also the period in which Frederick Douglass and Harriet Jacobs escaped slavery. Maritime escape from slavery had become a national issue.[8]

Maritime fugitives continued to arrive in Northern ports during the third phase of this history, from 1844 to 1850, as national tensions around the issue of slavery grew. Trade continued to expand, and the Northern dominance of Southern commerce continued apace, creating ever more opportunities for would-be escapees. Jonathan Walker's failed attempt to free seven people by sea in 1844 became a national issue after his release from prison. His book and the gruesome image of his branded hand circulated widely to illuminate the risks and promises of maritime escape. The high-profile trial and conviction of Captain Daniel Drayton for his part in trying to sail seventy-seven people to freedom roiled Washington, DC, including Congress, for several weeks in 1848. The persistence of runaways kept the issue of slavery before an increasingly polarized public and created pressure on members of Congress both North and South. The passage of the Fugitive Slave Act on September 18, 1850, reflected and in turn intensified a growing national crisis.[9]

Radical action taken by runaways prompted the Fugitive Slave Act of 1850 and the national fracas that followed it. Mimicking the evasive language of the US Constitution, legislators targeted "a person held to service or labor" and anyone who might help, setting up a complex coercive legal apparatus that put the power of the federal government behind the slave-owning ruling class of the South. Maritime fugitives inflamed the controversy by continuing to escape in great numbers, while urban Black workers threw fuel on the fire with numerous direct-action rescues. The solidarity shown to fugitives by sailors, dockworkers, market women, and other port-city abolitionists caused Congress to criminalize acts of assistance. During the 1850s maritime escapees Shadrach Minkins, Thomas Sims, Anthony Burns, and their thousands of supporters fought the enforcement of the Fugitive Slave Law in Boston, intensified the national debate, accelerated the growth of the abolition movement, and helped to polarize the country. By 1851 public opinion in the North began to shift toward abolition as the law galvanized fierce popular resistance.[10]

The 1850s also witnessed an important internal transformation within the maritime system of escape. At the very moment when runaways became a symbol of national conflict, several ship captains embraced the antislavery cause and began to carry fugitives from Southern ports, especially in Virginia and North Carolina, to Northern cities on a regular basis, often for a money payment. These captains also changed the technology of escape, constructing secret compartments in the holds of their vessels where escapees could hide, thereby expanding the Atlantic transit of freedpeople. As tensions around slavery soared nationwide, these mariners defied the Fugitive Slave Act and sailed an ever-larger number of people to the promised land of freedom.

Escaping slavery by sea did not come to an end with the outbreak of the Civil War in 1861, even though maritime trade shrank rapidly. Indeed, escapes expanded massively as enslaved people deserted the plantations, many of them by sea. Maritime mobility was part of what W. E. B. Du Bois called the "general strike" waged by enslaved people once the war broke out. Around Chesapeake Bay, thousands traveled by water to seek refuge with Union Army regiments, creating through their actions a partial military emancipation and a new category of worker that allowed them to be employed and protected. Frank Baker, James Townsend, and Sheppard Mallory escaped slavery by rowing a small boat to Fort Monroe, Virginia, in May 1861, demanding freedom. Union Major General Benjamin Butler declared them to be "contrabands of war," thereby freeing them, and soon nine hundred others, from their enslavers, and setting many of them to work. (Jonathan Walker showed up in 1864 to work with them.) On May 13, 1862, dockworker and ship pilot Robert Smalls commandeered a

Frank Baker, James Townsend, and Sheppard Mallory escaped slavery by sea in 1861, prompting Union general Benjamin Butler to emancipate them as "contraband of war."

Confederate transport ship, the *Planter*, and sailed it past several armed danger points in Charleston Harbor to US blockade vessels seven miles out to sea, turning over what would become a warship to the Union Navy. A year later Harriet Tubman led a major Union naval operation up South Carolina's Combahee River, resulting in the maritime liberation of seven hundred enslaved men, women, and children. Black watermen in North Carolina assisted the Union Army and Navy against the Confederacy throughout the Civil War. Amid the chaos of war, enslaved people continued to use the waterways to emancipate themselves.[11]

The success of these escapes, on a larger scale than ever, depended, like those of the previous thirty years, on a combination of social, natural, geographic, and technological knowledge, all of which now had to be integrated into a rapidly evolving knowledge of military operations. Freedom seekers had to study in new ways. The pathways of maritime escape shifted with the outbreak of war. People continued to abscond by merchant ships, but given the wartime disruption of commerce, many more now looked to opportunities created by the movement of armies and navies. The political importance of the intelligence provided by mobile workers increased exponentially. No one knew the battle zones like the people who had worked Southern lands and waterways. Many of the escapees possessed maritime skills and put them to good use under new circumstances. Some twenty thousand people of African descent would serve in the Union Navy during the Civil War, joining and working with a motley crew of other sailors. Those who would be free knew that they themselves must "strike the first blow" and many others afterward.

During the Civil War, in 1864, enslaved people of all ages left their homes in small watercraft to reach a Union naval vessel in the distance.

"INVISIBLE AGENCY"

For the last hundred years, most historians have kept the histories of abolitionism and slave resistance separate, with damaging results. For a long time, enslaved people were not considered abolitionists, when in truth they were the first and most important of them. "Abolition-ist" was coded white. This book makes it clear that the thoughts, voices, actions, and agency of enslaved people were indispensable to the origins and growth of the antislavery movement. By studying ab-olitionism from below, it becomes clear how maritime escapes helped to generate new ideas, labor alliances, and abolitionist institutions. Perhaps the most surprising question raised by this study of the social world of docks and ships is how we missed such a crucial zone of struggle for so long. Terracentrism had obstructed our vision of a powerful maritime engine of resistance.[12]

Keeping in mind the difficulty of estimating the number of fugi-tives owing to incomplete evidence, let us nonetheless assemble a general overview based on the numbers suggested in the previous pages of this book. If Jesse Olsavsky is right in saying that Vigilance Committees assisted as many as ten thousand people between 1835 and 1861 (I think he is), and if half to two-thirds of those arrived by sea as the reports written by William Still and Sydney Howard Gay indicate, that would amount to five to seven thousand maritime fugi-tives. Free Black communities in the Northern ports assisted the Vig-ilance Committees by providing food, shelter, and protection to those who arrived by sea, but it is important to recall that many escapees bypassed the Vigilance Committees altogether and went straight to Black churches, civic organizations, and homes on the waterfront. It is impossible to know how many used this route to freedom, but the number was probably as great or greater than those assisted by mixed-race organizations, primarily because of the issue of trust. As Harriet Jacobs reminded her readers in 1861, only those who had been en-slaved "would have known how difficult it was to trust a white man." The Vigilance Committees and the free Black communities were the greatest sources of support to maritime fugitives, but there were oth-ers, both organizations and individuals.[13]

Many who provided aid dealt primarily with maritime escapees. In New York William P. Powell and Albro Lyons assisted at least

2,500 runaways through the Colored Sailors Home, almost all of whom arrived by sea. Other boardinghouses for Black sailors—in Boston, for example—would have helped a smaller but still substantial number, perhaps a thousand. Another thousand assisted by Captain James Fountain came on his schooner, as did the large but unknown number carried by other captains in the 1850s. Between five hundred and a thousand, a large majority of them arriving by sea, found sustenance in the free Black community of New Bedford from 1830 until 1861. If we allow for exaggeration and overlap—many of Captain Fountain's fugitives, for example, went from his ship to the Philadelphia Vigilance Committee—we may conclude that maritime institutions and individuals assisted another three to four thousand runaways.[14]

By combining the mutual aid provided by institutions such as the American Anti-Slavery Society, the American and Foreign Anti-Slavery Society, and the Committee of Thirteen in New York, and the Fugitive Slave Church and Anti-Man-Hunting League in Boston, with the work of individual abolitionists such as Robert Purvis (who assisted 9,000), Louis Napoleon (3,000), Thomas Garrett (2,700), and Isaac Hopper (1,000), we would add to the total at least another two or three thousand maritime fugitives. The names of hundreds, if not thousands, of waterfront operatives, like the market women of Baltimore and Boston, remain unknown to us, as do the numbers they assisted. We should add Quakers, especially in Philadelphia, who often worked within their own networks and helped many, some of whom had come by ship. Let us also bear in mind that maritime fugitives arrived in other ports, especially in New Jersey and Connecticut, and in lesser numbers in Rhode Island, New Hampshire, and Maine, as well as in smaller ports of New York, Pennsylvania, and Massachusetts. Taken together, and allowing again for exaggeration and overlap, we can add another two or three thousand seaborne fugitives. A conservative estimate of the total number of fugitives arriving by sea in the thirty years before the Civil War would be fifteen to twenty thousand, or five to seven hundred a year for all ports, a substantial portion of the total number of people who escaped slavery during the antebellum years.[15]

The long, hidden, continuous history of escaping bondage by sea had profound historical consequences. As we have seen, maritime fugitives who stole away off vessels in Northern cities shaped the formation of new abolitionist organizations, from Vigilance Committees to colored sailors homes. They also shaped the subsequent evolution of those organizations and the wider antislavery movement, altering and improving communications, organizing, and strategy—especially, as we have seen, in Boston, the epicenter of abolitionism. William P. Powell and the seafarers who stayed in his boardinghouse in New York formed the first Black union and the first maritime union, the American Seamen's Protective Union Association, in 1863. Maritime fugitives and their fellow workers created the world's first migrant solidarity movement.[16]

Seaborne escapees also made a distinctive contribution to American literature as pioneers of the abolitionist genre, the escape narrative, which according to Boston minister and man of letters Theodore Parker was a kind of writing "wholly indigenous and original." William Grimes wrote the first such narrative about his escape from Savannah among the motley crew of the *Casket* in 1815, published without the help of abolitionists, other than himself, in 1825. Harriet Jacobs, who got away with the help of her seafaring uncles from Edenton, North Carolina, aboard the *Skewarky* in 1842, wrote the first woman's escape narrative, exposing to the public the sexual terrors she faced from Dr. Norcom. Maritime artisan Frederick Douglass, pretending to be a sailor named Stanley, dressed the part, then walked and talked his way to freedom as a sailor in 1838, publishing in 1845 the most famous escape narrative ever penned. Dozens of other tales dictated or written by maritime escapees became bestsellers of the abolitionist movement.[17]

Most of the stories in this book are about people who are unknown to readers, unknown even to history. I have named as many of these hidden historymakers as I could. I wanted to say their names and, when possible, the names of those who opened their way to escape. In some ways we know even less about the sailors, dockworkers, and market women who labored in the dark zones of danger than we do about the fugitives themselves. This leads us to another reason why the maritime system of escape has been largely overlooked: waterfront workers—men and women of the wharf, as they were called by Black activists in Boston—have rarely been considered part of the abolitionist movement. Brought together by dockside labor, these workers, together with the fugitives, exercised what Frederick Douglass and William Still called "invisible agency." A history of abolitionism from below, emphasizing lateral connections among the maritime proletariat, helps to restore them to their rightful place in history.[18]

This book has recounted a literal history of conspiracy—usually beginning with a hushed conversation between two people, a fugitive and a waterfront worker, in the dark hold of a ship, on a bustling wharf, or in a crowded dancing cellar amid music and merriment. We have seen dozens of examples of how this system worked. Talking and breathing together was the very definition of conspiracy. Others might or might not have joined as the plot advanced. The exchange of subversive whispers was the first breath of solidarity, which over thirty years would grow, through thousands of actors and actions, into an irrepressible, history-changing force.

The last words belong to Harriet Tubman, the fearless leader who used the waterways of Maryland in several of her missions to bring runaways to freedom. She revealed what may have been the deepest meaning of escaping slavery by water—she called it a Middle Passage to freedom. During her escapes, she ran a tight ship. She once explained to a group of discouraged, discontented North-bound fugitives that "they had to go through or die." She then added a threat: "a live runaway could do great harm by going back," but "a dead one could tell no secrets." She had a pistol at the ready but added that no one had to die as a "traitor." In her mind, and likely in the minds of many others, escaping slavery by sea reversed the historic voyage from Africa into the horrors of American bondage. According to her first biographer, Sarah Bradford, Tubman conveyed a coded Biblical message to a friend who worked with her on the passage to freedom: tell my brothers and sisters that "when the good old ship of Zion comes along, to be ready to step aboard."[19]

Acknowledgments

✥

This book has a long genesis. It commenced thirty years ago, disappeared from the world of scholarship for a quarter century, and reemerged five years ago before finally being completed. Many friends and colleagues have made the work possible.

My first thanks go to my editors at Viking, the incomparable Wendy Wolf and the brilliant Ibrahim Ahmad, who kindly took over as my editor when Wendy retired. Their knowledge of their craft is extraordinary, and I am grateful for it. Warm thanks to my team at the Sandra Dijkstra Literary Agency: Sandy, Elise Capron, and Andrea Cavallaro. They have done much to bring this book and several others into the world.

I called on three dear friends, Ed Baptist, Steve Hahn, and Maurice Jackson, to read the full manuscript. Their comments were learned, incisive, and invaluable. They helped me on issues big and small and showed me how to deepen the analysis. If I have gotten anything wrong, it's their fault. Many friends and colleagues offered expertise and assistance on one or another point: John K. Bardes; Ben Barson; Sean Bercaw and Mary Bercaw Edwards; David Blight; Doug Egerton; Kathryn Grover; Graham Hodges; Forrest Hylton; Kate Clifford Larson; Jules Lobel; Debra Campagnari Martin; Alaina Roberts; Jonathan Schroeder; Chris Smith; and Timothy D. Walker. Thanks to my former PhD student Jesse Olsavsky, who taught me a lot through his pioneering work on the Vigilance Committees. I wish Julius S. Scott were still alive so I could thank him personally for all I have learned from him; he lives on in this book as in so many others. I owe special gratitude to David Cecelski, Cassandra Newby-Alexander, and Timothy D. Walker, whose scholarship on escape by sea has been foundational for me and will be for everyone else who ever studies the subject.

I am delighted to thank those librarians and archivists who provided essential assistance: Chris Lemery at Hillman Library, University of Pittsburgh; Will Evans at the Boston Athenaeum; Paul O'Pecko and Maribeth Quinlan at the G. W. Blunt White Library at Mystic Seaport Museum; Daniel Hinchen and Peter Drummey at the Massachusetts Historical Society; Molly Silliman at the South Carolina Historical Society; Alison Thurman, Ian Dunn, and Dominique Romero at State Archives of North Carolina; Kevin Shupe and Victoria Garnett at the Library of Virginia; Matthew Turi at the Southern Historical Collection, University of North Carolina at Chapel Hill; Aaisha Haykal, Avery Research Center, College of Charleston; Julia Chambers at the Special Collections Research Center, Syracuse University; Elizabeth Dunn, Kaylee Alexander, and Katie Henningsen at the David M. Rubenstein Rare Book & Manuscript Library, Duke University; and Vincent Golden at the American Antiquarian Society.

I would like to thank two classes of students who studied the Underground Railroad with me: Carly Amann, Logan Biedermann, Karen Enomoto, Jonathan Feibusch, Mariah Forrey, Vito Gentile, Eli Gubernick, Matthew Miloszar, Alexander Phillips, Matt Picklo, Cole Privott, Addison Reckley, Sophie Shack, Sarah Stager, Maia Stephenson, and Carlee Stoner in 2021; and Elijah Carter, Jack Graham, Jamie Hackney, David Kim, Jack Lacianca, Arthur Lang, Morgan Meer, Christian Mendoza, Daniel Okren, Kyle Reed, Matthew Richards, James Rickard, Bella Tang, Benton Yurko, and Elizabeth Zwikl in 2023. I benefitted immensely from the curiosity, energy, and intelligence they brought to the classroom. I give especially great thanks to my talented, hardworking research assistants: Adel Mansour, Melina Xie, Matthew Anstatt, and Jaden Rankin-Wahlers. Adel deserves special commendation for his always-creative exploration of sources.

I owe much to my smart and engaged colleagues in the Department of History at the University of Pittsburgh: Reid Andrews, Eladio Bobadilla,

Alexandra Finley, Niklas Frykman, James Hill, Pernille Røge, Liann Tsoukas, and Molly Warsh. I owe Rob Ruck a special brotherly thanks as he has talked me through different parts of this project at many times and places, including courtside at Pitt basketball games. Thanks to Coach Tim O'Toole and the team for bringing so much joy into my life as I wrote these pages. Thanks too to David M. Friedland, whose brilliant talents have kept me going over many years. I also owe much to Deans N. John Cooper, Kathy Blee, and Adam Leibovich of the Dietrich School of Arts and Sciences at the University of Pittsburgh. They have generously supported this work and so many other projects over the years.

Many thanks to the people who engaged with me over several years about the arguments and themes of the book: Peter Cole and the Newberry Library Labor History Seminar; Matteo Aria and the program in History, Anthropology, and Religions at Sapienza Università di Roma; William Boelhower and the Departments of English and History at Università Ca' Foscari in Venice; Alessandro Buffa and the Department of Human and Social Science, Università degli Studi di Napoli L'Orientale; Alain Pascal Kaly and the Universidade Federal Rural do Rio de Janeiro; Joclyne Nunes and the New Bedford Whaling Museum in New Bedford, MA; Tony Bogues and the Center for the Study of Slavery and Justice, Brown University; Graham Hodges and the National Endowment for the Humanities summer seminar Abolitionism and the Underground Railroad, Colgate University; Martha Pallante and the organizers of the ninth annual V. W. Starr History Across the Humanities Conference, Youngstown State University; Martin Farr and the Britain and the World conference, Duquesne University; Marta Puxan Oliva at the Universitat de les Illes Balears, Mallorca, Spain; Julio Djenderedjian, Ludmila Scheinkman, and Juan Soria at the Universidad de Buenos Aires; Camilo Santibáñez Rebolledo at the Universidad de Santiago and Luis Thielemann Hernández at Universidad Finis Terrae, both in Santiago, Chile. I also wish to thank Gino Negro, Aldrin Castellucci, and their colleagues at Mundos do Trabalho who published a pilot essay from the project in 2022. All of you helped more than you know.

My family has lived this book with me. They are used to the tumultuous process by now, but that makes me appreciate them more, not less. My daughter Eva helped me think through several complicated issues. My son Zeke offered unflagging enthusiasm from our earliest discussions. My son-in-law Dylan Knight and my daughter-in-law Greer Donley have brought humane intelligence to this project and to our family. My granddaughters Leona and Cecilia Rediker didn't help with the book, but they sure have added meaning and adventure to my life. My wife Wendy Goldman has done more than anyone else, listening patiently to endless stories and helping me to find my way from beginning to end. I dedicate the book to two other family members, my late brother Shayne Rediker and my other brother Peter Linebaugh. I am a lucky man to have such family, friends, comrades, and colleagues. Love and gratitude to you all.

Illustration Sources and Credits

Page 4. Thomas H. Jones, *The Experience of Rev. Thomas H. Jones, Who Was a Slave for Forty-Three Years, Written by a Friend, as Related to Him by Brother Jones* (New Bedford, MA: E. Anthony & Sons, 1885), the New York Public Library Digital Collections.

Page 7. The New York Public Library.

Page 28. David Walker, *Walker's Appeal, in Four Articles; Together with a Preamble, to the Coloured Citizens of the World, but in Particular, and Very Expressly, to Those of the United States of America* (Boston: David Walker, 1829; repr. 1830), Cornell University Library.

Page 37. Collection of the Smithsonian National Museum of African American History and Culture, Partial Gift of Harry S. Hutchins, Jr. DDS, Col. (Ret.) and his Family, dedicated to the individuals these Slave Hire Badges represent and their descendants.

Page 57. Originally published in William Still, *The Underground Railroad: A Record of Facts, Authentic Narratives, Letters, &c., Narrating the Hardships, Hair-Breadth Escapes and Death Struggles of the Slaves in Their Efforts for Freedom* (Philadelphia: Porter & Coates, 1872).

Page 70. Eyre Crowe, *With Thackeray in America* (London: Cassell, 1893).

Page 85. *Harper's Weekly*, December 8, 1860.

Page 90. Originally published in William Still, *The Underground Railroad: A Record of Facts, Authentic Narratives, Letters, &c., Narrating the Hardships, Hair-Breadth Escapes and Death Struggles of the Slaves in Their Efforts for Freedom* (Philadelphia: Porter & Coates, 1872).

Page 115. Collection of the Massachusetts Historical Society.

Page 139. Jesse Hutchinson Jr., *The Fugitive's Song* (Boston: Henry Prentiss, 1845).

Page 199. Jonathan Walker, *Trial and Imprisonment of Jonathan Walker, at Pensacola, Florida, for Aiding Slaves to Escape from Bondage, with an Appendix, Containing a Sketch of His Life* (Boston: American Anti-Slavery Society, 1845).

Page 211. Bettmann/Getty Images.

Page 212. *Biography of Mahommah G. Baquaqua, a Native of Zoogoo, in the Interior of Africa (A Convert of Christianity), with a Description of that Part of the World, Including the Manners and Customs of the Inhabitants* (Detroit: George E. Pomeroy, 1854).

Page 218. Tonya Bolden, *Maritcha: A Nineteenth-Century American Girl* (New York: Abrams Books, 2005).

Page 238. From the New York Public Library.

Page 271. *Departure of the brig* Acorn *from Boston Harbor with Sims on board*, anonymous engraver with the firm Worcester & Co., Boston, 1851, from the National Parks Service.

Page 276. *Portrait of Anthony Burns, drawn by Barry from a daguerreotype by Whipple and Black* (Boston: R. M. Edwards, 1855).

Page 285. Originally published in William Still, *The Underground Railroad: A Record of Facts, Authentic Narratives, Letters, &c., Narrating the Hardships, Hair-Breadth Escapes and Death Struggles of the Slaves in Their Efforts for Freedom* (Philadelphia: Porter & Coates, 1872).

Page 286. Courtesy of Carrole Mabie, née Lambdin (great-grandniece of William H. Lambdin).

Page 296. Originally published in William Still, *The Underground Railroad: A Record of Facts, Authentic Narratives, Letters, &c., Narrating the Hardships, Hair-Breadth Escapes and Death Struggles of the Slaves in Their Efforts for Freedom* (Philadelphia: Porter & Coates, 1872).

Page 303. Courtesy of the Library of Virginia, Richmond, VA.

Page 322. Bettmann/Getty Images.

Page 323. *Harper's Weekly*, April 9, 1864. Schomburg Center for Research in Black Culture, Photographs and Prints Division, the New York Public Library. *Negroes Leaving Their Home*, New York Public Library Digital Collections.

Insert

Page 1. The Art Institute of Chicago, Chicago, IL.

Page 2. Wikimedia Commons.

Page 3. The Fine Arts Museums of San Francisco.

Pages 4–5. *Harper's Weekly*, August 4, 1869, courtesy of South Street Seaport Museum, New York.

Page 6. George Cruikshank, *A Sailor's Description of a Chase & Capture*, 1822. The Stapleton Collection/Bridgeman Images.

Page 7. *Steamer* Roanoke, *New York & Virginia Steamship Company, 1200 Tons*, 1855, courtesy of Royal Museums Greenwich.

Page 8. William James Bennett, *View of South Street, from Maiden Lane, New York City*, 1829, the Metropolitan Museum of Art, New York, NY.

Page 9. Pierre Jacques Benoit, *Voyage à Surinam; description des possessions néerlandaises dans la Guyane* (Bruxelles: Société des Beaux-Arts de Wasme et Laurent, 1839), the John Carter Brown Library, Providence, RI.

Page 10. Courtesy of the African American Museum in Philadelphia.

Page 11. Jonathan Walker, *Trial and Imprisonment of Jonathan Walker, at Pensacola, Florida, for Aiding Slaves to Escape from Bondage, with an Appendix, Containing a Sketch of His Life* (Boston: American Anti-Slavery Society, 1845).

Page 12. Daguerreotype by Southwark & Hayes, 1845, collection of the Massachusetts Historical Society.

Page 13. Boston Vigilance Committee Broadside, "The Plot Exploded! John H. Pearson & the Bloodhounds," (Boston, 1851), Digital Commonwealth, the Boston Public Library.

Page 14. Certificate of Inspection for Escaped Slaves, 1856, Captain Thomas P. Dunton Papers, Maine Maritime Museum, Bath, Maine.

Page 15. Portrait of Thomas Garrett by Bass Otis, 1838, courtesy of the Delaware Historical Society.

Page 16. Engraving by John Sartain, mid-nineteenth century. Schomburg Center for Research in Black Culture, Photographs and Prints Division, the New York Public Library. *Portrait of William Still*, New York Public Library Digital Collections.

Notes

Introduction: A Wave of Resistance

1. Thomas H. Jones, *The Experience of Rev. Thomas H. Jones, Who Was a Slave for Forty-Three Years, Written by a Friend, as Related to Him by Brother Jones* (1854; repr., New Bedford, MA: E. Anthony & Sons, 1885), 2, 8, 11, 31, 42–43, 60.

2. Jones wrote that Holmes "was at heart an Abolitionist, though he never professed as much in public." Jones, *The Experience of Rev. Thomas H. Jones,* 49.

3. Among the canonical works on the subject are Wilbur H. Siebert, *The Underground Railroad from Slavery to Freedom* (New York: Macmillan, 1898; Mineola, NY: Dover, 2006); Larry Gara, *The Liberty Line: The Legend of the Underground Railroad* (Lexington: University of Kentucky Press, 1961); John Hope Franklin and Loren Schweninger, *Runaway Slaves: Rebels on the Plantation* (Oxford: Oxford University Press, 1999); Fergus M. Bordewich, *Bound for Canaan: The Epic Story of the Underground Railroad, America's First Civil Rights Movement* (New York: Amistad Books, 2005); Eric Foner, *Gateway to Freedom: The Hidden History of the Underground Railroad* (New York: W. W. Norton, 2015); R. J. M. Blackett, *The Captive's Quest for Freedom: Fugitive Slaves, the 1850 Fugitive Slave Law, and the Politics of Slavery* (New York: Cambridge University Press, 2018); and Andrew Delbanco, *The War Before the War: Fugitive Slaves and the Struggle for America's Soul from the Revolution to the Civil War* (New York: Penguin Press, 2018). As David W. Blight has written, "The Underground Railroad is one of the most enduring and popular threads in the fabric of America's national historical memory." See his valuable collection of essays, *Passages to Freedom: The Underground Railroad in History and Memory* (Washington, DC: Smithsonian Books, 2004), 2.

4. For reflections on the origins and history of the phrase "Underground Railroad," see Scott Shane, *Flee North: A Forgotten Hero and the Fight for Freedom in Slavery's Borderland* (New York: Celadon Books, 2023).

5. On terracentrism, see Marcus Rediker, *Outlaws of the Atlantic: Sailors, Pirates, and Motley Crews in the Age of Sail* (Boston: Beacon Press, 2014), 2–3. Larry Gara was one of the few, and the earliest, to note the magnitude of maritime escape: "Of the slaves who fled to the North, probably the greatest number used water transportation."

See his *Liberty Line*, 50–51. See also Bordewich, *Bound for Canaan*, 239; and Franklin and Schweninger, *Runaway Slaves*, 33, 209.

6. Timothy D. Walker notes that few historians who have studied the Underground Railroad have been trained in maritime history and adds that "we have largely forgotten the centrality of the sea to early American economic and social life." He also writes that "seaborne escapes were potentially faster, safer, and more efficient than attempting to run away from enslavement overland." See his introduction and chapter in his edited collection of essays, *Sailing to Freedom: Maritime Dimensions of the Underground Railroad* (Amherst: University of Massachusetts Press, 2021), 8, 17–18.

7. The classic juxtaposition of running away and rebellion appears in Gerald W. Mullin, *Flight and Rebellion: Slave Resistance in Eighteenth-Century Virginia* (Oxford: Oxford University Press, 1974). Viola Franziska Müller makes a similar argument about the collectivism of running away in *Escape to the City: Fugitives Slaves in the Antebellum Urban South* (Chapel Hill: University of North Carolina Press, 2022), 5–7. Based on a database of 1,600 fugitives assisted by abolitionist Vigilance Committees, Jesse Olsavsky finds that 52 percent escaped in groups, most often of four to five people. See his *The Most Absolute Abolition: Runaway Slaves, Vigilance Committees, and the Rise of Revolutionary Abolitionism, 1835–1861* (Baton Rouge: LSU Press, 2022), 42–44.

8. R. J. M. Blackett tells the story of maritime fugitive John Anderson, who was reenslaved and held aboard the *Young America* until rescued by a mob in Savanna-la-Mar, Jamaica, in 1855. See his *Making Freedom: The Underground Railroad and the Politics of Slavery* (Chapel Hill: University of North Carolina Press, 2013), 22–31. See also Alice L. Baumgartner, *South to Freedom: Runaway Slaves to Mexico and the Road to the Civil War* (New York: Basic Books, 2020). The present study seeks to add the social spaces of docks and ships to Stephanie M. H. Camp's "rival geography" of resistance, *Closer to Freedom: Enslaved Women and Everyday Resistance in the Plantation South* (Chapel Hill: University of North Carolina Press, 2004), 1–11, and to other spatial approaches, including Robert H. Churchill, *The Underground Railroad and the Geography of Violence in Antebellum America* (New York: Cambridge University Press, 2020), and Damian Alan Pargas, *Freedom Seekers: Fugitive Slaves in North America, 1800–1860* (New York Cambridge University Press, 2022). See also the collection of essays edited by Pargas, *Fugitive Slaves and Spaces of Freedom in North America* (Gainesville: University Press of Florida, 2018), and Müller, *Escape to the City*.

9. This book owes a great deal to the classic work of N. A. T. Hall, "Maritime Maroons: 'Grand Marronage' from the Danish West Indies," *William and Mary Quarterly* 42, no. 4 (Oct. 1985), 476–98: David S. Cecelski, *The Waterman's Song: Slavery and Freedom in Maritime North Carolina* (Chapel Hill: University of North Carolina Press, 2001); Cassandra L. Newby-Alexander, *Virginia Waterways and the Underground Railroad* (Charleston, SC: The History Press, 2017); and Walker, ed., *Sailing to Freedom*. Cecelski's highly original essay, based, like this book, in labor history, deserves special mention as an influential approach: "The Shores of Freedom: The Maritime Underground Railroad in North Carolina, 1800–1861," *North Carolina Historical Review* 71, no. 2 (Apr. 1994): 174–206. Walker offers a deft overview of the limited scholarship on escape by sea in *Sailing to Freedom*, 14–17.

10. Newby-Alexander notes that the free Black communities were sanctuaries for fugitives. See her *Virginia Waterways*, 39. My research supports R. J .M. Blackett's argument that urban free Black communities were the "backbone" of the movement to escape slavery. See his *Making Freedom*, 2. For more on William P. Powell, see chapter 6.

11. Article originally published in the *Wilmington Aurora*, reprinted in the *Weekly North Carolina Standard*, October 30, 1850. On the history of African American sailors, see Martha S. Putney, *Black Sailors: Afro-American Merchant Seamen and Whalemen Prior to the Civil War* (New York: Greenwood Press, 1987), and W. Jeffrey Bolster, *Black Jacks: African American Seamen in the Age of Sail* (Cambridge: Harvard University Press, 1997). For a survey of sailors, see Paul A. Gilje, *Liberty on the Waterfront: American Maritime Culture in the Age of Revolution* (Philadelphia: University of Pennsylvania Press, 2004).

12. *Daily Union*, republished as "Skies Brightening at the North," *The Liberator*, November 11, 1850. The importance of free Black communities to escape networks has long been noted: see Leonard P. Curry, *The Free Black in Urban America, 1800–1850: The Shadow of the Dream* (Chicago: University of Chicago Press, 1981), 229–31; James Oliver Horton, *Free People of Color: Inside the African American Community* (Washington, DC: Smithsonian Institution Press, 1993), 62; and Cheryl Janifer LaRoche, *Free Black Communities and the Underground Railroad: The Geography of Resistance* (Urbana: University of Illinois Press, 2014).

13. Higginson to Wilbur H. Siebert, July 24, 1886, Siebert Notebooks, Houghton Library, Harvard University, vol. 13, quoted in Kathryn Grover, *The Fugitive's Gibraltar: Escaping Slaves and Abolitionism in New Bedford, Massachusetts* (Amherst: University of Massachusetts Press, 2001), 78.

14. The Vigilance Committees were made up of three committees: the New York Committee of Vigilance, the Vigilant Association of Philadelphia, and the Boston Vigilance Committee. Two stellar studies of the Vigilance Committees are Foner, *Gateway to Freedom*, and Olsavsky, *The Most Absolute Abolition*. Kellie Carter Jackson emphasizes how Black abolitionists affirmed self-defense and tactical violence, especially against kidnappers, that often put them at odds with Garrisonian "moral suasion" and pacifism. See her *Force and Freedom: Black Abolitionists and the Politics of Violence* (Philadelphia: University of Pennsylvania Press, 2019).

15. The Atlantic system was not the only maritime network of escape in antebellum North America; indeed, it was but one of five such systems. One, based in New Orleans and Mobile, operated in the Gulf of Mexico and the Caribbean Sea. A related freshwater system stretched up and down the Mississippi River and its tributaries. A third system spanned the Ohio River, from Pittsburgh to Cairo, Illinois. A fourth was based in the Great Lakes, especially after 1850 when the Fugitive Slave Law drove many fugitives to flee to Canada for safety. The Atlantic system was the largest of the five, and the one most closely connected to abolitionist organizations in port cities that could provide mutual aid. The last of these is the subject of this book, but lateral connections to the other four will appear throughout.

16. Marcus Rediker, *Between the Devil and the Deep Blue Sea: Merchant Seamen, Pirates, and the Anglo-American Maritime World, 1700–1750* (New York: Cambridge University Press, 1987); Peter Linebaugh and Marcus Rediker, *The Many-Headed Hydra: Sail-*

ors, *Slaves, Commoners, and the Hidden History of the Revolutionary Atlantic* (Boston: Beacon Press, 2000); Niklas Frykman, *The Bloody Flag: Mutiny in the Age of Atlantic Revolution* (Berkeley: University of California Press, 2020); Julius S. Scott, *The Common Wind: Afro-American Currents in the Age of the Haitian Revolution* (New York: Verso, 2018); *National Anti-Slavery Standard*, October 10, 1850.

17. David Walker, *Walker's Appeal, in Four Articles; Together with a Preamble, to the Coloured Citizens of the World, but in Particular, and Very Expressly, to Those of the United States of America* (Boston: David Walker, 1829; repr., New York: Hill and Wang, 1995); Peter P. Hinks, *To Awaken My Afflicted Brethren: David Walker and the Problem of Antebellum Slave Resistance* (State College: Pennsylvania State University Press, 1997), 66, 68, 79, 80, 84, 85, 116; Marcus Rediker, *The Amistad Rebellion: An Atlantic Odyssey of Slavery and Freedom* (New York: Viking, 2012); Jeffrey R. Kerr-Ritchie, *Rebellious Passage: The Creole Revolt and America's Coastal Slave Trade* (New York: Cambridge University Press, 2019). Important recent work on maritime marronage includes Linda M. Rupert, "Marronage, Manumission, and Maritime Trade in the Early Modern Caribbean," *Slavery and Abolition* 30, no. 3 (Sept. 2009): 361–82; and articles in a special issue of *Slavery and Abolition*, 42, no. 3 (Aug. 2021), edited by Theresa A. Singleton and Jane Landers: Kevin Dawson, "A Sea of Caribbean Islands: Maritime Maroons in the Greater Caribbean," 428–48; Fernanda Bretones Lane, "Free to Bury Their Dead: Baptism and the Meanings of Freedom in the Eighteenth-Century Caribbean," 449–65; Justin Dunnavant, "In the Wake of Maritime Marronage," 466–83; and Elena A. Schneider, "A Narrative of Escape: Self Liberation by Sea and the Mental Worlds of the Enslaved," 484–501.

18. I emphasize the early eighteenth century because seventeenth-century laws against runaways usually referred to indentured servants. Delbanco summarizes the federal laws on runaways in *The War Before the War*, chs. 3 and 4. The best treatment of the Fugitive Slave Act of 1850 is Blackett, *The Captive's Quest*, chs. 1 and 2, pp. 74, 312, 341, 457. Newby-Alexander notes that after the passage of the law, runaways increased from Richmond, Norfolk, Petersburg, and Portsmouth, Virginia. See her *Virginia Waterways*, 58. For an overview of Southern law on runaways, see Thomas D. Morris, *Southern Slavery and the Law, 1619–1860* (Chapel Hill: University of North Carolina Press, 1996), 340–46.

19. "Fugitive Slave Ads: Topics in Chronicling America," Library of Congress, https:// guides.loc.gov/chronicling-america-fugitive-slave-ads (accessed September 19, 2024). See also Franklin and Schweninger, *Runaway Slaves*, 48, 107, 278–79.

20. Estimates of the number of escapees varies widely, reflecting the limited evidence. Fergus Bordewich suggests that 70,000–100,00 escaped between 1830 and 1860, a quarter of them going to Canada. See his *Bound for Canaan*, 436–37. Cassandra L. Newby-Alexander places the number at 100,000 in *Virginia Waterways*, 95.

21. Frederick Douglass, *Narrative of the Life of Frederick Douglass, an American Slave, Written by Himself* (Boston: Anti-Slavery Office, 1845), 105–6; Frederick Douglass, *My Bondage and My Freedom* (New York and Auburn: Miller, Orton, and Mulligan, 1855), 321–24. The swamp maroon's comment was relayed by a Boston abolitionist named Mrs. Knox to James Redpath, who published it in *The Roving Editor; or, Talks with Slaves in the Southern States* (New York: A. B. Burdick, 1859), 295. I have

edited the statement to eliminate the original racist transcription: "'Spect I better not tell de way I comed: for dar's lots more boys comin' same way I did."

22. Frederick Douglass, *Life and Times of Frederick Douglass: His Early Life as a Slave, His Escape from Bondage, and His Complete History, Written by Himself* (Hartford: Park Publishing, 1881; repr., Boston: DeWolfe and Fiske, 1892), 197–98; Asa J. Davis, ed., "The Two Autobiographical Fragments of George W. Latimer (1820–1896): A Preliminary Assessment," *Journal of the Afro-American Historical and Genealogical Society* 1 (Summer 1980): 9–10; William Still, *The Underground Railroad: A Record of Facts, Authentic Narratives, Letters, &c., Narrating the Hardships, Hair-Breadth Escapes and Death Struggles of the Slaves in Their Efforts for Freedom* (Philadelphia: Porter & Coates, 1872).

23. Walker, ed., *Sailing to Freedom*, 1. Higginson added that some came by rail from Philadelphia and that the "direct land route" for the Underground Railroad "was through Ohio." See Thomas Wentworth Higginson to Wilbur Siebert, July 24, 1896, Wilbur H. Siebert Underground Railroad Collection, https://www.ohiomem ory.org/digital/collection/siebert/id/14422/rec/2, (accessed September 24, 2024), quoted in Olsavsky, *The Most Absolute Abolition*, 100. Kathryn Grover suggests that Virginia enslavers "had largely ceased" to place ads for runaways in the 1850s for those who had escaped by sea. See her *Fugitive's Gibraltar*, 242. On the percentages of escape by sea in Philadelphia and New York, see chapter 8.

24. "$20 Reward," *Wilmington Advertiser*, May 25, 1838. Megan Jeffreys notes that in a sample of 4,312 runaway ads in the Freedom on the Move Database, 14 percent revealed actual or suspected maritime methods of escape. See her "Freedom on the Move by Sea: Evidence of Maritime Escape Strategies in American Runaway Slave Advertisements," in Walker, ed., *Sailing to Freedom*, 216.

25. "$200 Reward," *Richmond Enquirer*, July 4, 1833; Newby-Alexander, *Virginia Waterways*, 56.

26. William Grimes, *Life of William Grimes, the Runaway Slave, Written by Himself* (New York, 1825; repr. 1855); Douglass, *Narrative of the Life*. See also Delbanco, *The War Before the War*, 11, 145, 159, 160; and Franklin and Schweninger, *Runaway Slaves*, 96. On the history of the runaway narrative see Zachary McLeod Hutchins, *Before Equiano: A Prehistory of the North American Slave Narrative*, (Chapel Hill: University of North Carolina Press, 2022); William L. Andrews, *To Tell a Free Story: The First Century of Afro-American Autobiography, 1760-1865* (Urbana: University of Illinois Press, 1986); Andrews, *Slavery and Class in the American South: A Generation of Slave Narrative Testimony, 1840-1865* (New York: Oxford University Press, 2020); and Michaël Roy, *Fugitive Texts: Slave Narratives in Antebellum Print Culture* (Madison: University of Wisconsin Press, 2022). All references to Grimes, *Life of William Grimes*, here are to the modern edition. An electronic version of the 1855 edition is available at docsouth.unc.edu/neh/grimes25/grimes25.html.

27. Sydney Howard Gay, "The Record of Fugitives," Sydney Howard Gay Papers, 1748–1931, Rare Book and Manuscript Library, Columbia University, New York, NY, exhi bitions.library.columbia.edu/exhibits/show/fugitives (accessed September 19, 2024).

28. William Still, "Journal C of Station No. 2 of the Underground Railroad, 1852–1857," Vigilance Committee of Philadelphia, Pennsylvania Anti-Slavery Society,

Pennsylvania Abolition Society Papers, Historical Society of Pennsylvania, edited by Peter P. Hinks, https://hsp.org/history-online/digital-history-projects/pennsyl vania-abolition-society-papers/journal-c-of-station-no-2-william-still-1852-1857-0 (accessed September 19, 2024). See also William C. Kashatus, *William Still: The Underground Railroad and the Angel of Philadelphia* (Notre Dame, IN: Notre Dame University Press, 2021), and Andrew K. Diemer, *Vigilance: The Life of William Still, Father of the Underground Railroad* (New York: Alfred A. Knopf, 2022). On the fugitive education of the abolitionist movement and the role of sailors in the Vigilance Committees, I am much indebted to the pathbreaking work of Jesse Olsavsky, *The Most Absolute Abolition*, 39–42, 68–69, 99–100.

29. Still, *Underground Railroad*.

Chapter One: The Art of Escape

1. Benjamin Drew, *A North-Side View of Slavery: The Refugee, or the Narratives of Fugitive Slaves in Canada, Related by Themselves, with an Account of the History and Condition of the Colored Population of Upper Canada* (Boston, 1856), 264–65. Fugitive Henry Bibb wrote about "the art of running away" in his *Narrative of the Life and Adventures of Henry Bibb, an American Slave, Written by Himself* (New York, 1849), 15. Historians have consistently underestimated the thought, planning, and knowledge required for successful escape, wrongly assuming that most anyone could run away, anytime, anyplace.

2. The requirements described here apply to escape by both land and sea. The following paragraphs detail additional requirements for getting away by sea.

3. Atlantic port cities were the first to establish modern police forces in the United States (New York, 1844; Philadelphia, 1850; Baltimore, 1853; Boston, 1854) in no small measure because of runaways; Edward E. Baptist, "Solidarity Versus Parastate," paper presented to the Department of History, Carnegie Mellon University, October 27, 2023.

4. William Grimes, *Life of William Grimes*, 31, 34, 35, 76, 65, 41, 82–85.

5. The concept "Baltimore front" was first explained to me by a dockworker, whose name is unknown to me, after a public lecture I gave at the Mariners' Museum in Newport News, Virginia, in 1991.

6. Tappan did not provide a date for his memorable encounter with the young woman. See Still, *Underground Railroad*, 709–10.

7. Henry Highland Garnet, *Walker's Appeal, with a Brief Sketch of His Life* (New York, J. H. Tobitt: 1848), v–vi. This section draws on the pioneering work of Peter P. Hinks, *To Awaken My Afflicted Brethren*, 28, 66, 68, 79, 80, 84, 85, 116, 118–51, 269.

8. David Walker, *Walker's Appeal*.

9. On the Negro Seamen Acts, see the outstanding work by Michael A. Schoeppner, *Moral Contagion: Black Atlantic Sailors, Citizenship, and Diplomacy in Antebellum America* (New York: Cambridge University Press, 2019), and Philip M. Hamer, "Great Britain, the United States, and the Negro Seamen Acts, 1822–1848," *Journal of Southern History* 1, no. 1 (Feb. 1935): 3–28.

10. James F. McRae to the Police of Mobile, Nov. 3, 1831, in Marshall Rachleff, eds., "David Walker's Southern Agent," *Journal of Negro History* 62, no 1 (Jan. 1977): 101.

11. South Carolina v. Edward Smith (1830), box 1, folder 5, Slaves, Slavery and Free Blacks Court and Legislative Materials, 1820–1835, Avery Research Center, College of Charleston, Charleston, SC. Smith admitted to knowing that the pamphlet "was something in regard to the imposition on negroes."

12. Walker quoted in Garnett, *Walker's Appeal*. Peter P. Hinks concludes that Walker died of tuberculosis; see *To Awaken My Afflicted Brethren*, 268–71. See also Rachleff, "David Walker's Southern Agent," 62: 100–103; William H. Pease and Jane H. Pease, "Walker's *Appeal* Comes to Charleston: A Note and Documents," *Journal of Negro History* 59, no. 3 (July 1974): 287–92; and Clement Eaton, "A Dangerous Pamphlet in the Old South," *Journal of Southern History* 2, no. 3 (Aug. 1936): 323–34. The power of Walker's *Appeal* can be glimpsed in a letter about Georgia newspaper editor Elijah H. Burritt, who possessed twenty copies of the "famous insurrectional pamphlet" and was forced by pressure to fly from the state in 1830. See William H. Torrance to George W. Crawford, February 5, 1830, collection number ms611, Hargett Rare Books and Manuscripts Library, University of Georgia.

13. Moses Roper, *Narrative of the Adventures and Escape of Moses Roper, from American Slavery. With an Appendix, Containing a List of Places Visited by the Author in Great Britain and Ireland and the British Isles; and Other Matter* (Berwick-upon-Tweed, UK: published for the author, and printed at the Warder Office, 1848), iii, xx, 4, 11, 16, 18, 23, 35, 36, 42. See also Christine Kinealy, "Moses Roper (1815–1891): 'A Religious Turn of Mind,'" in her book *Black Abolitionists in Ireland* (London: Routledge, 2020), 65, 69.

14. Roper deserted the *Fox* after he signed on and discovered the poor condition of the vessel, but after a fruitless search for another ship, he returned. See "Story of Moses Roper," *Chambers's Edinburgh Journal*, Sept. 1, 1838, 344.

15. A fine account of Roper's life, based on newly discovered sources, is Fionnghuala Sweeney and Bruce E. Baker, "'I am not a beggar': Moses Roper, Black Witness and the Lost Opportunity of British Abolitionism," *Slavery and Abolition* 43, no. 3 (Feb. 2022): 632–67. See also two important works by Hannah-Rose Murray, "'It Is Time for the Slaves to Speak': Moses Roper, White Networks, and 'Lying Inventions,' 1835–1855," in her *Advocates of Freedom: African American Transatlantic Abolitionism in the British Isles* (New York: Cambridge University Press, 2020), 48–80, and "'Did He Ever Hear of Egypt or Carthage'? Moses Roper's Literary and Oratorical Activism in the British Isles," *Kalfou* 9, no. 2 (2022): 415–36 (estimate of copies sold, 421).

16. Graham Russell Gao Hodges, *David Ruggles: A Radical Black Abolitionist and the Underground Railroad in New York City* (Chapel Hill: University of North Carolina Press, 2010), 30–31. For examples of Ruggles acting on tips from sailors, see Joseph Gavino to David Ruggles, January 4, 1837, published in the *Colored American*, October 7, 1837, and David Ruggles to the Editor of the *Evening Post*, Dec. 13, 1836, Black Abolitionist Papers #10986 and #14761.

17. *The First Annual Report of the New York Committee of Vigilance, for the Year 1837; Together with Important Facts Relative to their Proceedings* (New York: Piercy and Reed, 1837). Jesse Olsavsky argues that the very concept of "direct action" (also called "direct protest") originated in the actions of the Vigilance Committees in this era; see

his *The Most Absolute Abolition*, 52–71, 109–10. Mirelle Luecke notes that prior to the formation of the New York Vigilance Committee in 1835, enslaved people used informal maritime networks to make their escapes. See her "Claiming Liberty by Sea: The Port of New York as a Fugitive's Gateway from Enslavement," in Walker, ed., *Sailing to Freedom*, 131–36.

18. Jonathan Daniel Wells, *The Kidnapping Club: Wall Street, Slavery, and Resistance on the Eve of the Civil War* (New York: Bold Type Books, 2020), 91–92, 104–6.

19. Hodges, *David Ruggles*, 97–98.

20. Ruggles's account of the *Brilhante* and the subsequent attack on him appeared in the *Weekly Advocate*, January 14, 1837, Black Abolitionist Papers, #10536.

21. This and the next three paragraphs are based on James Matthews, "Recollections of Slavery by a Runaway Slave" first published in the *Advocate of Freedom* (Brunswick, Maine), August 2, 1838, then in the *Emancipator*, August 23, 1838, and most recently in Susanna Ashton, ed., *I Belong to South Carolina: South Carolina Slave Narratives* (Columbia: University of South Carolina Press, 2010), 49–82. See also Ashton's "Re-Collecting Jim," *Commonplace: The Journal of Early American Life* 15, no. 1 (Fall 2014). The steward must have been white because a Black steward would have been in jail according to South Carolina's Negro Seamen Act of 1822, unable to board the ship until it was ready to sail.

22. Paul Finkelman, "The Protection of Black Rights in Seward's New York," *Civil War History* 34, no. 3 (Sept. 1988): 211–34; Stephen J. Valone, "William Henry Seward, the Virginia Controversy, and the Anti-Slavery Movement, 1839–1841," *Afro-Americans in New York Life & History* 31, no. 1 (Jan. 2007): 65–80. For an overview of the personal liberty laws, see Thomas D. Morris, *Free Men All: The Personal Liberty Laws of the North, 1780-1861* (Baltimore: Johns Hopkins University Press, 1974).

23. William Henry Seward and Frederick William Seward, *Autobiography of William H. Seward from 1801 to 1834: With a Memoir of his Life and Selections from his Letters from 1831 to 1846* (New York: D. Appleton, 1877), 428–29.

24. Thomas W. Gilmer to the speaker of the Virginia House of Delegates, December 2, 1840, published in *Message from the Governor of Virginia, Communicating a Correspondence between the Governors of Virginia and New York, in Relation to Certain Fugitives from Justice* (Richmond: Samuel Shepherd, 1840), 1-3.

25. Leslie M. Harris, *In the Shadow of Slavery: African Americans in New York City, 1626–1863* (Chicago: University of Chicago Press, 2003), 215.

26. Legislators in Alabama, Louisiana, Maryland, and Missouri also passed resolutions to support Virginia in its battle against New York. See Herman V. Ames, *State Documents in Federal Relations: The States and the United States* (Philadelphia: Longmans, Green, 1911). Virginians decided not to appeal the legal case because they feared a ruling would strengthen federal power. They repealed the inspection act in 1846, suggesting that the profits they realized through New York–based shipping outweighed the value of the fugitives who escaped by sea. See also Michael D. Thompson, "Working on the Docks: Waterfront Labor, Coastal Commerce, and Escaping Enslavement from Charleston, South Carolina, in Walker, ed., *Sailing to Freedom*, 44–49.

27. Thomas W. Gilmer to William B. Seward, November 12, 1840, *Message from the Governor of Virginia*, 57, 58; Frederic Bancroft, *The Life of William H. Seward* (New York: Harper, 1900), 101–6. The case and the correspondence between the Virginia and New York governors are summarized in "New-York and Virginia," *The Liberator*, January 29, 1841.

28. The original lines (in racist dialect) were:

> I jump aboard de boat, ah, urly in de mornin',
> An I lebe Orleans, jist as de day was dawnin',
> I hide under wood, war de n——s just hab toss 'em.

See "A Faithful Account of the Life of Jim Crow the American Negro Poet," originally published as *Jim Crow's Vagaries, or, Black Flights of Fancy* (London: Orlando Hodgson, 1840), republished in W. T. Lhamon Jr., *Jump Jim Crow: Lost Plays, Lyrics, and Street Prose of the First Atlantic Popular Culture* (Cambridge: Harvard University Press, 2003), 402.

29. Laura Alexandrine Smith, *The Music of the Waters: A Collection of the Sailors' Chanties, or Working Songs of the Sea, of All Maritime Nations, Boatmen's, Fishermen's, and Rowing Songs, and Water Legends* (London: Kegan Paul, Trench, 1888), 331; "Creole Slave Songs," *Century Magazine* 31, no. 6 (Apr. 1886): 823. Thanks to Ben Barson for sharing this rare source with me. See also Bryan Wagner, *The Life and Legend of Bras-Coupé: The Fugitive Slave Who Fought the Law, Ruled the Swamp, Danced at Congo Square, Invented Jazz, and Died for Love* (Baton Rouge: Louisiana State University Press, 2019).

30. "Steward's and Cook's Marine Benevolent Society," *Colored American*, May 2, 1840.

31. The Society petitioned the New York state legislature for a charter in 1843: *New York Tribune*, December 20, 1843. We do not know precisely how long the society survived, but we do know it was still in existence eighteen years later, when the family of a recently deceased forty-five-year-old seaman named Samuel Burns, steward of the packet ship *St. Denis*, invited members of the society to attend the funeral. See the *New York Herald*, May 12, 1855.

32. *Colored American*, May 2 and August 15, 1840. Here, Mitchell quoted a poem titled "What is Charity?" by sailor-turned-printer Robert S. Coffin, *Oriental Harp: Poems of the Boston Bard* (Providence, RI: Smith & Parmenter, 1826).

33. Entry of July 24, 1855, Gay, "Record of Fugitives."

34. John Andrew Jackson, *Experience of a Slave in South Carolina* (London: Passmore and Alabaster, 1862), quotations at 26–28, 31. See also the first-rate biography of Jackson by Susanna Ashton, *A Plausible Man: The True Story of the Escaped Slave Who Inspired Uncle Tom's Cabin* (New York: New Press, 2024).

35. Foreman's boardinghouse had been the scene of a riot four years earlier that began with a fight between Black and white sailors. See "Disgraceful Riot on Ann St.," *Emancipator and Free American*, August 31, 1843 and "City Affairs," *Boston Semi-Weekly Atlas*, September 5, 1843; For an example of Jackson's activism in Britain, see "Lecture by a Runaway Slave," *Dumfries and Galloway Standard*, December 3, 1856.

36. J. W. Ellis v. S. M. Walsh, Court of Appeals, SC, January term, 1851, 4 Rich. 468 (1851), 38 S.C.L. 468, WestLaw.

37. "Hackey" was probably an alias. Efforts to discover anything more about the white gentleman's identity have been unsuccessful.

38. The jury "found a verdict for the plaintiff for $1,140." J. W. Ellis v. S. M. Walsh, Court of Appeals, SC.

39. Daniel Drayton, *Personal Memoir of Daniel Drayton, Four Years and Four Months a Prisoner (for Charity's Sake) in Washington Jail, including a Narrative of the Voyage and Capture of the Schooner Pearl* (1853; 2nd ed., Boston: Bela Marsh; New York: American and Foreign Anti-Slavery Society, 1854), 8, 20, 21, 22, 23, 119, 120. For general histories of the event, see Josephine F. Pacheco, *The Pearl: A Failed Slave Escape in the Potomac* (Chapel Hill: University of North Carolina Press, 2005), and Mary Kay Ricks, *Escape on the Pearl: The Heroic Bid for Freedom on the Underground Railroad* (New York: Morrow Books, 2008).

40. "Suicide of Capt. Drayton," *National Anti-Slavery Standard*, July 4, 1857.

41. "Escape of William Curtis and Samuel Glenn, Fugitive Slaves from Darien, Georgia," n.d., Massachusetts Anti-Slavery Society Papers, MSS Collection, New York Historical Society, https://digitalcollections.nyhistory.org/islandora/object/island ora%3A134156 (accessed September 19, 2024). On Black boatmen, see Lynn B. Harris, *Patroons & Periguas: Enslaved Watermen and Watercraft of the Lowcountry* (Columbia: University of South Carolina Press, 2014), and Craig Marin, "Coercion, Cooperation, and Conflict along the Charleston Waterfront, 1739–1785: Navigating the Social Waters of an Atlantic Port City" (PhD diss., University of Pittsburgh, 2008).

42. I date Curtis's escape as 1848 because a vessel he mentioned in his narrative, the *Elizabeth Eliza*, from Liverpool, called at Savannah in 1847 (see the Charleston *Courier*, November 10, 1847).

43. "The Banana Man," *Troy Daily Times*, May 7, 1874. Most of the quotations in this section come from this article. This article about Lobam suggested that he was forty-three years old in 1874, and therefore born in 1831, but the New York Census of 1860 listed his age as thirty-three, which meant that he would have been born in 1827. Captain Thatcher's sloop of war the *Decatur* was in Panama on Feb. 19, 1858. See *Weekly American*, May 6, 1858.

44. Foner, *Gateway to Freedom*, 140–42.

45. Samuel J. May, *The Fugitive Slave Law and Its Victims* (New York: American Anti-Slavery Society, 1856), 17; Thomas J. Davis, "Napoleon vs. Lemmon: Antebellum New Yorkers, Antislavery and Law," *Afro-Americans in New York Life and History* 33, no. 1 (Jan. 2009): 27–46; Blackett, *The Captive's Quest*, 388.

46. See the superb scholarship by Sarah L. H. Gronningsater, "'On Behalf of His Race and the Lemmon Slaves': Louis Napoleon, Northern Black Legal Culture, and the Politics of Sectional Crisis," *Journal of the Civil War Era* 7, no. 2 (June 2017): 206–41; and Marie Tyler-McGraw and Dwight T. Pitcaithley, "The Lemmon Slave Case: Courtroom Drama, Constitutional Crisis and the Southern Quest to Nationalize Slavery," *Common-Place* 14, no. 1 (Fall 2013). See also *Report of the Lemmon Slave Case: Containing Points and Arguments of Counsel on Both Sides, and Opinions of all the Judges* (New York: W. H. Tinson, 1860).

47. Noble placed runaway advertisements for Green in the *Baltimore Sun* on May 26, 28, 30, and June 1, 1857. On "fancy girls," see Alexandra Finley, *An Intimate Economy:*

Enslaved Women, Work, and America's Domestic Slave Trade (University of North Carolina Press, 2020), chapter 1.

48. This and the following two paragraphs are based on Still, *Underground Railroad*, 281–83.

49. Still helped Lear to travel on to Elmira, New York, where she reunited with and married William Adams, but their union was not to last as she passed away three years later.

50. Elizabeth Buffum Chace, *Anti-Slavery Reminiscences* (Central Falls, RI: E. L. Freeman and Son, 1891), 32–33. The comment by the runaway was originally transcribed as "De Cap'n called to de men to seize me, but dey never moved, an' I run up de street as fast as I could." The other man escaped the ship the following day; both men went on to Canada. For an example of a sailor sleeping three feet away from a stowaway among bales of cotton and having no idea he was there, see Thomas E. Taylor, *Running the Blockade: A Personal Narrative of Adventures, Risks, and Escapes during the American Civil War* (London: John Murray, 1896), 80.

51. Robert W. Young, *Senator James Murray Mason: Defender of the Old South* (Knoxville: University of Tennessee Press, 1998), chs. 1 and 4; Carl Schurz, *The Reminiscences of Carl Schurz* vol. 2, 1852–1863 (London: John Murray, 1909), 36–37.

52. Still did not record how William Carpenter escaped slavery. Coming from a northwestern region of Virginia he would have traveled over land a good distance, but he might have gone to Richmond or Norfolk and completed his escape by sea, as did hundreds of others in the 1850s. See Still, *Underground Railroad*, 454–55.

53. "A Disguised Runaway," *Baltimore Sun*, June 27, 1859; also in Ralph Clayton, *Slavery, Slaveholding, and the Free Black Population of Antebellum Baltimore* (Berwyn Heights, MD: Heritage Books, 2015), 40.

54. On the patrols, see Sally E. Hadden's *Slave Patrols: Law and Violence in Virginia and the Carolinas* (Cambridge: Harvard University Press, 2001).

55. Henry Bibb, quoted in Larry Gara, *The Liberty Line: The Legend of the Underground Railroad* (Lexington: University of Kentucky Press, 1961), 18, 147; Still, *Underground Railroad*, 75.

Chapter Two: The Structure of Escape: Port Cities, Trade, and Capitalism

1. Pepijn Brandon, Niklas Frykman, and Pernille Røge, "Free and Unfree Labor in Atlantic and Indian Ocean Port Cities (Seventeenth–Nineteenth Centuries)"; Marcus Rediker, "Reflections on the Motley Crew as Port City Proletariat" *International Review of Social History* 64, special issue 27 (Apr. 2019): 1-18, 255–62; Jacob Price, "Economic Function and the Growth of American Port Towns in the Eighteenth Century," *Perspectives in American History* 8 (1974), 121–86; Franklin W. Knight and Peggy K. Liss, eds., *Atlantic Port Cities: Economy, Culture, and Society in the Atlantic World, 1650–1850* (Knoxville: University of Tennessee Press, 1991).

2. Gary B. Nash, *The Urban Crucible: Social Change, Political Consciousness, and the Origins of the American Revolution* (Cambridge: Harvard University Press, 1979); Rediker, "Motley Crew," 255–62; Liam Campling and Alejandro Colás, *Capitalism and the Sea: The Maritime Factor in the Making of the Modern World* (London: Verso, 2021).

3. This paragraph and the next two draw upon Alex Roland, W. Jeffrey Bolster, and Alexander Keyssar, *The Way of the Ship: America's Maritime History Reenvisoned,*

1600–2000 (Hoboken, NJ: Wiley, 2008), 130, 145, 158, 171, 172, 174. See also Steven Hahn, *A Nation Without Borders: The United States and Its World in an Age of Civil Wars, 1830–1910* (New York: Viking, 2016), and Dale Tomich, "The Second Slavery and World Capitalism: A Perspective for Historical Inquiry," *International Review of Social History* 63, no. 3 (Oct. 2018): 477–501.

4. Tommy L. Bogger, *Free Blacks in Norfolk, Virginia, 1790–1860: The Darker Side of Freedom* (Charlottesville: University of Virginia Press, 1997), 21–22, 167; Charles Ball, *Slavery in the United States: A Narrative of the Life and Adventures of Charles Ball* (New York: John S. Taylor, 1837), 497; Jackson, *Experience of a Slave in South Carolina*, 24. John Hope Franklin and Loren Schweninger note that the larger Southern cities "attracted runaways from hundreds of miles away"; see *Runaway Slaves*, 131.

5. The precise sailing times to New York were, from Charleston, 6.7 days; from Savannah, 7.3 days; from Mobile, 17.7 days; and from New Orleans, 18.0 days. See Robert Greenhalgh Albion, *Square-Riggers on Schedule: The New York Sailing Packets to England, France, and the Cotton Ports* (Princeton, NJ: Princeton University Press, 1938), 63.

6. Albion, *Square-Riggers*, 2, 4, 52, 76; "Statement of the Tonnage of the Several Districts of the United States on the Last Day of June, 1850," in Thomas C. Cochran, ed., *The New American State Papers, 1789–1860: Commerce and Navigation*, vol. 32 (Wilmington, DE: Scholarly Resources, 1973): 699–709.

7. Individual steamship voyages began in the 1810s but were not regularized until the 1830s and 1840s. Even as late as 1850 steamships carried only 14.9 percent of all maritime commerce. See "Recapitulation of the Tonnage of the United States on the 30th of June, 1850," in Cochran, ed., *New American State Papers*, 32:710–11. For a survey of the US-based fleet of steamships in New York and elsewhere in 1853, see "American Steam Marine: The Great Lines of Sea Steamers Connecting American Ports, and the Old and the New World," *DeBow's Review* 14 (1853): 576–87.

8. Still, *Underground Railroad*, 58–65, 62, 256, 569, 283, 169, 201, 225, 245, 247, 249, 319, 393; Gay, "Record of Fugitives," entries for July 24, 1855, November 23, 1855, and March 20, 1856.

9. The precise number was 189,774 men and 6,097 boys. See "Statement Exhibiting the Number of Clearances of American and Foreign Vessels, with Their Tonnage and Crews, Cleared from Each District of the United States for Foreign Countries during the Year Ending June 30, 1850," in Cochran, ed., *New American State Papers*, 32:691–94.

10. Drew, *A North-Side View of Slavery*, 100. The lyrics to "Fire Maringo" were recorded by sailor Charles Nordhoff and quoted by Michael D. Thompson in his excellent book, *Working on Dock of the Bay: Labor and Enterprise in an Antebellum Southern Port* (Columbia: University of South Carolina Press, 2015), 20.

11. Steve Higginson and Tony Wailey, *Edgy Cities* (Liverpool: Northern Lights, 2006); Franklin and Schweninger, *Runaway Slaves*, ch. 6.

12. Thompson, *Working on the Dock of the Bay*, 76.

13. Thompson, *Working on the Dock of the Bay*, 71.

14. Thompson, *Working on the Dock of the Bay*, 88–89, 13; Scott, *The Common Wind*.

15. Cecelski, *Waterman's Song*, 213–20; Douglass, *Narrative of the Life*, 76.

16. Steven Hahn has suggested that free urban African Americans in this era constituted a kind of maroon community—a "renegade" social and political formation that

organized its own self-defense in a hostile world dominated by enslavers. See his chapter "'Slaves at Large': The Emancipation Process and the Terrain of African American Politics," in his *The Political Worlds of Slavery and Freedom* (Cambridge: Harvard University Press, 2009), 1–53; Harriet Jacobs, *Incidents in the Life of a Slave Girl, Written by Herself,* ed. L. Maria Child (Boston, 1861), 287; and Newby-Alexander, *Virginia Waterways*, 39. Eric Foner notes that free Black men who worked in New York's maritime jobs were in position to know about and help fugitives; see his *Gateway to Freedom*, 47.

17. Jacobs, *Incidents*, 244, 251; Frederick Douglass, *Life and Times of Frederick Douglass,* 202–4; Grover, *Fugitive's Gibraltar.*

18. Cecelski, *Waterman's Song*, 183. Fergus Bordewich writes: "The sea was, in a sense, a commercial extension of the Northern states, and every Yankee ship that touched at a Southern port like a piece of free territory that suddenly came within the physical reach of restive slaves," *Bound for Canaan*, 272. Michael S. Schoeppner notes that free Black sailors "embodied an alternative social order," *Moral Contagion*, 5.

19. "A Bill Providing Additional Protection for the Slave A Property of Citizens of This Commonwealth," 1856, in Jane Purcell Guild, ed., *Black Laws of Virginia: A Summary of the Legislative Acts of Virginia Concerning Negroes from Earliest Times to the Present* (Westminster, MD: Heritage Books, 2011), 89–90.

20. "An Act . . . to prevent the circulation of written or printed papers within this State calculated to excite disaffection among the coloured people of this state," 1829, in Howell Cobb, ed., *A Compilation of the Penal Code of the State of Georgia* (Macon, GA: Joseph M. Boardman, 1850), 216; "An Act more effectually to prevent Free Negroes and other Persons of Color from entering into this State; and for other purposes," 1835, in David J. McCord, ed., *The Statutes at Large of South Carolina,* vol. VII (Columbia, SC: A.S. Johnston, 1840), 471.

21. Guild, ed., *Black Laws of Virginia*, 54; Woodly (or Wooby): State v. Albert Woodly, Bertie County (NC) Superior Court Minutes, Spring Term 1855, North Carolina State Archives; "The Case of Alfred Woodly," *Semi-Weekly Standard* (Raleigh), March 29, 1856; Michel: Jacob Schirmer Diary, Schirmer Family Journals and Registers, 1806–1929, Call # 1149.00, Container 11/567/09, South Carolina Historical Society, entries for July 6, 1859, and January 28, 1860; "Pardoned," *Macon Daily Telegraph*, February 11, 1860. The legal systems of North and South Carolina showed mercy: neither Woodly nor Michel was hanged.

22. "Harboring, Enticing Away and Aiding the Escape of Slaves," Otho Scott and Hiram M'Cullough, eds., *The Revised Laws of the State of Maryland* (Baltimore: John Cox, 1859), 459; "Carrying Away Slaves, Advising or Aiding them, to Abscond," in Robert Ould and William B. B. Cross, eds., *The Revised Code of the District of Columbia* (Washington, DC: A. O. P. Nicholson, 1857), 530. Some of the women who assisted fugitives may have been fugitives themselves, as they were in Jamaica. See Shauna J. Sweeney, "Market Marronage: Fugitive Women and the Internal Marketing System in Jamaica, 1781–1834," *William and Mary Quarterly* 76, no. 2 (Apr. 2019): 197–222.

23. Guild, ed., *Black Laws of Virginia*, 84; "An Act Concerning Crimes and Punishments," in Frederick Nash, James Iredell, and William Horn Battle, eds., *The Revised Statutes of the State of North Carolina* (Raleigh: Turner and Hughes, 1837), 210;

"An Act to prevent Boat-owners or Patroons from permitting boat hands, or other negroes, from trafficking in corn, or other produce . . ." in Thomas R. R. Cobb, ed., *A Digest of the Statute Laws of the State of Georgia* (Athens, GA: Christy, Kelsea & Burke, 1851), 14; "An Act to Prohibit the Owners of Vessels, and other from Navigating the Same by and under the Sole Command of Negroes or Mulattoes," in *Laws Made and Passed by the General Assembly, of the State of Maryland* (Annapolis: Jeremiah Huggins, 1837), chapter 150, 537, available through Archives of Maryland Online: msa.maryland.gov/megafile/msa/speccol/sc2900/sc2908/000001/000537/html /am537–144.html (accessed September 19, 2024).

24. "An Act to Prevent the Taking Away Boats, Canoes, and Pettiaguas from Landings or Elsewhere without Leave," in Nash, Iredell, and Battle, eds., *Revised Statutes of the State of North Carolina*, 96; "Of Attachments," in *The Code of Virginia* (Richmond: William F. Ritchie, 1849), 602; "An Act to Prohibit the Owners of Vessels, and other from Navigating the Same by and under the Sole Command of Negroes or Mulattoes," in *Laws Made and Passed by the General Assembly, of the State of Maryland*, 537; "A Bill Providing Additional Protection for the Slave A Property of Citizens of this Commonwealth," 1856, in Guild, ed., *Black Laws of Virginia:* 89–90; "An Act to prevent the citizens of New York from carrying slaves, or persons held to service, out of this State," *Resolutions of the General Assembly of South Carolina* (Washington, DC, 1842), 7–10.

25. Guild, ed., *Black Laws of Virginia*.

26. Guild, ed., *Black Laws of Virginia*, 202–3, 206–8; "An Act to prevent the citizens of New York," *Resolutions of . . . South Carolina*, 7–10; "An Act to Better Secure and Protect the Citizens of Georgia in the Possession of their Slaves," *Acts of the General Assembly of Georgia* (Milledgeville, GA: Bought, Nisbet & Barnes, 1842), 125–28.

27. "The Fugitive Slave Case at Boston, Several Arrests, &c.," *Daily Constitutionalist and Republic* (Augusta, GA), February 22, 1851; "Great Excitement in Boston!," *New Orleans Weekly Delta*, April 21, 1848; *Daily Republic* (Washington, DC), April 8, 1851. Henry was captured and reenslaved four months later when he returned to Savannah as a ship's cook on a different vessel, likely to help "comrades or relations" escape by sea. See "Caught," *Charleston Courier*, March 27, 1851.

28. Emily P. Burke, *Reminiscences of Georgia* (Oberlin, OH: James M. Fitch, 1850), 63–64. My portrait of the Savannah waterfront draws on the classic work by Walter J. Fraser Jr., *Savannah in the Old South* (Athens: University of Georgia Press, 2005). See also Whittington B. Johnson, "Free African American Women in Savannah, 1800–1860: Affluence and Autonomy Amid Adversity," *Georgia Historical Quarterly* 76, no. 2 (Summer 1992): 265, 273.

29. Burke, *Reminiscences*, 46; J. S. Buckingham, *The Slave States of America*, vol. 1 (London; Fisher, Son, 1841), 118–19; Richard H. Haunton, "Law and Order in Savannah, 1850–1860," *Georgia Historical Quarterly* 56, no. 1 (Spring 1972): 17; Fraser, *Savannah in the Old South*, 281.

30. Fraser, *Savannah in the Old South*, 211.

31. Fraser, *Savannah in the Old South*, 216, 228, 278.

32. Timothy J. Lockley, "Trading Encounters between Non-Elite Whites and African Americans in Savannah, 1790–1860," *Journal of Southern History* 66, no. 1 (Feb.

2000): 25–48, and the same author's *Lines in the Sand: Race and Class in Lowcountry Georgia, 1750–1860* (Athens: University of Georgia Press, 2001). See also Jack K. Williams, "Georgians as Seen by Ante-Bellum English Travelers," *Georgia Historical Quarterly* 32, no. 3 (Sept. 1948): 158–74.

33. The members of the association sought laws limiting the hiring out of enslaved people, a stricter pass system and curfew, and a crackdown on the dramshops. It is not clear that they achieved any of their goals, and the association seems to have declined rather quickly. See *Preamble and Regulations of the Savannah River Anti-Slave Traffick Association* (Savannah, GA, 1846). Franklin and Schweninger note that fugitives frequently used the second economy while on the run, *Runaway Slaves*, 89–92.

34. Haunton, "Law and Order," 37; Charles S. Henry, Esq., *A Digest of All of the Ordinances of the City of Savannah* (Savannah, GA: Furse's Print, 1854), 446–56. Haunton studied 1,566 cases of illegal, usually interracial, trading, heard in the Savannah Mayor's Court.

35. Burke, *Reminiscences*, 63–64.

36. "Fifteen Dollars Reward," *Charleston Mercury*, December 24, 1831. For more on subsequent struggles at the rebuilt workhouse, see Jeff Strickland, *All for Liberty: The Charleston Workhouse Slave Rebellion of 1849* (New York: Cambridge University Press, 2022).

37. Walter J. Fraser Jr., *Charleston! Charleston!: The History of a Southern City* (Columbia: University of South Carolina Press, 1989), 208, 222–3, 232, 240; Thompson, "Working on the Docks," 46.

38. Fraser, *Charleston!*, 222; "Statement exhibiting the Number of American and Foreign Vessels, with their Tonnage and Crews, which Entered into Each District of the U. S., from for Foreign Countries, during the Year ending June 30, 1850" (July 1, 1849–June 30, 1850), in Cochran, ed., *New American State Papers*, 32:695–98.

39. Bernard E. Powers Jr., *Black Charlestonians: A Social History, 1822–1885* (Fayetteville: University of Arkansas Press, 1999).

40. Thompson, *Working on the Dock of the Bay*, 76. A second area of residence was the "Charleston Neck," north of Boundary Street, where a great deal of illicit trade was carried on.

41. Fraser, *Charleston!*, 212, 229, 239; Powers, *Black Charlestonians*, 24, 25, 44.

42. John Jonah Murrell to the South Carolina House of Representatives, 1829, in Loren Schweninger, ed., *The Southern Debate over Slavery*, vol. 1, *Petitions to Southern Legislatures, 1778–1864* (Urbana: University of Illinois Press, 2001), 106.

43. Fraser, *Charleston!*, 201–3.

44. Petition of the Trustees of the Charleston Port Society to the House of Representatives, Nov. 26, 1859, quoted in James David Altman, "The Charleston Marine School," *South Carolina Historical Magazine* 88, no. 2 (Apr. 1987): 76–82. See also *Rules of the Trustees of the Marine School of Charleston, adopted 12th April 1859, revised April, 1860: Also the Rules and Regulations of the School* (Charleston, SC: Walker, Evans, 1860) and "The Marine School at Charleston, South Carolina," *Harper's Weekly*, Dec. 8, 1860. The apprentice sailors later served the Confederate war effort.

45. As Bernard E. Powers, the leading historian of Black Charleston in the nineteenth century, explained, "The anonymity of the city and its position as a major seaport made running away one of the most common modes of resistance." See his *Black Charlestonians*, 27, and Thompson, *Working on the Dock of the Bay*, 42–43. On Carolina, see Thomas C. Marshall to John W. Mitchell, December 18, 1839, John Wroughton Mitchell Papers, Southern Historical Collection, University of North Carolina-Chapel Hill.

46. Fraser, *Charleston!*, 238–39; Powers, *Black Charlestonians*, 27, 33.

47. Fraser, *Charleston!*, 241; William Kingsford, *Impressions of the West and the South, during a Six Weeks Holiday* (Toronto: A. H. Armour, 1858), 77; Frederick Law Olmsted, *A Journey in the Seaboard Slave States; With Remarks on Their Economy* (New York: Dix and Edwards 1856), 404. See also Ivan D. Steen, "Charleston in the 1850s: As Described by British Travelers," *South Carolina Historical Magazine* 71, no. 1 (Jan. 1970): 36–45.

48. Captain Roberts [C. Augustus Hobart-Hampden], *Never Caught: Personal Adventures Connected with Twelve Successful Trips in Blockade-Running During the American Civil War, 1863–1864* (New York: W. Abbott, 1908), 26; "$50 Reward," *Wilmington Journal*, January 29, 1863. This section draws on Cecelski, *Waterman's Song* and Alan D. Watson, *Wilmington: Port of North Carolina* (Columbia: University of South Carolina Press, 1992).

49. Cecelski, *Waterman's Song*, 124 and ch. 5 more generally.

50. Letter to the Editor from a "Citizen," *Wilmington Journal*, October 19, 1849; Cecelski, *Waterman's Song*, 134.

51. The Clerk of the Commissioners made the decree public on May 20, 1850, as reported in "Orders and Enactments of the Commissioners of Navigation and Pilotage for the River Cape Fear," *Wilmington Journal*, June 7, 1850. See also "New Ordinances of the Commissioners of Navigation," *Wilmington Chronicle*, March 12, 1851. John Smith, William Furpless, and James F. Burnett were listed as the port's "fumigators" in the *Daily Times*, June 22, 1854. For documentation about fumigation between 1858–1861, see *Weekly Raleigh Register*, September 22, 1858; List of Vessels Searched and Fumigated, 1858–1862, Wilmington, North Carolina, Board of Commissioners of Navigation and Pilotage for the Cape Fear River and Bar, Records, 1857–1921; and Account of Records with William J. Love, Board of Commissioners of Navigation and Pilotage for the Cape Fear River and Bar; the latter two in the Rare Book and Manuscript Department, Rubenstein Library, Duke University, folios 256–66.

52. Watson, *Wilmington*, 56, 66, 68, 69; Cecelski, *Waterman's Song*, 136; Richard C. Rohrs, "The Free Black Experience in Antebellum Wilmington, North Carolina: Refining Generalizations about Race Relations," *Journal of Southern History* 78, no. 3 (Aug. 2012): 615–38.

53. *Peoples' Press and Wilmington Advertiser*, May 27, 1835, quoted in Watson, *Wilmington*, 58; "Notice," *Wilmington Journal*, January 30, 1852. Watson noted the prevalence of escape: "Many bondsmen stowed away. Others were befriended by captains or crews who opposed slavery and saw an opportunity to strike a blow for freedom." The dockworker snitched and Dowler was arrested as a runaway.

54. Article entitled "Free Negro Sailors" originally published in the Wilmington *Aurora*, reprinted in the *Weekly North Carolina Standard*, October 30, 1850.

55. Boston abolitionist Wendell Phillips told the story of Elizabeth Blakeley, a stow-away who survived three fumigations of her vessel as it departed Wilmington; see "Speech of Wendell Phillips at Faneuil Hall, Friday evening, January 30, 1852," *National Anti-Slavery Standard*, February 19, 1852.

56. Still, *Underground Railroad*, 155–58. For the full life of Galloway, who went on to become a hero of the Union army during the Civil War and a state senator in North Carolina during Reconstruction, see David S. Cecelski, *The Fire of Freedom: Abraham Galloway and the Slaves' Civil War* (Chapel Hill: University of North Carolina Press, 2012).

57. Still, *Underground Railroad*, 175–76.

58. This section is deeply indebted to Cassandra L. Newby-Alexander, *Virginia Waterways and the Underground Railroad*. See also her "Hampton Roads and Norfolk, Virginia, as a Waypoint and Gateway for Enslaved Persons Seeking Freedom," in Walker, ed., *Sailing to Freedom*, 86.

59. Bogger, *Free Blacks in Norfolk*, 121–23, 134–35. In a census of 1851, a majority of the free Blacks for whom an occupation was recorded worked on the waterfront. See "Accounts, Free Negroes in the City of Norfolk Return," 1851, Manuscripts APA 339, Library of Virginia, Richmond.

60. Still, *Underground Railroad*, 175, 225, 289, 242, 59.

61. Gay, "Record of Fugitives," entry for May 16, 1855. The United Order of the Tents still exists: Dodai Stewart, "A Secret Society Tied to the Underground Railroad Fights to Save Its Home," *New York Times*, December 20, 2022.

62. Bogger, *Free Blacks in Norfolk*, 122.

63. Henry Wadsworth Longfellow, "The Slave in the Dismal Swamp," 1842, hwlongfellow.org/poems_poem.php?pid=99 (accessed September 19, 2024); Frederick Douglass, "Slaves in the Dismal Swamp," *North Star*, March 31, 1848.

64. Important recent studies of maroons include Sylviane A. Diouf, *Slavery's Exiles: The Story of the American Maroons* (New York: New York University Press, 2016); Marcus P. Nevius, *City of Refuge: Slavery and Petit Marronage in the Great Dismal Swamp, 1763–1856* (Athens: University of Georgia Press, 2020); Daniel O. Sayers, *A Desolate Place for a Defiant People: The Archaeology of Maroons, Indigenous Americans, and Enslaved Laborers in the Great Dismal Swamp* (Gainesville: University Press of Florida, 2016); and J. Brent Morris, *Dismal Freedom: A History of the Maroons of the Great Dismal Swamp* (Chapel Hill: University of North Carolina Press, 2022). Jesse Olsavsky notes that running to the swamp was often the first step in getting away to the North; see his *The Most Absolute Abolition*, 38, 178.

65. Moses Grandy, *Narrative of the Life of Moses Grandy; Late a Slave in the United States of America* (London: T. Gilpin, 1843), 8.

66. Still, *Underground Railroad*, 590; Still, "Journal C of Station No. 2," 277; Newby-Alexander, *Virginia Waterways*, 52, 104, 116; Bogger, *Free Blacks in Norfolk*, 166–67.

67. Still, *Underground Railroad*, 42–44.

68. See the important work of Cheryl Janifer LaRoche, "The Underground Railroad in Maryland's Ports, Bays, and Harbors: Maritime Strategies for Freedom," in Walker, ed., *Sailing to Freedom*, 99–122. See also Christopher Phillips, *Freedom's Port: The African American Community of Baltimore, 1790–1860* (Urbana: University of Illinois Press, 1997), 14, 17, 195.

69. Phillips, *Freedom's Port*, 12, 29, 77, 78, 80, 81, 103, 104, 110. Phillips drew on a random sample of twenty ships entering Baltimore 1806–35 to discover that 22.4 percent of the crews were of African descent (80).

70. Phillips, *Freedom's Port*, 18, 110, 111, 132, 174, 229, 231.

71. "The Condition of the Coloured Population of the City of Baltimore," *Baltimore Literary and Religious Magazine* 4 (1838): 168–76; "Statisticks of Destitution in Baltimore," *Baltimore Literary and Religious Magazine* 3 (1837): 276–81; Phillips, *Freedom's Port*, 172.

72. Wilbur Siebert, interview with Harriet Tubman in Cambridge, Massachusetts, August 1897, transcription by Kate Clifford Larson, Wilbur H. Siebert Collection, "The Underground Railroad: Manuscript materials collected by Professor Seibert, Ohio [State] University," Manuscript collection: US 5278.36.25, Houghton Library, Harvard University. See also LaRoche, "Underground Railroad," 109–111, 118 (quotation). John Bowley acquired a schooner of his own in 1848: Dorchester County Circuit Court, Chattel Records, 1847–1852, vol. 776, 61–62, Maryland State Archives. See Larson's classic biography, *Bound for the Promised Land: Harriet Tubman, Portrait of an American Hero* (New York: One World Random House, 2005). See also Phillip Hesser and Charlie Ewers, *A Guide to Harriet Tubman's Eastern Shore: The Old Home Is Not There* (Charleston: The History Press, 2021).

73. "Robert Purvis Dead," *New York Times*, April 16, 1898. This section draws on the fine work of Margaret Hope Bacon, *But One Race: The Life of Robert Purvis* (Albany: State University of New York Press, 2007).

74. Purvis wrote this reminiscence at the request of R. C. Smedley, a physician who was compiling a history of abolitionists and fugitives in his native southeastern Pennsylvania. See his *History of the Underground Railroad: In Chester and the Neighboring Counties of Pennsylvania* (Lancaster, PA: Office of the Journal, 1883), 355.

75. Marion V. Brewington, "Maritime Philadelphia, 1609–1837," *The Pennsylvania Magazine of History and Biography* 63, no. 2 (Apr. 1939): 95–96, 112, 116; Frank H. Taylor and Wilfred H. Schoff, *The Port and City of Philadelphia* (Philadelphia: Commission of the 12th International Congress of Navigation, 1912), 19.

76. For the early history of Quaker abolitionism, see Jean R. Soderlund, *Quakers and Slavery: A Divided Spirit* (Princeton, NJ: Princeton University Press, 1985); Maurice Jackson, *Let This Voice Be Heard: Anthony Benezet, Father of Atlantic Abolitionism* (Philadelphia: University of Pennsylvania Press, 2010); Marcus Rediker, *The Fearless Benjamin Lay: The Quaker Dwarf who Became the First Revolutionary Abolitionist* (Boston: Beacon Press, 2017); and Paul J. Polgar, *Standard-Bearers of Equality: America's First Abolition Movement* (Chapel Hill: University of North Carolina Press, 2019).

77. Lydia Maria Child, *Isaac T. Hopper: A True Life* (Cleveland: John P. Jewett, 1853); Bordewich, *Bound for Canaan*, 47, 50, 51, 56. Some of Hopper's accounts of fugitives were compiled in Daniel E. Meaders, *Kidnappers in Philadelphia: Isaac Hopper's Tales of Oppression, 1780–1843*, 2nd ed. (Cherry Hill, NJ: Africana Homestead Legacy Publishers, 2009).

78. Robert Purvis, *Remarks on the Life and Character of James Forten, Delivered at Bethel Church, March 30, 1842* (Philadelphia: Merrihew and Thompson, 1842); Beverly C.

Tomek, *Slavery and Abolition in Pennsylvania* (Philadelphia: Temple University Press, 2021), ch. 7.

79. *Statistical Inquiry into the Condition of the People of Colour, of the City and Districts of Philadelphia* (Philadelphia: Kite & Walton, 1849), 17–18. Roughly two-thirds of all free Black women washed clothes or did day labor.

80. This and the next paragraph are based on Joseph A. Boromé, Jacob C. White, Robert B. Ayres and J. M. McKim, "The Vigilant Committee of Philadelphia," *Pennsylvania Magazine of History and Biography* 92, no. 3 (July 1968): 320–51. See also Foner, *Gateway to Freedom*, 79. In July 1838 Philadelphia's women established the Female Vigilant Committee. Its primary task was to raise funds to assist fugitives. Erica Armstrong Dunbar discusses the group's limitations of race and class in "Voices from the Margins: The Philadelphia Female Anti-Slavery Society, 1833–1840," in her *A Fragile Freedom: African American Women and Emancipation in the Antebellum City* (New Haven; Yale University Press, 2008), 70–95.

81. Alexandra Rosenberg, "Hiding in Plain Sight: Virginia Oystering and the Landscapes of Abolitionism," (master's thesis, University of Delaware, 2021); idem, "Escaping Slavery by Whaleboat, 1832," in Carl R. Lounsbury, ed., *The Material World of Eyre Hall: Four Centuries of Chesapeake History* (Baltimore: Maryland Center for History and Culture; D. Giles Limited, 2021), 132–38; idem, "Whaleboat Escape from Northampton County, Virginia, 1832," *Journal of Slavery and Data Preservation* 2, no. 3 (2021). Here I follow Jonathan Daniel Wells, who sees the arrival of the fugitives in 1832 as the beginning of a new phase in the history of New York. See his *Kidnapping Club*, 1–10.

82. William S. Floyd to Joseph Segar, January 19, 1838, and M. W. Fisher to Joseph Segar, January 19, 1838, Legislative Petitions, Northampton County, Library of Virginia. To replace Floyd, the governor of Virginia hired slave hunter Edward R. Waddey, who recovered nine more fugitives over the next several years. With each successive trip to New York, Waddey noted, he "found it more and more difficult & no one could go there for that purpose, nor can ever without hazarding his life." See the Petition of Edward R. Waddey to the Virginia General Assembly, January 1, 1838, Legislative Petitions, Northampton County, Library of Virginia.

83. J. D. B. DeBow, quoted in Leslie M. Harris, *In the Shadow of Slavery: African Americans in New York City, 1626–1863* (Chicago: University of Chicago Press, 2003), 189; William Johnston, *Fifth Annual Report of the New York Committee of Vigilance for the Year 1842, with Interesting Facts Relative to the Proceedings* (New York: G. Vale Jr., 1842), 14.

84. Harris, *In the Shadow of Slavery*, 191. Eric Foner notes that in the five years after the passage of the Fugitive Slave Act in 1850, the free Black population of New York declined from 13,815 to 11,840, which might be a good indicator of the number and percentage (14.3 percent) of fugitives and their families who left the city. See *Gateway to Freedom*, 136.

85. Wells, *Kidnapping Club*, 7, 9, 19; Harris, *In the Shadow of Slavery*, 208 9. For more on the dangers of kidnapping in New York and other Northern free Black communities, see Carol Wilson, *Freedom at Risk: The Kidnaping of Free Blacks in America, 1780–1865* (Lexington: University Press of Kentucky, 1994), and David Fiske, *Solomon Northup's*

Kindred: The Kidnapping of Free Citizens before the Civil War (Santa Barbara, CA: Praeger, 2016).

86. Report of a Negro Vigilance Committee, January 16, 1837, Black Abolitionist Papers, #1702; Foner, *Gateway to Freedom*, 65–66.

87. *First Annual Report of the New York Committee of Vigilance, for the Year 1837*, 30, 55, 51; David Ruggles, "New-York Committee of Vigilance, Secretary's Report for January 1838," *Emancipator*, March 1, 1838; Johnston, *Fifth Annual Report*, 32–36. By 1840 the Vigilance Committee had made it extremely difficult for enslavers to recover their wayward "property" in New York. See the complaints in the petition of Richard Reed to the Virginia General Assembly, Legislative Petitions, Accomac County, January 1840, cited by Franklin and Schweninger, *Runaway Slaves*, 159.

88. Wells, *Kidnapping Club*, 222; Foner, *Gateway to Freedom*, 59–60.

89. Valone, "William Henry Seward," 65–80; Harris, *In the Shadow of Slavery*, 215; Wells, *Kidnapping Club*, 169–70.

90. Daniel Ricketson, *The History of New Bedford, Bristol County, Massachusetts* [. . .]. (New Bedford: published by the author, 1858), 252–53. Timothy D. Walker notes that New Bedford was "not so much a stop along the Underground Railroad; rather, it was a *terminus*—a community where ex-slaves knew they could settle and prosper." See Walker, ed., *Sailing to Freedom*, 26.

91. Grover, *Fugitive's Gibraltar*, 126–27. This section is indebted to Grover's prodigiously researched book. She provides evidence of dozens of escapes by sea; for examples, see pages 1, 6, 13, 14, 45, 46, 68, 117, 118, 185, 196, 197, 198, 206, 228, 234, and 242.

92. Grover, *Fugitive's Gibraltar*, 16, 281; Herman Melville, *Moby-Dick; Or, the Whale* (1851; repr., Evanston, IL: Northwestern University Press, 1988), 32.

93. Grover, *Fugitive's Gibraltar*, 221; Len Travers, "Making a Living in the 'Fugitive's Gibraltar': People of Color in New Bedford, 1838–1845," in Walker, ed., *Sailing to Freedom*, 181, 188. Grover and Travers note that the number of Black mariners in New Bedford was declining over time.

94. Grover, *Fugitive's Gibraltar*, 40. For more on Powell, see chapter 6.

95. Charles Cook, *A Brief Account of the African Christian Church in New-Bedford* (New Bedford: B. T. Congdon, 1834), 7; Earl F. Mulderink, *New Bedford's Civil War* (New York: Fordham University Press, 2012), 41–45. Grover, *Fugitive's Gibraltar*, 113, 122, 134, 138, 248, 255, 261–62.

96. Douglass, *Narrative of the Life*, 114–15; Douglass, *My Bondage and My Freedom*, 347–48.

97. Jonathan D. S. Schroeder notes that at the end of his whaling voyage John S. Jacobs got $356 for his shares, an additional $22, plus two barrels of sperm oil, worth about $40 each, which comes to $19,426 in 2024 money. See his prologue to *The United States Governed by Six Hundred Thousand Despots: A True Story of Slavery; A Rediscovered Narrative, with a Full Biography*, by Jonathan Swanson Jacobs, ed. Jonathan D. S. Schroeder (Chicago: University of Chicago Press 2024), 122. For more on Harriet Jacobs, see chapter 4.

98. John Thompson, *The Life of John Thompson, a Fugitive Slave; Containing His History of 25 Years in Bondage, and His Providential Escape, Written by Himself* (Worcester, MA: John Thompson, 1856), 107–10.

99. George Teamoh, *God Made Man, Man Made the Slave: The Autobiography of George Teamoh*, eds. F. N. Boney, Richard L. Hume, and Rafia Zafar (Macon, GA: Mercer University Press, 1990), 7–9, 84–86, 106–7, 180–81; Grover, *Fugitive's Gibraltar*, 234–35; Morgan, quoted in Mulderink, *New Bedford's Civil War*, 47. Thanks to Kathryn Grover for consultation about whether a fugitive had ever been returned to bondage from New Bedford.

100. "Letter from Austin Bearse, Boston, [Massachusetts], to Samuel May, 1851 August 18." Correspondence, Boston, Massachusetts, August 18, 1851, *Digital Commonwealth*, digitalcommonwealth.org/search/commonwealth:2z110p75f (accessed September 19, 2024).

101. Still, *Underground Railroad*, 586. It should be noted that the number of Black seamen was declining in the 1850s. See Jacqueline Jones, *No Right to an Honest Living: The Struggles of Boston's Black Workers in the Civil War Era* (New York: Basic Books, 2023), 175–76.

102. James Oliver Horton and Lois E. Horton identified 129 Black activists in antebellum Boston and found that more than half of them were workers. See their *Black Bostonians: Family Life and Community Struggle in the Antebellum North*, rev. ed. (New York: Holmes and Meier, 1999), 59, 40, 52–53, 54. For a well-crafted portrait of Hayden, see Jackson, *Force and Freedom*, 67–75.

103. Matthews, "Recollections of Slavery by a Runaway Slave"; Jackson, *Experience of a Slave*; Horton, *Free People of Color*, 33. See the advertisements placed by Henry Foreman under the same title, "Genteel Boarding for Respectable Colored Seamen," *The Liberator*, September 16, 1842, and January 19, 1844.

104. Horton and Horton, *Black Bostonians*, 24, 34–35, 107; John Tidde to Arthur Jones, April 6, 1834, William Lloyd Garrison Papers, Boston Public Library; "Mr. Sewall's Remarks" to the Legislative Committee, *The Liberator*, March 26, 1836.

105. Austin Bearse, *Reminiscences of Fugitive-Slave Law Days in Boston* (Boston: Warren Richardson, 1880); Francis Jackson, "Treasurer's Accounts," October 9, 1853: "Austin Bearse services & boat in rescuing Sandy Swan a Fugitive in Boston Harbor in July 1853"; "Fugitive Slaves aided by the Vigilance Committee since the Passage of the Fugitive Slave Bill," Massachusetts Anti-Slavery Society Papers, MSS Collection, New York Historical Society, digitalcollections.nyhistory.org/islandora/object /islandora% (accessed September 19, 2024). See also Sidney Kaplan, "The *Moby Dick* in the Service of the Underground Railroad," *Phylon* 12, no. 2 (June 1951): 173–76; and Sandra Harbert Petrulionis, "Fugitive Slave-Running on the *Moby Dick*: Captain Austin Bearse and the Abolitionist Crusade," *Resources for American Literary Study* 28, no. 1 (2002): 53–82.

Chapter Three: Frederick Douglass's Maritime Dream

1. The best account of the life of Frederick Douglass is David W. Blight, *Frederick Douglass: Prophet of Freedom* (New York: Simon and Schuster, 2018). Crucial work on escape by sea in Maryland is being done by Cheryl Janifer LaRoche. See her "The Underground Railroad in Maryland's Ports, Bays, and Harbors: Maritime Strategies for Freedom," in Walker, ed., *Sailing to Freedom*, 99–122. The political economy of early nineteenth-century Maryland is expertly explored by Barbara Jeanne Fields,

Slavery and Freedom on the Middle Ground: Maryland during the Nineteenth Century (New Haven, CT: Yale University Press, 1985).

2. Frederick Douglass, *Narrative of the Life of Frederick Douglass, an American Slave, Written by Himself* (Boston: Anti-Slavery Office, 1845), hereafter cited as *Narrative*; Frederick Douglass, *My Bondage and My Freedom* (New York and Auburn: Miller, Orton, and Mulligan, 1855), hereafter cited as *My Bondage*; and Frederick Douglass, *Life and Times of Frederick Douglass: His Early Life as a Slave, His Escape from Bondage, and His Complete History, Written by Himself* (Hartford: Park Publishing, 1881; repr., Boston: DeWolfe and Fiske, 1892), hereafter cited as *Life and Times*. Michaël Roy explores the publishing history of the narratives in *Fugitive Texts: Slave Narratives in Antebellum Print Culture* (Madison: University of Wisconsin Press, 2022), 58–79.

3. *My Bondage*, 323; *Narrative*, 100; *My Bondage*, 321–24; *Life and Times*, 197–98. Douglass wrote to historian Wilbur H. Siebert on March 27, 1893: "My connection with the Underground Railroad began long before I left the South and was continued as long as slavery continued, whether I lived in New Bedford, Lynn, or Rochester, N.Y."; quoted in Jesse Olsavsky, "The Underground Railroad," in Michaël Roy, ed., *Frederick Douglass in Context* (New York: Cambridge University Press, 2021), 281.

4. Frederick Augustus Washington Bailey first appears in Maryland plantation records in Aaron Anthony's Ledger A, 1794–1826, Special Collections, Mary A. Dodge Collection, SC 564, page 1, Maryland State Archives. Blight begins his biography by calling attention to the role of water in Fred's life: "Douglass knew something of 'toil' and 'honest boatmen'; he was born a slave within yards of the Tuckahoe River on Maryland's Eastern Shore. He traveled in a sloop out the Wye and Miles Rivers and up the Chesapeake Bay to Baltimore as a youth, and he crossed the Susquehanna and the Hudson in his epic escape from slavery. He knew something of rivers," *Frederick Douglass*, 9. For a broad overview of the history of Maryland's waterways, see William S. Dudley, *Maritime Maryland: A History* (Baltimore, MD: The Johns Hopkins University Press, 2010).

5. *My Bondage*, 136; *Narrative*, 29.

6. *My Bondage*, 135; *Narrative*, 29.

7. *Narrative*, 29; *My Bondage*, 136–37.

8. *Narrative*, 31; Phillips, *Freedom's Port*, 14, 17, 195. The best portrait of the multiracial waged and unwaged working class of Baltimore in the early national era is Seth Rockman, *Scraping By: Wage Labor, Slavery, and Survival in Early Baltimore* (Baltimore, MD: The Johns Hopkins University Press, 2009).

9. This and the following two paragraphs, including all quotations, are drawn from *Narrative*, 42–43; *My Bondage*, 169–70; *Life and Times*, 113–14.

10. On the Irish entry into the American labor market and the resulting racial dynamics, see Noel Ignatiev, *How the Irish Became White* (New York: Routledge, 1995).

11. *Narrative*, 33; *My Bondage*, 146.

12. *Narrative*, 43; *My Bondage*, 171.

13. *Narrative*, 43; *My Bondage*, 171.

14. *Narrative*, 50.

15. *My Bondage*, 203; *Narrative*, 56; Blight, *Frederick Douglass*, 59.

16. *Narrative*, 63; *My Bondage*, 219.

17. This and the next two paragraphs draw from *Narrative*, 63–65; *My Bondage*, 220–21.
18. Blight calls these lines "artistry unparalleled in the genre of slave narratives." See *Frederick Douglass*, 62.
19. *Narrative*, 65; *My Bondage*, 220–21.
20. *Narrative*, 69–70.
21. *Narrative*, 71–73; *My Bondage*, 242–46.
22. This section, including quotations, is drawn from *Narrative*, 83–93, and *My Bondage*, 273–303.
23. Blight calls the plot "wildly ambitious and based on inadequate geographic knowledge." See *Frederick Douglass*, 70. As Fred prepared for his own escape, Maryland's legislators fought against maritime fugitives. They increased the reward for captured runaways fivefold, cracked down on clandestine trade and all-Black crews of vessels, limited the ability of enslaved people to work on vessels, and tried to hold vessel owners financially responsible for those who escaped by sea. See "An Act to Encourage the More Effectual Apprehending of Runaway Servants and Slaves" (1833), Maryland Sessions Laws, 1833, vol. 210, 130–31, Archives of Maryland Online, msa.maryland.gov/megafile /msa/speccol/sc2900/sc2908/000001/000210/html/am210–130.html (accessed September 19, 2024); "An Act to Prohibit the Owners of Vessels, and others, from Navigating the Same by and under the Sole Command of Negroes or Mulattoes," in *Laws Made and Passed by the General Assembly, of the State of Maryland, at a Session Begun and Held at Annapolis, on Monday the 26th Day of December, 1836*, vol. 537 (Annapolis: Jeremiah Huggins, 1837), Archives of Maryland Online, msa.maryland.gov/megafile /msa/speccol/sc2900/sc2908/000001/000537/html/am537–144.html (accessed September 19, 2024); "An Act, entitled, An Act to Prevent the Transportation of People of Colour, upon Rail Roads or in Steamboats," Clement Dorsey, *General Public Statutory Law and Public Local Law of the State of Maryland, from the Year 1692 to 1839 Inclusive*, vol. 141 (Baltimore: J. D. Toy, 1840), 1295, Archives of Maryland Online, msa.mary land.gov/megafile/msa/speccol/sc2900/sc2908/000001/000141/html/am141–1295 .html (accessed September 19, 2024).
24. This section is based on *Narrative*, 95–105, and *My Bondage*, 308–30. See also Manisha Sinha's illuminating discussion of "The Irish Question" in her *The Slave's Cause: A History of Abolition* (New Haven: Yale University Press, 2017), 359–63. Job competition with African Americans, along with the raw racism it spawned, and the proslavery outlook of the Democratic party and the Catholic Church made any kind of alliance between abolitionists and Irish workers impossible.
25. Seth Rockman notes that this incident of racial violence was neither uncommon nor typical on the Baltimore waterfront. See his *Scraping By*, 257.
26. Phillips, *Freedom's Port*, 78, 172.
27. This section is based largely on *Narrative*, 107; *My Bondage*, 333–34; and especially *Life and Times*, ch. 1. Based on the data about runaways incarcerated in Baltimore jails gathered and presented by Jerry M. Hynson, it appears that the 1830s was the most rebellious decade of the antebellum era, with more than twice as many captures (1,098) as the 1840s (216), the 1850s (287), and the 1860s (to 1864, 70) combined. See Jerry M. Hynson, ed., *Absconders, Runaways and Other Fugitives in the Baltimore City and County [Maryland] Jail, 1831–1864* (Westminster, MD: Willow Bend Books, 2004), 116–26.

28. Still, *Underground Railroad*, 136; *My Bondage*, 326.
29. *Life and Times*, 247.
30. This section is based on *Narrative*, 107–10, and *My Bondage*, 336–45. One of the best studies of a slave catcher is Milt Diggins, *Stealing Freedom along the Mason-Dixon Line: Thomas McCreary, the Notorious Slave Catcher from Maryland* (Baltimore: Maryland Historical Society, 2015).
31. See Wells, *Kidnapping Club*, 127–32; and Foner, *Gateway to Freedom*, 70–72.
32. Hodges, *David Ruggles*, 1–2, 132–35.
33. See Pennington's *The Fugitive Blacksmith; or, Events in the History of James W. C. Pennington, Pastor of a Presbyterian Church, New York, Formerly a Slave in the State of Maryland, United States* (London: Charles Gilpin, 1849). Kathryn Grover offers a good survey of Fred's maritime experience in her *Fugitive's Gibraltar*, 143–49.
34. The primary sources for this section are *Narrative*, 111–18; *My Bondage*, 341–59; and *Life and Times*, ch. 2.
35. Kathryn Grover notes that the dispute between Fred and the white caulkers is the only known "racially motivated labor action" in New Bedford before the Civil War. See *Fugitive's Gibraltar*, 267.
36. Olsavsky, "The Underground Railroad," 281.
37. Harris, *In the Shadow of Slavery*, 218, 239; *Narrative*, 102; Blight, *Frederick Douglass*, 77.

Chapter Four: Harriet Jacobs on a "Dark and Troubled Sea"

1. Like all other scholars who have studied the life of Harriet Jacobs, I am deeply indebted to the foundational research done by the late Jean Fagan Yellin: first, her annotated scholarly edition of *Incidents in the Life of a Slave Girl: Written by Herself*, 3rd ed. (1987; repr., Cambridge: Belknap Press of Harvard University Press, 2009); her comprehensive biography, *Harriet Jacobs: A Life* (New York: Civitas Books, 2003); and her collection of documents, *The Harriet Jacobs Family Papers*, 2 vols. (Chapel Hill: University of North Carolina Press, 2008).
2. Harriet Jacobs, *Incidents in the Life of a Slave Girl, Written by Herself*, ed. L. Maria Child (Boston, 1861), 5, hereafter cited as *Incidents*, docsouth.unc.edu/fpn/jacobs /jacobs.html (accessed September 19, 2024). See also John S. Jacobs, "The United States Governed by Six Hundred Thousand Despots, a True Story of Slavery," *The Empire* (New South Wales), April 25 and 26, 1855, recently discovered by Jonathan D. S. Schroeder and published as John Swanson Jacobs, *The United States Governed by Six Hundred Thousand Despots: A True Story of Slavery; A Rediscovered Narrative, with a Full Biography*. In his brilliant biography-from-below of Jacobs included in that volume, entitled "No Longer Yours: The Lives of John Swanson Jacobs," Schroeder notes the importance of the maritime family in the lives of Harriet and John, 106. See also John S. Jacobs, "A True Tale of Slavery," serialized in *The Leisure Hour: A Family Journal of Instruction and Recreation* (London) 476 (February 7, 1861), 477 (February 14, 1861), 478 (February 21, 1861), and 479 (February 28, 1861), docsouth.unc.edu/neh /jjacobs/jjacobs.html (accessed September 19, 2024). Harriet called Uncle Joseph Horniblow "Benjamin" and Uncle Mark Ramsey "Philip." Uncle Stephen (last name unknown, husband of her Aunt Betty Horniblow) is mentioned in the memoir but not named. (Schroeder identifies Stephen's enslaver as Edenton merchant Joseph

Bozman; see Jacobs, *United States Governed by Six Hundred Thousand Despots*, 93.) She called her brother, John, "William." See Grover, *Fugitive's Gibraltar*, 82. For a deft history of Harriet's narrative, see Roy, *Fugitive Texts*, 140–54.

3. *Incidents*, 11. John wrote later, "My father taught me to hate slavery, but forgot to teach me how to conceal my hatred." See "True Tale," 85–86.

4. "An Act for regulating the Pilotage and facilitating the Navigation of Cape Fear River" (1784), in *Acts of the North Carolina General Assembly*, vol. 24 (North Carolina General Assembly, 1784), 591; "An Act to Prevent the Taking Away Boats, Canoes, and Pettiaguas from Landings or Elsewhere without Leave" (1837), in Nash, Iredell, and Battle, eds., *Revised Statutes of the State of North Carolina*, 96–97; "An Act to prevent the transportation of Slaves upon Rail Roads, Steam Boats or Stage Coaches, without written permission from their owners" (1841), *Laws of the State of North Carolina* (Raleigh, NC: Wesley Whitaker, 1841).

5. *Incidents*, 72, 76; Cecelski, *Waterman's Song*, 26.

6. Owen and the *Edenton Gazette* quoted in Yellin, *Harriet Jacobs*, 34–35.

7. *Incidents*, 97–104.

8. This section draws on *Incidents*, 29–42.

9. Petition for Slave Manumission, Molly Horniblow, Edenton, N. C., April 10, 1828, N.97.4.264, State Archives of North Carolina.

10. Cecelski, *Waterman's Song*, xiii.

11. In "Bill of Sale No. 463," dated May 14, 1818, Joseph is described as a "mulatto boy slave"; see Yellin, ed., *Jacobs Family Papers*, 1:14–17.

12. Joseph planned to work his way to Turkey as a seaman. See Jacobs, *United States Governed by Six Hundred Thousand Despots*.

13. Jacobs, "A True Tale," 127, and Jacobs, *United States Governed by Six Hundred Thousand Despots*. Harriet provided additional evidence that it was Mark rather than someone named "Peter" when she narrated her escape to Snaky Swamp, explaining that only three people were involved, herself and her uncles Mark and Stephen. Harriet had good reason to want to protect Mark from involvement in her escape as he could have been imprisoned or reenslaved.

14. Jacobs, "A True Tale," 87, 108; Jacobs, *The United States Governed by Six Hundred Thousand Despots*.

15. Jacobs, "A True Tale," 126. Jonathan Walker is the subject of the following chapter.

16. "A Fugitive Slave" [Harriet Jacobs] to the Editor, *New York Tribune*, June 19, 1853, reprinted in the *Pennsylvania Freeman*, June 30, 1853.

17. Here and throughout the chapter I substitute the real names of the characters Harriet wrote about in her book.

18. *Incidents*, 149-150; "$100 Reward" (runaway notice for Harriet Jacobs), *American Beacon*, July 4, 1835, Digital History, https://www.digitalhistory.uh.edu/disp_text book.cfm?smtID=8&psid=2498&filepath=http://www.digitalhistory.uh.edu/pri marysources_upload/images/notice_1.jpg (accessed September 19, 2024).

19. This section draws on *Incidents*, 131, 152–54.

20. Jacobs, "A True Tale," 109; Jacobs, *United States Governed by Six Hundred Thousand Despots*.

21. Dr. James Norcom's Note to Repay for Sold Slaves (Joe and Louisa), Edenton, NC, August 4, 1837, N.97.4.263, State Archives of North Carolina.

22. This section is based on *Incidents*, 55, 148, 169–72, and 182.

23. *Edenton Gazette*, March 22, 1811, quoted in Yellin, *Harriet Jacobs*, 6. On Cheapside, see Yellin, 12, 18–19, 30–31; and Robanna Sumrell Knott, "Harriet Jacobs: The Edenton Biography" (PhD diss., University of North Carolina, 1994).

24. The quotations in this and the next two paragraphs come from *Incidents*, 172, 193, 224, and Jacobs, *United States Governed by Six Hundred Thousand Despots*.

25. Quotations for this section may be found in *Incidents*, 227–38.

26. Fanny was the fictional name Harriet used in her memoir. The woman's real name is unknown.

27. This section is based on *Incidents*, 237–41.

28. Knott, "Harriet Jacobs: The Edenton Biography," 320.

29. Levi Coffin to Lydia Maria Child, June 25, 1842, Anti-Slavery Collection, Boston Public Library, reproduced in "Correspondence," in Yellin, ed., *Incidents in the Life of a Slave Girl, Written by Herself*, 3rd ed., 312. See also Yellin, *Harriet Jacobs*, 65–66. Captain Wright was still trading to Edenton in the *Skewarky* two years later: see "Arrived," *Baltimore Sun*, November 29, 1844.

30. This section draws upon *Incidents*, 243–47.

31. Years later Robert Purvis recalled Harriet's story (with some errors), suggesting that he had met her: Robert Purvis to Sydney Howard Gay, August 15, 1858, in Yellin, ed., *Jacobs Family Papers*, 1:252–54.

32. The involvement of Durham, Purvis, and other members of the Vigilant Committee with Harriet soon after her arrival in Philadelphia strongly suggests that Ramsey had prior arrangements, as does a letter written by abolitionist Joshua Coffin to Lydia Maria Child, June 25, 1841, in Yellin, ed., *Jacobs Family Papers*, 1:40–42. On Powell, see chapter 6 and Philip S. Foner, "William P. Powell: Militant Champion of Black Seamen," in *Essays in Afro-American History* (Philadelphia: Temple University Press, 1978), 88–111.

33. *Incidents*, 248. Lymas Johnson is listed as a member of the Vigilant Committee in Boromé, White, Ayres, and McKim, "The Vigilant Committee of Philadelphia," 351.

34. *Incidents*, 257.

35. *Incidents*, 281, 300–301.

36. *Incidents*, 303.

Chapter Five: Jonathan Walker's Branded Hand

1. Jonathan Walker, *Trial and Imprisonment of Jonathan Walker, at Pensacola, Florida, for Aiding Slaves to Escape from Bondage, with an Appendix, Containing a Sketch of His Life* (Boston: American Anti-Slavery Society, 1845), hereafter cited as *Trial and Imprisonment*. See also Alvin F. Oickle, *The Man with the Branded Hand: The Life of Jonathan Walker, Abolitionist* (Yardley, PA: Westholme Publishing, 2011); Matthew J. Clavin, *Aiming for Pensacola: Fugitive Slaves on the Atlantic and Southern Frontiers* (Cambridge: Harvard University Press, 2015), 124–40; Bordewich, *Bound for Canaan*, 268–72, 283–92; and Sinha, *The Slave's Cause*, 394–97. After he retired from the lecture circuit, Jonathan wrote an autobiography, but he was never able publish it. No copy of the manuscript seems to have survived.

2. F. E. Kittredge, "Funeral Address," in *A Short Sketch of the Life and Services of Jonathan Walker, the Man with the Branded Hand, with a Poem by John G. Whittier and an*

Address by Hon. Parker Pillsbury, One of Walker's Anti-Slavery Friends, and a Funeral Oration by Rev. F. E. Kittredge (Muskegon, Michigan: Chronicle Printing House, 1879), 4. Kittredge's qualifications as Walker's first biographer were impressive: he "was his personal friend, was present at his deathbed, and spoke the word of tribute at his funeral, has had access to his papers and correspondence, and from these and other sources, including statements from his own lips, is able to bring together many interesting facts concerning him." He combined documentary and oral sources in his book, *The Man with the Branded Hand: An Authentic Sketch of the Life and Services of Capt. Jonathan Walker* (Rochester, NY: H. L. Wilson Printing, 1899), 12.

3. *Trial and Imprisonment*. See also Jonathan Walker, *A Brief View of American Chattelized Humanity, and Its Supports* (Boston: Published by the author, 1846). I include Jonathan in the Atlantic circuit of escape because he grew up in it, tried to use it in 1844, and returned to it after his stint in jail.

4. This section draws heavily on Walker, "Appendix, Containing a Sketch of His Life," in *Trial and Imprisonment*, 112–26.

5. Kittredge, "Funeral Address," *A Short Sketch of the Life*, 7. Alvin F. Oickle noted that Jonathan "maintained the spirit of the Quakers." See his *The Man with the Branded Hand*, 43.

6. *A Brief View*, 7. Elmer R. Koppelmann writes: "Perhaps the greatest lesson Jonathan Walker learned while serving on a whaler was that regardless of their color, men of the world have very much in common." See his *Branded Hand: The Struggles of an Abolitionist* (Sheboygan Falls, WI: Branded Hand Press, 1984), 1.

7. For an account of Jonathan's ordeal see "More of Mexico," *United States Gazette* (Philadelphia), July 20, 1836.

8. Parker Pillsbury, "Address," in *A Short Sketch of the Life*, 21.

9. Clavin, *Aiming for Pensacola*, 10, 77.

10. Clavin, *Aiming for Pensacola*, 89; George Livermore, *An Historical Research Respecting the Opinions of the Founders of the Republic on Negroes as Slaves, as Citizens, and as Soldiers* (Boston: John Wilson and Son, 1862), quoted in Clavin, *Aiming for Pensacola*, 77–83.

11. *The Home and Foreign Record of the Presbyterian Church in the United States of America: Being the Organ of the Boards of Missions, Education, Foreign Missions, and Publication* (Philadelphia: Presbyterian Church, 1850), quoted in Clavin, *Aiming for Pensacola*, 84.

12. Jonathan Walker, *A Picture of Slavery, for Youth* (Boston: J. Walker and W. R. Bliss, 1846), 11.

13. *Trial and Imprisonment*, 63; "Pensacola," *Pensacola Gazette*, July 29, 1844; Oickle, *The Man with the Branded Hand*, 40.

14. Jonathan recalled the case of William Cook in *A Brief View*, 8. The jailor's notice that Cook had been incarcerated as a runaway first appeared in the *Pensacola Gazette*, "William Cook," April 25, 1840, and for many weeks thereafter. See also Clavin, *Aiming for Pensacola*, 125–26.

15. Kittredge, "Funeral Address," *A Short Sketch of the Life*, 1; Oickle, *The Man with the Branded Hand*, 41.

16. *Trial and Imprisonment*, 102; Kittredge, "Funeral Address," *A Short Sketch of the Life*, 5. Jonathan originally returned to Pensacola to salvage a local shipwreck but discov-

ered that someone else had already claimed the rights. He then departed by sea to visit a friend thirty to forty miles away. When he returned a few days later, he began to plan the escape. See *Trial and Imprisonment*, 10.

17. Kittredge, *The Man with the Branded Hand*, 13.

18. Walker, *A Picture of Slavery*, 20–21; *Trial and Imprisonment*, 10; Kittredge, *The Man with the Branded Hand*, 13; Oickle, *The Man with the Branded Hand*, 41. We will never know the full breadth of Jonathan's conspiratorial network, as abolitionist Maria Weston Chapman explained in the preface to Jonathan's book: the author refused to include anything that could endanger the safety, lives, and liberties of both the free and enslaved people with whom he worked.

19. Kittredge, "Funeral Address," *A Short Sketch of the Life*, 6. When the Fugitive Slave Act was passed in 1850 Jonathan advised the creation of Vigilance Committees in every town and village. He also encouraged everyone to disobey the law. See Sinha, *The Slave's Cause*, 503.

20. This and the following paragraph draw upon email correspondence with master mariner Sean Bercaw and Mary K. Bercaw Edwards: Sean Bercaw to Marcus Rediker, December 6, 2020; Mary K. Bercaw Edwards to Marcus Rediker, December 8, 2020. For more on the whaleboat see Willits D. Ansel, *The Whaleboat: A Study of Design, Construction and Use from 1850 to 2014* (Mystic, CT: Mystic Museum, 2014).

21. Oickle, *The Man with the Branded Hand*, 60; Sean Bercaw to Marcus Rediker, December 6, 2020.

22. *Trial and Imprisonment*, 11; Kittredge, "Funeral Address," in *A Short Sketch of the Life*, 6. Kittredge, *The Man with the Branded Hand*, 17–18. For an account of another escape from Florida of seven men to the Bahamas that took place in 1843, just before Jonathan's adventure, see Irvin D. S. Winsboro and Joe Knetsch, "Florida Slaves, the 'Saltwater Railroad' to the Bahamas, and Anglo-American Diplomacy," *Journal of Southern History* 79, no. 1 (Feb. 2013): 51–78.

23. *Trial and Imprisonment*, 14; Kittredge, *The Man with the Branded Hand*, 17–18.

24. *A Picture of Slavery*, 23. In his first account of the capture, Jonathan called the seven men who sailed with him "passengers." See "Letter from Jonathan Walker," *The Liberator*, September 6, 1844.

25. *Trial and Imprisonment*, 59; *A Picture of Slavery*, 23; Pillsbury, "Address," in *A Short Sketch of the Life*, 21.

26. *Trial and Imprisonment*, 14; "Jonathan Walker to his Wife and Children," *New Jersey Freeman*, July 12, 1844.

27. Kittredge, *The Man with the Branded Hand*, 17–18. After he had gone to jail, Jonathan twice feared that vigilantes might break into his cell and kill him. Pillsbury, "A Short Sketch," 22.

28. *Trial and Imprisonment*, 17, 18, 20, 21; Pillsbury, "Address," in *A Short Sketch of the Life*, 21; Oickle, *The Man with the Branded Hand*, 79.

29. *Trial and Imprisonment*, 14, 17–18.

30. *Trial and Imprisonment*, 21, 23. Jonathan did not mention the name of the incarcerated man, but Matthew J. Clavin discovered that it was Silas Scott, having located the names of the other six in Pensacola documentary records during the 1850s; see *Aiming for Pensacola*, 131, 228.

31. *Trial and Imprisonment*, 75.

32. *Trial and Imprisonment*, 61; Kittredge noted that Jonathan, Jesus-like, forgave his enemies: he "never entertained hard feelings even toward slaveholders, or those who used him so harshly." See *The Man with the Branded Hand*, 21.

33. *Trial and Imprisonment*, 39, 55.

34. This section is based primarily on *Trial and Imprisonment*.

35. *Trial and Imprisonment*, 39–40, 66.

36. Quoted in Kittredge, *The Man with the Branded Hand*, 18.

37. *A Brief View*, 13.

38. *A Picture of Slavery*, 29–32. Jonathan kept a journal, which he included in his book *Trial and Imprisonment of Jonathan Walker*, for most of the time he was in jail: from July 19 through Nov. 20, 1844, and Nov. 26, 1844, through May 1, 1845, a little more than nine months altogether. He made notes about the people who occupied the jail with him, noting why each one was there. See also *A Brief View*, 27.

39. *Trial and Imprisonment*, 25, 30–31, 45.

40. *Trial and Imprisonment*, 25, 30–31, 45, 118.

41. *Trial and Imprisonment*, 25, 30, 46, 50–51.

42. *Trial and Imprisonment.*, 88.

43. Jonathan included the "Report of the Legislative Council of Florida" written by Ferguson and Anderson in his book *Trial and Imprisonment*, 87–93.

44. "Pensacola," *Pensacola Gazette*, June 29, 1844.

45. "Letter from Jonathan Walker," *The Liberator*, May 26, 1848; *A Brief View*, 30–31; Koppelman, *Branded Hand*, 22; Oickle, *The Man with the Branded Hand*, 216.

46. "Arrival of Jonathan Walker," *The Liberator*, July 18, 1845; "Letter from Jonathan Walker," *The Liberator*, April 9, 1847; *A Brief View*, 29–30. See also Sean O'Neill, "The Rebranding of Jonathan Walker," *Michigan Historical Review* 46, no. 1 (Spring 2020): 121–65.

47. John Greenleaf Whittier, *The Branded Hand* (Salem, Ohio: The Anti-slavery Bugle, 1845), Library of Congress, https://www.loc.gov/resource/rbc0001.2019gen30706/ (accessed September 19, 2024). Sophia L. Little was moved by Jonathan's story to write one of the first abolitionist plays, *The Branded Hand: A Dramatic Sketch, Commemorative of the Tragedies in the South in the Winter of 1844–5* (Pawtucket, RI: E. W. Potter, 1845).

48. Julia Wilbur Diary, 1847–1854, Julia Wilbur Papers, Haverford College Quaker & Special Collections, HC.MC.1158/mc1158_03_01_001, triptych.swarthmore.edu /cdm/compoundobject/collection/InHOR/id/89016/rec/11 (accessed September 19, 2024).

49. Marcus Wood, *Blind Memory: Visual Representations of Slavery in England and America, 1780–1865* (Manchester, UK: Manchester University Press, 2000), 246–49; "Arrival of Jonathan Walker," *The Liberator*, July 18, 1845, and "Jonathan Walker," *The Liberator*, November 11, 1847.

50. Frederick Douglass to Photius Fisk, July 15, 1878 (to be read at the funeral of Jonathan Walker), published in the *Chicago Tribune*, August 2, 1878. Another observer described how "an awful stillness pervaded the assembly" when Jonathan presented his scarred hand: "every beholder's countenance sunk to a graver expression"; "The Branded Hand," *Old Reflector* (Utica, NY), January 26, 1848.

51. *A Picture of Slavery*, 36; A. J. Grover, "Remarks," in *A Short Sketch of the Life*, 28–29; Koppelman, *Branded Hand:* 42; Oickle, *The Man with the Branded Hand*, 226, 244. See also Carl J. Guarnari, *The Utopian Alternative: Fourierism in Nineteenth-Century America* (Ithaca, NY: Cornell University Press, 1991), 408; and *Philadelphia Inquirer*, August 27, 1877. Jonathan's radicalism did not include the then-popular spiritualism that professed to bring the dead back to life. See his skeptical and humorous article "Spiritual Knockings," *The Liberator*, April 11, 1851.

52. Douglass, *Chicago Tribune*, August 2, 1878.

53. Stanley Harrold, "John Brown's Forerunners: Slave Rescue Attempts and the Abolitionists, 1841–51," *Radical History Review* 55 (Winter 1993): 89–110; Jonathan Walker, "Rights of Woman," *The Liberator*, February 23, 1849.

54. Douglass, *Chicago Tribune*, August 2, 1878.

Chapter Six: William P. Powell and Solidarity at Sea

1. William P. Powell, "Underground Railroad," *Elevator*, December 19, 1874. Additional evidence for this section has been gathered from "Things in New York," *Baltimore Sun*, July 14, 1847; "General News, etc.," *National Era*, July 15, 1847; "Important Slave Case," *New-York Evangelist*, July 22, 1847; "The Brazilian Slaves," *National Anti-Slavery Standard* (hereafter *NASS*), July 22, 1847; "The Brazilian Slave Case—Escape of the Slaves," *NASS*, August 12, 1847; and "In the matter of the writ of Habeas Corpus directed to Clemente José da Costa," *NASS*, September 2, 1847; "Brazilian Slaves," *Anti-Slavery Bugle*, July 30, 1847; "The Decision," *New York Herald*, August 7, 1847; and "Spirited Away," *Hampshire Gazette*, August 17, 1847.

2. For a brief portrait of Napoleon see Foner, *Gateway to Freedom*, 98–99. Maria da Costa decided, no doubt under great pressure, to return to the enslaver's family aboard the ship.

3. Baquaqua would become an important abolitionist in his own right, penning an autobiography in 1854 in which he described his ordeal in New York. See Mahommah Gardo Baquaqua, *The Biography of Mahommah Gardo Baquaqua: His Passage from Slavery to Freedom in Africa and America*, eds. Robin Law and Paul E. Lovejoy (Princeton, NJ: Markus Wiener Publishers, 2001).

4. Foner, *Gateway to Freedom*, 107–8. When Baquaqua published his autobiography seven years later, he still understood very little of what had happened in his court case or his escape. He saw his escape as an act of God, who had raised up "so many friends in a strange land." See *The Biography of Mahommah Gardo Baquaqua*, 171.

5. "Communications," *NASS*, September 4, 1851. William had held a fundraiser at the Colored Sailors Home for Douglass and the *North Star* the previous year (*NASS*, May 2, 1850) but criticized him after his break with William Lloyd Garrison in May 1851. For an account of the seafaring life of John S. Jacobs, see Jacobs, *The United States Governed by Six Hundred Thousand Despots*, 163–79.

6. Powell left no collection of papers and never wrote a book, but he was a vigorous newspaper correspondent throughout his life, contributing regularly to the *National Anti-Slavery Standard* based in New York and *The Liberator* in Boston. He worked as an assistant editor at a San Francisco–based African American newspaper called the *Elevator* and published several articles there in the 1870s. He also produced numerous reports, published and unpublished, about the Colored Sailors Home for the American Seamen's Friend Society, which supported his endeavors for decades. (See

the Records of the American Seamen's Friend Society, Manuscripts Collection 158, G. W. Blunt White Library, Mystic Seaport, Mystic, CT.) Powell appears briefly in several histories of abolition, but the only in-depth research about him remains Philip S. Foner, "William P. Powell: Militant Champion of Black Seamen," in his *Essays in Afro-American History*, 88–111. The documentation of Powell's extraordinary life is surprisingly rich and multifaceted.

7. "A Sensible Petition," *NASS*, July 17, 1851; "The Passport Case," *The Republic* (Washington, DC), August 16, 1849; "Passports Once More," *Salem Register*, August 23, 1849; *Old North State* (Elizabeth City, North Carolina), August 25, 1849; "Full!" *The Liberator*, August 1, 1851. William noted that "his grandfather and his father were slaves"; see *Freeman's Journal* (Dublin, Ireland), February 8, 1851.

8. William published his autobiography, "Letter of a Self-Made Colored Man," under the name "Simon Peter Barjona" in the *Christian Recorder*, June 2, 1866. Barjona was the surname of his grandmother Elizabeth, who was likely related to Cato and Phillis Barjona, free people of color who lived in Essex County, Massachusetts, according to the federal censuses of 1800 and 1810, respectively. "Simon Peter Barjona" was also the name Jesus Christ gave to the apostle Peter, a Jewish fisherman who was the son of Jonah, hence the name, Bar-Jonah or Barjona. William may have had a Jewish ancestor, or perhaps he chose the name based on Biblical knowledge.

9. Melville, *Moby-Dick*, 4.

10. "Coloured Seamen—Their Character and Condition, Pt. II," *NASS*, September 24, 1846.

11. "Coloured Seamen—Their Character and Condition, Pt. V," *NASS*, November 12, 1846, and "Colored Seamen—Their Character and Condition, Pt. IV," *NASS*, October 29, 1846.

12. William attended a "Temperance Convention for People of Color" in Providence, Rhode Island, in May 1836. Others in attendance included David Ruggles, cofounder of the New York Vigilance Committee six months earlier, and William Apess, the Afro-Pequot Methodist minister. See "Temperance Convention of the People of Color in New England," *The Liberator*, May 14, 1836. For Powell and Walker, see Foner, "William P. Powell," 94.

13. "Letter of a Self-Made Colored Man," *Christian Recorder*, June 2, 1866; "Coloured Seamen—Their Character and Condition, Pt. IV," *NASS*, October 29, 1846.

14. On Mercy O. Haskins's family background, see William's article "Full!," *The Liberator*, August 1, 1851. Advertisements appeared in the *New Bedford Mercury*, June 9, 1837, and September 22, 1837. William's emergence as a leader in New Bedford was reflected in his selection by the free Black community as one of three representatives to vet political candidates on their views of slavery; see the *Fall River Monitor*, November 4, 1837; and "Proceedings of the Meeting of Colored Citizens, N. Bedford, MSS," *Colored American*, November 18, 1837. In 1846 William wrote, "For seventeen years I have been associated with [seamen]; five of which were spent at sea, in the capacity of a sailor. I have been twelve years engaged in Seamen's affairs." This suggests that William began full-time seafaring in 1829 and opened the boardinghouse in New Bedford in 1834. See "Coloured Seamen—Their Character and Condition, No. V," *NASS*, November 12, 1846.

15. *Elevator*, November 21, 1874. William wrote in another context that he had just returned from a long whaling voyage in 1832, when he bought his first copy of *The*

Liberator. See his letter to *The Liberator*, March 13, 1862. It is important to note that "road" had a maritime meaning: a body of water sheltered from currents, a place where ships can lie safely at anchor.

16. Mercy O. (Haskins) Powell was also an abolitionist. She was named to the Board of Managers of the Manhattan Anti-Slavery Society in 1840. See "Manhattan Anti-Slavery Society," *NASS*, November 5, 1840.

17. "Boarding House for Seamen," *Colored American*, December 7, 1839. William made a deal to recommend workers to a progressive New York shipping company called Goin, Poole, and Pentz. Thomas Goin stood out during the 1830s as "the sailor's friend," not least because he opposed flogging in the US Navy. Powell acknowledged his work with Goin and his firm in *Sailor's Magazine* 15 (1842), 197. See also Thomas Goin, *Remarks on the Home Squadron and Naval School by a Gentleman of New York* (New York: J. P. Wright, 1840), v, 39–40.

18. Over the years William struggled to make financial ends meet, primarily because he served destitute seamen and fugitives without charge. The assistance of the ASFS was not enough, especially when he moved to new buildings in 1840, 1849, and 1862, and had to make repairs. William took on partners when he attempted to run the home without the support of the ASFS in the early 1840s: he worked with George A. Bodee (June 1840–July 1841) and soon thereafter with his Black seafaring abolitionist friend from New England, Nathaniel A. Borden, for an unknown length of time. (See *NASS*, July 22, 1841.) Both efforts apparently failed, requiring William to return to the ASFS, whose board renewed and sustained its support through the 1860s. William suffered "pecuniary embarrassment" and paid numerous expenses out of his own pocket. He occasionally appealed to both shipping agencies and fellow abolitionists for funding, apparently with some success. In May 1871 he opened "Powell House" at 153 Thompson Street, near Houston Street, seeking a broader clientele, but he continued to cater to Black sailors.

19. The portrait of the CSH that follows is a composite based on the following sources: "Boarding House for Seamen," *Colored American*, December 7, 1839; "Colored Seaman's Home," *Colored American*, May 8, 1841; "Colored Seamen's Home," *Emancipator*, July 2, 1840; "Inquest," *New York Morning Express*, January 20, 1841; *Sailor's Magazine*, February 1, 1842; "Colored Sailor's Home," *Sailor's Magazine*, August 1, 1849; "Sailor's Home, N.Y.," *Sailor's Magazine* (hereafter *SM*), December 1, 1849; "Sailor's Home, N.Y.," *SM*, February 1, 1850; "Home for Colored Seamen," *SM*, August 1, 1862; "Colored Seamen," *SM*, March 1, 1863; "Colored Sailor's Home," *SM*, June 1, 1866; "Report of the Colored Sailor's Home, No. 2 Dover Street," *SM*, May 1, 1867; "Boarding Houses for Colored Seamen in New York," August 1, 1869; Robert Purvis, "Visit to Eastern Pennsylvania," *The Liberator*, October 26, 1849; "Sailors' Home," *The Liberator*, January 18, 1850; "Ich dien," *The Liberator*, October 10, 1862; "The Colored Sailor's Home," *The Liberator*, July 24, 1863; "Worthy of Patronage," *The Liberator*, October 2, 1863; Records of the American Seamen's Friend Society, quarterly reports for April 1862, April 1864, December 1864, January 1865, and March 1866. The features of the various buildings in which the home was located were quite similar. The house at 330 Pearl Street seems to have been the largest of them all.

20. William estimated that about half of the sailors attended religious services. See "Report of the Colored Sailor's Home, No. 2 Dover Street," *SM*, May 1, 1867.

21. "Names of Shipwrecked and destitute colored seamen who received board & clothing, and sent to sea from July 1862 to April 1863," Records of the American Seamen's Friend Society. Purvis's comments appeared in "Visit to Eastern Pennsylvania," *The Liberator*, October 26, 1849. See also "Colored Sailors Home, New York," *NASS*, April 5, 1849.

22. "Colored Sailor's Home," *SM*, June 1, 1866. While William embraced the use of force in self-defense, he remained an orthodox Garrisonian in opposing the violence of armed insurrection by abolitionists or the enslaved. He specifically opposed emancipation that might involve "cutting their masters' throats." He applied the same view to sailors, discouraging them from taking part in mutinies. William boasted to the ASFS that very few who stayed in the Colored Sailors Home had suffered "imprisonment for mutiny or bad conduct." He did, however, work consistently throughout his life for what he called "*heel* resistance," helping "thousands to get their liberty on the peaceful underground railroad." He believed that "Moral power is greater than physical force." See "Wm. P. Powell to James Demarest Esqr. And gentlemen of the Sailors Home Committee, etc etc," December 27, 1864, Records of American Seamen's Friend Society, and his article "The Anti-Slavery Movement," *The Liberator*, September 30, 1864.

23. William estimated that 2,200 Black seamen worked out of New York in 1846; 2,500 in 1849; 3,271 in 1864; and 3,500 in 1870; "Coloured Seamen—Their Character and Condition Pt. II, Concluded," *NASS*, September 24, 1846; "Colored Sailor's Home," *SM*, August 1, 1849; Records of the American Seamen's Friend Society, April 1864; "Labor in New York," *New National Era* (Washington, DC), February 17, 1870.

24. "Gleanings by the Wayside," *North Star*, February 11, 1848.

25. "Third Annual Report of the Coloured Sailor's Home," *SM*, January 1, 1843; *NASS*, November 12, 1846.

26. "Wm. P. Powell to James Demarest, Chairman and members of the Sailors Home Committee, Annual report of the Colored Sailors Home, No. 2 Dover Street," April 25, 1866, Records of the American Seamen's Friend Society, 158.

27. On the Negro Seamen Acts, see Schoeppner, *Moral Contagion*; Hamer, "Great Britain, the United States, and the Negro Seamen Acts, 1822–1848"; Philip M. Hamer, "British Consuls and the Negro Seamen Acts, 1850–1860," *Journal of Southern History* 1, no. 2 (May 1935): 138–68; and Edlie Wong, "In the Shadow of Haiti: The Negro Seamen Act, Counter-Revolutionary St. Domingue, and Black Emigration" in Elizabeth Maddock Dillon and Michael J. Drexler, eds., *The Haitian Revolution and the Early United States: Histories, Textualities, Geographies* (Philadelphia: University of Pennsylvania Press, 2016), 162–88.

28. "Free Colored Seamen—Majority and Minority Reports, January 20, 1843," Report No. 80, House of Representatives, 27th Cong., 3d Sess., 3, 7, 38; "Black Seamen and Alabama Law," *NASS*, March 17, 1842; "A Petition for the Rights of the Col'd Citizen" to the "Honorable the Senate & House [from] the Commonwealth of Massachusetts," n.d. [c. 1843], Massachusetts Anti-Slavery Society, MSS Collection, New

York Historical Society, digitalcollections.nyhistory.org/islandora/object/islandora%3A134027#page/1 (accessed September 19, 2024). For more on struggle of free Black seamen in Massachusetts, see Edlie L. Wong, *Neither Fugitive nor Free: Atlantic Slavery, Freedom Suits, and the Legal Culture of Travel* (New York: New York University Press, 2009), 199–204.

29. "Coloured Seamen—Their Character and Condition, No. III, concluded," *NASS*, October 15, 1846.

30. "Coloured Seamen—Their Character and Condition," *NASS*, September 10, 1846; "Coloured Seamen—Their Character and Condition, *NASS*, No. II," September 17, 1846; "Coloured Seamen—Their Character and Condition Pt. II, Concluded," *NASS*, September 24, 1846.

31. For the petition of "Free Black Seamen of Boston," see "Free Colored Seamen—Majority and Minority Reports," House of Representatives, 3, 7, 38. The Massachusetts legislature demanded the repeal of the South Carolina Negro Seamen Act in 1839; see Paul Finkelman, "States' Rights North and South in Antebellum America," in Kermit L. Hall and James W. Ely Jr., eds., *An Uncertain Tradition: Constitutionalism and the History of the South* (Athens: University of Georgia Press, 1989), 132. Michael A. Schoeppner offers an important account of the resistance to the Negro Seamen Acts in Massachusetts in 1843; see his *Moral Contagion*, 138–59, 209.

32. "Coloured Seamen—Their Character and Condition, Statistics of Coloured Seamen Imprisoned in Southern and Foreign Ports, No. III," *NASS*, October 1, 1846, and "Coloured Seamen—Their Character and Condition, No. III, Continued," *NASS*, October 8, 1846. Michael Shoeppner recounts some of the misdeeds of captains against their Black sailors in Southern ports; see *Moral Contagion*, 202–4.

33. "Coloured Seamen—Their Character and Condition, No. III, Continued," *NASS*, October 8, 1846, and "Coloured Seamen—Their Character and Condition, No. III, Concluded," *NASS*, October 15, 1846. Kathryn Grover notes that William overestimated the number of Black workers on New England whalers; see her *Fugitive's Gibraltar*, 120. William's observations about New Orleans are borne out by John K. Bardes in "Soi-Disant Libre: Travelers of Color, Free Status, and the Slave Prison" in his *The Carceral City: Slavery and the Making of Mass Incarceration in New Orleans, 1803–1930* (Chapel Hill: University of North Carolina Press, 2024), 79–110.

34. "Coloured Seamen—Their Character and Condition, Pt. II," *NASS*, September 24, 1846, and "Colored Seamen—Their Character and Condition, No. III," *NASS*, October 15, 1846.

35. "Colored Seamen—Their Character and Condition, Pt. IV," *NASS*, October 29, 1846.

36. William Harned, Charles B. Ray, and Andrew Lester, "Circular of the New York State Vigilance Committee," 1849, Thomas P. Cope Family papers, HC.MC-1013, Box 3, Haverford College Quaker & Special Collections. This section draws heavily on reports of meetings held on October 1 and 4 published as "Meetings of Colored Citizens," in *NASS*, October 10, 1850.

37. Harned, Ray, and Lester, "Circular of the New York State Vigilance Committee." Since Powell and Attucks shared not only a seafaring background but also Afro-Indigenous parentage, it is not surprising that he kept an image of the revolutionary martyr in the Colored Sailors Home for inspiration.

38. "Meeting of Colored Citizens," *NASS*, October 10, 1850.

39. "Meeting of Colored Citizens"; "Letter from William P. Powell, Liverpool, [England], to Samuel May, April 5th, 1854." Correspondence. Liverpool, England, April 5, 1854. *Digital Commonwealth,* digitalcommonwealth.org/search/commonwealth: dv144h71j (accessed September 19, 2024).

40. "Letter from William P. Powell, 123 Field Street, Everton, L'pool [Liverpool, England], to Maria Weston Chapman, 21 Jan'y 1859." Correspondence. 123 Field Street, Everton, L'pool Liverpool, England, January 21, 1859. *Digital Commonwealth,* digitalcommon wealth.org/search/commonwealth:7s75fq633 (accessed September 19, 2024).

41. For a discussion of free Black runaways, see Franklin and Schweninger, *Runaway Slaves,* 189–92.

42. "Letter from William P. Powell," *The Liberator,* February 7, 1851.

43. Maritcha Lyons, quoted in Harris, *In the Shadow of Slavery,* 238–39.

44. "Letter from William P. Powell," *The Liberator,* February 7, 1851; "The Slave Girl and the Officer of Customs," *Liverpool Mercury,* March 19, 1856; "Wm. P. Powell," *Pennsylvania Freeman,* August 18, 1853; "Remarkable Escape of a Slave," *NASS,* April 19, 1856; "The Virginia Search Law," *NASS,* April 26, 1856; "Letter from Mr. W.P. Powell," *London Anti-Slavery Advocate,* June 20, 1856.

45. "Wm. P. Powell to James Demarest, Chairman of the Sailors Home Committee, Report of the Colored Sailors Home, No. 2 Dover Street," December 1862, Records of the American Seamen's Friend Society, Manuscripts Collection 158, G. W. Blunt White Library, Mystic Seaport, Mystic, CT.

46. "Wm. P. Powell to the Chairman and members of the Sailors Home Committee, Report of the Colored Sailors Home, No. 2 Dover Street," July 1863, Records of the American Seamen's Friend Society; Sidney Kaplan, "The American Seamen's Protective Union Association of 1863: A Pioneer Organization of Negro Seamen in the Port of New York," *Science and Society* 21, no. 2 (1957): 154–59.

47. "Sailor's Home—Monthly Report," *SM,* March 1, 1863. The editor of *Sailor's Magazine,* published by the ASFS, had seen the constitution, and complained that neither it nor the name of the organization indicated that it was primarily for "colored seamen." Perhaps William and the sailors hoped the organization would have broader appeal.

48. "Sailor's Home—Monthly Report," *SM,* May 1, 1863; Annual Report of the Colored Sailors Home, No. 2 Dover Street, April 1864, Records of the American Seaman's Friend Society. In conducting research for his book, *The Longshoremen* (New York: Survey Associates, 1915), Charles B. Barnes interviewed older maritime workers, some of whom recognized names among the founders of the American Seamen's Protective Union Association as dockworkers (255). How long the ASPUA lasted is unknown, but in a survey of Black labor in New York published in 1870, William noted that the organization was still alive. See the William P. Powell, "Labor in New York," *New National Era* (Washington, DC), February 17, 1870.

49. William, who was a careful record-keeper, noted that between 1839 and 1851 he served 6,533 boarders. From May 1862 to December 1864, he housed another 1,051. At that rate, he would have had another 125 for January through the end of the Civil War (April 9, 1865), bringing the total to 7,709. If Maritcha Lyons was correct that her father Albro assisted a thousand runaways during his years running the CSH, and if we compare that number to William's observation that Lyons received 5,300

sailors during the same period, the ratio of fugitives to seamen was 1:5.3. If the ratio was the same for William's boarders (it might have been larger), he would have assisted 1,454 fugitives between 1839–51 and 1862–65. See also William P. Powell to Gerrit Smith, September 4, 1861, Gerrit Smith Papers, Box 30, Special Collections Research Center, Syracuse University Libraries.

50. "Wm. P. Powell to James Demarest Esqr. And gentlemen of the Sailors Home Committee, etc etc," December 27, 1864; "Wm. P. Powell to James Demarest, Chairman and members of the Sailors Home Committee, Monthly report of the Colored Sailors Home, No. 2 Dover Street," March 28, 1866, Records of American Seamen's Friend Society.

Chapter Seven: Boston's War on the Waterfront

1. "Statement of the Tonnage of the Several Districts of the United States on the Last Day of June 1850," in Thomas C. Cochran, ed., *The New American State Papers,* 32: 699–709.

2. Horton and Horton, *Black Bostonians,* 24, 33–36, 40, 52–54, 59, 107; Jones, *No Right to an Honest Living,* 55–56.

3. *Right and Wrong in Boston, in 1836: Annual Report of the Boston Female Anti-Slavery Society* (Boston: Isaac Knapp, 1836); "Rescue of Slaves," *Salem Gazette,* August 5, 1836; "A Rescue in Court," *New Bedford Mercury,* April 5, 1836. The women were known in Baltimore as Ann Patten and Mary Pinckney, as the *Boston Post,* "Supreme Judicial Court, Extraordinary Rescue of Two Slaves," reported on August 2, 1836. I use the names they chose for themselves during the escape. It seems likely that they paid for their voyage, as Captain Eldredge said in court that he "had brought them as passengers." See "Outrage in Court," *Niles' Weekly Register,* August 5, 1836. On Adams, see Edward E. Baptist, "Solidarity Versus Parastate" (paper presented to the Department of History, Carnegie Mellon University, October 27, 2023). A good recent account of the event is Lyndsay Campbell, "The 'Abolition Riot' Redux: Voices, Processes," *New England Quarterly,* 94, no. 1 (Mar. 2021): 7–46.

4. Nina Moore Tiffany, *Samuel E. Sewall: A Memoir* (Boston: Houghton Mifflin, 1898), 63; "Rescue of Slaves," *Salem Gazette,* August 5, 1836. James Oliver Horton and Lois E. Horton have suggested that the African American women in the courtroom rescue were likely "washerwomen and domestic servants," *Black Bostonians,* 70. *The Liberator* noted specifically that "the liberated prisoners were borne out by the colored *females* in attendance, and not by the colored men." See "Rescue of Slaves," *Salem Gazette,* August 6, 1836. Edward E. Baptist notes that "Black crowds who freed those accused of the crime of escaping Southern slavery were typically made up of the poor and working class," in "Solidarity Versus Parastate," 36.

5. "Outrageous Violation of Justice," *Charleston Courier,* August 11, 1836, republished from the *Boston Atlas*; Tiffany, *Samuel E. Sewall,* 64; Leonard W. Levy, "The 'Abolition Riot': Boston's First Slave Rescue," *New England Quarterly* 25, no. 1 (Mar. 1952): 85–92.

6. "Outrageous Violation of Justice," *Charleston Courier,* August 11, 1836; Tiffany, *Samuel E. Sewall,* 64; "The Colored Citizens of Boston," *The Liberator,* December 10, 1852; Levy, "The 'Abolition Riot,'" 85–92.

7. The editor of the *Boston Evening Transcript*, quoted in Campbell, "The 'Abolition Riot,'" 39–40; letter from "A member of the Baltimore Bar" to "Sewall Esq. The Abolition Lawyer," August 2, 1836; Wm. A. Clarke to Samuel E. Sewall Esq., August 9, 1836, both in the Robie-Sewall Family Papers, 1611–1905, Ms. N-804, Massachusetts Historical Society. After a careful review of the surviving evidence, Campbell ("The 'Abolition Riot,'" 32) concludes that the women sailed aboard the British mail ship *Lady Ogle* to Halifax.

8. Benjamin Higgins, the mate of the *Wellington*, later stated that John got on board "Probably by the aid of sum of the crue." Charles Smith, who went aboard the *Wellington* in Boston and spoke to the fugitive as well as Captain James Higgins and his brother, Benjamin, thought John got aboard thanks to the ship's cook, who was almost surely Black. See the letter by Smith originally published in the *Boston Daily Mail*, June 17, 1841, reprinted in "Abolitionist Truth and Honesty!," *Newbern Spectator*, June 26, 1841.

9. According to Charles T. Torrey, the abolitionist who led the charge in this case, John may have had a child who accompanied Mariah to Philadelphia. Torrey wrote that John's plight "did touch the hearts of the common Sailors of the schooner Wellington." See his article "The Illegal Conduct of the Grand Jury for Suffolk County Exposed! The Laws of Massachusetts prostrated at the Footstool of Southern Slavery!" *The Liberator*, June 18, 1841. Benjamin Higgins noted that John "bought his wife by working on Shouse [shoes] in the night by help of friends"; "Boston Vigilance Committee," *The Liberator*, June 11, 1841.

10. "The Story of John Torrence," *The Liberator*, June 18, 1841.

11. "Extraordinary Case of Kidnapping by the Abolitionists of Boston," *Charleston Mercury*, June 14, 1841.

12. Testimony of John Gove, Josiah Brackett, and Oliver Smith, *The Liberator*, June 11, 1841. Both captain and mate "feared a mob might be raised to rescue [John]." It is significant to note that if a mob was threatened, the abolitionists around *The Liberator* knew nothing about it. The rescuers would likely have been African American waterfront laborers who worked on their own initiative. See also "Extraordinary Case," *Charleston Mercury*, June 14, 1841.

13. "Abolitionist Truth and Honesty!," *Newbern Spectator*, June 26, 1841.

14. This and the next paragraph are based on "Extraordinary Case of Kidnapping!," *The Liberator*, June 4, 1841, and "The Boston Vigilance Committee," *The Liberator*, July 2, 1841; "Anti-Slavery Events," *National Anti-Slavery Standard*, July 15, 1841. Charles Torrey and J. P. Bishop wrote in "To the Friends of the Slave, in New-England" (*The Liberator*, June 11, 1841): "It has been thought advisable to do as our New-York brethren have done, to organize a Vigilance Committee."

15. "The Illegal Conduct of the Grand Jury for Suffolk County Exposed! The Laws of Massachusetts prostrated at the Footstool of Southern Slavery!" *The Liberator*, June 18, 1841.

16. Mary D. Sayer, "$50 Reward," and James B. Gray, "$50 Dollars Reward," *Norfolk Beacon*, October 15, 1842; Newby-Alexander, *Virginia Waterways*.

17. George defiantly noted that Gray "made all his money by selling liquor to colored people. He bought stolen goods from colored people. I know this. Mr. Gray knows I

know it." Asa J. Davis, "The Two Autobiographical Fragments of George W Latimer (1820–1896): A Preliminary Assessment," *Journal of the Afro-American Historical and Genealogical Society* 1 (Summer 1980): 9.

18. Davis, "Two Autobiographical Fragments," 3–18. A large portion of the article is published as "The George Latimer Case: A Benchmark in the Struggle for Freedom," on the website of the Thomas A. Edison Papers, Rutgers University, edison .rutgers.edu/resources/latimer/the-george-latimer-case.

19. Eleven leading abolitionists, including Nathaniel Bowditch and Charles Sumner, immediately wrote a letter to the sheriff of Suffolk County demanding Latimer's release; Bowditch Family Papers, 1834–1882, Ms. N-49.61, Massachusetts Historical Society.

20. Sewall, quoted in Davis, "Two Autobiographical Fragments," 4.

21. Daniel Mann, *The Virginia Philosopher, Or Few Lucky Slave-Catchers: A Poem, by Mr. Latimer's Brother* (Boston: Printed for the Author, 1843).

22. *Proceedings of the Citizens of the Borough of Norfolk, on the Boston Outrage, in the Case of the Runaway Slave George Latimer* (Norfolk, VA: T. G. Broughton & Son, 1843).

23. "New England Freedom Association," *The Liberator*, December 12, 1845. See also Horton and Horton, *Black Bostonians*, 62–63.

24. "How it Ought to be Done," *Latimer Journal, and North Star*, Boston, November 12, 1842. Other issues were published November 1, 1842; November 14, 1842; November 23, 1842; and May 10, 1843, E187-XL, Massachusetts Historical Society.

25. *Latimer Journal*, November 11, 1842; November 14, 1842; November 16, 1842. Lemuel Shaw, chief justice of the Massachusetts Supreme Judicial Court, saw the *Latimer Journal* as a means "to excite a popular tumult" that would rescue the man from jail. See *An Article on the Latimer Case* (Boston: Bradbury, Soden, and Company, 1843).

26. Charles Francis Adams, *Report of the Joint Special Committee of the Massachusetts General Court on the Petition of George Latimer concerning Fugitive Slaves and Those who Aided Them*, including "An Act Further to protect Personal Liberty," (Boston: Commonwealth of Massachusetts, 1843). For more information about where the signatures originated, see "Final Report of the Latimer Committee," *Latimer Journal, and North Star*, May 10, 1843, E187-XL, Massachusetts Historical Society.

27. Information about the fugitive comes from the transcribed speech of Dr. Samuel Gridley Howe, delivered at Faneuil Hall, September 24, 1846. Howe had apparently gone down to the docks and talked to the sailors who worked aboard the *Ottoman*. See *Address of the Committee Appointed by a Public Meeting, held at Faneuil Hall, September 24, 1846, for the Purpose of Considering the Recent Case of Kidnapping from our Soil, and of Taking Measures to Prevent the Recurrence of Similar Outrages, with an Appendix* (Boston: White and Potter, 1846). See also "Letter from Samuel May, Boston and Leicester, [Mass.], to John Bishop Estlin, Sept. 26 and 29th, 1846." Correspondence. Boston and Leicester, Mass., September 26, 1846–September 29, 1846. *Digital Commonwealth* digitalcommonwealth.org/search/commonwealth:dv144346q (accessed September 19, 2024).

28. The ad, "$50 Reward," appeared in the *Daily Picayune*, August 11, 1846. The fugitive's age was given in "Astern All!" *The Emancipator*, October 7, 1846.

29. "$10 Reward," *Daily Picayune*, March 3, 1845. Pearson later wrote that "unless [George] was sent back to his owner [Captain Hannum] could never return [to New

Orleans] without being imprisoned from *two* to *ten* years and fined the value of the slave." John H. Pearson to *The Liberator*, October 23, 1846. For Pearson as a "merchant prince," see *The Emancipator*, September 23, 1846.

30. Hannum later wrote of George, "from the time of his discovery till his re-shipment he lived and fared as I did myself." This was one of many lies Hannum told during and after the ordeal. See "Letters of Messrs. Hannum and Pearson," *Address of the Committee*, 34. For Pearson's ownership of the packet line, see "The Atlas's Views of Kidnapping," *The Liberator*, October 9, 1846.

31. "The Great Faneuil Hall Meeting for the Prevention of Illegal Seizures of Slaves," *The Liberator*, October 2, 1846.

32. Hannum ascended from first mate to captain of the *Ottoman* in 1843 when Charles Inglee died on a voyage from Boston to Antwerp. See "Death of Capt. Charles Inglee," *Boston Post*, April 21, 1843. He subsequently wrote against the "wild proceedings" of "clandestinely bringing slaves to liberty" as destructive of relations between people like himself and Pearson and their "southern brethren," quoted in *Address of the Committee*, 34.

33. "The Great Faneuil Hall Meeting," *The Liberator*, October 2, 1846. See also "Letters from Boston," *Pennsylvania Freeman*, October 8, 1846. Pearson's wealth was mentioned in the *Southern Patriot* (Charleston), October 21, 1846.

34. Hannum later wrote that he left George "in the lower harbor on my arrival, while I came to the city for advice." See "Letters of Messrs. Hannum and Pearson," *Address of the Committee*, 34.

35. Testimony of William G. Reed, Mrs. Sarah Laforme, Henry Leonard, Daniel McGowen, Charles G. Cutter, John Fenno Jr., and James Topliffe before the Grand Jury, summarized in *Address of the Committee*, 41–42. The *Daily Picayune* reported in "Pretended Kidnapping," September 22, 1846, that Hannum "had a difficulty in getting the slave away from a mob, but finally succeeded by some device in doing so." Hannum later claimed that George had stolen his coat and purse but never provided evidence for a claim that was widely regarded as false; *Boston Journal*, September 12, 1846, quoted in *Address of the Committee*, 35.

36. "Kidnapping in Boston," *The Liberator*, September 18, 1846.

37. When John S. Jacobs went on a lecture tour with Jonathan Walker in 1847 and 1848, he spoke about the struggle to save George: see William Cooper Nell, "Jonathan Walker and John S. Jacobs," *North Star*, March 31, 1848.

38. Nell, "Jonathan Walker and John S. Jacobs"; Testimony of Pratt and Andrews, *Address of the Committee*, 42.

39. "Kidnapping in Boston," *The Liberator*, September 18, 1846. Newspapers in Louisiana, Maine, Massachusetts, Mississippi, Ohio, Pennsylvania, South Carolina, Vermont, and Wisconsin covered the case.

40. Hannum does not appear in the thousands of listings of vessels coming and going that appeared in the *Daily Picayune* after 1846. He shows up instead in the *Charleston Mercury*, June 15, 1847; September 29, 1847; January 15, 1848; and the *Charleston Courier*, May 22, 1848; January 15, 1849; November 14, 1850. The quoted text is Stephen C. Miller, *Address of the Committee* 15.

41. Boston's new Vigilance Committee incorporated and built upon the independent African American organization the Freedom Association, established after the

Latimer struggle in 1842 to assist fugitives, but it also radically changed its social composition: only eight of the two hundred members of the new Vigilance Committee were African American. Many free Black activists operated independently of predominantly white antislavery organizations.

42. *Address of the Committee*, 8, 40.

43. John W. Browne, "Committee of Vigilance, Agent's Record," 1846–1847, Blagden Papers, Houghton Library, Harvard University, published in full in Irving H. Bartlett, "Abolitionists, Fugitives, and Imposters in Boston, 1846–1847," *New England Quarterly* 55, no. 1 (Mar. 1982): 99–108.

44. "A Slave Case," *Public Ledger*, October 2, 1846.

45. In using the name Shadrach Minkins, I follow the lead of his biographer Gary Collison, whose *Shadrach Minkins: From Fugitive Slave to Citizen* (Cambridge: Harvard University Press, 1997) is a carefully researched and altogether magnificent biography from below.

46. Collison, *Shadrach Minkins*, 80. A few years later, Frederick Douglass agreed that people who "get a living by rolling casks on the wharves, and sweeping chimneys" were the ones who would "come to the rescue of the slave." See his "Agitate, Agitate: A Speech Delivered in Salem, Ohio on August 23, 1852," Frederick Douglass Papers, frederickdouglasspapersproject.com/item/8695 (accessed September 19, 2024), quoted in Olsavsky, *The Most Absolute Abolition*, 138.

47. J. W. Loguen, *The Rev. J. W. Loguen, as a Slave and as a Freeman, a Narrative of Real Life* (Syracuse: J. G. K. Truair, 1859), 339. Three likely family members—Nancy, John Seymour, and Edey Minkins—were listed in a census of Norfolk's free Black community the year after Shadrach escaped. See "Accounts, Free Negroes in the City of Norfolk Return," 1851, Accession APA 339, State Records Collection, The Library of Virginia, Richmond, Virginia.

48. Jacobs, *Incidents*, 286; Theodore Parker, *The Boston Kidnapping: A Discourse to Commemorate the Rendition of Thomas Simms, Delivered on the First Anniversary thereof, April 12, 1852, before the Committee of Vigilance, at the Melodeon in Boston* (Boston: Crosby, Nichols, & Co, 1852), 34.

49. Frederick Douglass, "Do Not Send Back the Fugitive: An Address Delivered in Boston, Massachusetts, on October 14, 1850," *The Frederick Douglass Papers*, frederickdouglasspapersproject.com/item/10185 (accessed September 19, 2024), and "The Fugitive Slave Law," speech to the National Free Soil Convention at Pittsburgh, August 11, 1852," *University of Rochester Frederick Douglass Project*, rbscp.lib.rochester.edu/4385 (accessed September 19, 2024).

50. William Craft, *Running a Thousand Miles for Freedom; Or, the Escape of William and Ellen Craft from Slavery* (London: William Tweedie, 1860). See also Ilyon Woo, *Master Slave Husband Wife: An Epic Journey from Slavery to Freedom* (New York: Simon and Schuster, 2023).

51. Broadside quoted in Collison, *Shadrach Minkins*, 111.

52. *Southern Press* (Washington, DC), February 20, 1851; Stanley W. Campbell, *The Slave Catchers: Enforcement of the Fugitive Slave Law, 1850–1860* (Chapel Hill: University of North Carolina Press, 1968), 149.

53. Daniel Webster to Hon. John P. Bigelow, Mayor of Boston, March 10, 1851, published as *City of Boston, Communication from the President of the United States* (Boston,

1851), copy in the Massachusetts Historical Society; Blackett, *The Captive's Quest*, 412–13; Delbanco, *The War Before the War*, 272; Millard Fillmore, "A Proclamation by the President of the United States," February 18, 1851, in Charles M. Wiltse and Michael J. Birkner, eds., *The Papers of Daniel Webster*, vol. 7, Correspondence (Hanover, NH: University Press of New England for Dartmouth College, 1986), 206–7.

54. Fillmore, "A Proclamation by the President of the United States."

55. "The Fugitive Slave Case at Boston, Several Arrests," *Daily Constitutionalist and Republic* (Augusta, GA), February 22, 1851; "Great Excitement in Boston!," *New Orleans Weekly Delta*, April 21, 1851; "The Fugitive Slave Case at Boston, Great Excitement," *Daily Republic* (Washington, DC), April 8, 1851.

56. *Daily Republic*, April 8, 1851. Sims's sister, Cornelia Sykes, did live in Boston, but his mother did not; she lived in Savannah. See "A Letter from Francis Jackson to Lydia Maria Child about Thomas Sims, who was arrested and reenslaved under the Fugitive Slave Law, 1860," Digital Public Library of America, dp.la/primary-source-sets/incidents-in-the-life-of-a-slave-girl-by-harriet-jacobs/sources/1140 (accessed September 19, 2024).

57. Edward Hartwell Savage, *A Chronological History of the Boston Watch and Police, from 1631 to 1865; Together with the Recollections of a Boston Police Officer, or, Boston by Daylight and Gaslight, from the Diary of an Officer Fifteen Years in the Service*, 2nd ed. (Boston: published by the author, 1865), 378–79.

58. Theodore Parker later regretted that Sims was "very imperfectly armed" and that his knife was "unlucky." See his *The Boston Kidnapping*, 36.

59. "Thomas Sims Again in Chains," *The Liberator*, May 2, 1851.

60. *Daily Republic*, April 8, 1851.

61. "The Plot Exploded! John H. Pearson & the Bloodhounds," broadside, 1851, Ephemera. Boston: s.n., [1851]. *Digital Commonwealth*, digitalcommonwealth.org /search/commonwealth:70796d03j (accessed September 19, 2024). See also *Trial of Thomas Sims, on an Issue of Personal Liberty, on the Claim of James Potter, of Georgia, against Him, as an Alleged Fugitive from Service* (Boston: Wm. S. Damrell, 1851).

62. "Remarks by Theodore Parker," *The Liberator*, July 4, 1851.

63. See the livid eyewitness account of Daniel Foster, Diary entry for April 14, 1851, Daniel Foster Papers, 1841–1884, Ms. N-1238, f.36, Massachusetts Historical Society. See also George R. Coffin journal, 1854–1857, Special Collections and University Archives, University of Massachusetts-Amherst Libraries, available online at credo.library.umass.edu/view/full/mums1000-i001 (accessed September 19, 2024); Leonard W. Levy, "Sims' Case: The Fugitive Slave Law in Boston in 1851," *Journal of Negro History* 35, no. 1 (Jan. 1950): 39–74. On armed rescues, see Baptist, "Solidarity Versus Parastate," 33–55.

64. Horton and Horton, *Black Bostonians*, 34, 61, 99, 116, 128, 129, 134.

65. "The Victim has Been Sacrificed," *The Liberator*, April 18, 1851.

66. Parker, *The Boston Kidnapping*, 47.

67. "The Sims Meeting," *The Liberator*, May 15, 1863.

68. Scholarship on the Burns case is extensive. Highlights include Jane H. Pease and William H. Pease, *The Fugitive Slave Law and Anthony Burns: A Problem in Law Enforcement* (Philadelphia: Lippincott, 1975); Albert J. von Frank, *The Trials of Anthony Burns: Freedom and Slavery in Emerson's Boston* (Cambridge: Harvard University

Press, 1998); Gordon S. Barker, *The Imperfect Revolution: Anthony Burns and the Landscape of Race in Antebellum America* (Kent, OK: Kent State University Press, 2010); and Earl M. Maltz, *Fugitive Slave on Trial: The Anthony Burns Case and Abolitionist Outrage* (Lawrence: University Press of Kansas, 2010). Manisha Sinha offers a concise summary of the Burns case in *The Slave's Cause*, 515–20.

69. Charles Emery Stevens was certainly the right person to chronicle the struggle of Anthony Burns. Stevens had taken part in the demonstrations, attended the trial, watched the procession of soldiers walk Burns to the docks, and most important of all, interviewed Burns at length when he returned to Boston after gaining his freedom. See his *Anthony Burns: A History* (Boston: John P. Jewett, 1856; repr., Williamstown, MA: Corner House Publishers, 1973), v–viii.

70. *Vermont Republican* (Brattleboro, Vermont), March 9, 1855; Campbell, *The Slave Catchers*, 124.

71. Higginson believed that they could have rescued Burns with "twenty more men."

72. The legal arguments are summarized in William I. Bowditch, *The Rendition of Anthony Burns* (Boston: R. F. Wallcut, 1854). For a list of 115 officers who were paid for their role in preventing the popular rescue of Anthony Burns, see "Military Actors in the Burns Rendition," 1854, Massachusetts Anti-Slavery Society, New York Historical Society, digitalcollections.nyhistory.org/islandora/object/islandora%3A130699#page /1 (accessed September 19, 2024).

73. Tiffany, *Samuel E. Sewall: A Memoir*, 81.

74. Anthony Burns to Richard Henry Dana, August 23, 1854, Dana Family Papers, 1853–1854, Ms. N-49.61, Massachusetts Historical Society. Rev. Grimes raised $700 ($25,500 in 2024) and Boston banker Charles Cushing Barry contributed $1,300 ($47,300 in 2024) to buy Burns's freedom. See the Barry Papers, 1834–1906, Ms. N-1809, Massachusetts Historical Society; and Blackett, *The Captive's Quest*, 427. In the aftermath of the Burns case, Asa Butman was attacked and almost killed by a multiracial crowd of one thousand in Worcester. See "Letter from Thomas Wentworth Higginson, Worcester, [Mass.], to Maria Weston Chapman, November. 30, 1854, Thanksgiving Day." Correspondence. Worcester, Mass., November 30, 1854. *Digital Commonwealth*, digitalcommonwealth.org/search/commonwealth:qz20t167k (accessed September 19, 2024). Higginson did not mention that he had helped Butman to escape. See also Blackett, *The Captive's Quest*, 429–30. For more on the dramatic cases of Minkins, Sims, and Burns, see Steven Lubet, *Fugitive Justice: Runaways, Rescuers, and Slavery on Trial* (Cambridge: Harvard University Press, 2010), and Stephen Kantrowitz, *More than Freedom: Fighting for Black Citizenship in a White Republic, 1829–1889* (New York: Penguin Press, 2012), 190–213.

75. For the broader context of resistance, see Lois E. Horton, "Kidnapping and Resistance: Antislavery Direct Action in the 1850s," in Blight, ed., *Passages to Freedom*, 149–73.

76. Mary E. Blanchard to Benjamin Seaver, May 29, 1854; B. L. Seaver to Benjamin Seaver, June 13, 1854, Letters to Benjamin Seaver (1795–1856), 1824–1854, Ms. N-2319, Massachusetts Historical Society. This is not to say that deeply embedded racism did not remain at all levels of society, including among some white abolitionists. This theme runs throughout Jones, *No Right to an Honest Living*.

77. Records of the Boston Anti-Man-Hunting League, 1846–1887, Ms. N-1875, Box 1, Folder 2, Massachusetts Historical Society, masshist.org/collection-guides/view/fa0420 (accessed September 19, 2024); Olsavsky, *The Most Absolute Abolition*, ch. 3.

78. Captain Pillsbury and stowaway Joseph Williams arrived aboard the *Growler* in Boston in 1856. Williams jumped into the water, was picked up by a sailor, and taken to the Vigilance Committee. When Williams came to court, no one appeared to prosecute. When the judge told Williams "to go free," the courtroom erupted in applause. *Columbus Enquirer*, July 22, 1856. R. J. M. Blackett notes that the cost of retrieval usually exceeded the market value of the runaway. See *The Captive's Quest*, 41.

79. Olsavsky, *The Most Absolute Abolition*, ch. 2. See also Blackett, *The Captive's Quest*, 69, 412, 439. This chapter supports Manisha Sinha's argument that "Slave resistance revolutionized abolitionist discourse and practice." See *The Slave's Cause*, 381.

80. Charles Sumner, "Union among Men of All Powers against the Slave Power and the Extension of Slavery, Speech before a Mass Convention at Worcester, June 28, 1848," in *The Works of Charles Sumner*, vol. II (Boston, MA: Lee and Shepard, 1875), 81.

Chapter Eight: Sea Routes to Philadelphia and New York in the 1850s

1. Ralph D. Gray, *The National Waterway: A History of the Chesapeake and Delaware Canal, 1769–1985*, 2nd ed. (Urbana: University of Illinois Press, 1989), 83, 111. See also Cheryl Janifer LaRoche, "The Underground Railroad in Maryland's Ports, Bays, and Harbors: Maritime Strategies for Freedom," in Walker, ed., *Sailing to Freedom*, 105–9.

2. In addition to Baylis, Fountain, and Lambdin, at least seventeen other captains willingly and consciously tried, with or without success, to carry fugitives out of the South to Northern ports: James Carter, Samuel Chadwick, John Dade, Daniel Drayton, Amos Hopkins, Edward Lee, Henry Lee, Robert Lee, John Minkins, [no first name] Mitchell, Capt. P, "Powder Boy," William C. Smith, David Teal, John Thomas, Jonathan Walker, and Thomas Walker. Most of these captains were active in the 1850s. See Newby-Alexander, *Virginia Waterways*, 114.

3. Thomas Garrett to Sarah Bradford, June 1868, published in James A. McGowan, *Station Master on the Underground Railroad: The Life and Letters of Thomas Garrett*, rev. ed. (Jefferson, NC: McFarland, 2005), 191. Garrett noted in convincing detail the slow increase in the number of people he assisted over time: 1,874 by 1854; 2,011 by September 1856; 2,028 by December 1856; and 2,072 by August 1857. Scholars have wondered whether the number could have been so high, but in my view the morally upright Garrett is not a man to be doubted.

4. Debra Campagnari Martin has definitively established that the captain long known as Albert or Alfred Fountain was James Watson Fountain. See her "The Rocks and the Underground Railroad: Captain Fountain," *The Quill: Newsletter of the Quaker Hill Historic Preservation Foundation* (May 2024). Priscilla Thompson was the first to identify Fountain as James rather than Alfred or Albert; see her "Harriet Tubman, Thomas Garrett, and the Underground Railroad," *Delaware History* 22, no. 1 (Sept. 1986): 15.

5. Still, *Underground Railroad*, 174; Gary A. Harki, "Escape," *The Virginian-Pilot* (Norfolk), an article in five parts, available at http://escape.pilotonline.com/index.html (accessed September 19, 2024).

6. Still, *Underground Railroad*, 174–75. One of "the twenty-one," Phyllis Galt (or Gault), told Still that she was "secreted in the hold of a vessel expressly arranged for bringing away slaves" (178).

7. Still, *Underground Railroad*, 135, 167-72, 346-48; Harry T. Sharp, "Information for the genealogy of [the] Sharp Family, Greenwood (Grinwode) Family, Christy Family, Fountain (Fontaine) Family, O'Donnell Family," unpublished typescript, 1965, Riverview Cemetery Office, Wilmington, Delaware. Thanks to Debra Campagnari Martin for providing a copy. Sharp was Captain Fountain's great-grandson.

8. "Personal," *Daily Republican* (Wilmington, Delaware), October 1, 1880; "Died," *Daily Gazette* (Wilmington, Delaware), October 1, 1880; *Bangor (Maine) Daily Whig and Courier*, August 13, 1860. Lambdin's name was also spelled Lamden, Lambden, and Lambson.

9. Thomas Garrett to William Still and James Miller McKim, May 11, 1856, in Still, *Underground Railroad*, 404–5; "Negro Stampede, Negro Stealers Caught," *Democratic Pioneer* (Elizabeth City, North Carolina), November 27, 1855; William H. Lambdin to Governor Henry A. Wise, June 18, 1856, Governor Henry A. Wise Executive Papers, 1856–1859. Accession 36710, State government records collection, the Library of Virginia, Richmond, Virginia. See also Lambdin's letters published in the *Smyrna Times* (January 9, 1856) and the *New York Herald* (January 14, 1856), in which he says he "discovered negroes secreted in my forecastle." Lambdin was highly respected by the citizens of Smyrna, Delaware, where he grew up, and Wilmington, where he currently lived. They sent numerous letters and petitions to Governor Henry A. Wise between 1856 and 1858 testifying to his character and urging a pardon. See Wm. B. Wiggins, mayor of Wilmington, to Governor Henry A. Wise, January 8, 1856; Petition of the Citizens of Smyrna to Governor Henry A. Wise, January 18, 1856; Petition of the Citizens of Wilmington to Governor Henry A. Wise, May 21, 1856; Edward R. Taylor to Governor Henry A. Wise, May 26, 1856; Petition of the Citizens of Wilmington "To His Excellency Henry A. Wise Governor of the Commonwealth of Virginia," October 1858; Thomas Young, mayor of Wilmington, to Governor Henry A. Wise, October 27, 1858; and Petition for the Pardon of Wm. H., Lamden, condemned to Pent'y for abducting slaves, Dec. 7, 1858, all from Wise Executive Papers, Library of Virginia.

10. *Anti-Slavery Bugle* (Lisbon, Ohio), June 19, 1858; Newby-Alexander, *Virginia Waterways*, 75; John T. Kneebone, "A Break Down on the Underground Railroad: Captain B. and the Capture of the *Keziah*, 1858," *Virginia Cavalcade* 48 (Spring 1999): 74-83.

11. Still, *Underground Railroad*, 74–75. Still did not approve of Baylis charging the runaways but added that this was not the business of the Vigilance Committee to decide.

12. Still, *Underground Railroad*, 76–79. The advertisement for the runaway Robinson first appeared in the *Richmond Dispatch*, January 30, 1855, and nine times thereafter.

13. "A Slave Dealer's Story," *Brookville (PA) Republican*, April 30, 1879.

14. Still, *Underground Railroad*, 147, 566; entry for Henry Johnson, November 24, 1856, Gay, "Record of Fugitives."

15. William Still, "Journal C of Station No. 2."

16. Still, "Journal C of Station No. 2." 104. Jesse Olsavsky sees the Vigilance Committees as schools in which fugitives did most of the teaching; see *The Most Absolute Abolition*, 110–23.

17. The remainder of this section is based on Still, *Underground Railroad*, quotations at 289, 484, 327, 137, 151, 276, 214–15, 221–23, 48–49, 99, 306–7, 54–59.

18. I have constructed my own database combining Still's journal and book, beginning with the first entry of the former (February 1852) and ending with the final entry in the latter (December 1860). This excludes two famous cases Still mentioned in his book: William and Ellen Craft, who ran away in December 1848, and Henry "Box" Brown, who escaped in March 1849, before Still began to keep his journal. See also the useful database compiled by James A. McGowen and William C. Kashatus, published in the latter's *William Still*, 221–77. John Hope Franklin and Loren Schweninger find that for period for the period 1838–60, 81 percent of runaways were male, with an average age of twenty-seven. See their *Runaway Slaves*, 210–12.

19. Still rarely recorded the means of transportation for the people who escaped from Maryland. It is not clear why. Perhaps it was because they were more likely than others to employ multiple methods of travel, using some combination of train, horse, and especially ship and foot. In any case, his notations about the means of escape from Maryland were not nearly as complete as those he noted for those from Virginia, which is why I concentrate on the latter.

20. The numbers adduced in this paragraph understate the importance of getting away by sea because, as Still's collected accounts make clear, almost all who escaped bondage had to make at least one portion of their journey over water, whether swimming, canoeing, ferrying across rivers, or by taking some kind of vessel for one passage in the journey. Many escapees used multiple forms of transportation. I counted as "escape by sea" only those cases in which the fugitive either made his or her initial escape from bondage or crossed into a free state while on the water. The finding that two thirds escaped by sea thus represents a conservative estimate.

21. Still's notations of vessel type show that eighty-one runaways (42.4 percent of the total number recorded) arrived on schooners, forty-three (22.5 percent) on steamers, and sixty-seven on unspecified watercraft Still generically called "boats" and "vessels" (35.1 percent). In the later 1850s Fountain skippered the *Chas. T. Ford*, a schooner of sixty-eight tons.

22. William Still to J. M. McKim, November 2, 1857, Elijah F. Pennypacker Anti-Slavery Correspondence, SFHL-SC-097, Swarthmore College Friends Historical Library.

23. Gay, "Record of Fugitives." Napoleon also made trips to Maryland to assist fugitives. See "A New York Character: The Old 'Engineer of the Underground Railroad,'" *New York Tribune*, October 12, 1875.

24. For more on Gay see Foner, *Gateway to Freedom*, 91–96. The 1838–40 split of the Tappan brothers from William Lloyd Garrison had no discernible effect on fugitives except perhaps to open another avenue for assistance.

25. Entry for September 5, 1855, Gay, "Record of Fugitives." On Louis Napoleon, see Don Papson and Tom Calarco, *Secret Lives of the Underground Railroad in New York City: Sydney Howard Gay, Louis Napoleon, and the Record of Fugitives* (Jefferson, NC: McFarland and Company, 2014), and Gronningsater, "'On Behalf of His Race and the Lemmon Slaves,'" 206–41.

26. Entries for November 19, 1855; July 9, 1856; November 30, 1855; and July 8, 1856, Gay, "Record of Fugitives." Franklin and Schweninger, *Runaway Slaves*, 210–13. For more on women runaways, see Karen Cook Bell, *Running from Bondage: Enslaved*

Women and their Remarkable Fight for Freedom in Revolutionary America (New York: Cambridge University Press, 2021), and Loren Ashmore Sorenson, "'So that I Get Her Again': African American Slave Women Runaways in Selected Richmond, Virginia Newspapers, 1830–1860, and the Richmond, Virginia Police Guard Daybook, 1834–1843" (PhD diss., College of William and Mary, 1996), 13.

27. Entry for April 9, 1856, Gay, "Record of Fugitives."

28. This and the following paragraph are based on the entry for October 13, 1855, Gay, "Record of Fugitives."

29. Entry for May 16, 1856, Gay, "Record of Fugitives"; Still, "Journal C of Station No. 2," 277. Gay recorded Winny's last name as "Patsy." Still used "Petty," which seems correct.

30. Entries for March 22, 1856, and July 8, 1856; Gay, "Record of Fugitives."

31. Entries for March 17, 1856, and July 23, 1856; Gay, "Record of Fugitives."

32. "Letter from James Miller M'Kim, Anti-Slavery Office, Phil[adelphi]a, [Penn.], to Maria Weston Chapman, Nov. 19th, [1857]." Correspondence. Anti-Slavery Office, Philadelphia, Penn., [November 19, 1857], *Digital Commonwealth*, digitalcommon wealth.org/search/commonwealth:qz20tz411 (accessed September 19, 2024).

33. Still, *Underground Railroad*, 587.

34. Gay reported the means of transportation for 134 of the 200 fugitives who arrived in his office: sixty-nine (51.5 percent) arrived by sea; thirty-two (23.9 percent) by carriage, wagon, or horse; twenty-one (15.7 percent) on foot; and twelve (9 percent) by train. Arrival by sea was more than twice as frequent as any other means of travel and more common than the others combined.

35. Edmund Ruffin, "Consequences of Abolition Agitation," *DeBow's Review:* 23 (1857): 547.

36. Still, *Underground Railroad*, 60–61.

37. This and the next two paragraphs draw on Tom Crew, "'Soon, The Grievance Will Cease To Exist': Chief Inspector of Vessels Reports," *The UncommonWealth: Voices from the Library of Virginia*, May 16, 2018, uncommonwealth.virginiamemory.com/blog /2018/05/16/soon-the-grievance-will-cease-to-exist-chief-inspector-of-vessels-reports.

38. Virginia Chief Inspector of Vessels, Quarterly Reports, 1856–1861. Accession 36456, State Records Collection, The Library of Virginia, Richmond, Virginia.

39. "An Act Providing Additional Protection for the Slave Property of Citizens of this Commonwealth," 1856, in Guild, ed., *Black Laws of Virginia*, 89–90.

40. J. J. Simkins to the Hon. Henry Wise, November 8, 1856, "Quarterly Report of Inspections, under the act passed March 17th 1856, in the Waters of Hampton Roads, and the mouth of the Chesapeake Bay," Virginia Chief Inspector of Vessels, Quarterly Reports, 1856–1861. See also *Buffalo Daily Republic*, April 8, 1856; *New York Herald*, April 9, 1856; "Resistance to the Virginia Search Law," *Richmond Dispatch*, April 15, 1856; "Seizure of a New York Vessel by the Authorities of Virginia," *Pittsburgh Gazette*, April 17, 1856; and "The Search Law," *The Liberator*, April 25, 1856. The captain's name was also spelled "Spike," "Spight," "Spright," and "Spaght."

41. This account of Thompson, Anthony, and the *Francis French* is pieced together from newspaper articles in the *Norfolk Day Book*, May 28, 1858 (reprinted in the *Anti-Slavery Bugle*, Lisbon, OH, June 19, 1858); "Under Ground Rail Road," *Richmond Enquirer*, June 1, 1858; "Negro Stealing," *Weekly Union* (New Bern, NC), June 11,

1858; and "The Isle of Wight Kidnapping Case," *The Liberator,* July 23, 1858. The cook of the *Francis French* might have been the same William Thompson who escaped Richmond in October 1855: he "accidentally met with y cook of a vessel + entered into some talk with him, + soon came to an understanding" that the cook would conceal and carry him to New York for five dollars; see entry for October 13, 1855, Gay, "Record of Fugitives."

42. *Norfolk Argus,* May 31, 1858, republished in the *Anti-Slavery Bugle* (Lisbon, Ohio), June 19, 1858. Dannenburg was likely guilty as charged: he had been a part owner of Baylis's *Keziah* only a year or two earlier. See Paul L. Singleton, "The *Keziah* Affair of 1858 and its Impact upon Underground Railroad Activities in Eastern Virginia" (master's thesis, Virginia State University, 1983), 51; and Kneebone, "Break Down in the Underground Railroad," 77.

43. *The Weekly Union* (New Bern, North Carolina), June 11, 1858.

44. *Weekly Union,* June 11, 1858. The *Francis French* subsequently sold at auction for $1,950, to Loveland; see the *Baltimore Sun,* August 20, 1858.

45. This section is based on "Negro Stealing," *Charleston Daily Courier,* June 3, 1858; "Under Ground Rail Road," *Richmond Enquirer,* June 11, 1858; "Pursuit and Recovery of Fugitive Slaves," *Petersburg Daily Express,* June 12, 1858; and "Fugitive-Slave Excitement at Norfolk, Va.," *Anti-Slavery Bugle,* June 19, 1858 (from the *Norfolk Argus*).

46. The best account of the capture of the *Keziah* is Singleton, "The *Keziah* Affair." A Petersburg newspaper reporter, who had visited the vessel, stated that it had "straw-matted flat stalls in the hold of the schooner where the four male captives had been stowed," quoted in Singleton, "The *Keziah* Affair," 55.

47. For information about the individual fugitives, see Singleton, "The *Keziah* Affair," 17–26. Petersburg authorities later arrested a white man, John M. David; a free woman of color, Eliza Parham; and enslaved man named George for having assisted the escape, but nothing came of the charges. See Kneebone, "Break Down in the Underground Railroad," 78, 82.

48. "Under Ground Rail Road," *Richmond Enquirer,* June 11, 1858. Even though Simkins must have known that five fugitives were aboard the *Keziah,* it was reported "that he knew nothing of the attempted escapes" and was acquitted. See the *Annual Report of the American Anti-Slavery Society, by the Executive Committee, for the Year Ending May 1, 1859* (New York, 1860), 99–100. Simkins was not in prison with Baylis according to the census of 1860.

49. Lucretia Mott to Martha Coffin Wright, June 13, 1858, Mott Manuscripts, SFHL-MSS-035, Friends Historical Library of Swarthmore College, item A00182010. The letter from Hill, dated June 5, 1858, is published in Still, *Underground Railroad,* 200.

50. Austin Bearse, *Reminiscences of Fugitive Slave Law Days in Boston* (Boston: Warren Richardson, 1880), 34. Bearse explained, "I intended with the 'Wild Pigeon' to go down [to Virginia] and resist the pilot boat as a pirate." He planned to "appeal to the courts" should he get arrested. Bearse either underestimated the hostility of judges and juries in Virginia or accepted the likelihood of going to prison.

51. J. J. Simkins to Gov. Henry A. Wise, March 31, 1857, "Inspection Return of 1st Quarter 1857, Hampton Roads, Potomac River," Virginia Chief Inspector of Vessels, Quarterly Reports, 1856–1861.

52. The *Francis French* was inspected April 30, 1858, and was apparently delayed almost a month in its departure, which allowed Anthony to steal aboard. See Entry for April 30, 1858, "Pilot Police Inspection for Hampton Roads, Potomac, and Rappahannock Rivers from 1st Day of Jany 1858 to 1st day of May 1858," Virginia Chief Inspector of Vessels, Quarterly Reports, 1856–1861.

53. Cassandra L. Newby-Alexander notes that of the twenty-seven men held in the Virginia penitentiary for assisting fugitives between 1842 and 1860, only thirteen were convicted after during and after 1856, a modest increase suggesting the limited effectiveness of the inspection law of 1856, *Virginia Waterways*, 118–19; Third Ward, Richmond City, Henrico, Virginia, United States Census, 1850 and 1860. Baylis would be pardoned by the governor of Virginia in March 1865, just before the Union Army took Richmond.

54. A modest decline in the number of runaways arriving by sea over time can be seen by comparing Still's notations in Journal C to what he included in *Underground Railroad*. In the former, which spans December 1852 to February 1857, 72.2 percent arrived by sea, while for the later period (March 1857 to February 1860) the proportion declined to 64.4 percent. Some of this modest decline can probably be attributed to the Virginia law of 1856.

55. R. J. M. Blackett notes that the number of fugitives flowing into Philadelphia and New York continued, and indeed increased, in the late 1850s. See his *The Captive's Quest*, 337, 391.

56. List of Vessels Engaged in the Piloting Business, "Report of the Chief Inspector under the law for additional protection for the Slave Property in the Commonwealth of Virginia, passed March 17th 1856, for the quarter ending September 30th 1858," Virginia Chief Inspector of Vessels, Quarterly Reports, 1856–1861. In his thorough overview of the body of law against runaways in Virginia, Philip J. Schwarz concludes, "No matter how the government of the Commonwealth [of Virginia] tried, it never caught up with the determination, ingenuity, and intensity of fugitives and their allies." See his *Slave Laws in Virginia* (Athens: University of Georgia Press, 2010), 148.

57. Anne Brown Adams quoted in Louis A. DeCaro Jr., *The Untold Story of Shields Green: The Life and Death of a Harper's Ferry Raider* (New York: New York University Press, 2020), 1–2.

Epilogue: The Middle Passage to Freedom

1. Maria Dietrich, Henry Louis Gates Jr., and Carl Pedersen, eds., *Black Imagination and the Middle Passage* (New York: Oxford University Press, 1999); Marcus Rediker, *The Slave Ship: A Human History* (New York: Viking, 2007).

2. In 1860 the *New York Times* estimated that only one in ten fugitives was ever returned, but R. J. M. Blackett suggests that this overestimates the number. The percentage of successful escapees by sea would have been even higher. See Blackett's *The Captive's Quest*, 458, 459.

3. Bennett's interview, taken January 7, 1937, was published in Charles L. Perdue Jr., Thomas E. Barden, and Robert K. Phillips, eds., *Weevils in the Wheat: Interviews with Virginia Ex-Slaves* (Charlottesville: University Press of Virginia, 1976), 29. I have modernized the original transcription: "Whut cause war was white folk searchin Yankee vessel wen dey come in harbor. Wite man go de boat jes' lookin.

Say, 'N——, get outten heah!' Catch n—— runnin away and kill 'im. Yankees got mad." Other formerly enslaved people who recalled sea escapes in Virginia were Rev. C. W. B. Gordon (110), Mrs. Fannie Nicholson (218), Mrs. Jane Pyatt (234), and Richard Slaughter (272). Eric Foner notes that the fugitive slave issue "played a crucial role on bring about the Civil War"; see his *Gateway to Freedom*, 26. R. J. M. Blackett agrees: fugitives were "a major contributing factor" to the coming of the Civil War; see *The Captive's Quest*, xv. Jesse Olsavsky makes a bolder, and more comparative, argument: "In the United States, as had been the case in Haiti, the runaway took the lead in pushing the nation from sectional crisis, to secession, to war, and then to emancipation." See *The Most Absolute Abolition*, 9.

4. William C. Nell, Henry Weeden, Thomas Cummings, and James L. Giles, "New-England Freedom Association, December 2, 1843," in Yellin, ed., *The Harriet Jacobs Family Papers*, 1:61–62.

5. Scott, *The Common Wind*. I agree with Eric Foner, who sees the origin of the Underground Railroad in the formation of the New York Vigilance Committee in 1835, although he does not emphasize its maritime character. See his *Gateway to Freedom*, ch. 3.

6. "The Illegal Conduct of the Grand Jury for Suffolk County Exposed! The Laws of Massachusetts prostrated at the Footstool of Southern Slavery!," *The Liberator*, June 18, 1841.

7. James Sagurs, Henry Sagurs, and Joseph Felt, "1837-06-16 Affadavit of James Sagurs, owner of Atticus" (1837), *Atticus the Slave*, 2. Maine State Archives, digitalmaine .com/atticus_docs/2/. This and the next paragraph draw on Paul Finkelman, "States' Rights North and South in Antebellum America," in Hall and Ely, eds., *An Uncertain Tradition*, 125–58.

8. Andrew Delbanco and R. J. M. Blackett emphasize that the personal liberty laws outraged the South and created severe obstacles to recapturing fugitives in the 1840s and 1850s. See Delbanco, *The War Before the War*, 169, 186, 209, 345–46; and Blackett, *The Captive's Quest*, 5, 6, 436, 449. John C. Calhoun saw the laws as "one of the most fatal blows ever received by the South and the Union": John C. Calhoun, "The Southern Address," *Charleston Courier*, February 1, 1849.

9. Bordewich, *Bound for Canaan*, 303–4.

10. Bordewich, *Bound for Canaan*, 341; Blackett, *The Captive's Quest*, 86.

11. W. E. B. Du Bois, *Black Reconstruction in America, 1860–1880* (1935; repr., New York: Free Press, 1997); Newby-Alexander, *Virginia Waterways*, 147–49; Delbanco, *The War Before the War*, 356–62; Oickle, *The Man with the Branded Hand*, 243; Cate Lineberry, *Be Free or Die: The Amazing Story of Robert Smalls' Escape from Slavery to Union Hero* (New York: Picador, 2018); Edda L. Fields-Black, *Combee: Harriet Tubman, the Combahee River Raid, and Black Freedom during the Civil War* (New York: Oxford University Press, 2024); Cecelski, *The Waterman's Song*. Newby-Alexander notes that the actions taken by Baker, Townsend, Mallory, and Butler opened the way to the Confiscation Acts of 1861 and 1862 and the Emancipation Proclamation of 1863, *Virginia Waterways*, 146. The experience of a "contraband" is recounted in William B. Gould, *Diary of a Contraband: The Civil War Passage of a Black Sailor* (Stanford: Stanford University Press, 2002). For more on the politics of mobility see Wong, *Neither Fugitive nor Free*.

12. Major exceptions would be W. E. B. Du Bois, *Black Reconstruction*, and C. L. R. James, *The Black Jacobins: Toussaint L'Ouverture and the San Domingo Revolution* (1938; repr. New York: Vintage, 1989). For important works that have connected abolitionism and resistance by the enslaved, see Sinha, *The Slave's Cause*; Blackett, *The Captive's Quest*; and Olsavsky, *The Most Absolute Abolition*.

13. Olsavsky, *The Most Absolute Abolition*, 11, 20–21; Jacobs, *Incidents in the Life of a Slave Girl*, 240. R .J. M. Blackett notes that not all fugitives who arrived in Philadelphia and New York contacted the Vigilance Committees. The same was true for Boston. See *The Captive's Quest*, 328, 392.

14. Kathryn Grover notes that Powell and other Black abolitionists began to assist fugitives well before the establishment of Vigilance Committees and operated more or less independently of them afterward. See her "Seaborne Fugitives from Slavery and the Ports of Eastern Massachusetts," in Walker, ed., *Sailing to Freedom*, 161.

15. For maritime escapes to and through Rhode Island, see Chace, *Anti-Slavery Reminiscences*, 27–36. Horatio T. Strother called New Haven Connecticut's "Gateway from the Sea." See his *The Underground Railroad in Connecticut* (Middletown, CT: Wesleyan University Press, 1962), 107–20. For maritime escapes in New Jersey, see Graham Hodges, *Root and Branch: African Americans in New York and East Jersey, 1613–1863* (Chapel Hill: University of North Carolina Press, 1999). Maritime escapes can also be found in the trilogy by William J. Switala, *Underground Railroad in Delaware, Maryland, and West Virginia* (Mechanicsburg, PA: Stackpole Books, 2004); *Underground Railroad in New York and New Jersey* (Mechanicsburg, PA: Stackpole Books, 2006); and *Underground Railroad in Pennsylvania*, 2nd ed. (Mechanicsburg, PA: Stackpole Books, 2008).

16. Viola Franziska Müller makes the creative argument that antebellum runaways were "undocumented migrants" seeking sanctuary in urban areas. See her *Escape to the City*, 2–5. Cassandra L. Newby-Alexander calls the Underground Railroad "America's first nonviolent resistance movement." See her *Virginia Waterways*, 163.

17. Theodore Parker, *Speeches, Addresses, and Occasional Sermons by Theodore Parker, Minister of the Twenty-Eight Congregational Church in Boston*, vol. 3 (Boston: Horace B. Fuller, 1867), 391, quoted in Delbanco, *The War Before the War*, 159.

18. Douglass, *Narrative*, 102; Still, *Underground Railroad*, 43.

19. Tubman quoted in Still, *Underground Railroad*, 312–13; Sarah H. Bradford, *Scenes in the Life of Harriet Tubman* (Auburn, NY: W. J. Moses, 1869), 57. Thanks to Kate Clifford Larson for discussing with me Tubman's thoughts on escape as a new Middle Passage.

Index

Italicized page numbers indicate material in photographs or illustrations.

100 YEARS of PUBLISHING

Harold K. Guinzburg and George S. Oppenheimer founded Viking in 1925 with the intention of publishing books "with some claim to permanent importance rather than ephemeral popular interest." After merging with B. W. Huebsch, a small publisher with a distinguished catalog, Viking enjoyed almost fifty years of literary and commercial success before merging with Penguin Books in 1975.

Now an imprint of Penguin Random House, Viking specializes in bringing extraordinary works of fiction and nonfiction to a vast readership. In 2025, we celebrate one hundred years of excellence in publishing. Our centennial colophon features the original logo for Viking, created by the renowned American illustrator Rockwell Kent: a Viking ship that evokes enterprise, adventure, and exploration, ideas that inspired the imprint's name at its founding and continue to inspire us.

For more information on Viking's history, authors, and books, please visit penguin.com/viking.